THE MARRIAGE OF CONTINENTS

Multiculturalism in Modern Literature

Guy Amirthanayagam

University Press of America,® Inc.
Lanham • New York • Oxford

CONTENTS

PREFACE:

THE BOOK'S TITLE AND SHAPE

One of the greatest adventures of the twentieth century is the growing contact of cultures. In its classical configuration, the meeting of cultures is that of the East and the West, meaning at one time the "Orient" and Europe, but now enlarged to include America: in fact, because of its position as the dominant superpower, many think of America as typifying the West. The interaction of cultures may be seen either from a broad international perspective, or at a more intimate level as an interplay of subcultures within national or regional spheres – for example, the Black, Jewish or the American-Indian minorities within the United States.

A rich fruit of this multiple meeting of cultures, both within and among nations, is a type of modern literature which has great artistic merit and social significance. This modern literature consists of writings that are directly generated by the meetings of cultures, namely those works in which the central experience is cross-cultural, and where the nature and the destiny of character is shaped in some fashion by the cross-cultural encounter.

To validate the timeliness and topicality of a study of this literature one has only to point to the degree of inter-cultural misunderstanding that persists in the modern world, even though cross-cultural contact has greatly increased and the opportunities for interaction between cultures are constantly growing both in frequency and range. The literature of cross-cultural contact mirrors this situation well, since it embodies the actual processes of interaction, and demonstrates in complex, multifaceted ways the harmonies and disruptions which are their consequence. This kind of demonstration has an intimacy, immediacy, inwardness and subtlety unavailable from any other source.

There has also been in recent years a flowering in the study of such subjects as relations between literature and society, the position of the writer in society, and social problems as material for the creative artist. A literary-cultural discipline, if it may be so called, has many uses. It could explore the ways in which literature is a key to the understanding of culture. It could illuminate culture's intellectual and imaginative life. It could investigate how literature not only reflects and "refracts" but also "lives" and forms the values, social habits and assumptions of cultures. It could help to identify the conditions in a civilization which foster or discourage creative achievement in literature and the arts, and study the ways in which literature activates or inspires social concerns. Familiarization with the creative processes in a culture, while ministering to personal enrichment, should contribute to inter-cultural understanding, as the study of literature, because of its concern with "universal values", is a potent means of transcending the confines of particular cultures.

But the studies we have, such as they are, have not always served the cause of international understanding. They have tended to be culture-specific and even ethnocentric. Despite the greater exposure of the rest of the world in the twentieth century, several important thinkers in Europe and America still behave as though the countries outside their region are marginal and have little to contribute to an understanding of their own situation; they neglect even the more obvious evidence of interpenetration. When writers condemn modernization, industrialization or centralization, they often embrace the anti-rational, and appeal to a past which is no longer recoverable, even in traditional societies. Composing poetry on the tongue may be feasible for the visionary, but may not be possible where the social conditions for such communal participation no longer exist. Imagistic spontaneity is a virtue, but must it be accompanied by the loss of a sense of art as a form of intellectual sentience, an act of the total mind? In societies which are learning to identify tradition with cultural backwardness, a recommendation of anything less than the exercise of one's total intelligence may seem designed to perpetuate stagnation.

The greater closeness of diverse geographical regions in our time has brought comfort to some and insecurity to others; it has been seen as especially threatening to weaker nations and small cultures with ancient traditions. On the other hand, the almost incestuous concern with their own societies shown by many Western writers has not been reassuring to the outsiders who want to partake in the great movements and changes of this century.

In the modern world the pull towards expressing, or making accommodations to, an international or global culture has had a considerable, sometimes beneficial, sometimes devastating impact on writers, regardless of the country of origin or livelihood. But it must also be recognized as true that several writers have fashioned their art out of their very struggle to resist such a homogenizing and universalizing force.

The problems, though less acute, were not less important in countries which have not suffered the colonizing experience, or had not been exposed to any major traumatic break in their cultural continuity. Britain is such a case, with a relative calmer picture, in spite of the industrialization which writers from Wordsworth on have inveighed against. The need for modernity seems to have always been contained by an equally strong need for conserving the continuity of the literary experience. Just as capitalism did not abruptly rupture the organic community, and a measure of balance was retained by absorbing sectors of the community into the power structure with a gradualness which did not bring hierarchial society crashing down with undue suddenness, so also in literature the revolutionaries were absorbed, or relegated as eccentrics to the fringes of the scene, until they could be accepted as serving the cause of tradition itself.

Obviously, the kind of cultural conflict caused by the relationship of colonizer to colonized was not at the center of the stage as it was in the colonies themselves; a typical modern work in India shows the interaction of cultures more vividly than a typically English or even American work. But this is not to deny that the British have been influenced by, and are listening to, the assertions of modernity in Asia, Eastern Europe or even Japan.

In America, however, a primordial anti-establishment tendency and a desire to draw from as many cultures as possible in order to build a unique cultural base has often resulted in a medley of superficial borrowings. The encounter between cultures does not often take the form of a mature interpenetration. A country of immigrants had necessarily to cope with a desire to draw on separate, external cultural sources, if only to assert a personal voice in the chaos of a vast, unopened country. Very soon, however, the universalizing tendencies became dominant on the American scene, and even the protesters wanted to fall back on something which they tried to identify as typically American. Poets like Ginsberg and Snyder, while ostensibly seeking Oriental sources of nourishment, are also drawing on residual elements in the American heritage; this is not without its difficulties, as for example when the ecologist's love of the wilderness sometimes fails to recognize that anything like modern American civilization would have been impossible if the wilderness had not been tamed in the first place.

The issues of national or cultural identity, creative authenticity, the writer's language, his relation to his own and external societies, the concern over the vanishing of small cultures in the face of increasing homogenization, are not separate or inseparable questions, but merely aspects of the central problem for the artist and the fabulator in our time. The artist struggles to give form to a double experience: attachment to his own culture, and the umbilical stretching caused by his confrontation with other cultures.

The twentieth century has compelled writers to consort with extremities, the most extreme of which is the condition of exile with different kinds of human and artistic consequences. A taxonomy of writers in exile is fascinating. There was the self-chosen flight from potential danger: Bertolt Brecht and Thomas Mann from Nazi Germany; Solzhenitsyn from communist Russia. There was also a self-imposed response to constraints or circumstances, or the result of personal or cultural preferences; from the United States, Ezra Pound went to Italy, Henry James and T. S. Eliot to England, Lafcadio Hearn to Japan and Richard Wright to France.

The condition of exile need not involve departure from the home country. It could be an accepted internment on principle within a flawed mother culture; Boris Pasternak in the U.S.S.R., Alan Paton in South Africa, or Nick Joaquin in the Philippines. The complex negotiations required to sustain life and art undertaken by writers in the various situations of exile must be studied by the writer--and therefore by his critics--at different levels: for example the strategies, so different from each other employed by Henry James in Europe; by Hemingway in Spain and Cuba; by Robert Louis Stevenson in California, Hawaii and Samoa; and by Lafcadio Hearn in Japan.

There is also the matter of the directions of exile or sojourn: for example, the flow from the European modern to the primitive, Lawrence in Mexico; from the "raw" frontier to the European, James and Eliot; from the industrial-modern to the ancient-traditional, Hermann Hesse to Asia, Gary Snyder and Allen Ginsberg to India; from the totalitarian to the relatively free, Solzhenitsyn: from the post-colonial to the cosmopolitan, V.S. Naipaul, Raja Rao and G. V. Desani. There could also be returns to lands of ancestral memory, Issac B. Singer to Jewish middle-Europe and Russia; Naipaul to India.

As far as criticism is concerned, the very relevance of literature, let alone its centrality, has become a matter of earnest dispute. Broadly speaking, art and literature have positioned themselves on three points on a continuum. First they have been seen as autonomous, *sui generis*, vulgarized and debilitated as "art for art's sake". Second, they have been considered agents, making society, while at the same time being mirrors and reflections of it. Third, they have been seen as by-products, outcrops, epiphenomena of society as in the classic Marxist schema. Wherever one wants to locate oneself on this continuum, it has to be accepted that criticism itself, if not determined, is conditioned by culture. Modern culture has seen such scientific, industrial and technological advancement as to make a novelist and man of science like C. P. Snow speak of "two cultures" much to the chagrin of critics like F. R. Leavis in Britain and Lionel Trilling in America who want criticism to retain its Johnsonian and Arnoldian role of an unambiguously central relevance. Raymond Williams and Richard Hoggart, since Leavis, have further widened and democratized the concept of culture, trying to move it away from kinds of establishment culture, or at least the hegemony exercised by the prominent poets, critics, men of letters, dictating standards of artistic taste to the largely uncivilized majority. In the United States, where the ambition was to find new frontiers not only in art but in social organization and religious sensibility, what was applauded was the creation of the new, making something out of almost nothing; and even though important works have been written on aspects of cultural life, no one has dared, or been able to offer a truly centralist vision. Europeans, however, have had a long tradition of phenomenological concern and present a very different picture of their function from that of the British giants of the nineteenth century: Wordsworth, Coleridge, Mill, Arnold and William Morris.

But there are other major dimensions bedeviling a consideration of our area of interest. Once upon a time, English was the language only of England. Today it is the language of the United States, Canada, Australia, New Zealand, many countries of the former British Empire, now the Commonwealth, the Caribbean, parts of South Africa and Africa itself, and enjoys official status in countries ranging from India to Sri Lanka, to Singapore, to Malaysia, to Fiji and other regions in the Pacific. Besides it is the dominant world language.

Another dimension is that English is not just an international language, it is an international literature. Its bulk, proliferation and sheer variety frustrate any attempt to project an inclusive view.

It is difficult to find a major writer today who is not cross-cultural in the sense in which Jane Austen may be said to be monocultural. But as Edward Said in his recent *Culture and Imperialism* has pointed out, the colonial enterprise of Sir Thomas Bertram is of crucial importance to Mansfield Park as the material basis for the way of life, its sustenance, its emotional quality, its moral underpinnings, but also as a frame for the heroine Fanny's own movement from a near indentured laborer to mistress of the house. It is not sufficient to be a regional or "geographical" specialist: one has to seek a total picture however daunting the task.

It would also seem that it is no longer enough to be a literary critic of the old humanist variety; the problem is further compounded by the fact that the physiognomy of literary criticism appears to have changed beyond recognition. Rarely in the history of intellectual life have so many thinkers whose primary interest is not literature or creative writing or even *belles-lettres* so strongly influenced the way we look at imaginative writing in our time. University departments of literature are rife with professors who spend their time wrestling with the demons unleashed by these thinkers, eminent men in their own domains but of ambiguous relevance when applied out of context, away from the breathing texts which should be the reader's main concern. Literary critics have to double up as sociologists, psychologists, philosophers, linguistic theoreticians, cultural historians and the like.

The impact of these intellectuals has been such that it is possible to designate different periods in modern literary criticism as the Age of Structuralism, the Age of Psychoanalytic Criticism (a la Lacan), the Age of Deconstructionism, the Age of Post-Structuralism and so on, though the time-frames and boundaries are inexact and ever shifting.

The early influence was of course that of Ferdinand de Saussure whose famous distinction between *langue* and *parole* continues to affect different branches of the human sciences. For him *langue* is a finite structure while *parole* is infinite, made of particular, individual utterances. Language is a system of signs which acquire meaning only in terms of the system as an entirety. Saussure himself puts it best as in this extract from *Cours de linguistique generale*:

> In itself, thought is like a swirling cloud, where no shape is intrinsically determinate. No ideas are established in advance, and nothing is distinct, before the introduction of linguistic structure.
>
> But do sounds, which lie outside this nebulous world of thought, in themselves constitute entities established in advance? No more than ideas do. The substance of sound is no more fixed or rigid than that of thought. It does not offer a ready-made mould, with shapes that thought must inevitably conform to. It is a malleable material which can be fashioned into separate parts in order to supply the signals which thought has need of. So we can envisage the linguistic phenomenon in its entirety -- the language, that is -- as a series of adjoining subdivisions simultaneously imprinted both on the plane of vague, amorphous thought, and on the equally featureless plane of sound....
>
> Just as it is impossible to take a pair of scissors and cut one side of paper without at the same time cutting the other, so it is impossible in a language to isolate sound from thought or thought from sound. To separate the two for theoretical purposes takes us into either pure psychology or pure phonetics, not linguistics.

The importance of this formulation is that it separates the linguistic sign, that holistic totality of what signifies and what is signified, from reality, understood as something existing out there which has a validity of its own. The word has "meaning" only within a linguistically articulated structure.

Such an approach robs reality of a determinable meaning. This grew into the wide-ranging movement known as Structuralism, which spread across various disciplines of thought and research, which in general terms attributes meaning to a cultural fact by reestablishing and interpreting its place within the system of relationships to which it belongs rather than by positing a direct linkage between it and reality. Claude Levi-Strauss applied structuralism to the study of myth, rites and kinship systems. Roland Barthes looked at *haute cuisine* among other social ensembles. Roman Jakobson extended Saussure's theory that languages are marked by "oppositions" and has had a major influence on literary theory and criticism. His distinction between metaphor and metonymy as tools of literary analysis has been put to good use, notably by David Lodge in essays of practical criticism. Jacques Lacan has strengthened the portfolio of Freudian psychoanalysis, not least by adapting Saussure's linguistic theories: as Lacan puts it,

> And how could a psychoanalyst of today not realize that his realm of truth is in fact the word, when his whole experience must find in the word alone its instrument, its framework, its material, and even the static of its uncertainties...what the psychoanalytic experience discovers in the unconscious is the whole structure of language.

In what is clearly the post-structuralist phase (how much more "post" can one go in chronology!) we encounter Jacques Derrida, the most potent hijacker on the intellectual scene: while the attempt to dismantle the Western metaphysical tradition, which has corralled the world of meaning for so many centuries, has its admirers, what Derrida offers is a notion of the word as being intrinsically incapable of achieving its full signification: it is imprisoned within a system of differences, *differences* in the more inclusive and expressive French, and has a built-in tendency to undermine, in fact detonate, its purported meaning. The sense too dissipates into a number of readers or signifiers: it is not just the disappearance of a recognizable author, but his very death and, to the delight of Stanley Fish, the only arbiter of meaning is a group of himself and like-minded academic critics. The above remarks may seem somewhat dismissive of Derrida, who I know is an impressive philosopher but I like to contrast him with a thinker I admire even more, Michel Foucault, in a limiting way. Foucault does not, like Derrida, reduce all our problems to the dominance of the Western metaphysical tradition but relates them to *pouvoir*, the structures and institutions of power. His scope is therefore the real world. In the most perceptive essay on Derrida and Foucault, Edward Said, in *The World, the Text and the Critic* says of Foucault that

> Although it is true that he has been mainly interested in two sides of the same coin – the process of exclusion, by which cultures designate and isolate their opposites, and its obverse, the process by which cultures designate and valorize their own incorporative authority – it is not certain that Foucault's greatest intellectual contribution is to an understanding of how the will to exercise dominant control in society and history has also discovered a way to clothe, disguise, rarefy, and wrap itself systematically in the language of truth, discipline, rationality, utilitarian value, and knowledge.

Said takes Foucault further and into the more precise areas of Colonialism and Imperialism. His magnificent study, *Orientialism*, now almost a classic, showed how European powers endorsed, nay created a body of scholarship designed to stereotype the colonized Orient in order to buttress an imperial hegemony. His extension from the text is justified:

> Criticism cannot assume that its province is merely the text, not even the great literary text. It must see itself, with other discourse, inhabiting a much contested cultural space, in which what has counted in the continuity and transmission of knowledge has been the signifier, as an event that has left lasting traces upon the human subject. Once we take that view, then literature as an isolated paddock in the broad cultural field disappears, and with it too the harmless rhetoric of self-delighting humanism. Instead we will be able, I think, to read and write with a sense of the greater stake in historical and political effectiveness that literary as well as other texts have had.

Our area of interest – the literature of cross-cultural contact – has another important theme which keeps knocking at the door at every turn – I refer to the topic of colonialism and the current post-colonialism which is still hyperactive in many respects. Said is very pertinent here. Though his *Orientalism* filled a much required space, it did not adequately consider the distortions produced by the colonies not only in understanding their situation but in devising modes of handling it. I do not want to delay with this here because I deal with this more concretely in Part III of this book. I merely want to draw the reader's attention to the very important contributions to colonialism and post-colonialism theory in thinkers like Frantz Fanon, Antonio Gramsci and Jose Karlos Mariategui, which are very apropos to the concerns in this book. It is vital that we read them in conjunction with the colonized writers who are the "resisters", able to afford a nuanced articulation of their discontents and their hope.

T. S. Eliot published *Notes towards the definition of Culture* in the late forties. His approach still has a centrality though the tentativeness of the title suggests a radical uncertainty on the part of the writer. It is surprising, however, that it increased the choler and raised the gall of so many sociologists: the only explanation is the overweening ambition of modern sociologists which has blinded them to the fact that their darling science does not, if considered as an empirical science, offer a self-sufficing discipline. True, Eliot spoke of culture as the incarnation of a religion: he believed that what is distinctive in a culture, what constitutes, so to speak its *form* is its psychic life and that the primary determinant of the psychic life of a culture is its religion. But in this view, Eliot is in good company, and has a respectable ancestry. Emile Durkheim, whose theories of sociology are very different from Eliot's, put it this way:

> Since it has been made to embrace all of reality, the physical world as well as the moral one, the forces that move bodies as well as those that move minds have been conceived in a religious form. That is how the most diverse methods and practices, both those that make possible the continuation of the moral life (laws, morals and art) and those serving the material life (the material, technical and practical sciences) are directly or indirectly derived from religion.

Now that the thorny subject of religion has entered these pages, it is as well to draw a parallel between the parts played by religion and the arts in culture, and how their respective functions must be treated in cultural studies. My remarks must needs be elementary in nature; my excuse is that in a consideration of such a complex and important problem first principles have been almost forgotten. To take religion first: perhaps the clearest way of formulating this is to state that though religion and culture are for the purpose of the sociologist different aspects of the same, there is a real distinction between religion, *qua* religion and culture, *qua* culture. Religion considered apart from the problem of culture and defined for its own sake is the relation between the human being and a super-human transcendent power or, to put it more simply, between man and God. Both aspects of this definition are important: man is the only creature open to religious experience. The other half of the definition involves Transcendent Being; it is a difficult task, and this is hardly the place, to discuss the notion of religious experience: suffice it to say that whether it be the experience of the mystic piercing the naked Being of God with "the sharp dart of longing love" or the natural religion of ordinary men, the element of transcendence is an essential datum.

The supernatural is a necessary constituent of religion: to possess even the faintest of religious intuitions is to enter the world of the Other. "The ultimate ache of man is his ache for Being": the loss of Being is his ultimate agony. This is why it has been said that the most fully human existence is not to be found in social or "cultural" being: the fully personal life, that mode of life which engages the deepest desires and touches the deepest levels of the personality, is the life lived in communion with God. Religion, then, considered in itself is supra-social and trans-cultural: the intrinsic or "eternal" truth of a religion does not depend on its cultural fruits or accomplishments.

In the area of desire and the relationship between religion and culture, the most fruitful contribution in modern times has been made by Rene Girard. Girard describes the mimetic nature of desire; we want things or objects because others want them. When we try to claim the objects as our own, whether the "object" is a woman, a toy, or a piece of land, we do so under the illusion that our desire preceded the desire of the other. There is a rivalry over who is first, in effect, and thus conflict is born. The object of the conflict fades to the background and now at center stage are the two rivals, and these rivals are doubles. Conflict is contagious as we are witnessing outbreaks of violence in virtually every area of society and in the verbal battles in our intellectual community.

In order to free ourselves from conflict we need to seek the help of another. In the larger scope of society we band together and choose an arbitrary victim, a scapegoat, who is held responsible for the crisis. Girard follows his "victimage mechanism" through myths and other texts of persecution, of which the Bible is representative. After the sacrifice there is a period of rest, which soon enough becomes ordinary. We imitate desires for new and greater experiences, and this commences yet another crisis. Girard has already spoken about the structure of mimetic desire in literature in *Deceit, Desire, and the Novel*. He discusses at length the part played by religion in the transformation of culture in *Things Hidden Since the Foundation of the World*.

One must not forget that the end of sociology is a human end: it is therefore wrong to talk of sociological as distinct from human values -- equally meaningless is the analogical notion that art is concerned not with moral but with "aesthetic" values, art being thought as of a special territory with its autonomous standards. I do not wish to simplify the problem: the moral judgement of art does not depend on the application of externally conceived notions of "good" and "bad" derived from codes constructed by others. It is indeed a superficial conception of both art and morality that would see an enmity between them: one can be called truly moral only if one lives by moral standards that accord with the deepest personal intuitions of one's living experience: it is this same quality of deeply felt experience in one's inner life that is the parent of great art.

An adequate definition of culture involves not so much a knowledge of techniques of sociological research as well-clarified notions about man and human society: by this I do not mean that a sociologist should study culture in order to see exemplified in it his notions of man. We all agree that the ideal sociologist should not distort what he studies in order to strengthen his own bias: sociological generalizations in so far as they claim our attention should be inductive, not a priori assertions with which facts are made to accord. But it is well to remember that the term "sociological generalizations" does not include the definition of man. One's notions about the nature of man would condition the choice of methods and the conclusions reached: A Marxist sociologist, for example, would interpret the W*eltanschauung* of a community in terms of its methods of production, influenced as he is by his belief that culture is an epiphenomenon of material factors (the mind-matter dialectic is, as we know, specious and can ultimately be reduced to a materialist monism).

I have already said that sociology is not a self-sufficient discipline; the object of investigation -- man -- is not exhausted in the discipline of such empirical knowledge as sociology affords. The answer to the question, what is man, is pre-sociological and can perhaps be determined only by a rational metaphysic, concerned with first principles.

Just like art itself, criticism too provides an interesting parallel with sociology particularly in the matter of moral judgements.

I have already pointed out that there is no valid antagonism between art and morality – by this I did not mean that criticism of art is merely a branch of moral knowledge. There is a function which the literary critic alone can perform; the moralist with a deficient sensibility is not competent to judge literature since he has not mastered those standards and tools of analysis that are the proper concern of literary criticism, and has not acquired the discriminating responsiveness to literature that characterizes the literary critic. It is obvious that a literary work does not become great art merely because of the highly moral nature of the ideas and sentiments when abstracted from the particular piece of work in which they are embodied: It is also important to note that an experience which is trivial cannot be considered serious art even if it were "formally" perfect and "technically" adequate -- what is not worth saying is never worth saying, however "well" it may happen to be said. Literary criticism has to be completed by moral criticism, but the word "completed" should not imply any succession in time: in good criticism the critical and moral judgements are simultaneous, the moral valuation of art includes the critical, and cannot do without it. The problem for sociology is similar: the relation between the critical and moral judgments in art and literary criticism bears a resemblance to the relation between the ascertained facts and the moral judgments in the social sciences. One agrees with Evans-Pritchard when he makes the following observation,

> It is unsatisfactory that the sociologist....should often be the person who knows the facts best and yet should be self-debarred from making judgments on them. It is even more unsatisfactory that the moral philosopher, who is the person best fitted to make judgments, should do so, as often happens, without an adequate knowledge of social theory and fact.

but in his further statement there lurks a hidden danger to which it is worth calling attention:

> The answer would seem to be that the sociologist should also be a moral philosopher and that, as such, he should have a set of definite beliefs and values in terms of which he evaluates the facts he studies as a sociologist. He must make, and keep apart, two different kinds of judgement within the same field: a judgment on the significance of social facts to scientific theory and a judgment on their significance to moral theory.

Just as the literary critic should also be a "moral arbiter", it is true that the sociologist should be a moral philosopher as well: but I think the relation between sociologist and moral philosopher within the province of this science should be expressed better than in the quoted sentence. I daresay that Professor Evans-Pritchard may agree with my own statement of this "relation", since we are not disagreed on the fundamental question of the relevance and necessity of value-judgements in sociology: but, since the point of view I am trying to present is not widely accepted today, inexact formulations on this important question may lead to confusion. The reason why such a presentation as what I propose to offer does not now enjoy a wide currency is due, I submit, to the methodological weakness of present-day sociologists – that laziness of intelligence which avoids methodology under the pretence that such speculation is abstract and unprofitable.

Evans-Pritchard suggests that sociology differs from the "natural sciences" mainly in this regard – the sociologist not only studies facts but has the additional task of evaluating them in terms of moral judgements. The problem seems to me more complex: the sociologist is by no means a mechanical union of statistician (collector of facts) and moral philosopher. One cannot distinguish sociology from other sciences by asserting that in sociology value-judgments are super-added to the normal scientific discovery, analysis and grouping of facts. It is true that sociology, like other sciences, depends on the constant correlation between general laws and empirical verification: however, to say that sociology differs from some natural sciences because it deals with the classification of facts plus moral judgments is to reveal a wrong understanding of the way judgments of value are made.

Evans-Pritchard thinks of a moral valuation as a necessary but subsequent imposition on facts one has already observed. A sociologist is always making moral judgements not merely because he is like other men, and cannot, by virtue of his being a human being, avoid such judgements but for the more important reason that value-judgements are inherent in the kind of knowledge this science imparts, being due to what may be called the formal object of sociology itself. In order to clarify this, we should discuss the difference – and this distinction, though not easy to establish, is vital – between "facts" in sociology and "facts" in other disciplines among the natural sciences with which we are familiar.

One may choose an illustration from physiology: the physiologists studying the function of, say, the *opisthonephros* in *scoliodon* deals with facts that are ultimately observable: I make this remark with great exactness since my intention is not so much to discuss the general differences between the natural and social sciences as to point out, by the use of particular examples, the essential nature of sociological knowledge. Now it should be evident that the sociologist inspecting what Sorokin calls super-organic phenomena has to deal with "facts" of a very different kind. If a number of sociologists were to study the same human community it is likely that on certain levels, such as population statistics, the investigation will yield uniform results, but on the more fundamental issues there is likely to be a wide divergence of opinion. Different sociologists will give different accounts, all claiming to be factual: the facts will vary because the interpretations vary, or rather "fact-interpretation" is a unity, it being impossible to separate, where the deeper levels of sociology are concerned, the fact from the interpretation given. It is not possible to decide with any definiteness which account gives us the truth: sociological knowledge does not offer the possibility of demonstration with certainty like, for example, the discipline of chemistry where the report of a chemical analysis can be justified by an appeal to experiment. Unlike in a chemical experiment, we cannot in a sociological survey control everything that takes place: it is perhaps this characteristic of sociological knowledge that has made several empirical sociologists apply to fields of investigation those quantitative methods that bring definitive results in some of the natural sciences. The tendency to make of sociology an exact science is deplorable because it exhibits an insensitiveness to the peculiar nature of sociological knowledge, alike to its misery and grandeur, its exigencies and its fruits: the attempt to reduce its many--colored language to the referential terminology of the natural sciences reveals the intellectual habit that confuses the discipline of sociology with the discipline of mechanics. Further, sociology justifies itself as a legitimate branch of knowledge: it is not necessary to defend its claim to be considered a science by identifying its methods with those of the natural sciences – such an attitude proceeds from a crude notion of what constitutes scientific knowledge and scientific method.

It must not be inferred from what has been said that sociology does not deal with objective truth: a sociological conclusion is objectively true or false but there is no way of showing the one or the other, one cannot prove one's judgement in the way a logician demonstrates the final term of his syllogism. The analogy offered by literary criticism is helpful: sociological knowledge, like criticism, is approximation towards the truth. The poem is good or bad in itself but the critic can offer no definite proof: this is due to the mode of knowledge of the object, the work of literature; this is the inevitable condition of the discipline, and does not affect the essential objectivity of one's knowledge of literature. Similarly one's sociological knowledge is objectively valid, even though one cannot show that a particular conclusion is true in an absolute sense (except of course in the case of statistical or other information that can be empirically verified).

The explanation for this essential characteristic of sociology is to be found in the nature of its "formal object" – human life, and more specifically, man in society. The social life of man cannot be described fully with the tools of measurement and analysis: the way of life of a people has to be grasped as a pattern, the sociologist must "possess" intellectually the life of a community of spiritual beings: the only scientific procedure in such a case is to make one's methods suit the nature of the "object" one studies – sociology is as valid a science as botany though the methods are not the same.

To explain more adequately the reason why human life imposes on those who wish to study it this peculiar feature we have associated with sociological knowledge, it may be useful to contrast human with animal society: I have suggested this comparison not in order to repeat the current academic cliché that the differences between human and animal society are a matter of varying degrees of flexibility in response to the environment: the detestable crudity of this notion rests on the inability to make proper distinctions, when such distinctions have to be made. Most of us will agree that when two students of animal biology study termites they will not differ in regard to the facts relating to the biology of termites or if they do, there is a way of showing that one is definitely wrong: if, on the other hand, two sociologists, one from Eire and the other from Malaya, study an African "primitive" community, they almost certainly will differ in their conclusions, for here are no common "facts" which are varyingly interpreted but the "facts" themselves will appear differently to different observers. I hope I have hinted at my notion of "sociological fact": what I wish to stress is that the differences among sociologists cannot be explained as different measurements and notations of common material or phenomena: the very notion of measurement is out of place since we are here dealing with the sociologist's intellectual "possession" of the life of a community in its living concreteness: the mode of understanding has no analogy with the kind of measurement to which we are accustomed in the natural sciences. When a sociologist observes a phenomenon, he simultaneously interprets it in relation to his values, or, more broadly speaking, to his previous experience: the observation and the valuation are contemporaneous, and form a unity. The essential difference between the social organization in animal society and in human community is that social organization among animals is predetermined by the genetic endowment and under special circumstances by certain "extrinsic" factors: for example, in the bee community the modes of behavior among the members are determined both by the genetic make-up and external factors such as food: while a male bee has to remain such all its life as a result of its genetic constitution, individuals which are genetically female may become either workers or queens: this depends on whether or not they are fed on "royal jelly", according to the needs of the colony.

A human community obviously is not determined by any of these factors: the modes of social behavior among human beings are not explained physiologically or by any other uniform laws. We are now concerned with no less an issue than the fundamental question of what distinguishes man from the animal: it is enough to say here that the distinction is one of kind, and not merely a matter of different degrees of "mental power": the possession of symbolic intelligence, manifested in human language, and the power of free-will are qualitative distinctions that separate human from animal nature. It should be evident that the science which has man as its "object" must employ an unique discipline: not only must the sociologist assess the community in relation to his own experience, he must also attempt to see what makes it a community in itself: he must live the life of the community he studies and at the same time guard himself lest he becomes too absorbed into the community he has set out to study.

What is most important is not methodologies of research but more the prior identification of what is to be studied.

The new reality in the world of letters, dwarfing all others, is not structuralism or its even more recent variations, which however useful, are lenses from which to view the cultural text, but the very nature and content of the new realities – the multi-cultural, cross-cultural, "global" nature of the experience itself. We need new strategies, new emphases on different facets to see the reality right.

Though there is nothing new under the sun, the configurations are vastly different and ever changing.

The lack of a defined social setting which was available, say in Victorian or earlier England, throws on the writer the task of digging deeper into his personal resources to give interest or even piquancy to his creative efforts. The situations have to be more atypical, exceptional, even bizarre. The characters who were eccentrics at worst in Dickens have become grotesques as in the novels of Salman Rushdie. The writer's *Weltanschauung* is privately fabricated as against the earlier movement away from, and to an established frame. There has to be a straining after setting and place, as in Salman Rushdie, to whom I have devoted a chapter, or even in Anita Desai, to whom I have given substantial space, especially because there are no landmarks or road signs as in earlier times. Even the topics, subjects or themes have to be even more a matter of individual, almost idiosyncratic creation rather than a take-off from what has been given.

Of course the problems of global inter-relatedness are not peculiar to writers and artists: even the head of the Roman Catholic Church is a peripatetic Pope, who visits his flock in remote parts of the world. But it is the writer who is called upon more and more to live amid life's extremities: how much more extreme or, in a favorable sense, more of an oddity can one get than in the recent novel of Kazuo Ishiguro, a winner of Britain's most prestigious award for fiction, the Booker prize. His novel *The Remains of the Day* is about an English butler, that quintessentially British figure. Ishiguro is a man born in Japan and settled in England, the degree of whose acclimatization can be seen in the following extract from the book:

> It is sometimes said that butlers only truly exist in England. Other countries, whatever title is actually used, have only menservants. I tend to believe this is true. Continentals are unable to be butlers because they are as a breed incapable of the emotional restraint which only the English race are capable of. Continentals – and by and large the Celts, as you will no doubt agree – are as a rule unable to control themselves in moments of strong emotion, and are thus unable to maintain a professional demeanor other than in the least challenging of situations. If I may return to my earlier metaphor – you will excuse my putting it so coarsely – they are like a man who will, at the slightest provocation, tear off his suit and his shirt and run about screaming. In a word, 'dignity' is beyond such persons. We English have an important advantage over foreigners in this respect and it is for this reason that when you think of a great butler, he is bound, almost by definition, to be an Englishman.

I do not wish to dwell on, or even adumbrate, the underlying thematic structure of my book: what form or unity it has must emerge from itself as a completed piece of work.

The attempted progression in this book is from greater and more inclusive levels of generalization to a consideration of examples intended to illustrate the theories and to prove a concrete fidelity to the literature which has been chosen. Such a procedure was adopted largely because the analytic perspectives offered could be reckoned uncommon in modern literary and cultural criticism. However, since it is impossible within the compass of one book to adequately flesh out these theories, the first part of the book may be considered a project for criticism in general rather than as a promise of what will be accomplished in this particular book. It may therefore be seen as a section having its own particular validity.

Part I begins with an exposition of the principal and multi-form issues of study generated by the topic of the international convergence of literature and culture in the modern world. Though such a convergence is a fact of life, language and letters, academic departments have fought shy of dealing with its many implications or even of recognizing its significance.

In the second chapter of Part I, the presentation is more specific, even though it is largely concerned with periodization of theoretical constructs.

In the third chapter, *American Responses to the New Realities*, the situation in the United States, which has the greatest effect on literary taste and standards, and because of its importance has considerable influence in the field, is briefly examined.

Part I is followed by an *Interlude* which is meant as a transition to Part II. It looks briefly at a form of cross-cultural *belles-lettres*. It is not "fictional" in content or shape. In searching for a book which best exemplifies this genre, I have chosen one of the volumes of Leonard Woolf's autobiography, *Growing*, which is an excellent example of the work of a serious sojourner, a participant observer who directly describes in the first person his involvement in a foreign culture. Many candidates could be found among works of travels and other kinds of commentary, born of direct observation, by writers who have lived from time to time in different lands, but Woolf's book was selected because of its clear literary merit and for the way it accurately reveals the intellectual equipment, the literary credentials, the writer's sensibility, as well as the cultural specifics of the society he encounters and interprets.

In Part II, the geographical area is limited to Europe and Asia, and more particularly to the interactions between Britain and South-east Asia. It has chapters on Kipling's *Kim*, Leonard Woolf's *The Village in the Jungle*, Forster's *A Passage to India*, George Orwell's *Burmese Days*, L. H. Myers' *The Root and the Flower*, Anthony Burgess' *The Malayan Trilogy* and Paul Sacott's *Staying On*. The novels range from Imperialism at its apogee as in *Kim* to the Empire in dissolution and retreat as in *The Malayan Triology*, and its aftermath as in *Staying On*. No apologies are made about the fact that the bulk of the present work is about the British-South and Southeast Asian connections; it is, however, almost a survey of the modern British novel since it includes Kipling, Forster, Orwell, L. H. Myers, Burgess and Paul Scott. It is no accident that the notable absentees, Joseph Conrad and D. H. Lawrence, also had as part of their intellectual disposition and literary endeavor a strong migratory instinct and a concern for the exile. The same analytic perspectives could be applied to them as well as to other areas and confrontations: one has to keep one's efforts within a manageable focus.

Part III breaks away from the Anglo-centric emphasis of Part II and deals with the opposite side of the coin. It unveils Indian responses in philosophy, poetry and the novel to the East-West encounter and discusses an area of presentation where the problems and issues raised by biculturalism and bilingualism are even more visible. There are chapters on Indian poetry in English, the Indian novel in English and on a comparatively early but still relevant philosophical attempt to bring together the East and the West under the umbrella of a common Great Tradition.

The book ends with a return to one of its major preoccupations in an Epilogue titled *Place as Anima* where the role of "place" or landscape is examined with the use of two extreme and contrasting examples, Conrad's *Heart of Darkness* and Graham Greene's *The Quiet American*. It is hoped this brief comparison will further establish the differences possible within this typology. I have included as an Appendix a previously published essay "Literature and Culture" which still seems to me the best general statement I am capable of making on this subject. It may help the reader to appreciate in a simple way the main presuppositions that govern my writings in this field.

I am planning another book which will consider another facet of the cross-cultural encounter, this time the relations between the United States and Europe as illustrated by the work of Henry James. It is not intended to be a point by point parallel with the Asian-European studies but will endeavor to provide another basic vantage-ground from which to observe and chart comparable and contrasting cross-cultural spaces.

This will not be another book on Henry James, as, apart from brief references to other pertinent works, I have selected only three novels from different stages of his career; it is rather a commentary on the trans-Atlantic experience from the viewpoint of cross-cultural convergence and confrontation. The movement is from the raw frontier, which has already become for some writers a self-sustaining repository of cultural strength and variety, to the sources of the

Imperialist European mission. The victimization is cultural; exile from the United States is generated not only by an assumed lack of sufficiency in American culture but also by increasing American wealth; after all, it is money which makes it possible to buy one's way into Europe. Beginning from a sense of cultural inferiority, the attempt to conquer Europe becomes a form of imperialism in reverse, foreshadowing America's present role as super-power and global policeman. It is evident that it is not necessary to assume the civil government of a country in order to perform the function of a colonizing power.

However, the present work must stand on its own two feet. If the reader finds Part I forbiddingly abstract and theoretically dense, he is encouraged to read the subsequent parts first and return to Part I if he chooses. But the earnest and scholarly-minded reader, it is hoped, will follow the sequence in the book.

Acknowledgments

There are only a few acknowledgments, as the book was a lonely endeavor without benefit of institutional affiliation or regular secretarial help.

Apart from the constant encouragement of my wife, I must mention the sharp affectionate scrutiny of my friend, the late Reuel Denney, an insufficiently recognized philosopher-king, who could have received adequate gratitude only if he had agreed to be named as my co-author. I am beholden, as always to my beloved teacher and longtime friend, the late Stuart Gerry Brown. Malcolm Bradbury's high praise of my work represents another of my unpayable debts.

My good friend and erstwhile Research Assistant Dr. Margaret King drafted most of Chapter III when she was a member of a research team which I directed at the East-West Center in Hawaii.

I am particularly grateful to my son Aruna for his vigilant encouragement, my son Indran for his unremitting impetus in all my literary endeavors, my son David for his scholarly counsel, for his wife Anne for meticulously proof-reading the final text and my daughter Mareeni for loving help and advice.

Very special thanks to my niece, Chemeli Cherubim, for retyping the entire text to make it "camera ready" for my publisher and to another niece Shankari Bastiampillai for her help.

I would like to add here that I have used some paragraphs and sentences from earlier books which I co-authored in order to make as complete a presentation as I can at the present time and to benefit the reader who can find most of what I have to say on this topic between two covers and within a single spine.

Chapter I

MODERN LITERATURE IN THE CONFLUENCE OF CULTURES: THEORIES AND CATEGORIES

1. Cervantes As Progenitor.

Though the novel, which is the major form of literary modernism since Gutenberg, has been carefully investigated as a subject of comparative literary studies, its cross-cultural nature and origins have not been sufficiently emphasized. If one takes the most important locus in the development of the genre, the publication of *Don Quixote* in 1605 (Part One) and 1615 (Part Two), it will be seen that this book, the primordial ancestor of the novel, anticipated most of the transformations of the genre between its own time and that of Franz Kafka. Although it has accumulated more commentary than perhaps any other work of prose fiction ever written, its cross-cultural lineage sometimes goes unmentioned. This is particularly unfortunate in its implications for the study of prose fiction in our own time.

The purported genesis of the book is an inventive fiction fathered by Cervantes. Marthe Robert says, in *L'Ancien et Le Nouveau*, (translated *The Old and the New*), by Carol Cosman, University of California Press: 1977).

According to this fiction, Cervantes is not the author of his book. He has contributed to its elaboration, and of course, takes credit for it; but in all honesty he is simply, like Homer, the editor who arranges and presents to the public an old, familiar story. He finds the completed work already written; his task is merely to transcribe it faithfully in the most attractive form. At first glance, the existence of this prototype seems to be a distinct inconvenience, since it considerably limits the author's rights to his creation and diminishes his glory. But in fact, it is his passport to the epic heights where, for good or ill, he is determined to cling. Thanks to Cid Hamete Benengeli, to whom he delegates the functions of divine memory, Cervantes assumes a position at least comparable, if not equal, to Homer's...we know at least three authors of *Don Quixote*: the anonymous author who has dealt with only several episodes: Cid Hamete Benengeli, who apart from a few regrettable lapses, furnishes almost all of the material of the novel; and Cervantes, whose role is limited to collecting and ordering the texts he has acquired. But these are not all. Others have collaborated on the work, notably the Spanish-speaking Moor whom Cervantes recruits on the spot to translate his manuscript (on Benengeli) and the authors of the parchments, which are found by mere chance in a lead box...(It may be added that the Benegeli manuscripts are obtained just in time: they were in notebooks whose paper was attractive to silk-workers.) Marthe Robert further notes that an even more distant "author" of the work is, in a sense, the author of Amadis de Gaul, since that chivalric romance is the one that Don Quixote sets out to imitate in loyal detail.

Marthe Robert accepts the general interpretation that Cervantes uses Benengeli in the manner he does in order to provide a fictionally obscure provenance for the tale. It could even be thought that, by fobbing it off on a non-Christian, Cervantes avoids responsibility for anything offensive or heretical a Christian reader might find in it. But at this point I would like to be foolhardy enough, by proposing an addition to the numberless interpretations of the book and its author, to suggest another possible set of integral connections with which one may have to reckon.

Cervantes in his lifetime, suffered not only from the Moorish masters of slavery in Algiers, where he was captive of war, but also from the Spanish Inquisition, which threatened his life and liberty in an obscure pursuit. He was therefore personally familiar with the unlimited ideological power and violence of both sides of the cultural war of his time. Moreover, the knightly romances he describes as the seducers of Don Quixote, although they generally supported the

Christian side of the long struggle with the Saracens, sometimes had room for heroes on both sides of the fray.

For these reasons, his extraordinary decision to credit an infidel with the writing down of an exposé of knight-errantry, and his purported employment of a Moorish translator to help him get the materials into Spanish, has rich cross-cultural overtones. Is it possible, for example, that *only* a Moor would bother to save and record memories of a Christian fanatic such as Quixote whose very actions satirized Christian-written romances, or, by an alternative explication, actually imagine and invent them in the act of writing them down? In that event one level of the great novel consists in the invitation it has offered to a Islamic chronicler to make a basic contribution to a travesty of Christian muddle-headedness.

The point perhaps acquires additional interest with respect to the historical origins of the novel and the imperial colonialism which provides one of the major backgrounds of the modern novel of culture contact. The expulsion of the Moors in the fifteenth century has been considered by Fernand Braudel, author of *The Mediterranean and the Mediterranean World in the Age of Philip the Second* (trans. Sian Reynolds, Harper & Row, 1972) as a step coordinate with the beginning of colonial rivalry between Catholic powers on the one hand, and Protestant powers of Holland and England on the other.

Cervantes wrote soon after this, at a time when Spain had reached the height of its colonial accomplishment and was already beginning its decline. In short, the book appeared just at the point when the spread of English power to both the New World and Asia was just beginning to get in gear. It was this development, more than anything else, that led to the Post-Spanish, modern forms of colonialism and imperialism, and to the creation of the conditions in which the literature of cross-cultural contract has arisen. This should be kept in mind, I think, as I turn to more contemporary reflections on this type of literature, before returning to Cervantes at a later state of my analysis. In the meantime, it would appear that the cross-cultural novel is the earliest, not the latest, manifestation of the novel.

2.   The Current Situation

The twentieth century is an age in which, more than any other, several writers have come to take an interest in literatures remote from their own. Pound found inspiration in the Orient as well as in Rome and Provence. He gave a new direction to the long-standing concern of American writers and philosophers with the creativity of the East. My studies in literature in cross-national perspective are concentrated on the East-West axis and North-South axis and for obvious reasons are highly selective rather than comprehensive; but they are the descendants of the interest in world literature expressed by Goethe in the eighteenth century and Matthew Arnold in the nineteenth century.

When the study of comparative literature began to develop in the late eighteenth and early nineteenth centuries, it was characterized by two particular cross-national and cross-historical perspectives. What was clearly shared by all the cultivated Europeans in the enterprise, was a common knowledge of Latin (and often Greek), and a realization that the literary cultures of those languages, along with the Bible, were the ancestors of European written literature as a whole. However, since the national vernacular languages had already come to be accepted by as early as 1500, European comparatists of the eighteenth and nineteenth centuries became interested in the ways in which these were still affiliated with each other even though they had gone their separate ways. One unifying thread was found in the common dependence on classical literature and civilization and on the transmission of this to later times by such cultivated masters of the vernacular as, for example, Dante in Italian and Chaucer in English.

It is well known that an entirely new stage of European comparative studies had begun in the seventeenth century, when Leibniz brought China to the attention of Europe in a new and influential way; and in the eighteenth century, when Sir William Jones discovered the affinity of Sanskrit with the European languages and inaugurated the age of studies in Hindu and Pali Buddhist literature and philosophy. Anything that goes on today in the study of cross-national literary connections in my own area of interest, the Pacific rim countries and South Asia, including the magnificent contribution of the twentieth century to translations of the literatures of these regions, owes a great debt to these founding fathers and, of course, the other later linguists and commentators who enriched their insights, for example, the great American scholar William Dwight Whitney in the field of Sanskrit studies, Max Muller, Arthur Waley, and in science, Joseph Needham.

If we look back to the Renaissance or even the Augustan Age, we find strikingly few attempts to try to justify the cross-national study of literature and language. Scholars such as Dr. Johnson could still carry on a conversation in Latin, and the clergyman of a small English parish was considered ill-educated if he was not able to read the New Testament in Greek. In most places, Latin was still the language of diplomacy and international science reporting; and the new vocabulary of science was being built up out of new applications of the roots of both Greek and Latin. Moreover, Johnson was a self-taught reader of French and Italian. Until recently, what needed defending was the odd idea that an educated man could get by on his mother-tongue alone. Today few feel the need to defend the self-sufficiency of one's own native language especially if it is a "World Language" like English.

As the relative decline in foreign language study in the United States seems to show, there are many people who adopt an isolationist stance and are content to ignore changes in the rest of the world. That these rapid changes are unintelligible to many Americans, the rise of Islamic fundamentalism being only the current major example, is a concomitant of the relative decline of the productivity and competitiveness of America compared to other places in the world. On the other hand, Americans who read widely have taken an increased interest in the translation of works from other languages and are proud if they hear that Faulkner has been translated in so many countries which are geographically remote.

It is more to the point, however, that since World War II, the United States has shown a strong and undiminished interest in religious, philosophical and literary messages from Asia. While some of this is at a sensational level that does no credit to American taste or intelligence, much of it is deserving of serious consideration and understanding. Furthermore there is no doubt that American writing has had a strong influence on cultures as diverse, for example, as Indian and Japanese. Thus, there is indeed a highly active cultural osmosis through literature taking place at present between East and West. The "problem" is to describe its general dimensions and channels, to grasp its themes, to understand its processes, to evaluate its effect, and to judge its implications for modern man.

3.   Changing Conditions of Literary Creativity

National Literature, World Literature, Comparative Literature.

This is a categorization with which we have become familiar since about 1800. I do not suggest that literary institutions, world-wide, have entered into a period of change and development since the peaking and subsequent decline of European colonialism. The peak is dated variously by various scholars, but I do not think that many of them would consider it wide of the mark if I placed the date at the time of the British Imperial Durbar in India in 1911. Since that time, literature has entered a phase that is observably different, in some important respects, from the phases which preceded it. This is partly a matter of the changing conditions of literary institutions, partly a matter of the way writers themselves helped to bring about those changes, and partly a matter of literature's response to such changes.

The dating that I have suggested is not an invention of my own. Suzanne Howe, writing at mid-century in the little known book *Novels of Empire* (Columbia University Press, 1949), saw three stages in the definition of the "problem" of colonialism and colonial culture contract by writers of fiction. The earliest, from about 1825 to 1880, saw the conquered people and their culture in a casual way as merely another exotic source of the clutter of the nineteenth--century novel. From 1880 to World War I writers began to see the relation between the occupier and the occupied as the problem, while after World War II, the tendency was to see the occupier himself as the problem, and to face directly the matter of retreat from imperialism. We might now add a fourth definition of the problem, as evidenced in post-1950 work done by Burgess and others: what good and bad effects have been brought on the occupier and the occupied by the experience of conquest and retreat? It can be seen that my selection of the Durbar of 1911 harmonizes with later stages of this typology.

The largest alteration, of course, is the European retreat from imperialism and colonialism. In one sense this has meant a decline of these patterns of power in general; in another it has meant that powers outside of Western Europe, especially the United States and the USSR, have picked up some of the pieces of a dismantled hegemony. In the 1980's the existence of a "Second World" and a "Third World", as well as the implied "First World" tells us something about what has happened. This shift in the centering and organization of political and economic power is one of the major transformations affecting the modern writer. But to a certain extent, literary influences themselves helped to bring some of this about. An anti-imperial view fuelled later on by literary talents such that of E. M. Forster had appeared in Britain as early as the 1880's. In the colonized countries, literary genius such as that of Mohammed Iqbal and Rabindranath Tagore in Moslem and Hindu India, helped to foster ideas of national self-determination.

The response of literature to the vast alternations I have spoken of cannot be discussed without first taking account of the technological revolutions that have set in since about eighty to one hundred and ten years ago. It was around this time that we began to move into the modern age of telecommunications by leaping far ahead of mid-nineteenth century telegraphy-cum-cable techniques. After Edison, it was no longer a requirement for a world defined as literary that it should be written, as opposed to spoken and memorized in oral form. The recorded electric sound-wave preserved the work in as permanent, repeatable, and distributable a form as the page of print. Some aspects of the literature to be studied here are the result in large part of this much-discussed transformation. This development alone, without regard to other causes and conditions of literary affairs, would be sufficient to establish the literary period of which I am speaking as markedly different from all that had preceded it. This is often summarized by the observation that these great technological changes have brought the literary man into a new relation with his own language and audience while at the same time they have brought all the languages and literatures of the whole world into a new relationship with each other.

There were two major effects. On the one hand, national cultures possessing substantial control over the world media of communication, notably Britain, extended what had already become a powerful diffusion of her own language, even further from her shores. On the other hand, cultures still in a pre-literate stage achieved an important kind of "literacy" even before they learned to write and read their own language, when it was recorded for them and for the rest of the world by visiting anthropologists and literary historians.

In between these two major consequences at the extremes, there were many other effects of a mixed sort, such as: the rise of interest in indigenous languages as contrasted with colonial imports of language; the linking of linguistic autonomy with national and cultural autonomy; the rapid increase of multi-lingualism in various classes and professionals outside literary and scholarly circles; the appearance of language-planning efforts in the Third World; changes in the methods and ideology of foreign-language teaching and learning; the proliferation of translation, especially of scientific, technological materials and the commodities of popular culture, such as the movie-dubbing and the mass-marketed "formula" types of fiction; the new acquisition of power over the tongues of colonizers of "home" countries by Indians and Africans; and the achievement of literary equivalence, if not ascendancy, in Spanish and Portuguese, by the Latin Americans over their European progenitors.

It is safe to say that not all of these effects--among others that have not been mentioned—were anticipated in the Belle Epoque. For at that time, for example, no one would have predicted that major poets in French would be emerging, not just from France itself, but, in the person of Leopold Senghor, from Africa or in Aime Cesaire from the Caribbean.

Yet, what we have already seen in the twentieth century is even more fateful that this. Within many nations, both in Europe and the Second and Third Worlds, there has been a high percentage increase in literacy. Thus, it is not enough to say that we have been observing an enlargement of the scope of world literature and a broadening beyond Europe and the Americas of comparative literature, but we have also seen a growth in the internal audiences and the literary institutions of many separate nations--including many new ones. And not a few of even the newest—for example, Nigeria, with writers of the calibre of Achebe and Soyinka--have produced authors who have been heard and acclaimed by the older literary centers.

Given these conditions and situations, it is fair to claim that this is a period of literature influenced, to a degree not known before, by global cross-national, cross-cultural and cross-linguistic contacts. But in order not to overstate or to misstate this point, it is of course necessary to admit that analogous processes of a smaller but nevertheless pivotal character, did occur in earlier periods. I have already acknowledged this factor in my introductory remarks on the older comparative literature, with its European-centered approach, its interest in the divergences and parallels in the writing in various European language families, and the long-standing historically pervasive influence upon their literature of Greece, Rome and the Old and New Testaments. But it is now necessary to take notice of more recent developments in regard to European involvements with the thought and literary art of non-European cultures, especially, because of the scale and prominence and problematic nature of the "Oriental". For the purposes pursued here, Oriental will be taken to include the Near Eastern, as for example, Persian literature.

4. Contact Literature in Cross-National Perspective

It would be foolhardy on my part to attempt a definition of literature or justify its uses or even classify its various genres. But I would like to say here that for the purposes of this book, literature is limited to creative writing, and includes fiction, drama, and poetry. The ancient Indians gave the general name of "poetry" to all forms included in this category, subdividing in again into "poetry that is heard", meaning, thereby, lyric and epic poetry as well as narrative couched in verse or prose, and "poetry that is seen," by which they meant the drama or the theatre. Some critics have dismissed questions about the uses of literature on the ground that these are attempts to look for utilitarian merit in creative achievements the value of which is intrinsic. But here there seems to be a confusion of terminology. It is possible to ask for the purposes or uses of literature even if the answer is that it has no uses other than the enjoyment or *rasa* it provides. The question then could be, what value is to be attached to the enjoyment of literature for its own sake?

In India, the experience of *rasa* was equated with, or compared to, the highest rung of spiritual experience regarding the worth of which there was no question in the context of the society of the time. But Indian theorists of literature did not always have their heads in the clouds. Their approach to literature had empirical supports--they postulated that literature had its practical uses and was relevant to the business of living.

Literature helped in understanding life and the complexities of human nature and human relations. Literature explored the human mind and the human heart, unearthed the hidden springs of action and laid bare motives that were not always apparent to other modes of understanding. Literature, therefore, provided a view of life from the inside.

The important thing to recognize is that a distinction must be made between the manner in which literature sets out to perform its task and the manner in which the other disciplines carry out theirs. First, disciplines like psychology and sociology try to observe "facts" concerning the human mind or society and make generalizations based on the "facts", while literature forms its own fictive recreation of the world of facts and experience in order to relive, understand, criticize and perhaps to transcend it. Second, whereas the scientific disciplines give us factual knowledge or information about life, literature gives us the opportunity to involve ourselves, imaginatively, with the life situations themselves, and to take part in a total "conative-effective" experience, if this clumsy phase is forgiven.

It will be seen, therefore, that an understanding of life or human nature based on any of the empirical sciences, philosophy or history, can be at best only partial. What it lacks is sympathy, in the basic sense of the word, and could lead to wrong judgement or inappropriate action. This is what Whitehead has in mind, when, in his *Science and the Modern World*, he makes the following remark: "It is in literature that the concrete outlook of humanity receives its expression. Accordingly, it is to literature that we must look, particularly in its more concrete forms, namely in poetry and drama, if we hope to discover the inward thoughts of a generation."

At the heart of our interests is the realization that one of the important facts of the twentieth century is the proliferating contact of cultures. It is a marriage of continents, such as America, Europe, Asia and others: it is also the interaction of sub-cultures, large and small such as the Black or Jewish minorities within the United States with the dominant majority culture. India is an excellent example of a country where each state can be considered a separate cultural entity in which the pull towards unity exerted by a dominant native language exists alongside of other unifying or divisive claims urged by language, race or religion.

So important is contact literature, and so distinctive of our times, that one may be tempted to call it the quintessentially modern *form* of literature. This "literature of cross-cultural contact" (we shall hereafter, for the convenience of abbreviation and critical shorthand, substitute the term "contact literature") is not a literature which merely describes or expresses a writer's reactions to another culture. Pearl Buck's *The Good Earth* or Graham Greene's *The Quiet American* may be less likely candidates for consideration within the category of superior contact-literature than, for example, E. M. Forster's *Passage to India* or Henry James' *The American*.

Contact literature is a burgeoning literature growing very strongly, which brings to light the problems that arise when the cultures of the world, which possess vastly different histories, and often uphold conflicting and even contradictory value-systems, come into contact and conflict with one another as is happening in the world of today. Creative writers see these problems not so much as economic or political or social problems but as human problems that affect the happiness of people, their satisfaction with life and their ability to integrate themselves into the society to which they belong. The literature naturally focuses on the more sensitive individuals of a culture, those who have an awareness of other cultures and have dreams of an ideal pattern of life. They are the people tormented by the chaos that results from the confrontation, even collision of one set of moral values with another, and the difficulty in choosing between them.

Contact literature has assumed a special importance in recent times. In the U.S., for example, Black, American-Indian, Hispanic-American and other literatures of "subcultural contact" are being drawn to the forefront of study largely because of their roots in identifiable cultures. In Asia, on the other hand, many modern literatures have been shaped, if not engendered, by contact with Western culture. Nonetheless, such literature has not been seen from the perspective of cultural contact. Even writers like Kipling or Forster who have received ample critical attention, have not been viewed from the standpoint of contact literature even though they obviously exemplify it.

The study of contact literature can contribute both to humanistic knowledge and to currently available resources for research in the humanities. In the first place the resulting generalizations and hypotheses will prepare the way for a better understanding of some aspects of modern literature and provide a means of re-evaluating and refashioning existing critical tools. Secondly, it will offer new insights not only about individual literatures, but also about the literary-creative process in terms of the cross-cultural experience.

In more general terms the study of contact literature will provide both a key to the understanding of culture and a means of perceiving and grasping the responses of one culture to other cultures. Such study can also evaluate certain prevailing notions about the relationship between literature and culture, particularly notions that are unduly restricted by ethnocentric critical values. One of the principal issues is whether the closer contact of cultures that occurs in modern times brings about a merging of aesthetic criteria or has the paradoxical effect of promoting separation in the field of aesthetics. Is there any explanation for the persistence of classical aesthetic criteria besides reverence for tradition? Or is such persistence a reaction to the "internationalization" of literature? On the other hand, has the close cultural exchange of modern times brought about a melding of aesthetic norms, necessitating a new set of criteria?

Contact literature is a fertile ground for investigating not only such general questions but also specific issues such as whether modern Indian literature is best assessed in terms of Western critical criteria (for example, Aristotelian or Coleridgean), the Indian theory or *rasa*, or of something entirely new.

Research and writing on contact literature can follow a number of directions. These may be stated interrogatively as follows:

1. What does contact literature reveal about the nature of the cross-cultural experience?
2. How does literature articulate the contact of cultures--what are the modes, the levels and the forms of its occurrence? What is the range of experience represented?
3. What are the conditions and the factors which lead to and influence the expression of cross-cultural interaction in literature?
4. In what manner, if any, does contact literature act as an influence upon the process of cultural contact?

As I approach some questions of classification and periodization, I am keenly aware that their investigation always, even when it does not appear to do so, involves matters of taste and standards. And since taste and standards are for the most part established by critics, it is well to remember that critics themselves are subject to cross-cultural influences. To take just the example of English, the major critics of literature, Dryden, Johnson, Coleridge, Hazlitt and Arnold, were all energized in their critical creativity by cross-cultural influences and by examples of creative writing and theoretical and practical criticism from foreign lands.

Dryden could hardly have achieved his thoughtful, if narrow, critical writings without stimulus from the French neo-classicists, Johnson, the most insular of them all, but in some ways the most broad-minded, lived and wrote partly in reaction to the French and Scottish Enlightenment. Hazlitt was influenced by French intellectual and political revolt against the Old Regime, even to the point of honoring, like Beethoven, the mixed genius of its Thermidor product: Napoleon. Coleridge, as we know, was saturated in the German metaphysicians and psychologizers who supposedly fed him theories of the literary imagination. Arnold found refreshment as well as some puzzlement at the tides of taste which accompanied the beginnings of the Celtic renaissance. And one could add that Henry Fielding, who helped to lay the ground for a theory of English prose fiction, was inspired in many ways by Cervantes with whom I began.

5.   Periodization and its Problems

It is important to remember that literature in cross-national perspective is not a discipline but an area of interest. It draws on several different disciplines in and related to literary studies. A project which I once directed at the East-West Center in Honolulu was inevitably concerned chiefly with current literature, with writing in the Pacific Rim countries, and with writing which gives evidence that cross-national and cross-cultural influences are at work. These influences, needless to say, run from East to West as well as from West to East. It is as important to consider the influence of Asian thought on important young American poets as it is to consider the influence of the English language on the writers of fiction and poetry in modern India. It should be added that the emphasis on current writing does not mean that the literary past is neglected: modern poetry in India, in both the indigenous languages and in English, is marked, for example, by inspiration drawn from classical sources within India itself.

Mention of the further past is relevant but it is not to our profit to discuss here the early historical and cross-cultural chains of connection and influence between East and West. I leave to specialized scholars such matters as the creative adoption of Eastern motifs in the literature of the Greeks, for example, the Thracian Orpheus myth, and the imaginative absorption of Eastern mystery religions into Christianity. Likewise I leave aside the religious affiliation of Indian and Western epic forms from some common sources and the question of whether the European Aesopian fable and animal tale have debts to the traditions of the Indian subcontinent. However, it is worth referring to the seventeenth and eighteenth centuries when, as a result of direct contacts and the exchange of Asian manuscripts and texts, European literature began to respond to these events.

In the broad sense this response was chiefly in the fields of travel--writing, geography, history, and the translation of religious and historical texts. To be sure, these channels flowed in two directions in some cases, as we see in the Jesuit importation into China in the seventeenth century, of texts of Aristotle as well as Aquinas. But for my purposes the main lines to be emphasized are those that were related to the translation of important and later influential Oriental texts into European languages, as for example, those by Sir William Jones in the eighteenth century; the adoption of allegedly Oriental scenes, topics and themes by Westerners, as in Johnson's *Rasselas* (of course there were similar precedents in earlier times such as Marlowe's *Tamburlaine* in the Elizabethan period); and the artful exploitation of alleged Eastern character and scene to provide indirect if obvious commentary on the European scene, as in *The Persian Letters* by Montesquieu. With such *loci* in mind, I hardly need to emphasize that not a few European accounts written in the form of travel literature, from Marco Polo to Richard Burton, have exhibited great literary merit in non-fictional forms.

During almost all of the period from 1600 to 1900, the Europeans were dominant actors in the drama of culture contact and, generally speaking, they belonged to the "elite" forces of pirates, tradesmen, military men, missionaries and plenipotentiaries. On the Asian side of the transaction, it was also the elite that took the preponderant role of dealing with the European stranger, even if the general populace, especially near the seaboards and in the maritime areas felt the effects of the culture-contact almost immediately. Thus, even at the end of the nineteenth century, the cultural interchanges between East and West were mediated by powers and figures at the higher levels of their respective societies.

But there were asymmetrical aspects as well. Asians became acquainted with the West as a result of economic, missionary and educational intrusions, as in India for example, and developed a coherent if simplistic view of the foreigner through actual contact with him on their native soil. Quite the other way in the West, Europeans and Americans had to depend almost entirely on their travellers and expatriates for a view of the East; and even when this view was modified by the entrance of South Asian populations into the Caribbean, and Chinese and Japanese into the U.S. in the late nineteenth century, the general Western ignorance of Asia was not much dissipated. Moreover, the literary connections with foreign cultures were of an even more elitist character than the literary institutions growing up within the European and American civilizations of the period.

The creative literature of the West did not begin to concern itself with fiction and poetry that involved East-West interactions as a subject until the early nineteenth century. Johnson, Montesquieu, Goldsmith, and others were fictional romancers of the Asian exotic implicitly regarded as such. It was not until around the time of James Monier's *Haji Baba of Ispahan* in 1824, that Europeans began to take into their fiction a somewhat realistic and contemporary view of Asian character and institutions. In the middle and later nineteenth century, European and British fiction admitted more direct interactions between European and Oriental into their constructions, as in Wilkie Collins' *The Moonstone*; but the Asians were still fetched-in minor agents in a basically European action.

With the appearance of Forster's *A Passage to India* in 1924, we saw a high fictional talent dealing with close-range transactions between Easterners and Westerners, transactions rendered more problematic and powerful because they were located on Indian soil. This is the work that we take to be the grand beginning, for the English reader at least, of the modern period I have spoken of. Kipling, I may venture to assert, in such books as *Indian Tales* and *Kim*, represents the close of the old period. Kipling, that is to say, is suffused with the army, the civil service, the missionary, the telegraph, the imperial struggle seriously pursed in the line of duty, and his world is closer to the world of Warren Hastings that it is to that of Gandhi, just as Forster's is closer to that of Ayatollah Khomeini than it is to that of Kipling.

I offer here the proposition that it was not only for the British but for Europeans and Americans as well that Forster's book inaugurated the new period of which I have spoken. This is a period of literature that is cosmopolitan in context and tenor to a degree that is new on the world scene. I realize that it was not unheralded in the eighteenth and nineteenth centuries. The stimulating influence of the European Enlightenment and Romantic movement on Russian literary expression breaking up the old southwestward-looking pattern, is well-known. Perhaps even better recognized is that rebound effect by which Russian nineteenth--century writing, combining "Western" formal invention and feeling with "Eastern" sensibility, conquered Europe and the U.S. through such cosmopolitans as Turgenev as well as Pan-Slavists like Dostoevsky.

Moreover, the Russians were masters of cross-cultural fiction in works such as Gogol's *Taras Bulba* and Tolstoy's *Cossacks and Other Tales of the Caucasus*. But these were triumphs of print and translation and the genre of prose narrative in particular, and coming as they do from a nation state without external and far-flung colonies, they do not figure in the way that the work of which I speak figures, in the lines descended from Forster.

6. Some Angles of Approach

This new literary actuality I speak of is occurring in so many fronts that it is quite natural, and not necessarily unproductive, to look at it in a somewhat piecemeal manner. There is nothing odd and much to the good in the interest of British scholars such as William Walsh--and kindred sprits the world over--in the use of English in fiction, poetry and criticism in the world of the British Commonwealth and some linguistically associated former dependencies. There is political as well as intellectual logic in Russian references to its internal ethnic literatures and its policy of translating foreign languages as well as Russian works into four major non-Russian USSR languages; and translating from the same four--and more--into Russian and foreign languages. It is historically determined that Japan, the first eager Eastern cross-cultural learner outside of India, should continue its longtime interest in Greek, German, Russian and English writing with an interest in American writing and a developing interest in Latin American writing. (It is also understandable that British publishers and reviewers should be interested in former imperial markets. The same applies to French publishers, critics and schoolmasters.) No less expedient and relevant to national interests is the cultural communication of modern China with its considerable and very influential overseas population, many of its members being skilled multi-linguists who are themselves often the brokers of inter-cultural exchange in their own regions of extra-Chinese settlement.

Yet the important thing to notice is that from an historical and ideological point of view it is certain that the new literature I speak of reflects and induces certain states of the penetration of one culture by another, of the dependency of one on another, and in some cases the appearance of a new symbiosis between one culture and another. These states are evidence in various confrontations, reflected and refracted in the literature between diverse and often disparate systems of beliefs and values, different artistic norms with respect to notions of expression, and even different paradigms of knowledge. This sort of encounter occurs in all the fields of human effort, including even that of the self-purported universal field of science. However, our question here is, how must we view these encounters when the field and the channel of such cultural interaction is creative literature?

One such way is to try to see the literary scene as a meeting place in which authors, books, critics, reviewers, readers and publishers come toward each other from different literary structures with different viewpoints.   The so-called rules of the game that underlie literary institutions are not the same in all times and places and are, in fact, as John Galtung pointed out in a lecture at the East--West Center in Honolulu, closely related to the social structures of which they are a part. For this reason, as well as others, the professional networks of literature are involved in a constant re-examination of standards that sometimes harmonize and sometimes are in conflict.   Moreover, the very discussion of these harmonies and disharmonies is subject to powerful political and ideological forces: the movement of texts, writers and ideas is subject to distortion in the free enterprise world by influences as various as literary marketing agreements, constricting definitions of the writer, notions of the book as an escapist commodity, and in the controlled societies of the former USSR, China and parts of the Third World, by control from above not only of the writer's creative ambitions and products but also of his income and lifestyle.

In the theory-building and methodology of such investigations, it is of the most basic theoretical importance that any research that is planned should 1) avoid exploitation of the researched (i.e., authors, texts, reviews, for example); 2) avoid the kind of intellectual penetration which assumes that the researched must be revealers while the researchers are not, 3) avoid, if possible, the fragmentation of literature and the human experience by failing to share discovery and knowledge with the researched and, 4) avoid if possible, at least some of the ethnocentric tendencies that make some topics of research "central" and some "marginal" not for good intellectual reasons, but by reason of national and cultural habits institutionalized in the observers and researchers.

Certain lines of investigations that are closely related to each other but differ in the matters of data, variables and method may now be mentioned:

1.   The topic of the new literature in relation to present-day cultural pluralism;

2.   The topic of the new literature in its relation to the extensive sway of English as an international language;

3. The topic of the new literature in its relations to the survival or revival of oral literatures during the transition from the oral to the written or recorded forms of literature;
4. The topic of the new literature in its relation to the careers and crises and trajectories of the modern writers as exile.

7. The Major Themes of Research

The questions above are so general, that they require explication in specific terms. The following remarks spell out the range of these questions in terms of the major themes that need to be investigated.

Contact literature is a vast field, and its various aspects suggest ways in which we might approach its study. Consideration by region--e.g., the Pacific, South Asia, the U.S.--is in itself self-limiting in concept and possible development. It seems better, therefore, to select some points of departure for the study of contact literature. These points of departure are not seen as individual or separate sub-topics within the broader subject of contact literature. They have been adopted because of the valuable analytical perspectives they provide. They are also points of return.

a) Contact literature and cultural pluralism:

Cultural pluralism is a dominant reality in the world of today. Of course, some form of cultural pluralism has existed as a fact of life from early historical times, but its conceptualization and transformation into a desired and consciously pursued ideal is of recent origin. The notion that equates national entity with cultural entity is no longer widely held; cultural unity is no longer regarded as a prerequisite for national integrity. In the U.S., the idealized concept of the "melting pot" has given way to an equally idealized concept of "cultural pluralism" which is not seen as damaging to American nationhood. In Asia, on the other hand, anti-colonial feelings, which until recently helped to bind together disparate linguistic and ethnic groups into nation-states, have now lost some of their unifying potency. The resultant cultural pluralism threatens the new sense of nationhood.

The ideology of an assertive cultural pluralism that seeks recognition of, and protection for, small subdominant or partly submerged ethnic groups and cultures gives to the study of contact literature an important basic role. Contact literature can serve as material in which the range of feelings toward cultural pluralism can be measured. More important, it is the best source for the discovery of this ideology's inward expression, an expression which cannot find an adequate voice in public statement or political rhetoric.

Studies from this perspective illuminate the query "What does contact literature reveal about the nature of cross-cultural experience?" For in this case, the cross-cultural experience is intra-national as well as trans-national. One of the chief indicators of its dynamic is evidenced in that limited portion of the indigenous literature which is the voice of a particular cultural or ethnic group, which itself is only a part of the given nation state although it may and often does have cultural links outside that nation state. This, for example, is true of the writing of Indian and Chinese groups scattered in Southeast Asia and the Pacific Islands.

b)   Contact literature and its linguistic bases: the role of English

One of my research questions asks: "how does literature articulate the contact of cultures-what are the modes, levels and the forms of its occurrence? What is the range of experience represented?"

The role of English was admirably surveyed as early as twenty years ago in a set of papers, *The Spread of English,* edited by Fishman, Cooper and Conrad (Newbury House Publishers: 1977). In the use of English as an additional language, there are certain themes that are of special interest to the student of contact literature. English is the dominant language of diplomacy, or written messages whether postal or faxes or e-mail, of aviation, of broadcasting and of commerce. My statistics are derived from this early publication simply because I do not have access to a big library but it is safe to say that both numbers and percentages have risen considerably since then. On a recent visit to India I saw for myself the dominance of English as the language of government, as the link language between the states and between educated elites all throughout the country, the main language of banking, finance and business and the medium in recent years for an astonishing surge of creativity in poetry and fiction and the cause of what is now a commonplace: India now is one of the largest markets for publications in English throughout the world. Even as of 1972 English was then the first language of over 300 million people and the additional language of about the same number. India then had 18 million English-knowing bilinguals. The West Indian novel is an English language form and boasts from its tiny countries and islands the likes of V.S. Naipaul, Derek Watcott, Caryll Phillips, Roy Heath and Earl Lovelace. There is also a large and impressive literature in English as well as French in Africa. Also at the time, in Asia, the percentage of primary students in English language classes was 22 million or 16% of the total; in secondary schools, 40 million or 97% of the total. Book production in English was high, 14% of all publishing. Asia in 1972 published about 9,000 titles in English compared to 60,000 titles in all languages. English book production in the non-mother tongue was more than double that of French. When we look at literary vehicles and channels, we note that *Time, Newsweek, The International Herald Tribune* and *West Africa* were widely read outside the English speaking countries. Five Asian countries had English as one of the officially designated languages and five others gave some official role to English. They had 97% or 8 million of the English-language newspaper circulation in Asia. These millions of readers are key figures in Asia, in commerce and literature.

With respect to the spread of English, the main factors that have been studied are those that were used by Brosnahan in 1963 in his study of the spread of Arabic, Greek and Latin in historic times. The main factors were military imposition, duration of authority, linguistic diversity and material advantage. But scholars such as Fishman, Cooper, and Conrad add five other factors: urbanization, economic development, religious composition, and political affiliation. As for changes that are not going on, Fishman has opinions on the "recurring need" of an endless array of nationalities to protect their mother tongues against world languages such as English, Arabic, French, Russian and so on.

All this has additional implications for my theme of cultural pluralism. We have today become as interested in ethnicity as in language but hardly know more about ethnicity that we did some time ago. Fishman says it is given little attention by leading social theoreticians; but this remark should be qualified; Glazer and Moynihan, along with others, have written on the topic intelligently (*Ethnicity*, [ed.] N. Glazer and D.P. Moynihan, Harvard University Press, 1975) but in any case, Fishman wants the best of two worlds-- availability of an international language such as English to ethnic groups, *and* preservation of their own tongues. His observation on multi lingualism and the bilingual individual are also important. His work is especially useful in pointing out that it is the large languages that run the risks of parochialism, provincialism--because they are not at risk, their members are lulled by the complacent feeling that they do not have to learn about their languages. This risk may be especially great for the United States. Finally, the major world-role language previous to English was French, but it had an elite and aesthetic role that is only one part of the English role.

As we have seen, the English language has become, for better or worse, the chief linguistic "mode" of the literary contact between Western and Eastern cultures and between one Eastern culture and another. In effect, this may both widen and narrow the range of the experience represented. It may widen the range if its use in any manner succeeds in bringing deeper knowledge and feeling for more non-English speaking cultures to the attention of its readers. It may narrow the range if its use by an author to write about a non-English speaking culture (possibly his own) forces a constriction and dulling of the picture that is conveyed.

But this is not all. Nationally as well as internationally the existence of a dominant language generates many conflicting forces which are of special relevance to the study of contact literature. Since English has become the principal medium for literatures of cultural contact, it is frequently used for many purposes even in cultures where it is a minority tongue. The cross-cultural experience is central to such writing in the English language. How the usage of English affects not only the structure, but also the lexical and idiomatic content of the language has been a subject of continuing study. My concern, however, is to probe the ways in which the English language functions in the expression of contact between cultures, that is, English itself seen as a significant element in the process.

Contact literature arises, in part, as a result of the rise of bilingualism--although bilingualism is not a necessary condition for all productions of contact literature. However, as bilingual writers from a non-English speaking culture undertake to deal with themes of culture-contact, as they so often do, they have to make linguistic choices. For example, they must choose between publishing in 1) their native tongue; 2) their native language plus translation into English; or 3) solely in English.

Their choices will, in no little time, have an influence on the process of contact between their own culture and those that are outside it, as for example, by influencing directly or indirectly the policies of language-education and language-publishing within their own culture. These decisions tend either to widen or narrow the contact with cultures outside; and to influence the roles assigned to the various institutions, such as schools and the mass media, which mediate that contact.

Thus, the phenomenon of bilingualism is directly related to my question; English is not only the dominant element in bilingual configuration, but in its literary functions illustrates the process of culture-contact. An Indian poet of distinction who writes in English has observed that bilingualism has set up a "painful but nevertheless fruitful tension" in his poetry and has induced a dialogue between him and his cultural inheritance. This cultural "confrontation" is not untypical.

In exploring the use of English in the process of cultural contact, some crucial questions need to be asked. Does the use of English for literary purposes in non-English speaking cultures suggest an effort by writers to "educate" the reader? What conflicts, values and attitudes toward English-speaking cultures are generated by the literary presence of English in non-English speaking cultures? Does the place occupied by literary English in a culture affect in any fashion its contact with other cultures?

South and Southeast Asia best illustrate the problems raised above. In this geographical region, English is a well-established literary presence while at the same time the native languages are of great age and have rich literatures of their own. The Hawaiian example (with Hawaiian, Japanese, Chinese, Korean and Filipino languages present), provides an interesting contrast.

c) Contact literature and the transition from oral to written or print culture

The transition from oral to written culture is still proceeding in many parts of Asia and the Pacific today. It is widely known that this process is set in motion and fed by a variety of forces, of which contact with another culture, mostly Western and English-speaking, is the primary determinant.

The manifestations of contact in such literatures, however, vary considerably from region to region. For example, the impact of recently arrived forms on literatures with highly developed traditions, produces complexities in the creative blending of the two. On the other hand, writers who do not have a written literary tradition sometimes exhibit greater freedom in their use of adopted forms.

The examination of selected examples of literature produced under these conditions is expected to cast light on some troublesome issues of scholarship. How is the foreign culture viewed in the cross-cultural meeting reflected in the literary work? Is the encounter seen as useful and enriching, or, according to the official rhetoric of many Third

World countries, destructive and corrupting: Or both? What is the nature of protective, preservation-minded, or conservation-minded attitudes that seem to be generated in the minds and feelings of those who wish literature to play a part in a program of maintaining or reviving the integrity of the native culture?

The various stages and modes of transition from the oral to written or print culture lie at the very center of the literary aspect of the cross-cultural experience in many parts of Asia and the Pacific.

d)   Contact literature and the modern writer as exile

The exile of the writers is a familiar aspect of modern as well as past times. In my preface, I have tried to adumbrate a taxonomy which exhibits the variety of reasons, motives and impulsions that drive writers to become exiles from their own counties. If these exiles are to be seen as offering evidence that throws light on relations between one culture and another, the best place to start is with the writing itself, with a focus on works that are executed, though not necessarily begotten, in a culture other than the writer's own. A work of this sort may reflect a concern largely with the culture of origin, for example, Mann's *Dr. Faustus*. On the other hand, it may reflect a concern with the interpretation of the culture of reception: Hearn's *Japanese Ghost Stories*. In other cases, it may reflect a concern with a culture-contact that has been activated by the travels and writing of the author himself: Henry James on the trans atlantic experience, especially the American-English transaction.

A very important aspect of all these patterns is that the writer is often in the position of exploring his own minority relation, either to the culture of the place that he left under duress, or to the national culture that has seen fit to receive him as an exile, as for example Joyce, Pound, and Nabokov.

By and large, the recent, overwhelming tendency has been a retreat to the traditional from the modern, even though the writer has retained as his reading public, the modern metropolitan audience. Many moderns seem to assume that traditional cultures are the last repository of values that Western society has been losing. In Japan, on the other hand, the pursuit of modernity is encompassed in a paradoxical way--an acceptance of the older culture and at the same time, a rejection of it.

8.   The General Approach and the Sample

The first great English critic to contribute to the theory of the novel, according to Charles Patterson, was William Hazlitt, a judgement which is adopted and developed by John Kinnaird in his book *William Hazlitt, Critic of Power* (Columbia Univeristy Press, 1978). The argument is that 1) he was right in drawing his ideas about the novel not only from the actual work of Fielding, Richardson and Scott, but also from his studies of the Restoration Drama, 2) he was probably the first to put his finger on the sociological theme that is developed in Ian Watt's *The Rise of the Novel*—the connection of the novel form to the rise of the middle class, 3) he understood the rapprochement between the novel and the historical imagination that was occurring in the nineteenth century and 4) he correctly distinguished the "truth" of the novel from that of factuality, romance and theater.

Since distinctions like this are relevant to literature of cultural contact, it is important to state here that 1) the historical consciousness which can be helpful in the study of such literature can also stand in the way of understanding it as art and 2) it is useful to learn not only from the art-minded critics such as Forster and Percy Lubbock, but also from the New Critics and the Structuralists.

Although I disagree with much of what the Structuralists have written, the best focus for the structuralist and formalist viewpoints that I have found is in Robert Scholes's *Structuralism in Literature* (Yale University Press, 1974). I take the liberty of quoting from him and from extracts he himself quotes. In the words of the structuralist, Boris Eichenbaum, with whom I agree:

> Instead of utilizing under a new conceptual sign the earlier observations of the specific features of literary evolution (and those observations, after all, not only do not contradict but actually support an authentic sociological point of view), our literary "sociologists" have taken up the metaphysical quest for the prime principles of literary evolution and literary forms. They have had two possibilities at hand, both already applied and proved incapable of producing any literary-historical system: 1. Any analysis of works of literature from the point of view of the writer's class ideology (a purely psychological approach, for which art is the least appropriate, the least characteristic material) and 2. The cause-and-effect derivation of literary forms and styles from the general socio-economic and agricultural-industrial forms of the epoch.

Since literature is not reducible to any other order to things and cannot be the simple derivation of any other order, there is no reason to believe that all its constituent elements can be genetically conditioned. Literary-historical fact is a complex construct in which the fundamental role belongs to literariness--an element of such specificity that its study can be productive only in immanent evolutionary terms.

These, however, are quite *general* critical approaches. I should now like to add that one of the Formalists, Victor Shklovsky, also discussed by Scholes, suggested an important variation on the mimetic theory of the novel which I find useful. This is the idea that the novel, by the exercise of selective viewpoint, for example, achieves a *defamiliarization* of our view of the world. Scholes quotes from Shklovsky's discussion of a passage from Tolstoy's *Diary* and makes his own comment.

Habitualization devours objects, clothes, furniture, one's wife, and the fear of war. If all the complex lives of many people go on unconsciously, then such lives are as if they had never been.

Art exists to help us recover the sensation of life; it exists to make us feel things, to make the stone stony. The end of art is to give a sensation of the object as seen, not as recognized. The technique of art is to make things "unfamiliar", to make forms obscure, so as to increase the difficulty and the duration of perception. The act of perception in art is an end in itself and must be prolonged. In art, it is our experience of the process of construction that counts, not the finished product.

In quoting this passage, I initially intended simply to use the Lemon and Reis version. But their treatment of the last sentence in particular, seemed strange to me. Their version reads this way "Art is a way of experiencing the artfulness of an object; the object is not important." This reading is too open to a narrowly "aesthetic" or "art-for-art's sake" interpretation. In my judgement Todorov's French version is more satisfactory: "l'art est un moyen d'eprouver le devenir deja devenu n'importe pas pour l'art." With the aid of Professor Thomas Winner of Brown University, I consulted the Russian text, which reads as follow, "iskusstvo jest sposob perezit delan'e vesci, a sdelannoe v iskusstve ne vazno" A close literal translation would be: "art is the means for experiencing the making of the thing, but the thing made is not important in art."

While I recognize the dangers implicit in this way of formulating the distinction, the reader will have guessed that I regard the novel of cross-cultural experience, when well written, as an employer *par excellence* of this tactic. The notion of defamiliarization is important for the writer of contact-literature--who, in penetrating another culture, undergoes the complex process of making his prior world "unfamiliar," and creating a language to encompass the new world while simultaneously engaged in the artistic process of dehabitualizing the world in order to experience it as new and see it with a fresh vision. It is equally important for the reader who has to suspend the preconceptions of his familiar social and literary world while responding to an amalgam which has absorbed the shock of the new.

The distinction drawn between the making of the thing and the thing made could also be used to serve in important ways in a study of contact literature. The task of expressing one's entry into another culture in artistic terms is a process. Though the writer may be reflecting back on a completed experience, he cannot hope to encapsulate it fully in this work nor, by extension, can the culture be fully accommodated in the original experience. The particular difficulties encountered by the writer in adapting his sensibility, his language and his literary conventions to the recording of the cross-cultural experience render the creative process more relevant to the evaluation of the work than any structural elegance it may contain as a work of art. For the reader too, the art-object is not a self-sufficient artifact but part of an experiential continuum which modifies and is modified by subsequent reading and experience. Inevitably one must respond to the poem or the novel as a finished product but one has to bear in mind that the product is itself part of a process. For example, where contact literature is the result of colonialism, it often initiates a chain of literary response which is born out of the need to correct distorted images or more adequately record the actualities of the encounter. Achebe as reaction to Joyce Cary and colonial historians, Albert Wendt as a revision of Stevenson and Michener, Nirad Chaudhuri's answer to Indian attitudes to British colonialism are some of the examples which come to mind.

It is worth stating here that the critical concepts of the great Russian theorist, Bakhtin, are of acute relevance in this area, though an application of them would take me further afield and cost me too much space.

I would like to conclude this section with the truism that formal analysis, however, subtle, cannot exhaust the human response to a work of art. On the other hand, it can be sadly deficient. Even if the reader or the critic can apprehend the sense, discern the intention, appreciate the tone, empathize with the feeling, he may still fail to fully understand the work unless he knows its context, historical and social, and is able to visualize the human frame in its geographical setting. The context or contextuality of a work is an important determinant of the total experience, for reader and writer alike.   Ignorance of the conditions of life in a remote and primitive village in Sri Lanka at the turn of the last century is the only reason I can discover for the neglect of that exceptionally fine novel *The Village in the Jungle* by Leonard Woolf: the villagers imbued with a sense of Buddhist transcendence and defeatism, an almost insuperable burden of privation, lose out in their struggle with the jungle but despite their defeat and violation show a heroic quality of human prowess and dignity.

At mid-century, Suzanne Howe, reviewing works of fiction with imperial and colonial backgrounds by British, French and German authors, suggested an informal typology of the works (*Novels of Empire*). I summarize here from her chapter on the novels about India.

1.   *The Burden.* Novels which illustrate the burdensome aspect of life in India for an Englishman--the forbidding climate, the unfriendly natives, the unrewarding work, the difficulty of relating to an intricate and aged civilization produce a homesickness; a sense of impasse which disfigures even the better novels such as W.D. Arnold's *Oakfield* or *Fellowship in the East*.

2.   *The Happy Years.* There were "happy years" where writers were not too troubled by the Indian connection and where novels with an Indian setting harmonized with attitudes prevalent in the society at home.   The period was roughly from Plassy to the take-over of power by the Crown from the East India Company in 1858. This category is further subdivided into:

   a.   *Edification*, which consists of didactic or pedagogic books written partly for and about children. They have a strong Evangelical flavor.

   b.   *Ladies in Exile*, where the Englishwoman in India in historical progression begins by being passive, becomes frivolous and ends up by being flirtatious and even promiscuous, a predatory female who hunts for a family or breaks up a family.

   c.   *Younger Sons.* There are several novels dealing with the fortunes of younger sons who come to India because there is no professional employment for them at home.   Some of them are disagreeable, some daring soldiers, others are imbued with a bumptious idealism. They are the variants in an Indian setting of familiar types in the English life and fiction of the time.

    d.   *In the Lord's Vineyard.* This is the fiction of missionary efforts and trials, the services to Empire where the Bible followed the flag.

    e.   *Half and Half.* These are the works populated by half-caste or half-breed, the Anglo-Indians who are seen equivocally either with sympathy or as both unfortunate and disreputable in terms of middle-class Anglo-Saxon morals.

    f.   *Blood and Thunder.* Where the novels are about a rogue-hero in an atmosphere of violence.

3.   *Battle Pieces.* In the post-mutiny era, India comes to the forefront of the stage and novels about the Mutiny become popular. According to Carlyle, this was also the age of serious heroes and India offered an opportunity to portray great Anglo-Saxons fighting abroad for King and Country.

4.   *Lightening the Burden.* This is about the lighter side of British rule and is the fiction of manners dealing, generally in a light-hearted way, with the escapist pleasures from the white man's burden--sports and drinking for the men, music and flirting for the women, dances and gossip for them all.

5.   *Work.* This fiction chronicles the other side of the coin--the gospel of work which drove hard the conscientious district officer, the policeman, the soldier, the builder of roads and bridges.

6.   And finally, *the mystery* itself; the puzzlement, the tendency to get lost in the fog of Indian complexity, the difficulty of making a coherent statement about the reality of this intricate subcontinent. The final impression of these novels is the tremendous sense of waste, an inability "to connect" which even Forster could not overcome.

It can be seen that this useful classification works chiefly in terms of content and theme. As such it points toward certain types of cultural interaction that are analytically distinct in certain ways: for example, the interaction between the native Indian and the British military man on the one hand and the British missionary on the other. In the discussion that accompanies this typology, Suzanne Howe does a remarkably good job, within the limited space for specific cases offered by the survey shape of her book (*Novels of Empire*), at suggesting some of the modes and qualities of cultural interaction portrayed in the works she mentioned. And she implies that there are important differences in the fictional intents, sub-forms and skills of the authors as they approach this topic. I have spent some time with her categories because they do show how multiform these cultural meetings are and how they help determine the contours as well as the substance of the fiction. It is not my purpose in this paper to quarrel with Howe's helpful sorting-out of diverse materials. However, I would like to suggest that we must now think in categories that go more deeply into 1) the depth with which the cross-cultural interaction is portrayed by a work of fiction and 2) the craftsmanlike and experimental resources that feed into this depth of sounding.

9.   Literary Significance in Classification

Keeping in mind the comments that have been made on the *conditions* under which this new and interesting literature has developed, let us now take a more clearly literary approach to the question of classification. I should like to develop this, at least in part, by a series of contrasts and oppositions. They refer to the works which, because they are famous and widely read, merit the first attention in this field.

E. M. Forster's *A Passage to India* (1924) is deservedly known as a great progenitor of English writing in the types of work that we are studying. The rich commentary on the work appears to agree that is striking and successful not only because it portrays in an imaginative way, a cultural scene that is exotic to most English and readers in the English language (of course to some Indians) but for another reason as well. It does not use this cultural setting and baggage merely as a background for the acting out of Western characters and concerns nor is it a mere tract on the theme of race-relations. It dramatizes the interaction of the characters from East and West and, in fact, places its central emphasis upon this interaction.

This is in sharp contrast to a host of works, many of them of the highest literary merit and topical interest, which might be represented here by Graham Greene's *The Heart of the Matter*. In this work, the African setting is evoked with a high degree of persuasive and evocative skill. Yet, for the purposes of the novel and author, it remains as background. African character and circumstance are not envisioned in deep interaction with the Western protagonist. It is not so much that Greene's book is less interesting or important than Forster's-although that may seem to be the case to some experienced readers--but that it is a different endeavor. Nor does it claim to be other than it is. My first conclusion is that in the literary field of which I am speaking, the Forster novel is an appropriate case for study; the Greene novel, except for the purpose of helping to establish the contrast I have ventured to suggest, is not. Following this line of analysis, I would group with Forster certain works by Conrad, Naipaul, Raja Rao, Desani and Burgess, for example; and with Greene's book, certain works by Maugham, Lowry, Stevenson and Melville. No literary judgement is yet implied.

At this point, I should like to argue that Forster's *A Passage to India*, is, as a novel, not only a great descendant of that supreme ancestor of modern Western fiction *Don Quixote*, but also to remind the reader that *Don Quixote* is itself a masterpiece of the contact literature of which I have been speaking. It achieved this priority for many reasons. In the first place, the manuscript which is the principal purported source of the life and adventures that Cervantes relates was, according to Cervantes, the product of a writer with an Arabic name. This chronicler, Cervantes says, may have been Arabic in culture but Christian (or Crypto-Christian) in cult. In any case, the fable or content, as contrasted with the *recit*, or *representation* of the Quixote mock epic is derived from a source with Moslem connections. Cervantes leaves quite open the answers to the obvious conjecture that the satiric approach to the derring-do of largely Christian-type knightly heroes, which we find in Don Quixote is the result, in part, of a critical view of European Christian culture from the outside. Again the content, context, and interactions developed in both Parts I and II of the famous work are offered as arising in part from the great, bloody, adventurous and portentous struggle between Christian Europe and Levantine and African Islam. In the first place, the author unabashedly represents himself and his favorite characters as Christian Spanish Europeans who are delighted that the Moor was thrown out of Spain a few generations before (in the fifteenth century under Ferdinand and Isabella); and that the Moor was very recently trounced in the decisive naval battle of Lepanto (1571). This is no surprise to readers who know that Cervantes not only lost his arm in the battle of Lepanto but was for a time a prisoner of the Moors in Algiers. Not only a prisoner, but as he claims an unusually free-spoken and rebellious one--a captive who tried to escape twice while waiting for ransom, and managed to sweet talk his way out of death at Moorish hands when he was recaptured. It was such an experience, we presume, that Cervantes drew on when he pulled into the orbit of Don Quixote's crusading not only a Moorish lady who had become Christian and escaped from Algiers to Spain but also certain unfortunate Moors who had been driven out of Spanish towns by Spanish religious and racial persecution.

Despite Cervantes' obvious and understandable partisanship against the one-time invaders, later refugees, the Moors, he handles this material I have mentioned with great cross-cultural empathy and insight. As a result, his great fictional work is still worth re-interpretation--perhaps especially in these days of Islamic and Arab resurgence--as a study of the interpenetration of two powerful cultures.

The emphasis placed on Forster may suggest that my perspective leaves out entirely the consideration of more popular works that achieve less of the quality supremely exemplified by him. But this is not so. The romantically adventurous quality of *Kim* by Kipling places it in a different genre from that of *A Passage to India* and ensures it a wider audience. But it not only possesses to a high degree the qualities I have praised in Forster, but also is one of the major ancestors of certain works of international derring-do and intrigue that are written for a mass-market while observing the inter-cultural transactions involved. An example of this is Joseph Hone's fine spy novel about Alexandria, *The Private Sector* (1971). Here again it is important to notice that Hone does not use the Egyptian background as E. Phillips Oppenheim or the author of *Graustark* uses his exotic background: he has a good sense of culture contact and collaboration.

The more direct line of descent from Forster, at the higher literary levels, is to be found in works in which a realistic and, one might say, humanistic tradition of the novel is still at work. An example is *The Malayan Trilogy* of Anthony Burgess, with its broad range of characters drawn from different layers and segments of both South Asian and European society. The involvement of these actors with each other is seen against a background of school life, army organization, police affairs and the semi-institutionalized rivalries of the various national, linguistic and ethnic groups represented in the book. Burgess deploys high comic talent to probe the ambiguities and paradoxes of the cross-cultural bargains that are struck—and come unstuck—in the course of the story.

Quite different in method, *The Alexandria Quartet* of Lawrence Durrell attains some of the same subtlety in following the interplay of characters molded in sharply contrasting cultural conditions. Durrell is proficient in the comic mode, but commits himself and his fictional project to a much more indulgent use of stylistic color. Every setting is evoked by a luxuriance of metaphor and each episode is magnified, mirrored, and diffracted by a flow of tinted and sensuous figures of speech.   These traits are intimately connected with Durrell's dramatization of particular national and cultural traits and they do serve to differentiate characters who, at times, in the comic perspective threaten to become stereotypes.

A second class of works comes to mind when we read the highly illustrative work of R.K. Narayan. He is a master in presenting the middle class in a small town in India, which is the setting of many of his novels, as a vivid, organically interrelated congeries of family relationships conditioned by habit, custom, religion, and morals in a style which is itself an inimitable mix of Narayan's own wit, urbanity and sense of local color. Part of that mastery lies in his ability, as in *The Financial Expert*, to refract in it his vision of the influences of the West. Narayan is the master of this genre, but he is not the only one who has practiced it. It has, in fact, been attempted with some success by Europeans writing about small communities in Asian countries that are largely foreign to the authors themselves. Almost at the opposite end of the spectrum is an under-rated novel, *A Village in the Jungle* by Leonard Woolf, which is a work of high literary merit, honest and accurate   perception,   and   written   with   great   cross-cultural understanding. It deals with a disappearing community in Sri Lanka during the early years of this century which is unable to cope with the new ways and must be obliterated by the inexorable spread of the jungle, at once poetic symbol and immense fact of life.

A third distinct form which is most difficult of execution is represented by very few highly successful examples. It involves the work of fiction in which a Westerner attempts to give an "insider's" view of a foreign culture by writing about fictional characters who are entirely or almost entirely members of that culture. We think immediately for example of *The Good Earth Trilogy* by Pearl Buck. The ambition of that series is high, and the literary lapses are overwhelming. Yet the books can claim to have done something to evoke the everyday life of pre-revolutionary China for many Western readers. By comparison, some of Robert Von Gulik's *Judge Dee* stories deserve high marks for historical and cross-cultural insight.

A fourth form of fiction with aspirations and qualities of its own is the novel of a cross-bred hero and his experiences. A masterpiece in this field is *All About H. Hatterr* by H. V. Desani, a fine comic work of the twentieth century. There are many examples of this in Latin American literature, including the work of Machado de Assis. In Hawaii, it is represented if not on the same level by the fiction of John Dominis Holt. In Samoa, it is a feature of the writing by Albert Wendt.

A fifth form is exemplified in some of the work with Mexican or Australian backgrounds by D.H. Lawrence. In these stories and novels, the exotic scene, while it acts partly as a background to the actions and the thoughts of the Europeans, is also the source of a contrast that dramatizes European values in a symbolic confrontation with the ways of another culture, often in order to highlight the decline of Western civilization.

A novel such as George Orwell's *Burmese Days* may be said to represent still another category. It is cross-cultural in that Orwell not only draws on his direct experience of Burma, but also presents a group of Englishmen interacting, whether they like it or not, with at least some of the "natives" and responding in their own way to the unfamiliar environment. The Burmese too, are visibly present even though the Burmese way of life is not imaginatively or deeply probed: they are seen in their relationship with Europeans as imitative entrepreneurs, lackeys, servants, mistresses, what have you. The novel is distinguished for its verisimilitude, its accurate, if malicious guying of the Englishmen in the European Club, as well as of the small number of Burmese and Indians who aspire to European standards of power and behaviors.

However, the main thrust of the novel seems to me not so much to explore the ramifications of cross-cultural interpenetration, as to exorcise Orwell's own demon of anti-imperialist and anti-colonialist sentiment, and to resolutely come to terms with a malaise within.

While in Forster's work, where the main characters, both English and Indian represent a complex and evolving portraiture, in Orwell, the characters, with the exception of Flory, are caricatures. This is not to damn the book with faint praise, a book which is extraordinarily interesting in the fast pace of its action, its strong moral purpose and its close recreation of a tropical landscape that seems to press on your eyelids with its humidity, and blind your sight with its flaming patches of floral color in the noonday glare.

The personal tragedy of the protagonist seems to mirror the environment, but a question remains, despite the even-handedness of Orwell's treatment, of how much he understood or tried to appreciate the less disabling aspects of Burmese civilization.

Yet another type, though obviously not equally germane to our purposes, is the type of fiction which chooses as its settings a foreign country of the same or different time, both in order to distance the action and to bring to the foreground similarities and differences between far-flung cultures and periods of history.

A good example of this type is the tetralogy, *The Near and the Far* by L. H. Myers. In his own words: "This is not a historical novel, although the action is placed in time of Akbar the Great Mogul (who was a contemporary of Queen Elizabeth's), nor is it an attempt to portray Oriental models of living and thinking."

However, the novel is cross-cultural because Myers is interested in counterpointing Western religious and philosophical values against Eastern spiritual ideas, notably such concepts as "*maya*" and "detachment". The energy of the intellectual discussion does not make this purely a novel of ideas: Myers is able to give his preoccupations a high degree of concreteness because of his satiric treatment of ethical and social problems much nearer home, as for example his portrayal of Bloomsbury, which in the novel becomes a "Plesaunce of the Arts," presided over by prince Daniyal, a compellingly acid delineation of a way of life glorifying an aestheticism and a triviality, out of which comes evil.

Categorization can proceed a great deal further: the above are only some of the main types which can be subsumed under the heading of contact literature.

But I cannot conclude this section without referring to the literature produced by what I would like to call "the resident alien" - the person who is from a foreign culture but raised, if not born, in the country of adoption. He is not an expatriate. Of course, V.S. Naipaul exemplifies in some of his work this particular niche but I am thinking more of such writers as Salman Rushdie in his novel, *Midnight's Children*. These are writers who belong to marginal sections of society: they are foreign, or mixed ethnic, and have not yet acquired the social normalities of citizenship. As a form this is not only historically new but novel in content and literary shape. It is bound to be an increasingly current phenomenon as the immigrants grow into the host society without altogether forgetting their countries of memory and origin. If one surveys literary talent in Britain, one finds that a large percentage of important writing is produced by these "peripheral" writers, overshadowing, in fact, the writers who slavishly follow the worn out tracks of the class-bound novel inherited from a Jane Austen, George Eliot or Trollope. They deserve a separate study, and it is perhaps premature to undertake such an exercise now. The differences between Britain and America are also notable: while in the United States, the writer who hails from a minority culture soon acquires an outsider-insider relationship to the national civilization, in Britain the pressure to assimilate does not seem to be so intense, so that the minority writer retains his own heritage for a longer period. This category of literary work deserves special and separate study.

10. In Conclusion

With respect to the East-West Axis, we have to be aware that Asian nations vary greatly in their reception of Western writing. The extremes might be represented by Japan and by Muslim Afghanistan. Beginning in the Meiji period, Japan undertook to translate practically everything that had been written by Europeans into Japanese; and in the twentieth century, especially after World War II, the Japanese often read a Japanese version of a new book in English, French, German or Russian before European and American readers did. On the contrary, Afghanistan undertook no such mission and such a mission was on a small scale in most Arabic-speaking and Muslim countries. (There are of course, exceptions in the case of Egyptian and Persian interest in English and French modern literature.)

Moreover, the acceptance of European work in China from 1860 on, was highly selective and pretty much the monopoly of the literati and Westerners in China, including the diplomats and missionaries. Finally, there are large parts of Southeast Asia, notably Indonesia, as an example, which are at the far end of the extreme from Japan. For various historical reasons, Indonesia, in sharp contrast to Sri Lanka, was less penetrated by Western literary artifacts, forms, and interests.

Second, we have to notice that in all Asian countries, with the possible exceptions of Japan and India, the notion of literary form and theme, either in the native language, or in the works written today in imported languages, is "frozen". Especially in the written forms of the native language, we notice the absence of an experimental and modernist form in fiction. In drama and poetry, to be sure, the situation is rather different. The French Symbolist poetry had such a strong influence on Iran early in the twentieth century that new forms of poetry spring up in Farsi. And in India, there are writers of poetry in the native languages and even in English, such as Ezekiel and Ramanujan, who write in what can be called a modernist mode, even when they are drawing on indigenous sources for the lyric. For all this, the young writer in Asia may feel oppressed by the "frozen" state of the tradition, and run to cosmopolitan Western modes and languages in order to achieve contemporaneity and secure receptive audiences.

Other concerns emerge from current criticism: the problems of translation; the use of English as an international language; the use of lesser-known languages; the influence of the shift from the oral tradition to print; the influence on audiences of spreading education and the impact of mass-media; and the break-up and renewal of traditional cultural art forms. One of the conclusions which is indubitable is that in the best literary products, there is a distinctively modern adaptation to tradition, as well as to cross-cultural experience. This adaptation has unique features which are not found in past literatures or in the literatures of relatively monocultural countries.

For example, the spread of English in India has articulated India's contact with the English--speaking world in both positive and negative ways--positively by creating a class of English-speaking Indians who can control resources of literacy and knowledge in English, including science, and negatively by promoting a new element of separation between this elite and the non-English speaking Indians. What price has been paid by Indian authors who have made gains in the size of their audience by writing in English? For one thing, they have stepped away from their native speaking audience. For another, they have risked the misrepresentation of aspects of human relationships by writing in a tongue that is not their mother tongue. The levels of their work are high with respect to their capacities in "book-English" but low with respect to their capacities in live spoken English. Thus, this literature, while articulating connections between Indian and English-speaking cultures in certain ways, blunts the quality of the articulation in others. The chief blunting may be the suppression of Indian sensibilities and tastes.

Another interesting point, originating from the other direction, as it were, is made in an unpublished paper by Reuel Denney on the

American poet Snyder: it appears that is some cases, an Asian cross-cultural experience in which a writer has participated can lead to the production of a work of contact literature in which the Asian encounter has had the effect of re-energizing and transforming his inheritance of his own native culture. This is not surprising, since it has certainly been observed in the writing of Asians influenced by their contact with the West. However, with this Western case added to the picture, it suggests new angles of vision on cross-cultural experience in general. Is it possible that one of the most fruitful aspects or results of any kind of cross-cultural experience is the stimulus it gives to deeper participation in previously untapped resources of one's own heritage?

There is also the case of the evolution of a new literature: for example, in the literature of the newly independent island nations of the South Pacific, it appears that the literary genesis or evolution cannot be traced to a single "prime mover" such as economic growth or literacy, but rather to a concatenation of factors. The work of the more mature writers who are aware of their craft derives stimulus from three sources: the existing oral traditions; the literature created by expatriate Anglo-American and European writers using the South Pacific as a backdrop, and the writer's own education in the English, European and Commonwealth literary traditions.

In essence, the literary process is found to be dialectical: the South Pacific writer reacts in his own terms to the distorted images projected by outsiders. In order to adapt the forms he borrows from the West, the short story and the novel, to serve local and artistic needs, he invests them with the narrative styles and forms of oral literature. The common identity that he expresses is firstly with the Pacific region. Many of the Pacific Island countries are former British colonies and the writers are aware that the South Pacific is the last of the "Commonwealth" regions to develop a literature. They are therefore interested in what has been achieved elsewhere in the Commonwealth, even more than in the new literature of the "mother country". They want to salvage their past and create a unique identity in order to become respectable and respected members of the modern world community of leaders.

It may appear from this essay that too many "extensions" are being made from the literary object to the worlds of history and culture. However, it is my conviction that when art is seen under the penumbra of culture, not only do we acquire fresh insights and new knowledge about the contemporary world, but the work of literature itself is better understood. And what is more, the recognition of literature's intrinsic value is not threatened. One proceeds after all, from life to literature, and returns from literature to life.

CHAPTER II

AMERICAN RESPONSES TO NEW REALITIES

In order to give the concerns outlined already a more specific habitation, I would like to pay some attention to American responses in the world of letters to World literature in the 1980's and 90's with particular reference, of course, to the literature available in English.

A.   A Change of Windows

Since World War II American letters have greatly increased their prestige and influence abroad. For example, the fame of Faulkner has reached even secondary school students in nearly all parts of the world. It is salutary to recognize this in view of the mistaken notion in the United States that only the popular and populist culture of Westerns, Disney, Rock Music and Ronald Reagan have spoken for this nation abroad.   At the same time, American letters have shown a commendable receptivity to literary currents from abroad, as is seen in translations from Japan, the post-war literature of France, Central Europe, the Soviet satellite countries (no longer satellite at the time of writing) and, of course, the secessionist literature of the U.S.S.R. Major poetic influence, such as that of Snyder and Ginsberg have learned from Eastern lore and writings as well as from experiences derived from direct travel or sojourn.   What may be even more gratifying is that young American readers have, since World War II, departed in some numbers from the old provincialism, and shed the unwarranted snobbism about the literary artists of Latin America. For the first time, Latin American genius in poetry and fiction has an attentive, even adulatory, audience outside the academy in the United States.

The reader can supply his own various explanations for these developments: World War II, the Korean War and the Vietnam War; the increasingly large number of Americans living and working abroad; great increases in travel and tourism; global interdependence, and the like. Obviously, the relative importance of factors such as these is harder to measure, even harder is it to estimate the influence of ethnic-centered concerns in the United States, especially since about 1960. In this respect, the United States is of course part of a movement which is world-wide but for the moment our interest is the American chapter of this wide spread impulsion towards ethnic and linguistic autonomy. In the United States, the social and linguistic self-consciousness of young Oriental-Americans has fostered American reading in Oriental literatures, ancient and modern, and a similar pattern may be observed among the Latins in the United States. Moreover, literate and sensitive young American Indians are interested not only in the aborigines of North America but also of Central and South America. These are only three examples of a widely diffused tendency and fashion. On the other hand, it is not at all clear that the Germans, the Irish, the Italians or the Poles in the United States share very deeply in this trend; the reason may be that they have been so acculturated and Anglicized that it has little meaning or relevance for them.

The emerging, or rather the evolving, picture suggests some rather strong contrasts to the literary situation of the United States between the first and the second World Wars. Paris was then for a while a literary and artistic Mecca for Americans, and this helped to sustain a flow of French influence ranging from that of the Symbolists to the work of Proust and Gide. Berlin became thereafter, for a briefer while, a literary center for some of the British and Americans, and this helped to promote a Weimar flow of interest in Rilke, Brecht and many others. After the Twenties, the exodus of immigrants from Hitler's Europe to America brought in many new names and influences – the most famous were in science, the somewhat less famous were in the social sciences, but the literary and philosophical influences were also introduced. During this entire period, for which particular dates cannot be set down, the attention of American writers and readers was, of course, synchronously engaged by British and Irish writing in English – Shaw, Joyce, Virginia Woolf and others. Auden played an important part in influencing the style of American poetry after he became familiar to United States readers in the late 1930's.

How different in many ways the scene is today! German authors in translation are far from getting the attention they deserve in the U.S. but American fiction has been transformed by an infusion of Jewish influences from German and Slavic Jewry. French literary impact consists at the moment of a rather narrow and extremely sharp critical cutting edge which is affecting American cultural definitions and concepts of prose fiction and poetry. This movement may have more favorable consequences for the British and Americans than for the French. One of the reasons for this, on the French side, is the realization that the French language ceased to be a world language after World War II, and, as to be expected, there was a corresponding shift in French linguistic and literary self-concerns.

Two of the most fruitful "adventures" for American readers today, mostly absent in the years from 1920 to about 1950, are the openings to Asia and Latin America. The Asian interests are largely Northeast Asian for understandable reasons; and within Northeast Asia, the scanty traffic, the slender exchange between China and the U.S. reader is partly explained by the rise and consolidation of the Communist government there. The "understandable" reasons -- the new U.S.-- Japan friendship, the liberation of Korea from Japan and the U.S. – U.S.S.R. détente. High stakes of peace and war are associated with Northeast Asia, which is already the Boom Region in the late twentieth Century and likely to stay that way beyond. It is also the locus of key blockages to international harmony.

The Latin interests are very various and have developed during a period in which U.S. political and economic attention towards Latin America has moved erratically towards a higher level of comity. Young radical Americans might be motivated to "go Latin" because of Castro or Guevara or, on another level, of Neruda; young wandering Americans might make the same turn as in connection with pot and peyote and wonder herbs in Mexico; still other young Americans seem to have developed enough interest in Latin American social and intellectual concerns and backgrounds to be outraged by U.S. interference in Chile and Nicaragua, while at the same heartened and impressed by "positive" aspects of U.S. policy in Mexico, Venezuela, Brazil, Columbia, and Panama. The last-named country had, at the close of 1989, become a different case altogether which only goes to show that it is premature and rash to specify countries as the kaleidoscope changes in dizzy fashion. It would be too much to say that the average American college graduates of the 1980's or early 1990's have the faintest ideas of the Latin American lands and their past tragic relationships with themselves and Europe. But hundreds more of them are working and teaching in Latin America than in any previous period of history.

These openings of eyes and ears owe a great debt, of course, to the scholars and writers and translators who laid the groundwork for this in the past, first the Orientalists and the Hispanists of the late Nineteenth Century, then the translators and publicists of the 1920's and 1930's.

B. The New Imbalances

In spite of these changes in American literary taste and receptivity there are some prominent "imbalances" in the picture and there are late century tendencies in American literary life which are isolationist and provincial.

First of all, the "imbalances":

American interest in the Oriental arts, literature and religion made its first firm connection in a focus on South and Southeast Asia about 145 years ago. At that time Japan was closed, China was in siege against the West, but India was open and three forces worked together to stimulate American interest in the Indian subcontinent. One was the obvious presence of the English imperialists in India; the second, the gathering crisis in religious thought; the third was the partly religiously inspired interest in linguistics. The greatest American "Orientalist" before 1900 was the Sanskrit scholar William Dwight Whitney and the most prominent visitor to the Religious Conference in Chicago in 1893 was Vivekananda. Today, American intellectual and literary interest in South and Southeast Asia, despite the appearance of many swamis and the sprouting of a variety of Indian and Tibetan inspired cults is at a rather less intense and sophisticated level that the involvement with Northeast Asia. Indonesia, for example, attracts little interest from Americans and the same can be said of the whole region of Basa-Malaysian and Basa-Indonesian speech. U.S. interest in Philippine writing continues to be almost non-evident, despite the prominent use of English in that country. This may well be because creativity in

English has not exhibited any great originality of technique or expressiveness.

The greatest imbalance with respect to South and Southeast Asia, however, is the ignorance of even well-read Americans about the literary revolutions that have been taking place in India since independence. In the first place, there has been a steady rise of productivity in the regional languages. In the second place, there has been the strengthening of South Indian cultural confidence marked by the emergence of a strong regional spirit, both literary and political, sharply distinct in some ways from Bengal and North India. In the third place, some of this work is now becoming available both in English and in translation into English. It includes work by writers who write with great effect both in a local language and in English. Finally, English writing by Indians is on an even higher level than it is recognized to be by those who are aware of the work of Desani, Narayan, Raja Rao and the fiction of the writer of Caribbean-Indian origin, Naipaul. *All About H. Hatterr*, written several years ago by G. V. Desani, is one of the most remarkable English comic novels of the Twentieth Century. Some of the poetry in English of Nissim Ezekiel, A.K. Ramanujan, Arun Kolatkhar is as impressive in some ways as the best poetry written in English today in the United States and Britain. Most of these developments are unknown even to the more than a quarter of a million readers of the *The New Yorker*, *The New York Review of Books* and the *American Poetry Review*, who are the most knowledgeable readers, an audience that includes Americans who are best read in and about foreign literatures. Of course, Salman Rushdie, with his fame and notoriety alike, has changed the picture somewhat: Rushdie has remained Oriental in sympathy though considered a renegade or at least a maverick. It is not clear whether Rushdie is appreciated in the West because of his original adaptations of Twentieth Century literary forms, Western in shape and origin, while it is quite clear that the popularity of V.S. Naipaul is because he has moved sternly and steadily towards an endorsement of Western values. It is no accident that he was knighted by the Queen, though there are true-blue British novelists who are at least equally deserving of the honor.

The fact that writing in English has such a vital life outside of Britain and the United States is more evident to the British than it is to the Americans for the obvious reason of Commonwealth associations.

But the British have been almost obtuse about some portions of the former Empire, not excluding Australia and New Zealand.

Americans find it surprising to be told that Tom Kinneally's *Larks and Heroes*, for instance, is the product of a finer talent than that of many Americans of his generation. Janet Frame of New Zealand is not neglected in the United States, but is not sufficiently known, either. Broadway and off-Broadway have not yet produced any of the poetic drama in English of the Nigerian Nobel prizewinner, Wole Soyinka. American university departments of English will not teach Naipaul's *A House for Mr. Biswas* until, perhaps, he has received, or narrowly escaped receiving the Nobel Prize. The idea that some poetic talent in India could be comparable in quality to American poetry in the 60's, 70's or 80's is one that never occurs to American critics and commentators. American reviews of a good English translation of a play such as Euripedes' *Iphigenia in Aulis* make no reference to the creative use of English in Soyinka's fine version of Euripedes' *The Bacchae*, which shows a transposition and congruity between the mythologies of ancient Greece and modern Nigeria. Finally, important and distinguished incorporations of Asian thought and poetry by Americans such as Gary Snyder float almost awash in other work by exoticizers and poetasters who combine unreadable English with a mish-mash of Zen and other unassimilable foreign imports.

No less surprising is the reluctance of American observers to understand that the "oral" American poetry of the 1960's was not a nationally separate event but part of a trans-national and trans-cultural movement. It developed first out of the political use by young people, in India, Indonesia and elsewhere, of the tradition of oral composition and tree-posting that have had a long life there. The original political setting was the need to provide anonymous, unsigned and unprinted (though sometimes hand-lettered and wall-posted) poems dealing with matters of acute concern, crisis and forbidden cultural expression. It was well adapted for transmission by telephone, radio and the public address system. The "breath" school of American poetry was and is, without being aware of it, a single part of the much larger movement away from, and in some cases even against print.

C. The Absence of Comparative Judgements

The day is past when writings in English and American were regarded as quite separate streams. Due to quick trans-Atlantic communications, co-publications, exchanges of books and periodicals, readers and critics are now familiar with contrasts and comparisons between the two. It may be, as Malcolm Bradbury has suggested, that a major American literary trait is hyperbole or at least overstatement and a major English trait is understatement, and that is connected with an American desire to flaunt convention as contrasted with an English desire to accept and work with it; and that, finally, the convention-centered English find it easier to exploit deliberate parody of conventions in order to develop new literary modes, while Americans are all too often likely to fall into unintended parody. But to make such observations is already to possess a keen sense of the mutuality or even coherence of British letters with American. But this contrastive view ends there and one can offer examples to prove this. William Carlos Williams has been re-evaluated in a sensitive and admirable critical biography by the American poet, Reed Whittmore. The book contains an equable discussion of William's major poetic opus, *Paterson,* and a review of varying critical opinions -- largely from Americans, in this case -- that it has inspired. Reading this record, it is quite clear that the last thing that the critics thought of was to find other contemporary work in English (with the exception, of course, of Pound's *Cantos*) with which it might profitably be compared.

Now there is one long poem in English of not too distant a vintage which bears many resemblances in purpose, form and method to *Paterson*: this is *A Drunk Man Looks at a Thistle*, by Hugh McDiarmid. Both poems are concerned with a "regional" setting, with the expression of populistic values, with the relation between a poet-protagonist and a specified regional and cultural landscape; both employ "experimental" methods of organizing a long poem out of a sequential mosaic of pieces – the pieces being realized in a manner that combines elements of vernacular speech, expressionistic form, and multiple levels of meaning and symbol. The relatively high evaluation of *Paterson* by some critics could be corrected, in an informed way, if it were realized that McDiarmid's poem is in most respects a much more successful piece of work. It has many of the good qualities of *Paterson*, and far more than *Paterson*. It exploits drama, ambiguity, changes of identification in the agents, better managed narrative and satire, the work of an idiosyncratic Scottish genius. The absence of such comparison and contrast is habitual to American critics whose tunnel-vision makes it impossible for them to see that in many cases

American products are inferior to similar achievements in Britain or at the edges of the empire that is now bequeathed to us.

Though the phrase "Global Village" is often parroted, what we have to reckon with is a Global Metropolis, not a condition of stasis but a confusing, dizzily changing reality.

CHAPTER III

PROLEGOMENON: THE INTERNATIONAL CONVERGENCE OF LITERATURE AND CULTURE: THEORETICAL ISSUES IN A NEW FIELD OF STUDY

A Critical Prospectus for the above topic would pursue the following lines of study and research: contact literature (works expressing the interaction of two or more cultures): literature as an index to differing cultural values and aesthetic sensibilities; the contrast between myths and values expressed in the literatures of the technologically "developed" and the "developing" world; literature as both a reflection and catalogue of social concerns, as well as source of inspiration for their solutions; literature as an instigator of social consciousness and artistic sensibility; literature as a creator of universal human values, including cultural universals, and as a record of unique cultures and subcultures; the position of the writer within his own culture and against the background of the international literary scene; and the role of literature, of its creators, and of its readers, in cross-cultural awareness and international understanding.

The topic itself poses some problem areas and tentative hypotheses – often in the form of dialectic oppositions of ideas – about literature as an expression of modern concerns reaching across the international literary and social spectrum, fed into by writers of traditional, transitional, and developed nations. How are the common concerns of this emerging "global reality" in every area of human life from industrialization to personal relations and the intimacies of the individual psyche, perceived and elaborated upon by the modern writer, in his choice and treatment of subject, in his time and literary technique. How do these choices and concerns unite or divide the international community of writers?

For the very reason of its ability to comprehend all human experience, and to set that experience up for careful scrutiny, literature is also one of the most challenging subjects facing the social scientist as well as the humanist. Two versions of the world are open for observation. One is the imaginative, literary construct. The other is the grand total of real life out of which literature gleans its organized vision of man. Students of literature are thus faced with the world, as well as the reflection of that world, in the unique mirror of literature, as one attempts to discern the refracted image from the original "object" and as one seeks to grasp the artist's personal modification of that object.

Obviously, such a subject must be approached from a number of different perspectives, producing a great many questions and concerns which can be conveniently, if loosely, placed under several headings. However, because these concerns cover a vast scope of subjects ranging from the very private and individual nature of the creative experience to questions of world culture in contact across many historical epochs, all set against the background of a fast-moving, steadily-converging international culture, these questions are not easily distinguishable; they double back on each other, lead into one another's territories, and address, from what at first seem unrelated perspectives, many of the same issues in the interdisciplinary approach to the exploration of literature.

One of the great adventures of the twentieth century, and perhaps the most notable one, has been the contact of world cultures, and their emerging perceptions of each other. A major part of the record of this adventure can be found, naturally enough, in the literature which deals with cultures in contact and reflects the growing awareness that traditional and developed countries have of one another, marking the rising tide of inter-cultural consciousness. The complex relationships between local and global cultures are played out on the world literary scene. A current of interest is the survey of rudimentary facts of world history concerning the diffusion of cultures, the dominance of certain cultures over others, and the essential trends of cultural interpenetration and exchange. The culture critic has a need to be more sensitive to the phenomena of imperialism, monopolistic capitalism, state socialism, neocolonialism and the role of the multinationals and their impact on social structure, culture and intellectual activities.

One fact of cultural convergence is of central importance. The "mutual images" that predominate in contact literature are not the result of a multi-lateral cultural balance. The Western style dominates. While Asians and other Third-World readers, for example, are familiar with the English-language literary tradition, few Westerners are familiar with literature outside their own culture. The fact that writers and poets from Asia were more well-versed in the literary traditions of the West gives insights into what happens in a situation in which one partner is the colonizer and the other is the colonized. Since its inception in 1901, the Nobel Prize in Literature has been overwhelmingly favorable to Westerners. It has been awarded only thrice to Asians; the Indian poet Tagore and the Japanese novelist Kawabata, and recently to a Nigerian, Wole Soyinka, an Egyptian, Naguib Mafouz and another Japanese, Kenzaburo Oe.

The emerging global culture – heavily Western in both technological and artistic aspects – includes this imbalance as part of its perplexing challenge to the survival of the more traditional cultures. This challenge poses a number of interrelated questions, pointing in various directions and addressing a number of concerns.

How can this "global" culture, consisting in part of the "international style," be described, and how is its spirit the result of the confluence of Western (developed) and non-Western (traditional) styles? Is this new culture monolithic, or does it operate on a number of levels, in a variety of fields? For example, the world technological and business culture is quite distinct in character from the world "literary guild" and art world. How do each of these spheres compare to that of international politics? The basic questions for developing nations is how to resolve the conflict between the style of internationalism and the maintenance of their own cultural traditions. This simple statement of the problem quickly becomes complicated when related aspects are considered: the disparity between discrete nations and discrete cultures, along with the long history of cultural contact, which is itself an historical process of constant change due to colonization, trade, military conquest, or whatever.

Since the linguistic character of cultures varies among a number of modes, including the traditional, the imported, homogenized, heterogeneous, colonized, oral, or oral/written, therefore linguistic imperialism becomes perhaps the most critical aspect of culture exchange. Cultures are variously affected by the domination of English and other colonial languages. For cultures with an ancient literary tradition of their own (such as India), this issue has a very different emphasis than for exclusively oral cultures (such as African examples) which may suffer from various sorts of linguistic victimization. While this imperialism, especially at present, is seen as a serious obstacle to the resolution of cultural identity problems, any common language, however it was foisted upon non-native speakers, also provides an indispensable lingua franca by which nations divided by language barriers and torn internally by balkanized linguistic patterns can communicate, both within and without. From this double-edged situation arises a great ambiguity of feeling toward English as the international medium of exchange that it is.

One can build a three-part descriptive model for categorizing broad types of world literature resulting from the convergence of cultures. The first group of works are those written in English from cultures closely allied by language, culture, and political ties to England and the United States (e.g., Canada). The second group of works emerges from ancient classical traditions of written language, such as Sanskrit. The third group describes works from Third World verbal cultures with a limited material culture, heavily based on an oral tradition which is well-integrated within a self-contained and rather insular scope of experience, so that modern and imported concepts are brought into these cultures through contact with the English language. English is then adapted to fit their own cultural needs for expression.

A related set of questions deals with the effects of political and economic relations upon literature and its cross-cultural exchange. There appears to be an unavoidable correlation between economic or political hegemony and cultural eminence. But the image of dominant and subordinate cultures must be tempered by other considerations of communication than simply power relationships between the strong and the weak -- sharing of language, technology, and knowledge; the exchange of cultural concerns and values; the international elite – the "jet set" of artistic as well as economic and political preeminence; and finally, the possibility of the multilateral sharing of common themes as a set of mutual concerns, largely through the agency of these international or cross-cultural artists and their heterogeneous audiences.

One aspect of this intercultural situation is the question of which literary forms dominate as channels for cross-cultural understanding. Can these same forms be understood as ideally suited for this purpose? This ideal genre, when discovered, could then by extension serve as a consciously-selected medium of cultural exchange for writers with that purpose in mind.

The modern tradition of the novel, a Western creation growing out of the industrial state and the middle-class experience, might in fact be considered a reliable index to modern national economic and social development. But is the novel a culture-bound form in this sense, and therefore a cultural imposition upon traditional cultures; and is it a necessary, perhaps ideal form of self-expression for cultures undergoing the "Western experience?" Looking at the same question from a different perspective, one observes that many modern non-Western writers whose works are well-read in the West are likely to use Western literary forms and styles, especially the novel; examples such as Mishima, Kawabata and Rushdie come readily to mind. But the adaptation of Western styles and genres by the East is open to many sorts of interpretation. Is this use of Western forms to be viewed simply as another instance of cultural or artistic imperialism? Or does Western influence persist in this way because the form of the novel, although its origins are Western, is also somehow naturally suited to cultural expression by writers of all "modern" cultures? Put another way, do Third World writers adopt the novel out of an imitative impulse, or does the form, with its opportunities for elaborate description and psychological probing, uniquely express problems of emerging nations?

The case for poetry takes a slightly different direction, pointing to the compact focus and symbolism of the poem, with its links to the musical and epic poetry common to all linguistic traditions in their earliest oral, and later recorded, stages. Poetry is thus offered as an additional candidate for cross-cultural literary expression. But the novel is the ascendent modern medium of cultural exchange.

Questions about the nature of literary genres and their power to communicate cultural sensibilities may appear at first to be purely artistic and aesthetic ones. But, like all the issues which emerge in the "literature-culture" discussion, artistic and social matters are assumed to be inextricably intertwined. The exact balance between them is in fact very complex. Is literature to be considered as part of a large sociological framework? Or, as often postulated by critics and teachers of literature, is it contained within society as an autonomous system of symbols and conventions whose artistic integrity exists without direct connection with the society, which it makes use of only as a kind of warehouse of raw materials for a refined artistic vision? The issue of artistic integrity is often proposed, even by specialists in the connections between literature and culture, to underline the special functions performed by the artist, which, they claim, cannot be compared to the other kinds of "reactive" human behavior studied and described by the social scientist.

Great literature is considered to explore an independent and universal form of human experience removed from the specific, temporal conditions of life at any given moment. This is an accepted principle of literary study. But the evidence from inter-cultural discussions points to traditions outside the West which are more in touch with the realities of social and economic life than is usually granted. Out of these contrary (or complementary) views of literature comes the question of whether literature leads, or whether it reflects, culture: or to put the matter more precisely, to what extent it does both.

A corollary to this concern is the question of whether the writer creates culture, or culture creates the writer. The writer's relationship to his culture differs from society to society; in the U.S., for example, writers may be closely related to academic life, through departments of English, as teachers and critics of literature themselves; in Japan, on the other hand, the study of literature and its practice are strictly separated.

In Third World countries or countries under communist rule dedicated to the business of nation-building, literature poses an even more vexing challenge to the view of the separation of life and art. Their writers may come to have a primarily political and propaganda purpose. Some leading practitioners of this role find no difficulty in admitting that they are more like journalists, even propagandists, than they are like the Western version of the alienated, detached, isolated, creative artist. In democratic nations, the "outsider" image of the writer is the expected characterization. Between the extremes of writers as culturally supportive (largely positive in their views of a cultural vision) and writers as critical, suspicious, and catabolic, with a negative outlook on the entire notion of "culture," writers from both camps and from positions in between them play a number of roles, dependent on their position with respect to the social order. Ultimately, this role rests on the writer's own acceptance or rejection of that prescribed place and on his ability to create a different version of the artist's persona. One culture may also accept what another culture rejects; writers may also exchange prominence within a subculture for mainstream acceptance, or vice-versa.

But do works which best capture a cultural zeitgeist also then become its exemplary literature? Obviously a gap does exist between the most characteristic types of literature (and its practitioners), and those which becomes internationally acclaimed. The writer who does the best job of capturing his culture on paper may not be the same one who acquires an international following of eager adulators who prefer works appealing to a sense of international sensibility and taste which differs from the native standard.

The disparity between local cultural expression and world taste is a critical influence on the way the writer sees himself. What degree of self-consciousness promotes his concerns; is he intimately personal or frankly nationalistic? Writing for himself, or with what audience – wide or focused, like or unlike the writer himself? In terms of purpose – his vision of the writer's mandate – how does this sense of identity and choice of subject rely on or take its cues from his public reception, either on the local level, or through international repute? Does he (or should he) write consciously in order to help a local culture experience and examine itself, or to publicize and proclaim local issues and sensibilities to an outside audience, which may be national or global? How does he embody or interpret his culture to itself? Does this self-consciousness, arising out of the writer's self-proclaimed role as sensitive reader of his own culture, belie his identification with "the People" on whose behalf he writes? Here the outside audience for localist writing plays the questionable role of "outside adulator," whose praise and enthusiasm for these works, by putting them through the lionizing process, may not be doing the work, or the writer's identification with the work, any favors. Can writers thus address international issues through their discussions of specific culture-bound situations, or can these be considered to make a more direct mythological contact with universal issues, and by extension, create a sense of global human values?

The issue here is clearly one of the qualitative differences between local, national, and world concerns as these appear in the concerns of the writing which deals with these spheres.

A global mythology can be seen to be emerging, based not on the traditional myths and values of any single culture, but on a wide scope of commonly-held values. The form of this emerging culture is materializing through the mass media in such electronic productions as film and television, distributed as Western exports to the Third World. A descriptive scheme can set forth a loose pattern of five "international subjects:" the heroic avenger, catastrophe on a grand scale, the great caper, conspiracy in high placcs, and pornography. Clearly these global topics are conveyed through widely-diffused electronic media and not by literary models, which, by comparison, except in the widely publicized cases such as that of Salman Rushdie, begin to take on quite an arcane and rarified appearance.

The trend toward mass media, marked by the waning of the general capacity for the careful, critical judgements which are involved as part of the skill and practice of literacy, have become a matter for world concern, not simply on the part of the literati, but as part of the larger and more immediate question of the educated populace which is crucial to the support of democratic governments.

What is the developing relationship between literature, especially between the novel form and the more popularly accessible force of the mass media? Does popular culture radically depart from the tradition of high literature, or does it in some ways, as a modern counterpart to more classical forms, continue some of the literary, stylistic and mythic archetypes and images?

The "high culture versus popular culture" debate, in its cross-cultural dimension, usually relies on the Western, industrial notion which postulates a dichotomy between literary or artistic concerns and the manufactured culture of applied science. This construct assumes that these are two separate and irreconcilable modes of human thought and expression which can be sharply differentiated and whose basic philosophies are radically opposed.

The distinction between high culture and popular culture reflects stratification systems both within a country and among nation-states. It is essentially a power relationship. One line of thinking may be that the popular culture of the West has a harmful impact on the rich and high culture of the less developed nations. The other argument could be that it is necessary to import Western technology and science to transform the "primitive" indigenous culture. In fact, the transformation of indigenous culture cannot be stopped and it is not desirable to impede modernization within a country. While popular culture could have a damaging effect on high culture, it is true that it has weakened class and caste lines and contributed to egalitarian and democratic tendencies within countries.

However, this divided image of culture cannot be assumed for non-Western, traditional cultures, even from an elitist perspective. Recent work in both the social sciences and the humanities, in addition, points to a much less antagonistic picture of these forces, and indeed indicates a much better integrated model of modern culture, even for the West.

No clear consensus can be reached on the problems raised here but a more subtle kind can be reached in the awareness that every issue has two or more dimensions, and that these contrasting views could usually be formulated comprehensively as a series of paradoxes, oppositions, dilemmas, or ironies:

1. The more aware and self-conscious the writer, and the better-known his work, the looser and more tenuous is his connection with his indigenous culture. Contact with other cultures can lead to a greater understanding of one's own culture, but at the same time that very awareness prevents the writer from unself-consciously embodying it, in effect separating him from his less sophisticated countrymen, making him less "authentic" in a cultural sense.

2. The literature popular within a culture is usually not the literature by which the country is known to outsiders. Also, one country's popular culture may become another's elite culture – in other words, removal from its original cultural context may alter the character or evaluation of a work.

3. Literature performs the dual functions of both reflecting and shaping culture. These two versions of the literature and culture relationship are commonly thought of as mutually exclusive; when one image is employed to describe and analyze a literary event, the other is ignored or obscured. But clearly both operations are in force and must be considered within some sort of larger framework which can allow for this apparent contradiction, widening the conventions of study in both the field of literature and the study of literature as sociology.

4. Use of a Western (e.g., English) language facilitates international exchange, but at the same time begins to lessen cultural distinctions and specificity. In similar fashion, by using English (or another Western language) an "emerging" nation can gain access to technological advancement and communication with

others, but in this process hastens the dilution of cultural identity. But simultaneous with the shaping of emerging nations by the resources of the English language, they themselves "stretch" English by adapting folk traditions from their own languages to its structure.

5.   Countries having economic and political hegemony often achieve a corresponding artistic hegemony that feeds ethnocentrism. For example, many Asians read third-rate Western writers but may not be familiar with their own brilliant ones. The paradox is that a culture self-confident enough to learn from other cultures, and powerful enough to require cultural sensitivity in order to avoid self-centered arrogance, receives adulation or criticism rather than the inspiration it requires from the rest of the world. Contrariwise, the countries that are most in need of developing a strong sense of individuality and indigenous culture are the most likely to imitate and borrow from others, especially the dominant nations.

What is needed is conclusive and summary statements in the many areas of interest introduced.   But much more that this, more comprehensive clarification and description of the individual issues is called for in order to arrive at a deeper appreciation of these paradoxes and conflicts – their underlying features, supporting framework, and levels at which these oppositions and contrasts operate. For this research, of course, the existing resources of the study of literature as a cultural force will have to be assessed, annotated, and evaluated to arrive at a general catalogue of available materials, both primary and secondary.

We need a number of case studies based on individual writers or collection of works, chronologically, or by genre, from a cross-cultural perspective. These studies can be accumulated to form a typology of socioliterary study. Finally, the development of curricula for secondary and college level study based on this research is essential.

What is the utility of findings and inquiries suggested here? Among the suggestions for studies which would be of immediate and practical benefit in relieving, if not solving, some of the perplexities are the following: models of the formation and interaction of processes of literature, between cultures and on the international scale; clarification of the theoretical framework of literature in its social role; identification of major areas of interest in the field;

principles of selection of literary works from a variety of cultural traditions; the determination and definition of "classics," within and across cultures; problems of translation; the influence of the national and international publishing situations; the relationships between literature and other art forms, including the mass media; and the description and explanation of contextual materials -- all these are salient factors which make up the background and nurturing ecology of the international literary scene.

Finally, the questions pertaining to literature, social commitment, and nation-building create some dilemmas.   The two opposed positions are: 1. that writers and poets should be actively involved in nation building and in counteracting Western cultural and intellectual colonialism and imperialism, 2. that writers should work in a value-free mode, disregard political or social involvement, and should only conform to international standards of the discipline.

Are Western forms applicable to the needs of Third World nations? Are they capable of bringing and reinforcing liberation movements in the Third World? These are complex issues and more serious attention has to be given to fundamental, historical, and genetic questions. The writers and poets in the Third World should search for new intellectual forms in literature which will facilitate the liberation process.   Also, it should be the social responsibility of writers and poets as intellectuals to reflect on the processes which retard the emergence of new forms capable of weakening colonial and dependency relations.   Social responsibility and intellectual activity should be combined. The writers and poets should overcome the fear that the acceptance of social responsibility would somehow destroy intellectual creativity. Creative activity could be constructive as well as destructive.

Intellectuals should not feel too timid to function in normative-critical modes and shy away from the tedious problem of making judgements about socially relevant values. After all, how can the question of values be avoided in human activity?   Literary intellectuals must continue searching for social justice, democracy and human community. The search for significant ideals and socially relevant values does not mean an adherence to some absolute goals and values.   Significant goals can be determined after critically analyzing the historical experiences of nation states, the social conscience of a society and the world ecosystem.   Some of the meaningful human aims include democratic ideas and social justice in all countries. In defining intellectual ends, intellectuals should take into account the bases of social justice and the hope of developing a worldwide human community within the limits set by the planet Earth.

INTERLUDE

Chapter IV

CROSS-CULTURAL *BELLES-LETTRES:*
LEONARD WOOLF – *GROWING*

    Leonard Woolf's *Growing*, the second volume of his autobiography, which tells the story of his seven years from 1904 to 1911 as an administrator for the British Raj in Ceylon, (now known as Sri Lanka) soon became a source of controversy. A narrative which deals with events that took place over sixty years before the book was published is bound to contain inaccuracies, however honest the author and however good his memory. I do not propose to consider the kind of questions raised by his erstwhile administrative subordinate, the Mudaliyar, in one of the Sunday papers in Sri Lanka: there seems to have been little love lost between the Assistant Government Agent and his officer, and even the passage of fifty years has not chastened the Mudaliyar's rancor. I myself have doubts about the accuracy of Woolf's version of one of the incidents: I refer to the accusation, which he denies, that he hit H.A.P. Sandrasagra, an eminent Tamil lawyer, in the face with his riding whip. Harry Sandrasagra was a great uncle of mine, and the story, as has been told in family circles and by independent witnesses, is that Sandrasagra was driving down Main Street, Jaffna, in his horse and trap when

Woolf riding on horseback obstructed him and refused to make way. Sandrasagra, thereupon, is supposed to have whipped him. Whether the family story is false – the reaction of a proud native family to a cheeky foreign oppressor – or whether Woolf even in his old age cannot admit to himself that he was whipped by a "native", is a matter that can hardly be resolved today. Anyway, it is not of great importance to consider this book merely from the point of view of its correctness as a factual record, particularly in regard to its details.

One should evaluate this book in terms of Woolf's own professed intention:

> If one has the temerity to write an autobiography, then one is under obligation not to conceal. The only point in an autobiography is to give, as far as one can, in the most simple, clear and truthful way, a picture, first of one's own personality and of the people one has known, and secondly of the society and age in which one lived.

and, accordingly, the merit of the book appears to be twofold. Firstly, it reveals an interesting personality, highly individual and at the same time representative of a special British intellectual and social ethos. Secondly, it gives a vivid picture of different regions of Ceylon at the beginning of the twentieth century, recalls a way of life that is past or passing, a period of our history that is not too remote from us for our interest to be merely an "antiquarian" one. In fact, one cannot separate the two aspects: what makes the book valuable is that the picture of Ceylon is drawn by a special kind of individual who is able to give not merely a description of places, persons and incidents but the *feel* of what it was like to live in Ceylon at that time, an assignment that can be successfully accomplished only by a person who is exceptionally sensitive, and imaginative enough to recreate for his readers an inward portrayal of the country in which he lived and recapture with specificity and vividness the individuals and groups of people among whom he spent seven years of his life. This cannot be done by a sociologist, however expert he may be: it can only be achieved by a writer with "creative" gifts. And if you want further proof that Leonard Woolf had these outstanding special qualities you have only to read *The Village in the Jungle* which is still to my knowledge the best imaginative work in English on a Ceylon theme.

There is no false modesty about Leonard Woolf: he says often that one of his main liabilities was his intelligence. His family, St. Paul's and Cambridge helped to nurture a lively mind; though the "Bloomsbury" set had its own inbred confines, his friends were among the most "intelligent" in the England of his day: his circle included Lytton Strachey, E.M. Forster, John Maynard Keynes, Clive Bell, Roger Fry, Thoby Stephen and their common mentor the "great" G.E. Moore. But Woolf is quite honest about his own defects of character: in fact, he tends to overstate:

> At the age of 24 I was an arrogant, conceited and quick-tempered man"... "What in fact happened was that I had put the finishing touches to a façade behind which I would conceal or camouflage my intellect and also hide from most people, both in Ceylon and for the remainder of my life, the fact that I am mentally, morally and physically a coward.

His conceit never appears excessive and as for moral cowardice there is no trace. He seems to have been a man with most engaging personal qualities, humane, witty, cultivated, morally supple, conscientious to a fault, shrewd with a highly individual sense of humor. The book is enlivened by several humorous incidents as when he mentions how his dog "dashed up to a Sinhalese man standing on the pavement, turned around, and committed a nuisance against his clean white cloth as though it were a London lamp-post" and witty asides such as the following: "in 1905 kissing was much rarer, less public and more significant that it is in 1960"

Though his cast of mind is rationalistic, his style felicitously incorporates a near-poetic bravura even when he is being ironical. This is how he makes fun of a superstitious Ceylonese dignitary, a Muhandiram who, like most Ceylonese dignitaries, and like most Ceylonese then and now, consults astrologers about birth, marriage and death and nearly everything in between:

> And the Muhandiram, through whom I was attempting to impose our rule upon them, so quick witted, so intelligent, so Anglicised and Europeanised – scratch the surface of his mind and you found that Halley's comet, the bearing constellations above our heads, the planets in their courses, the spiral nebulae, the infinite galaxies flaming away into space, had been created and kept going through billions and billions of years in order that a grubby little man in the Hambantota bazaar could calculate the exact day and hour at which the Muhandiram's infant daughter would have her first menstrual period.

The book abounds in witty comments on persons, though on occasion the tone is quite merciless. He says of Dutton, one of his colleagues:

> Every evening Dutton wrote poetry, poetry incredibly feeble and of a sickly, sticky simplicity which, had I not read it – hundreds of lines of it – I should not have believed attainable by an adult in the 20th century .... When not writing poetry, Dutton either read or played, with distressing incompetence, on a wheezy, out of tune piano. Some of the notes of this piano had fallen in pieces and were now tied up with string, and he played on it for hours. Gilbert and Sullivan, Mozart, the Gaiety and other Girls and impossibly sentimental German abominations ... The only possible way I could imagine he might have cheated fate or God or the Devil would have been for him to have obtained a safe, quiet post in the Inland Revenue or the Post Office and to have lived a life bounded on the one side by Somerset House or St. Martin's-le-Grand, and on the other by a devoted mother and a devoted old servant in Clapham or Kew.

Although Woolf was fundamentally irreligious he can evoke a sense of the individual's desolation in the cosmos, an experience which afflicted men of stronger religious fiber, like Pascal; he preferred Buddhism to all other religions, he saw it as a "philosophy rather than a religion, a metaphysic which has eliminated God and gods, a code of conduct civilized, austere, springing ultimately from a profound pessimism." However fundamentally irreligious he may be, Woolf is no superficial materialist: if he were, *The Village in the Jungle* would not be the moving book it is.

Several passages in the book evoke vividly the places in Ceylon where Woolf lived and worked: Jaffna, Kandy, Hambantota – especially Hambantota where the "feel" of the dry zone is captured in passage after passage of charged prose. He has recorded a civilization which has now largely disappeared. As he himself says:

> I am glad that I had for years, in what is called the prime of life, experience of the slow pushing life of this most ancient type of civilization. I lived inside it to some extent, at any rate Hambantota, and felt a curious sympathy with the people, born and bred to its slowness, austerity, harshness, so that something of its rhythm and tempo, like that of the lagoons and the jungle, crept permanently into my heart and bones. It was almost the last chance for anyone to see it or live in it.

Even the minor elegiac melancholy that descended on the white colonial administrator over whisky and soda after the day's work was done, and the ritual of British conversation which followed British exercise is captured:

> When in the tropics the glaring, flaring day ends ... and darkness creeps rapidly up the sky and over the earth, it is impossible not to feel the beauty, the emptiness, the profoundity, the sadness in the warm, gently stirring insect-humming air.

What is missing, however, in this account of Ceylon is a more complete picture of the civilization of that time. Woolf does not seem to have had any contact with the Sinhalese and Tamil middle classes: as a Colonial administrator, even though he was fond of the people and conscientious about his duties as can be seen in the way he coped with such mundane administrative problems as the outbreak of rinderpest, he steered clear of the local elite society that was to determine and mold the country's future. He is strongly critical of imperialism and indeed not sufficiently appreciative of the benefits of British Colonial Administration: but in his social behavior he seems to have remained true to type. When I met him in London in 1956 he made some very penetrating comments on some of the men he had known or heard of in Ceylon, men who were later to become the leading figures of their day – men such as Sir Ponnambalam Ramanathan, Sir Ponnambalam Arunachalam, Sir Baron Jayatilleke.   I remember he spoke of the communalism that was already – in 1910 – visible beneath the surface and has since surfaced several times since Ceylon obtained its independence.   He told me that all the Sinhalese leaders he knew, despite their charm, hospitality and liberalism, were communal in that they wanted Sinhala culture to be dominant in Ceylon. Though in later years in England as a prominent left-wing liberal and political commentator Woolf took a deep and abiding interest in the struggle of the former colonies for freedom, while in Ceylon, despite his professed hatred of imperialism, he remained a devoted and conscientious servant of the British Raj. His comments on the people, with which I want to conclude, are ambivalent at best, however honest his attitude may have been: they provoke the perhaps unfair question, how less primitive are most people all over the world today?

I do not think that I sentimentalize or romanticize them. They are – or at least were in 1905 – nearer than we are to primitive man and there are many nasty things about primitive man. It is not their primitiveness that really appeals to me. It is partly their earthiness, their strong mixture of tortuousness and directness, or cunning and stupidity, of cruelty and kindness. They live close to the jungle (except in the Europeanized towns) that they retain something of the litheness and beauty of jungle animals. The Sinhalese especially tend to have subtle and supple minds. They do not conceal their individuality any more than their beggars conceal their appalling sores and ulcers and monstrous malformations. Lastly, when you get to know them, you find beneath the surface in almost everyone a profound melancholy and fatalism which I find beautiful and sympathetic – just as something like it permeates the scenery and characters of a Hardy novel.

TRANSITION

The preceding comments on Leonard Woolf's *Growing* represent a transition to my Part II, where individual works of creative literature are considered in somewhat greater depth. My intention in including this interlude is to show that the direct observation of a society can sometimes shed less equivocal light than fictional or imaginative treatment. The observer not only throws all his cards on the table, bares his fangs as it were, but speaks in the first person singular of his involvement in the encounter. Of course this is not always the most credible or compelling evidence. For example, Woolf's book discloses not only his strength but also his limitations. E. M. Forster's *A Passage to India*, despite its many-sided, sometimes profound insights into Indian society, remains a passage rather than an integration; his more direct descriptions in *The Hill of Devi* are perhaps easier for the reader to assimilate, though less interesting as art. On the other hand, Kipling's *Kim*, which is the subject of my first chapter in Part II, achieves in fictional terms a much closer identification with the Indian culture of its time than either Forster's novel or Woolf's autobiography. This is not to place Kipling higher than either of the others; it is merely a recognition of a higher degree of inwardness in cross-cultural reportage and penetration.

CHAPTER V

KIPLING'S *KIM*: ITS ANCESTRY, NATURE, AND ACHIEVEMENT

When planning this essay on Kipling's *Kim* I made two decisions which may seem surprising for a responsible critic or commentator; one, not to read for this purpose any other work by Kipling; two, also for this purpose, not to read any of the critical literature on Kipling. The reason was to preserve a directness, a freshness of view, to write, as it were, within the afterglow of the experience offered by reading the novel. I did not want to see the book as part of Kipling's *oeuvre* or locate its place in the history of the English novel. Nor did I wish to be influenced by the see-saws in his reputation--he has been called a genius and an adolescent, a humane writer and an arch-imperialist, a master of English prose and a journalist, a poet as well as a poetaster of copy-book maxims. All that matters to me is my sense of the book as a work of art and as the best thing he ever did: it is also one of the finest examples of cross-cultural interpenetration in any literature.

Though much attention has been paid to the time-sanctioned categories into which literary art is broken down in order that the mind may seize them for its own convenience--material and theme, political, social and economic milieux, feeling and tone, as well as the writer's intentions as disclosed in the work of art, there is another neglected element, the reality of its context. By this I do not mean simply a sense of "place," atmosphere or even an enveloping geography. I mean the deeply subsisting ground of a moral and cultural locale. Kipling has this in *Kim* and this is why it is a great text of cross-cultural intervention, analysis, conquest and absorption.

If one were to establish a continuum for different forms of the novel, it would be possible to plot the positions of the great figures--for example, Hawthorne, Melville, Jane Austen, George Eliot, Conrad, Henry James, Lawrence, Tolstoy--with reasonable accuracy. The extremities would be occupied on the one hand by the highly allegorical or symbolical writers such as Borges and even so-called absurdists or practitioners of the "anti-novel", and on the other by the detailed naturalists, though naturalism is as much a technique as a social philosophy. Naturalism would exclude such a novel as Thomas Keneally's *Schindler's List* which while not a docu-drama claims to be based entirely on truth: its relative success is due to the novelist's skill, his strong plot-line, and his ability to conjure up a character of such variety, copiousness and magnitude as Schindler. Realism and naturalism are terms that no sooner used have to be defined in particular contexts. If, however, one were to limit this continuum to a manageable length, a more tractable segment, say, from the sifted, analyzed and pondered art of Henry James, to the greater freshness and immediacy of experience, moving towards a profounder realism because driven by a search for the meaning of life, as in Tolstoy, it has to be said that Kipling, if a lesser writer than either, is at the Tolstoyan end of this useful if arbitrary continuum.

The greatness of *Kim* lies partly at least in its magical clarity of utterance, even though the setting is foreign. That this is not a commonplace quality may be seen if one compares the relation between character, action and setting or social context in *Kim* with the relation in, for example, Hawthorne's *The Scarlet Letter*. It cannot be said that Hawthorne had more difficult problems, whether in terms of his interests or of his milieux, than Kipling: the sense of sin is as refractory as the search for the River of Healing. Though Hawthorne complained about the cultural thinness of his society,

> No author without a trial, can conceive of the difficult of writing a romance about a country, where there is no shadow, no antiquity, no mystery, no picturesque and gloomy wrong, nor anything but a common-place prosperity, in broad and simple daylight, as is happily the case with my dear native land.

and Henry James listed what was disablingly absent in America:

No State, in the European sense of the word and indeed barely a specific national name. No sovereign, no court, no personal loyalty, no aristocracy, no church, no clergy, no army, no diplomatic service, no country gentlemen, no palaces, no castles, nor manors, nor old country-houses, nor parsonages, nor thatched cottages, nor ivied ruins; no cathedrals, nor abbeys, nor little Norman churches; no great Universities nor public schools--no Oxford, nor Eton nor Harrow; no literature, no novels, no museums, no pictures, no political society, no sporting class--no Epsom nor Ascot!

Hawthorne knew his New England remarkably well. So much so that James can also say of him:

Out of the soil of New England he sprang--in a crevice of that inimitable granite he sprouted and bloomed. Half of the interest that he possesses for an American reader with any turn for analysis must reside in his latent New England savor; and I think it no more than just to say that whatever entertainment he may yield to those who know him at a distance, it is almost an indispensable condition of properly appreciating him to have received a personal impression of the manners, the morals, indeed of the very climate of the great region of which the remarkable city of Boston is the metropolis. The cold bright air of New England seems to blow through his pages, and these, in the opinion of many people, are the medium in which it is most agreeable to make the acquaintance of that tonic atmosphere . . . I have alluded to the absence in Hawthorne of that quality of realism which is now so much in fashion, an absence in regard to which there will of course be more to say; and yet I think I am not fanciful in saying that he testifies to the sentiments of the society in which he flourished almost as pertinently (proportions observed) as Balzac and some of his descendants--Flaubert and Zola--testify to the manners and morals of the French people. He was not a man with a literary theory; he was guiltless of a system, and I am not sure that he had ever heard of Realism, this remarkable compound having (although it was invented some time earlier) come into general use only since his death. He had certainly not proposed to himself to give an account of the social idiosyncracies of his fellow citizens, for his touch on such points is always light and vague, he has none of the apparatus of a historian, and his shadowy style of portraiture never suggests a rigid standard of accuracy. Nevertheless, he virtually offers the most vivid reflection of New England life that has found its way into literature . . . Hawthorne's work savors thoroughly of the local soil--it is redolent of the social system in which he had his being."

I have permitted myself this extended quotation in order to suggest that Hawthorne's New England is no less authentic than Kipling's India and that the differences between the writers' modes of presentation cannot be explained in terms of definitions of "realism". One has to fall back on the more basic criterion: Kipling in *Kim* is able to transmute his experience into art with a greater openness and luminosity than Hawthorne in *The Scarlet Letter* (of course, no relative evaluation is intended, as the material to be transmuted is of overriding importance, and is another matter.) Kipling has no dark corners, no shadowy mysteries; in Hawthorne, however, something dark, hidden and recalcitrant is not fully brought into the light, it is the interest and the problem of his art that his psychology is in excess of his technical gift and his derived morality.

What is even more remarkable about Kim is that the locale is brought to felt life with a precision, an integrity and a parity with the other constituent elements of the fiction which is rare in literature; even Conrad for whom the setting is more than a mere backdrop, but blends intimately with the themes, characters and the action does not, except perhaps in *Nostromo*, succeed in elevating the physical and social geography to a parity with the other interests that are being transmitted: in *The Heart of Darkness,* for example, the African scene is so dominated by the figure of Kurtz, the distortions in the human heart caused by imperialism, and the isolation of the European from his native culture, that the physical setting remains somewhat shadowy, however powerfully evoked.

It is time now to turn to a special quality in *Kim*, its excellence as a novel of the cross-cultural encounter: the place is India, the hero born English but a "native" Indian under his skin, the characters a mix of Indian and European. The word "cross-cultural" can be used here in two senses: first, as a fiction generated by the relationship between two or more nations, societies, peoples and cultures; second, as the relationship between a subgroup and the larger society which surrounds and includes it. In the second sense, the sub-culture here is the sub-culture of youth. We may dwell briefly on this, as it helps to describe an important element of the novel and also to disclose its progeny.

Youth had first appeared as a world-shaking force earlier as for example in Joan of Arc who though a female and not a male had her first vision when she was about thirteen (1425 A.D.) and the final result was the end of the English-French "local" war and the establishment of France. But the use of the young heroine had to wait till the appearance of industrialism and Romanticism to exhibit its modern form. The first growth was slow, though the young age at which Robinson Crusoe ran away from home and Moll Flanders had to fend for herself in the world (both in the early seventeenth century) are noteworthy. But partly for various historical and sociological reasons, the great era of the juvenile and early adolescent protagonist is the nineteenth century.

In a rough order of appearance in the nineteenth century, we have *The Heart of Midlothian*, Jack Easy in *Mr. Midshipman Easy, Oliver Twist*, Nicholas Nickleby, David Copperfield, Amyas Leigh in *Westward Ho, Tom Brown, Lorna Doone, Huckleberry Finn*, David Balfour and at the turn of the century, *Kim*. The author of *Kim* clearly took an existing genre learned from his predecessors, especially Dickens, Mark Twain and Stevenson, and transformed it into something new and of his own.

In what is now called the "sub-culture" of youth, the transactions that take place between older and younger persons, for instance between schoolmasters and pupils, often occur across sub-cultural barriers. In past times differences in religion were called differences in "culture"; young heroes and heroines often have adventures which involve their relationships with people of another religion. Since differences in culture often arise out of differences in ethnicity, young heroes and heroines, even within their homeland, may find themselves, as for example, English with Welsh or Scottish or consorting with Irish--groups different in ethnicity and cultural pride.

The eighteenth and nineteenth centuries were periods of great migrations and migrants are relatively young compared to the population as a whole. Thus, the notion of cross-cultural experience is more often connected with the fact of being young, even very young, than with being old or even mature. It is important to note that these remarks are not limited to external and colonial migrations. In the eighteenth and nineteenth centuries, young people were dragged into, or raced into, the vast movements of labor from north to south in England, from south to north in France. This was equally true of other countries and regions, and included the great shifts in the Mediterranean and Germany. In this labor market, a move was often a move into a rather new cultural as well as social setting. These transferences of population were anything but voluntary, a further important cause being the European wars. There had always been a twelve year-old drummer boy. But Waterloo had segments of juveniles on each side, and many of the victims of Trafalgar were teenagers.

Those who survived saw foreign cultures and some stayed on to live in them.

Increased "public" attention to youth came partly out of the rise of support for music, science, art and, of course, the military. Perhaps the growth of schools would not have been so fast if it had not been noticed, that, especially where science is stressed, young talent when it makes an early appearance, has a great chance. The same early revelation of talent in preceding European stages of culture would not have attracted the same attention and support. Conversely, the larger numbers of educated young people increased the reading-public for literature concerned with youth.

From Tom Jones and Crusoe to Kim, there are visible trends. In the earliest work, the young hero is just another young adult, whether fourteen or twenty-four; he is treated as an adult in process. In the later work, the young hero is clearly adolescent, early adult, and the reader is invited to share the distinctions that accompany this difference.

Along with this shift in life-stage role definition, comes a change in the distance intended by the author between the author himself and his reader and between the hero and the reader. After *Humphrey Clinker* the distance between reader and protagonist is gradually decreased, allowing for, and asking for, more identification, more empathy, more sharing of the intimate and inner thought. In Dickens, this takes the form of introducing the "child's eye" as a standard point of view. I do not mean that all distance is obliterated. Since the book is read by both young and old, it sometimes falls between being a "juvenile" and a novel and sometimes, irridescently, works as both. They have different kinds of distances, but they are there. There is the prospective identification of the young reader and the nostalgic retrospective identification of the older one. The friend until early in the twentieth century has been one of increased identification and empathy as principles of reader appeal and fictional form.

In general, these works are as much "romances" as novels: within the romance form, they are more directed towards headlong, chronological and sequential narrative; and within that form, it is required that they command pathos and laughter and terror but not tragic feeling; they are in the larger sense comic. Within all the forms, they are a variation of the novel of self-development, the *Bildungsroman*. Their heroes do not die before the book ends. They have another stage of life beyond them. They almost always involve a key episode with a parent or parent figure; ambivalence about this often provides a very important emotional tone to the work. Women often appear near the end, as both promise and menace. Themes of loyalty, and conflict of loyalty are often present, though perhaps not more so than in all other fiction. A major source of interest, however, is the way young people before they are fully aware of it, are drawn into taking sides in the great national religious and cultural conflicts that absorb the adults around them. This involvement is part of what has been called the "loss of innocence" theme.

One of the ways the reader's emotional interest is secured is by the use of the first-person narrative as in *Robinson Crusoe, Huckleberry Finn*, and *Kidnapped*. The third person is used in *The Heart of Midlothian, Lorna Doone, Tom Brown's Schooldays, Westward Ho* and *Kim*. But *Kim* "frames in" some first person narrative in functional and imaginative ways. The narrator in Dickens employs the third person but the author and the narrator enter so empathically into the viewpoint of the third person protagonist that the effects, as in *David Copperfield* are practically cinematic.

A fine example of the cross-cultural experience in literature, shortly before *Kim*, was Stevenson's *Kidnapped*. It is in some senses more simple and derring-do, but not at all levels. The hero is gradually forced to realize that a highland Catholic Scot, compared to a lowland Protestant Scot, is still a Scot and a man, and not a Devil. This is significant cross-cultural knowledge and education. There is a strong political cast to the action since loyalty to a whole sovereignty is at stake. There are loyalists and dissidents; and good as well as bad men on both sides of the fratricidal war.

However, the great predecessor of *Kim* as a novel of cross-cultural encounter is Mark Twain's *The Adventures of Huckleberry Finn*. Even though the action of this novel takes place in Twain's own country, it spans the important cultural divide between white and black ethnicities. The hero narrator Huck describes, in his own in-group language which Twain obliges his reader to share as against an improbably standard English, the inner conflict that stems from his growing moral commitment to a view of a black man and slavery which is not accepted even in his own "free-state" society. Here two major "cultures" are involved, American White and American Black, the shifting sub-cultures of anti-slave and pro-slave in both north and south, as well as the differences between Big House whites and poor whites. It is important to note that the regions dealt with are also "colonial" in nature, in the North-South balance of relationships.

There are major affinities with *Kim*. In both novels, there is a relationship between a young man and an older person from another racial group; in fact, it is more than just a relationship, it is more of a deep connection with a blood-brother from another culture. What is significant is that the moral growth of the protagonist depends on the cross-cultural encounter. If the garnering of wisdom and maturity had happened within a single culture, *Kim* would have in his circumstances been priggish, prejudiced and the possessor of an undeveloped heart in the Forsterian sense. The mixture is important for the novel's ecology: Kipling believed India could not be protected without the combined contributions of Mahbub Ali, Hurree Chunder Mukerjee, Lurgan and Creighton. The lama's way of life and search for peace needs the reassuring cover of the military and the spy machine. The lama flees religious turmoil and cold ritualism in his monastery in order to look for the river of healing but his journey paradoxically activates the plot of intrigue. Also, paradoxically, it is Kim's worldly action on behalf of the Game that enables him to reach an almost spiritual state through sheer exhaustion and the lama to balance renunciation and enlightenment with his now Bodhisattva-like attachment to his fellow human beings. A youth's worldly cunning and sophistication are needed to direct and safeguard the progress of an unworldly person who is the repository of spiritual knowledge.

The special and seemingly original uses of language also link Kim with *Huckleberry Finn*. But the use of language in Twain is not as novel and free of the linguistic heritage as it has been made out to be. Hemingway's remark that "all modern American literature comes from one book by Mark Twain called *"Huckleberry Finn"* has led to an erroneous notion of Mark Twain's line of descent: I see him as much as the product of a literary language with its roots in Shakespeare and Bunyan as an original of the American vernacular. I could analyze his language to show that he is as much a master of the traditional language as the originator of a new American style, a finding that would place him in the line of Hawthorne, Melville and James and in continuity with the English tradition rather than as the progenitor of Dreiser, Fitzgerald and Hemingway. But this is not the place to demonstrate such an approach from his use of language, but rather to draw out the resemblance to Kipling. Kipling too departs from the literary language in order to bring alive the texture of Indian society but as will be seen in quotations later on, he is a master of the language that keeps putting forth new branches from the old tree of the English tradition. Kipling uses some two hundred and fifty vernacular and place names and devotes much care to the transitions from standard English to the vernacular, Babu English, the notation of languages used by persons of different castes and different social levels and altogether to the connection between language, mind-set and cross-cultural behavior. These are not exercises in virtuosity; they are employed in necessary situations, such as when Kim uses the vernacular to resist Lurgan's attempt to hypnotize him.

Of course, novelists were quick to discover that it is easier to trace the psychological and moral development of a character in a novel which deals with the growth of an adolescent to an adult: in the case of mature characters, the change has to result entirely from the nature of the experiences faced. Lear, in order to develop his deep humanism, has to be pitted against exceptional circumstances, while the growth of a young man's personality can be credibly and naturally presented as a part of the process of maturation.

The main thread of the story is Kim's "growing up". An associated thread is the lama's search for enlightenment. It is also an adventure and a spy story: the Game is an important part of the plot. *Kim* is also a vivid portrayal of the actuality of India, not just its physical geography of mountain, foothill and the plain through which runs the Great Trunk Road, but of its culture and civilization. It is too a record of India at a particular historical moment when India was a colony in the heyday of the British Empire. There are representatives of Anglo-India who are however treated as individuals and not also as a social group, as in Forster's *Passage to India*, or Orwell's *Burmese Days*. I do not propose to schematize too much by considering these aspects separately but follow the sequence of the plot, commenting on what I have not emphasized already, even though it is impossible sometimes to avoid clustering one's observations regardless of the chronological flow of the narrative. His nature and the qualities of his character are incipient in *Kim* from the beginning of the novel. He is seen as a creature of the conjunction of two cultures:

> Though he was burned black as any native; though he spoke the vernacular by preference, and his mother-tongue in a clipped uncertain sing-song; though he consorted on terms of perfect equality with the small boys of the bazaar; Kim was white--a poor white of the very poorest.

In fact he is more of a "native" Indian than a white; the closeness to a world of magic and superstition is suggested by the amulet he wears and his belief in his father's prediction that one day a Red Bull and a Colonel on a horse will come and do great things for him. He has the capacity "to do nothing with a great success" and is nicknamed "Little Friend of all the World" in the wards of the town. He is completely free of racial bias or prejudice of any kind and his gibes directed at his friends are without any animus: "thy father was a pastry-cook, thy mother stole the ghi." His taste in friends is truly catholic: the Hindu son of a half-millionaire, the sweetmeat seller's son, the Punjabi policemen, the museum carpenter, the water-carrier, the low caste vegetable seller and ash-smeared faquirs.

He loves adventure, the game for its own sake, and disguise, being an accomplished shape-shifter:

> It was intrigue, of course, --he knew that much, as he had known all evil since he could speak,--but what he loved was the game for its own sake--the stealthy prowl through the dark gullies and lanes, the crawl up a water-pipe, the sights and sounds of the women's world on the flat roofs, and the headlong flight from housetop to housetop under cover of the hot dark. ... The woman who looked after him insisted with tears that he should wear European clothes--trousers, a shirt and a battered hat. Kim found it easier to slip into Hindu or Mohammedan garb when engaged on certain businesses.

The disguises pose the question, what are the appurtenances, what the real man? Thrice in the novel, at crucial moments, Kim raises the question of his identity: Who is Kim? The disguises however are essential for the Game and later in the novel Lurgan puts Kim through his paces:

> The shop was full of all manner of dresses and turbans, and Kim was apparelled variously as a young Mohammedan of good family, an oilman and once--which was a joyous evening--as the son of an Oudh landholder in the fullest of full dress. Lurgan Sahib had a hawk's eye to detect the least flaw in the make-up, and lying on a worn teak-wood couch, would explain by the half-hour together how such and such a caste talked, or walked or coughed, or spat or sneezed, and, since "hows" matter little in this world, the "why" of everything... a demon in Kim woke up with joy as he put on the changing dresses, and changed speech and gesture therewith.

The Way, the Game and the Road--the three great things in *Kim*--are introduced quite early in the novel. The Way makes its appearance in the figure of the lama, a distinguished looking man full of religious wisdom but still seeking for the river of perfect healing, a man innocent of the ways of the world and so very much in need of the protection a worldly-wise Kim can offer as a chela: the lama is so naive as to think the prostitute from Amritsar is a nun, but it is not naivete alone that distinguishes him. Even though as the Rissaldar remarks, military strength is needed to safeguard the way of life of "weaponless dreamers", what the lama represents is a fundamental criticism and repudiation of the way human societies depend on violence. A compromise must be reached, and even though Kim in the end joins the spy service, the last word in the novel is with the lama.

Besides, the Great Game in later nineteenth-century India does not have the ominous nature of modern espionage. It is altogether a milder affair, and this is why it is futile to ask the question why Kipling permits Kim to join a service which would be used to preserve India in colonial subjection and force Kim to work against the very people with whom he is so intimately identified. There is no complicated death-dealing gadgetry in the spy's equipment: surveyor's tools play as important a role as the firearm. Mahbub Ali, who next to the lama is Kim's major mentor, is registered in the books of the Indian Survey Department as C.25.1B.

> Twice or thrice yearly C.25 would send in a little story, badly told but most interesting and generally--it was checked by the statements of R.17 and M.4--quite true. It concerned all manner of out-of-the-way mountain principalities, explorers of nationalities other than English, and the gun-trade--was, in brief a small portion of that vast mass of 'information received' on which the Indian Government acts.

The most recent information implicated five confederated kings, a sympathetic Northern Power (Russia), a Hindu banker in Peshawar, a firm of gun-makers in Belgium, and an important, semi-independent Mohammedan ruler to the south. Mahbub had this information and it was imperative that he should have it delivered to the proper hands as soon as possible. This is how Kim is recruited as the carrier, "as unremarkable a figure as ever carried his own and a few score thousand other folk's fate slung around his neck." This is how he and the lama encounter the Great Road, the backbone of all Hind, the broad, smiling

river of life which carries all castes and kinds of men, all kinds of
traffic, country arts and heavy carts, wedding processions and strolling
jugglers, Brahmins and chumars, bankers and tinkers, barbers and
bunnies, pilgrims and potters--all the world coming and going.

The indifference of the lama to this vast panorama of life, his mind
concentrated on the search for his own river of healing, is in sharp
contrast to Kim's obvious joy in all this novelty and variety. Even
though an otherworldly figure cannot give us the sense of the physical
India, he remains a part of the Indian ethos which Kipling recreates as
well as the best writer of Indian ethnic origin. The India of plain,
foothill and mountain is captured in several passages of remarkably
evocative prose, but what is important is the blending of the natural and
the human scene. This may be the place to disregard the strict
chronology of the plot and draw attention to the brilliant picturing of
the geographical ground of Indian culture. The longer quotations I will
use are supplemented by several incidental descriptions which only a
painstaking attention to the novel will disclose.

> But Kim was in the seventh heaven of joy. The Grand Trunk at this
> point was built on an embankment to guard against winter floods from
> the foothills, so that one walked, as it were, a little above the country,
> along a stately corridor, seeing all India spread out to left and right. It
> was beautiful to behold the many-yoked grain and cotton wagons
> crawling over the country-roads: one could hear their axles,
> complaining a mile away, coming nearer, till with shouts and yells and
> bad words they climbed up the steep incline and plunged on to the hard
> main road, carter reviling carter. It was equally beautiful to watch the
> people, little clumps of red and blue and pink and white and saffron,
> turning aside to go to their own villages, dispersing and growing by
> two and threes across the level plain. Kim felt these, though he could
> not give tongue to his feelings, and so contented himself with buying
> sugar-cane and spitting the pith generously about his path.

What is special about Kipling is the intimate interpenetration of the
natural and the human, as will be seen in this description of the onset of
evening.

> By this time the sun was diving broad golden spokes through the
> lower branches of the mango trees, the parakeets and doves were coming
> home in their hundreds; the chattering gray-backed Seven Sisters, talking
> over the day's adventures, walked back and forth in twos and threes

almost under the feet of the travellers; and shufflings and scufflings in the branches showed that the bats were ready to go out on the nightpicket. Swiftly the night gathered itself together, painted for an instant the faces and cart-wheels and the bullocks' horns as red as blood. Then the night fell, changing the touch of the air, drawing a low, even haze, like a gossamer veil of blue, across the face of the country, and bringing out, keen and distinct, the smell of wood-smoke and cattle and the good scent of wheaten cakes cooked on ashes. The evening patrol hurried out of the police-station with important coughings and reiterated orders; and a live charcoal ball in the cup of a wayside carter's hookah glowed red while Kim's eye mechanically watched the last flicker of the sun on the brass tweezers.

Just as the fall of darkness transforms the human and animal communities, the rising dawn wakes them all. It is the change and variety of nature and life on the Great Trunk Road which is breath to Kim's nostrils:

> The diamond-bright dawn woke men and crows and bullocks together. Kim sat up and yawned, shook himself, and thrilled with delight. This was seeing the world in real truth; this was life as he would have it--bustling and shouting, the buckling of belts, and beating of bullocks and creaking of wheels, lighting of fires and cooking of food, and new sights at every turn of the approving eye. The morning mist swept off in a whorl of silver, the parrots shot away to some distant river in shrieking green hosts: all the well-wheels within earshot went to work. India was awake, and Kim was in the middle of it, more awake and excited than any one, chewing on a twig that he would presently use as a toothbrush; for he borrowed right- and left-handedly from all the customs of the country he knew and loved.

It is Kim's heightened sensitivity and excitement that are infectious; as will be seen in this account of the foothills on the climb to Simla:

> But it was all pure delight--the wandering road, climbing, dipping and sweeping about the growing spurs; the flush of the morning laid along the distant snows, the branched cacti, tier upon tier on the stony hillsides; the voices of a thousand water-channels; the chatter of the monkeys; the solemn deodars, climbing one on top of the other in the down-drooped branches; the vista of the Plains rolled out far beneath them; the incessant twangling of the tonga-horns and the wild rush of the led horses when a tonga swung around a curve; the halts for prayers (Mahbub was very religious in dry-washings and bellowings when time

did not press); the evening conferences by the halting places, when camels and bullocks chewed solemnly together and the stolid told the news of the Road--all these things lifted Kim's heart to song within him.

But as Kim and the lama approach the mountains, Kim is out of his element: he says it is the abode of the Erds and no place for men. The lama takes over, he is now the leader and guide:

> But it was on the steep downhill marches three thousand feet in three hours, that he went utterly away from Kim, whose back ached with holding back, and whose big toe was nigh cut off by his grass sandal-string. Through the speckled shadow of the great deodar-forests; through oak feathered and plumed with ferns; birch, ilex, rhododendron, and pine, out on the bare hillsides' slippery sunburnt grass, and back into the woodlands' coolth again, till oak gave way to bamboo and palm of the valley, the lama swung untiring. . . . Thus, after long hours of what would be reckoned very fair mountaineering in civilized countries, they would pant over a saddle-back, sidle past a few landslips, and drop through forest at an angle of forty-five on to the road again. Along their track lay the villages of the hill-folk--mud and earth huts, the timbers now and then rudely curved with an axe-- clinging like swallows' nests against the steeps, huddled on tiny flats half-way down a three thousand-foot glissade; jammed into a corner between cliffs that funnelled and focused every wandering blast; or, for the sake of greener pasture, cowering down on a neck that in winter would be ten feet deep in snow. And the people--the sallow, greasy, duffle-clad people, with short bare legs and faces almost Esquimaux-- would flock out and adore. The Plains--kindly and gentle--had treated the lama as a holy man among holy men. But the Hills worshipped him as one in the confidence of all the devils. Theirs was an almost obliterated Buddhism, overlaid with a nature-worship fantastic as their own landscapes, elaborate as the terracing of their tiny fields; but they recognised the big hat, the clicking rosary, and the rare Chinese texts for great authority; and they respected the man under the hat.

In Kipling, the transitions from the natural scene to the comment on the religion of the people, an adaptation of a higher religion of an otherworldly character to nature worship and polytheism, is easy and unforced: it is in accord with the treatment of popular Buddhist pessimism in Leonard Woolf's *The Village in the Jungle* and the remarks in letters by D. H. Lawrence about Ceylon and its version of Buddhism:

We were at the Perahera here for the Prince of Wales. It was wonderful, gorgeous and barbaric with all the elephants and flames and devil dances in the night. One realizes how very barbaric the substratum of Buddhism really is. I shrewdly suspect the highflownness of Buddhism altogether exists mostly on paper ...

I've been in Ceylon a month and nearly sweated myself into a shadow. Still, it's a wonderful place to see and experience. There seems to be a flaw in the atmosphere, and one sees a darkness, and through the darkness the days before the Flood, marshy, with elephants mud-grey and buffaloes rising from the mud, and soft-bonded voluptuous sort of people, like plants under water, stirring in myriads.

I have permitted myself these lengthy quotations from Kipling because his fidelity to the specific and the concrete in natural description and his ability to unite his observations of the natural scene with its human resonances are not sufficiently understood or appreciated. I have myself seen in India the huts still clinging like swallows' nests on the steep hillsides, a view so different of similar elevations in European mountain ranges. Kipling has his version of the cosmic grandeur and loneliness one finds in European literature from-Pascal to Robert Frost, but with a distinctively Indian ambience:

Above them, still enormously above them, earth towered away towards the snow-line, where from east to west across hundreds of-miles, ruled as with a ruler, the last of the bold birches stopped. Above that, in scarps and blocks upheaved, the rocks strove to fight their heads above the white smother. Above these again, changeless since the world's beginning, but changing to every mood of sun and cloud, lay out the eternal snow. They could see blots and blurs on its face where storm and wondering wullie-wa got up to dance. Below them, as they stood, the forest slid away in a sheer of blue-green for mile upon mile; below the forest was a village in its sprinkle of terraced fields and steep grazing-grounds; below the village they knew, though a thunderstorm worried and growled there for the moment, a pitch of twelve or fifteen hundred feet gave to the moist valley where the streams gather that are the mothers of young Sutluj.

At the beginning of the novel, Kim has no special interest in religion: his affinity to the lama begins with a taste for the exotic, he accepts the lama's "Eternal Law" as a new god to be added to the few score he already knew. He kicks the sacred bull of the world on his moist blue nose in order to drive him away with an irreverence that fits

his use of derogatory sayings about the local religion: "For the sick cow
a crow; for the sick man a Brahmin." But it cannot be gainsaid that
there appears to be something preternatural about Kim's choice of the
lama as his guru, a belief shared by many Indians about their choice of
spiritual mentor. The criticism of Christianity and of Anglo-India
represented by Bennett and Father Victor is based on their interest in
Kim only because he is white and on their belief that the non-Christian
world is merely pagan, unredeemed and unredeemable. Father Victor as
a Catholic is the less prejudiced because he sees some merit in the lama
and is more inclined to respect the friendship between the lama and
Kim. Colonel Creighton is interested in Kim as a potential spy but is
shrewd enough to make the journey to the proposed school attractive by
telling Kim that he will see and hear new things all the way. The
preference of Catholic over Protestant may be linked to Kipling's own
distaste for the Christianity he knew and to the growing acceptance of
the Catholic religion in England:

> Between himself and the Roman Catholic chaplain of the Irish
> contingent lay, as Bennett believed, an unbridgeable gulf, but it was
> noticeable that whenever the Church of England dealt with a human
> problem she was likely to call in the Church of Rome.

Lurgan, another European figure, is detailed to teach Kim the
techniques of disguise and hypnosis as utilitarian tools in his education
as a spy, as contrasted with the lama's attempts to train Kim for the
religious quest for salvation. The dice are heavily loaded on the side of
the lama, except for the development of a parallel relationship on Kim's
part with Mahbub Ali who also assumes a paternal role in equipping
him for survival in a world of intrigue where the race is to the most
cunning.

The lama himself is not just a static representative of an arcane
creed: his growth as a fuller human being is as important a part of the
novel as Kim's development. Paradoxically, the more the lama comes
to love Kim, the more threatened is his search for Nirvana and the
freedom from the fetters of human life on this earth. The way Kipling
modifies, nay transforms the nature of the lama's quest is of crucial
significance in the unfolding of the novel's vision, culminating in its
conclusion.

There are very few novels in the history of the world's literature
where an unabashed delight in life is combined with an equally strong

value attached to its renunciation. Kim is not full of the joy of life in himself, he generates it in others, even in the most unlikely ones: the prostitute in the train is so captivated by him that she gives him money for a ticket, and more, another prostitute does a painstaking job in painting his body to disguise him for little more than his jests and calls him a breaker of hearts. Sahiba is a rich comic character worthy of comparison with Chaucer's Wife of Bath who comes to love Kim as much as she venerates the lama; the woman of Shamlegh wishes she could get to know him better. Lurgan's Indian boy is jealous of the great attractiveness of Kim, and even Mahbub Ali is jealous of Kim's unqualified devotion to the lama. Hurree Chunder Mukherjee, who is no stereotypical Bengali, is a comic figure of Dickensian proportions with an obvious relish in Kim's company.

The most important crisis in the lives of the lama and Kim occurs when they meet the Russian and the French spy, guided by the Babu, on their journey through the hill country. The spies for whom the lama is no more than an unclean old man haggling over a dirty piece of paper wants to buy his chart of the Wheel. When the Russian snatches at the chart, the lama is provoked beyond endurance and his hand reaches for his weapon, the heavy iron pen-case. He is attacked and Kim, every unknown Irish devil awake in his blood jumps at the Russian's throat and makes him roll over and over down hill. The hillmen prevent any further violence, and Kim is able to retrieve the kilta which contained all the spy material the Babu was after.

It is a clear victory for Kim in the Great Game but an occasion for soul testing for the lama. Even though he has prevented the hillmen from killing the foreign spies, he is tormented with remorse at the evil in him which was aroused.

> Had I been passionless, the evil blow would have done only bodily evil--a scar, or a bruise—which is illusion. But my mind was not abstracted, for rushed in straightaway a lust to let the Spiti men kill. In fighting that lust, my soul was torn and wrenched beyond a thousand blows. Not till I had repeated the Blessings (he meant the Buddhist Beatitudes) did I achieve calm. But the evil planted in me by that moment's carelessness works out to its end. Just is the Wheel swerving not a hair! Learn the lesson, chela.

The experience in the hills convinces the lama that he should not pride himself in the strength the climate gives him but descend to the plains where his River is to be found. Kim, though exhausted himself, nurses the lama as faithfully as Ananda nursed the Lord Buddha:

> Never was such a chela. I doubt at times whether Ananda more faithfully nursed our Lord. Art thou a Sahib? When I was a man--a long time ago--I forgot that. Now I look upon thee often, and every time I remember that thou art a Sahib. It is strange?

> Thou hast said there is neither black nor white. Why plague me with this talk? Holy One? Let me rub the other foot. It vexes me. I am not a Sahib. I am thy chela, and my head is heavy on my shoulders.

The cross-cultural encounter is full and complete: there is no distinction of color or status in the search for Freedom. Kim's loyalty to the lama is stronger than his obedience to the State and the Great Game.

> Kim thought of the oilskin packet and the books in the foodbag. If some one duly authorized would only take delivery of them the Great Game might play itself for aught he then cared.

Kim now needs to recuperate his health: after a period of skilled nursing by the Sahiba and her entourage, he has his own moment of awakening.

> He tried to think of the lama--to wonder why he had tumbled into a brook--but the bigness of the world, seen between the forecourt gates, swept linked thought aside. Then he looked upon the trees and the broad fields, with the thatched huts hidden among crops--looked with strange eyes unable to take up the size and proportion and use of things--stared for a still half-hour. All that while he felt, though he could not put it into words, that his soul was out of gear with its surroundings--a cog-wheel unconnected with any machinery, just like the idle cog-wheel of a cheap Beheea sugar-crusher laid by in a corner. The breezes fanned over him, the parrots shrieked at him, the noises of the populated house behind--squabbles, orders and reproofs--hit on dead ears.

> "I am Kim. I am Kim. And what is Kim? Kim?" His soul repeated it again and again. He did not want to cry,--had never felt less like crying in his life,--but of a sudden easy, stupid tears trickled down his nose, and with an almost audible click he felt the wheels of his being lock anew on the world without. Things that rode meaningless on the

eyeball an instant before slid into proper proportion. Roads were made
to be walked upon, houses to be lived in, cattle to be driven, fields to be
tilled, and men and women to be talked to. They were all real and true--
solidly planted upon the feet--perfectly comprehensible--clay of his
clay, neither more nor less.

Kim, though touched by the spirit, realizes that he has to live in the
world and therefore his anagnorisis inheres in a pragmatic realism:
"roads were made to be walked upon." The lama is convinced that Kim
will attain Freedom in the end and even Mahbab's cynical compromise
takes account of the lama's role: "No matter at all, but now I
understand that the boy, sure of Paradise, can yet enter Government
service, my mind is easier?"

The novel concludes with the lama's account of his own awakening:
there is a profound transformation of the original basis of Buddhism
which shows in a creative way how the clash of cultures can result in a
new reality and how a spiritual journey can take an unexpected, more
inclusive and more human shape. The lama's own words deserve full
quotation because it is one of the rare occasions in literature when a
mystical experience is conveyed without fuzziness or sentimentality.

> "I took no food. I took no water. I sat in meditation two days and two
> nights, abstracting my mind; inbreathing and outbreathing in the required
> manner . . . Upon the second night--so great was my reward--the wise
> Soul loosed itself from the silly Body and went free. This I have never
> before attained, though I have stood on the threshold of it. Consider for it
> is a marvel!"

The lama proceeds to describe the experience as follows:

> "Yea, my Soul went free, and wheeling like an eagle, saw indeed that
> there was no Teshoo Lama or any other soul. As a drop draws to water,
> so my soul drew near to the Great Soul which is beyond all things. At
> that point, exalted in contemplation, I saw all Hind, from Ceylon in the
> sea to the Hills, and my own Painted Rocks at Suchzen; I saw every camp
> and village, to the least, where we have ever rested. I saw them at one
> time and in one place; for they were within the Soul. By this I knew the
> Soul had passed beyond the illusion of Time and Space and of Things.
> By this I knew that I was free. I saw thee lying in thy cot, and I saw thee
> falling downhill under the idolator--at one time, in one place, in my soul,
> which, as I say, had touched the Great Soul. Also I saw the stupid body
> of Teshoo Lama lying down, and the hakim from Dacca kneeled beside,

shouting in its ear. Then, my soul was all alone and I saw nothing, for I was all things, having reached the Great Soul. And I meditated a thousand thousand years, passionless, well aware of the Causes of all Things."

But this experience of extinction in the Great Soul, of a merging and disappearance into its Essence, is not the final event; the ultimate word is Love, for the liberated soul has to return to the human world in order to save the beloved. This is not in accord with strict Buddhist doctrine but a profound Kiplingesque variation of a deeper, more satisfying, humanist, even Christian vision:

> "Then a voice cried: 'What shall come to the boy if thou art dead?' and I was shaken back and forth in myself with pity for thee; and I said: 'I will return to my chela, lest he miss the Way.' Upon this my soul which is the soul of Teshoo Lama, withdrew itself from the Great Soul with strivings and yearnings and retchings and agonies not to be told. As the egg from the fish, as the fish from the water, as the water from the cloud, as the cloud from the thick air; so put forth so leaped out, so drew away, so fumed up the soul of Teshoo Lama from the Great Soul. Then a voice cried: 'The River! Take heed to the River!' and I looked down upon all the world, which was as I had seen it before—one in time, one in place--and I saw plainly the River of the Arrow at my feet. At that hour my soul was hampered by some evil or other whereof I was not wholly cleansed, and it lay upon my arms and coiled upon my waist; but I put it aside, and I cast forth as an eagle in my flight for the very place of the River. I pushed aside world upon world for thy sake. I saw the River below me--the River of the Arrow--and, descending, the waters of it closed over me; and behold I was again in the body of Teshoo Lama, but free from sin, and the hakim from Dacca bore up my head in the waters of the River. It is here! ... So thus the Search is ended. For the merit that I have acquired, the River of the Arrow is here. It broke forth at our feet, as I have said. I have found it. Son of my Soul, I have wrenched my Soul back from the Threshold of Freedom to free thee from all sin--as I am free, and sinless. Just is the Wheel! Certain is our deliverance. Come."

He crossed his hands on his lap and smiled, as a man may who has won salvation for himself and his beloved.

The evil of which he is not yet wholly cleansed is the evil attendant on the selfish search for individual perfection; personal holiness has to be further sanctified by human love and a participation and involvement in the salvation of others. It is only when the lama realizes this that he sees the River of the Arrow: healing is holiness and wholeness, to be achieved when a commitment is made to the world of men. The images of natural process and fruition, "as the egg from the fish, as the fish from the water, as the water from the cloud, as the cloud from the thick air" suggest the creatively positive nature of the experience: the lama's beloved represents the human world. The River is near, "behind the mango-tope here," and the lama's realization is in accord with Kim's acceptance of the world in which he has to spend his days. It is rarely in literature, and especially so in the English tradition, that such a fructifying and full experience emerges from a brilliant tale of adventure and intrigue, a nearly miraculous achievement considering that it comes from the pen of a writer who elsewhere often fails to transcend the neurotic and real agonies of his life and became almost the very type of a jingoistic chauvinism and imperialism. Kim demonstrates that art can tell more than the author knows.

CHAPTER VI

LEONARD WOOLF: *THE VILLAGE IN THE JUNGLE*

Leonard Woolf's *The Village in The Jungle* is one of the most underrated novels published in this century. In this respect, it can be compared to L. H. Myers' *The Root and the Flower* except for the difference that the Myers novel enjoyed the attention of major British critics at least for a time. It can also be compared to the neglect of T.F. Powys' *Mr. Weston's Good Wine,* a novel as unlike Woolf's work as it is possible to imagine. But Powys' novel at least earned a coterie cult and occupied a niche in the history of English literature, though I would imagine hardly anyone reads him nowadays.

The fate of the Woolf novel can be attributed to many causes. Woolf himself did not for the major portion of his life devote his energies to creative writing in the technical sense, except for his major and remarkable autobiographical sequence, *Sowing, Growing, Beginning Again , Downhill all the Way,* and *The Journey not the Arrival Matters,* published in the sixties and worthy to be ranked with the best in this genre. However, these volumes are not cast in the fictional mode. He was a busy editor of influential political journals, an active member of several committees, author of books on Government, Politics, History,

Imperialism and Peace, and a publisher with little outside help of a forward-looking and heroic press. (He was the first English publisher of T.S. Eliot's *The Waste Land*). He was an active socialist. His own literary reputation was overshadowed by the rising fame of his wife Virginia Woolf who soon became the center of a group and acquired the status of a genius. Perhaps also the setting and the subject-matter of *The Village in the Jungle* appeared somewhat remote to the average British reader—an isolated village in a jungle of Ceylon, now called Sri Lanka, a faraway outpost of Empire characterized by a way of life almost infinitely distant from the complex urban and rural society of contemporary England.

But the society of the novel itself has its own complexities, and my purpose here is to untangle the strands of its theme in order to show that the work is indeed a masterpiece. Its closeness to the Ceylon scene and its empathy with important features of its way of life are such that Ceylon critics consider it the best fictional work in English on a Ceylon subject: some go even so far as to say that it is the best novel about Ceylon in any language, not excepting the two indigenous languages, Sinhala and Tamil.

Unlike George Orwell's *Burmese Days,* which does not really get under the epidermis of Burmese culture, Woolf's novel is written almost entirely from the inside, as it were; it is in this sense one of the most successful works of fiction written by an European about Asia. To my mind it is, at least in some aspects, even more successful that the more celebrated *A Passage to India,* where though Indians and Englishmen come together as individuals or as groups, one is never sure how much of the material and the treatment is truly of India or how much it is a grafting onto India of Forster's own sense of the European norm with its aspiration towards order and harmony, how much of his attitude is modified by his human pessimism, his melancholy awareness of the void which environs all human ties and relationships, and his perception of the aura which encircles all attempts by human beings to relate to each other.

Unlike the other novels I consider in this book, Woolf's *The Village in the Jungle* is the only work, apart of course from Myers' *The Root and the Flower,* set as it is in a time long before the colonial encounter, which has local characters at its center, where all the main figures are natives of the country which provides the setting. Even though it is under colonial rule, the Ceylon Woolf observes in seen in its internal workings, in its autonomy as it were, thus providing him with a directly focussed vision.

The Village in the Jungle is so well organized as a work of art that one way of dealing with it would be to conduct a "running commentary" on the book following the sequence of the pages in which it is written. This method, however, does not do sufficient justice to its spatial organization of theme and symbol: the best that one can do therefore is to combine a consideration of its movement in time with its spatial interrelationships, despite the inevitable disjointedness of such an approach.

The first chapter of this novel is an excellent example of Woolf's prose style at its best. Though the intention seems to be a matter-of-fact, realistic depiction of the jungle environment, the language is so poetically charged, the rhythms so evocative that one cannot miss the symbolic dimension. The novel's first paragraph in as follows:

> The village was called Beddagama, which means the village in the jungle. It lay in the low country or plains, midway between the sea and the great mountains which seem, far away to the north, to rise like a long wall straight up from the sea of trees. It was in, and of the jungle; the air and smell of the jungle lay heavy upon it--the smell of hot air, of dust, and of dry and powdered leaves and sticks. Its beginning and its end was in the jungle, which stretched away from it on all sides unbroken, north and south and east and west, to the blue line of the hills and to the sea. The jungle surrounded it, overhung it, continually pressed in upon it. It stood at the door of the houses, always ready to press in upon the compounds and open spaces, to break through the mud huts, and to choke up the tracks and paths. It was only by yearly clearing with axe and katty that it could be kept out. It was a living wall about the village, a wall which, if the axe were spared, would creep in and smother and blot out the village itself.

The jungle frames the book with an equally moving evocation at the end of the novel but it is not merely a frame, it is an active, moving reality. Man can only stake his territory by assiduously striving to keep it at bay: he has to halt its inexorable infiltration by yearly clearing with axe and katty. At the outset, even before introducing the main characters, the author establishes the tone of the insider by recounting the incident of a man who knew the jungle intimately, "he knew the tracks better than the doe who leads the herd.." He would boast that he did not fear the jungle but eventually he did become its victim: his bones were found scattered on the ground "gnawed by the wild pig and the jackal, and crushed and broken by the trampling of elephants." Nature in the form of the jungle is innately evil and hostile to man. Here is no Wordsworthian sense of Nature as a source of tranquil restoration:

> All jungles are evil, but no jungle is more evil than that which lay about the village of Beddagama. If you climb one of the bare rocks that jut up out of it, you will see the jungle stretched out below you for mile upon mile on all sides. It looks like a great sea, over which the pitiless hot wind perpetually sends waves unbroken, except where the bare rocks, rising above it, show like dark smudges against the grey-green of the leaves. For ten months of the year the sun beats down and scorches it; and the hot wind in a whirl of dust tears over it, tossing the branches and scattering the leaves. The trees are stunted and twisted by the drought, by the thin and sandy soil, by the dry wind. They are scabrous, thorny trees, with grey leaves whitened by the clouds of dust which the wind perpetually sweeps over them: their trunks are grey with hanging, stringy lichen. And there are enormous cactuses, evil-looking and obscene, with their great fleshy green slabs, which put out immense needlelike spines. More evil-looking still are the great leafless trees, which look like a tangle of gigantic spiders' legs--smooth, bright green, jointed together-- from which, when they are broken, oozes out a milky, viscous fluid.

The jungle is almost the main character in the story: it is established as a presence, the most important one, in page after page of descriptive enactment. The fear, hunger and thirst in the jungle is paralleled in the people who live in it:

> The spirit of the jungle is in the village, and in the people who live in it. They are simple, sullen, silent men. In their faces you can see plainly the fear and hardship of their lives. They are very near to the animals which live in the jungle around them. They look at you with the melancholy and patient stupidity of the buffalo in their eyes, or the cunning of the jackal. And there is in them the blind anger of the jungle, the ferocity of the leopard, and the sudden fury of the bear.

But it is important to realize that, even though many of the characters are depicted as having animal attributes, the novel is not a "beast-fable" nor are the pervasive analogies of the human and the animal world intended to support a Swiftian vision. Nor is the portrayal of a cruel Nature merely a backdrop for a Man versus Nature statement.

The closeness to the jungle is also a closeness to the hale, the vigorous and the instinctual as opposed to the so-called civilized and sophisticated: Silindu's two daughters have skins smooth and blooming, "like the coat of a fawn when the sun shines on it"

Though it would not be customary to provide a synopsis of the plot or resort to lengthy quotations from the text in a critical piece of this nature, I have to do both in order to make my comments intelligible, as the novel is very little known. *The Village in the Jungle* is the story of a man, Silindu, and his family. Silindu, whose outer and inner life is profoundly shaped by the jungle, lives on its edges, and ekes out his existence by hunting game and by "slash and burn" cultivation of seasonal crops, a form of planting known as "chena". His family is one of a small settlement in a tiny village in one of the remotest parts of Sri Lanka. The toll taken by the climate is heavy but heavier still is the cruelty of other human beings in the village. Silindu has two daughters, Punchi Menika and Hinnihami. His enemies include the village chief or Headman, who cannot forgive the family because his nephew, the honest and simple-minded Babun, has married the elder daughter; a medicine-man, a practitioner of demonology and witchcraft, ugly and wicked, who wants to marry the younger one, and an unscrupulous money lender who wants to have the married daughter as his mistress. Babun is framed as the perpetrator of an arranged burglary, is tried and sent to prison where he dies, a broken relic of his former self. Silindu. like an animal goaded beyond endurance, kills the headman as the only way he has of getting his revenge. He is also sent to prison. The family is now shrunk and so is the village, decimated by the harshness of nature. We are finally left with Punchi Menika as the sole resident, clinging to her hut and the jungle, as it is the only life she knows till the jungle finally swallows her hut and overwhelms her.

The novel is suffused with Buddhist pessimism, Hinduism, animism and devil worship which are all parts of the local religious sensibility: that a skeptic like Woolf could acknowledge without a sense of superiority such a diverse blend is a tribute to the open and hospitable nature of his imagination. Karlinahamy, Silindu's sister, sings a chant which expresses very well the Buddhist sense of fatalism. It is not inappropriate to note that the following is a moving lullaby, a fine poem in its own right.

Sleep, child, sleep against my side,
Aiyo! Aiyo! the weary way you've cried;

Hush, child, hush, pressed close against my side.

Aiyo! Aiyo! will the trees never end?
Our women's feet are weary; O Great One, send
Night on us, that our wanderings may end.

Hush, child, hush, thy father leads the way,
Thy mother's feet are weary, but the day
Will end somewhere for the followers in the way.

Aiyo! Aiyo! the way is rough and steep,
Aiyo! the thorns are sharp, the rivers deep,
But the night comes at last. So sleep, child, sleep.

Buddhist love figures in the narration by the same Karlinahamy of a Jataka story to her fellow pilgrims, sitting around the evening fire. The Buddha disguised as a tailor marries a maiden called Amara. He tries her patience and loyalty repeatedly until at last he is satisfied that she is worthy of him. Finally she is brought by force to him and he is unrecognizable because he is dressed in state in his kingly robes. She wins his heart by addressing his thus:

> "Lord, I smiled with joy to see your divine splendor and the merit acquired by you in innumerable births; but when I thought that in this birth you might by some evil act, such as this, by seducing another's wife, earn the pain of death, I wept for love of you."

It in only then that the Buddha convinced of her worth reveals his true self to her and makes her his queen.

The Buddhist belief in rebirth is very much a part of the spiritual topography of this novel. Even Silindu the hunter, half animal, half man is converted on his way to being condemned for murder by an old beggar who preaches the virtues of non-violence. But Buddhism co-exists with devil-worship as it still does in the popular religion of Ceylon: that Woolf with his profoundly agnostic turn of mind should accept the notion that a devilish charm could cause Silindu a deadly illness is a tribute not merely to his suspension of disbelief but to the artist's capacity to identify with the inner springs of an alien culture. He also sees with a perceptiveness rare in one who is not a trained anthropologist how Buddhism is an overlay on a more down-to-earth Hindu and animistic belief and practice. The pilgrimage to the Hindu

God (obviously a reference to the Hindu temple at Kataragama, is one of the most momentous acts of the Sinhalese worshipper who feels much closer to this God, much nearer to his own life than the remote, world renouncing Buddha of their dagobas and viharas:

> "The god, therefore, is of the jungle; a great devil, beneficent when approached in the right manner and season, whose power lies for miles upon the desolate jungle surrounding his temple and hill. A power to swear by, for he will punish for the oath sworn falsely by his hill; a power who will listen to the vow of the sick or of the barren women; a power who can aid us against the devils which perpetually beset us."

This is the God who can answer their prayers, whether it is for their betterment or the misfortune of their enemies.

Religious chicanery so endemic in that part of the world is a major factor in the lives of the people. The Sannyasi with his long black beard, a big hooked nose, twinkling black eyes, hair plaited and matted into long coils, speaking an unintelligible language which needs a translator, is obviously in collusion with the medicine-man who wants to possess Hinnihami, Silindu's daughter, as part of the deal which will free her father from his illness. The Sannyasi's verdict is that something must be given, either the man or the girl, and all the listeners to a man, have no doubt what has to be done--Hinnihami has to be sacrificed. Hinnihami herself is the only one who experiences the ecstasy of the religious rite without the distractions of prayer and supplication:

> But Hinnihami felt the power of the god in her and over them all: she felt how near he was to them, mysteriously hidden beneath the great cloth which lay upon the elephant's back. She felt again the awe which great trees in darkness and the shadows of the jungle at nightfall aroused in her, the mystery of darkness and power, which no one can see. And again and again as the procession halted, and the cry of the multitude rolled back to them, her breath was caught by sobs, and again she lifted her hands to the god and called upon his name. She formulated no prayer to him, she spoke no words of supplication: only in excitement and exaltation of entreaty she cried out the name of the god.

There are two major occasions when an agent of British colonialism, the Magistrate, has to deal with native "crime". Well-meaning but

because of ignorance of local life, totally incapable of dealing with it,
British justice cannot be fair; but the problem is not merely colonial
because the natives themselves are evil-doers who prey on each other.
With a foreign ruler there is the chance of redress or at least the
semblance of judicial procedure. The hope however is dwarfed by the
vista of nature just as the courthouse seems small and insignificant
suspended over the vast and soundless world of water and trees:

> The court-house stood on a bare hill which rose above the town, a
> small headland which ran out into the sea to form one side of the little
> bay. The judge, as he sat upon the bench, looked out through the great
> open doors opposite to him, down upon the blue waters of the bay, the
> red roofs of the houses, and then the interminable jungle, the grey
> jungle stretching out to the horizon and the faint line of the hills. And
> throughout the case this vast view, framed like a picture in the heavy
> wooden doorway, was continually before the eyes of the accused. Their
> eyes wandered from the bare room to the boats and the canoes, bobbing
> up and down in the bay, to the group of little figures on the shore
> hauling in the great nets under the blazing sun, to the dust storms
> sweeping over the jungle, miles away where they lived. The air of the
> court was hot, heavy, oppressive; the voices of those who spoke
> seemed both to themselves and to the others unreal in the stillness. The
> murmur of the little waves in the bay, the confused shouts of the
> fishermen on the shore, the sound of the wind in the trees floated up to
> them as if from another world.

In the second instance when Silindu has confessed to murder, it is
the British judge who understands Silindu's predicament better than the
local chief headman:

> "This man, now: I expect he's a quiet sort of man. All he wanted was
> to be left alone, poor devil.   You don't shoot, I believe,
> Ratemahatmaya, so you don't know the jungle properly. But it's really
> the same with the other jungle animals, even your leopard, you know.
> They just want to be left alone, to sleep quietly at night. They won't
> touch you if you leave them alone. But if you worry'em enough;
> follow'em up and pen'em up in a corner or a cave, and shoot .450
> bullets at them out of an express rifle; well, if a bullet doesn't find the
> lungs or heart or brain, they get angry as you call it, and go out to kill.
> I don't blame them either. Isn't that true?"   "I believe it is, sir."
> "And it is the same with these jungle people. They want to be left
> alone, to reap their miserable chenas and eat their miserable kurakkan
> [a grain], to live quietly, as he said in their miserable huts. I don't think

that you know, any more than I do, Ratemahatmaya, what goes on up there in the jungle. He was a quiet man in the village, I believe that. He only wanted to be left alone. It must take a lot of cornering and torturing and shooting to rouse a man like that. I expect, as he said, they went on at him for years. This not letting one another alone, it's at the bottom of nine-tenths of the crime and trouble; and in nine-tenths of that nine-tenths there's one of your headmen concerned--whom you are supposed to look after."

There are two major attempts to destroy Silindu and his family—the first by the medicine-man who succeeds in getting Hinnihami but is more than defeated by her; and the second by the money-lender who wants Silindu's married daughter as his mistress. She rejects him, even though it may mean utter destitution for her husband and herself because the moneylender has a stranglehold on the entire village. Punchi Menika refuses him with the fatalism which is an essential part of her culture:

> "What is there to say, aiya? I cannot do it. If this thing must come to us, what can we do? Always evil is coming into this house--from the jungle, my father says. At first there was no food. Then the devil entered into my father. Then more evil, upon my sister and her child, and upon my child. The children died; they killed Punchi Appu; they killed my sister. And now evil again."

Silindu himself is a man of the jungle: he knows it well but he fears it. He has the right humility before the unknown but the relationship is coloured by love:

> But though he feared it, he loved it in a strange, unconscious way, in the same unconscious way in which the wild buffalo loves the wallow, and the leopard his lair among the rocks. Silent, inert, and sullen he worked in the chena or squatted about his compound but when he started for the jungle he became a different man. With slightly bent knees and toes turned out, he glided through the impenetrable scrub with a long slinking stride, which seemed to show at once both the fear and joy in his heart.

He calls his daughter "little toad", "little crow"; he gives Hinnihami a baby fawn whom she suckles at her breast along with her own child. Though this may seem an extreme example of the human-animal nexus, it does not sound obnoxious except to over-"civilized" taste.

Hinnihami's child dies, as do most children in the village in the month of August.

Everyone shares this sense of determinism because unmerited adversity is part of the scheme of things. The killing of the fawn and the accompanying death of Hinnihami reminds one of witch-hunts and the extremist forms of cruelty perpetrated by the human animal. Silindu has been hunted by the rascally Headman, the devilish medicine-man, and the mercenary money-lender; he is overcome but not before he destroys his enemies.

The village shrinks due to its own inequities as well as nature's cruelty: the book concludes with a moving enactment of the jungle encroaching on the village and blotting it out, along with its sole surviving inhabitant, who would rather perish amid the fear, hunger and thirst of the jungle which she had known all her life:

> The village was forgotten, it disappeared into the jungle from which it had sprung, and with it she was cut off, forgotten. It was as if she was the last person left in the world, a world of unending trees above which the wind roared always and the sun blazed. She became one of the beasts of the jungle, struggling perpetually for life against hunger and thirst; the ruined hut, through which the sun beat and the rains washed, was only the lair to which she returned at night for shelter. Her memories of the evils which had happened to her, even of Babun and her life with him, became dim and faded. And as they faded, her childhood and Silindu and his tales returned to her. She had returned to the jungle; it had taken her back; she lived as she had done, understanding it, loving it, fearing it. As he had said, one has to live many years before one understands what the beasts say in the jungle. She understood them now, she was one of them. And they understood her, and were not afraid of her. They became accustomed to the little tattered hut, and to the woman who lived in it. The herd of wild pigs would go grunting and rooting up to the very door, and the old sows would look up unafraid and untroubled at the woman sitting within. Even the does became accustomed to her soft step as she came and went through the jungle, muttering greetings to them; they would look up for a moment, and their great eyes would follow her for a moment as she glided by, and then the heads would go down again to graze without alarm ... She was dying, and the jungle knew it; it is always waiting; can scarcely wait for death. When the end was close upon her a great black shadow glided into the doorway. Two little eyes twinkled at her steadily, two immense white tusks curled up gleaming against the

darkness. She sat up, fear came upon her, the fear of the jungle, blind agonizing fear.

"Appochchi, Appochchi!" she screamed. He has come, the devil from the bush. He has come for me as you said. Aiyo! save me, save me. Appochchi!" As she fell back, the great boar grunted softly, and glided like a shadow towards her into the hut.

The jungle was Punchi Menika's home as well as her habitat. She was linked to it because of an indissoluble kinship, based both on fear and love.

Fear of the jungle is the beginning of wisdom. The jungle provided sustenance for Silindu and his family and when the time was ripe, it was the agent of their retrieval. As the novelist states it early on in the book,

> Silindu slept with his eyes open like some animals, and very often he would moan, whine, and twitch in his sleep like a dog; he slept as lightly as a deer and would start up from the heaviest sleep in an instant fully awake. When not in the jungle he squatted all day in the shadow of his hut, staring before him and no one would tell whether he was asleep or awake. Often you would have to shout at him and touch him before he would attend to what you had to say. But the strangest thing about him was this, that although he knew the jungle better than any man in the whole district, and although he was always wandering through it, his fear of it was great. He never attempted to explain or deny this fear. When other hunters laughed at him about it, all he would say was, 'I am not afraid of any animal in the jungle, no, not even of the bear or the solitary elephant (whom all of you really fear) but I am afraid of the jungle.' But though he feared it he loved it in a strange unconscious way, in the same unconscious way in which the wild buffalo loves the wallow, and the leopard his lair among the rocks. Silent, inert, and sullen he worked in the chena or squatted about his compound, but when he started for the jungle he became a different man. With slightly bent knees and toes turned out, he glided through the impenetrable scrub with a long, slinking stride, which seemed to show at once both the fear and the joy in his heart.

Leonard Woolf's *The Village in the Jungle* embodies a tragic vision, alike in its defeatism and its profound pessimism, as well as its epic portrayal of a peasant family's struggle against the cruelty of man and the malignancy of nature.

CHAPTER VII

E. M. FORSTER: *A PASSAGE TO INDIA*

It is an interesting and important fact that, were it not for the encouragement and persuasion of Leonard Woolf, Forster may never have completed *A Passage to India*, the classic novel in critical and popular acclaim of the East-West encounter. Woolf himself, one of the early percipient critics, said of the book that it "marches firmly, triumphantly .... through the real life and politics of India, the intricacy of personal relations, [and] builds itself up, arch beyond arch, into something of great strength, beauty and also of sadness." Forster was diffident and hesitant about writing this novel as he felt he was dealing with subjects outside his accustomed range. In *The Hill of Devi* he makes this revealing comment about *A Passage to India:*

> I began this novel before my 1921 visit, and took out the opening chapters with me, with the intention of continuing them. But as soon as they were confronted with the country they purported to describe, they seemed to wilt and go dead, and I could do nothing with them. The gap between India remembered and India experienced was too wide. When I got back to England the gap narrowed, and I was able to resume. But I still thought the book bad, and probably would not have completed it without the encouragement of Leonard Woolf.

Bridging the distance between memory and experience is a problem for all literary art but it becomes more formidable in cross-cultural fiction as the geography, which has to be vividly recreated, is detailed and specific. That Forster does minimize this gap is part of the singular success of this novel. *A Passage to India* has been so much written about that it is difficult to say anything fresh about it: Forster's words have so many associations and reverberations, his poetic symbolism despite the pervasive comedy is so weighty and intricate that a proper commentary would require a monograph of some length. Besides, these aspects have been so well covered by so many critics that any further attempt on my part would be otiose. But since I cannot ignore this novel in this book because it is of central relevance, my essay will be as brief as possible, highlighting only those features which I think have been ignored or understated.

Criticism of Forster has been replete with such questions as, is he fair to imperialism, is his view of Anglo-Indians stereotypical, does he show sufficient understanding of Indians, is he patronizing to them, does he concentrate too much on the discouraging reality while neglecting the richness of tradition, does he prefer Muslims to Hindus, or vice versa? I think most of these questions and the possible ensuing judgements are tangential if not irrelevant. For my purposes the novel's elements are the social comedy of human intercourse, the meetings and confrontations of individuals and groups, or within groups, the political context of Empire and the distortions which accompany it, the clash of religions and the search for life's meanings, the impact on a liberal, Western sensibility of the muddle and mystery of an alien culture and finally speculation not only about the future of India and of its ties with its colonial master but about personal relationships in the broadest sense. It has been wisely remarked that the book is a passage to more than India.

The rape, or attempted rape, of a white woman by a colonial subject is the quintessential insult, the ultimate social crime and while the incident of the alleged rape and the subsequent trial are the climaxes of the narrative sequence, the total meaning of the book rests on the treatment of personal relationships, both generally and in the context of the colonial nexus, and on the human being's orientation in relation to God, the non-human and the void.

Throughout the book the themes are inextricably interlinked: even in the first chapter the city of Chandrapore is divided between the mud huts of the locals and their mud-moving inhabitants, "a low but indestructible form of life", and the civil station which charms not neither does it repel. We are introduced to the pre-historic Marabar caves, non-human but resembling human attributes such as fists and fingers extruding from the earth in grotesque shapes. The question whether Indians can be friends with Englishmen or not is also raised very early in the novel at a party where the gregarious intimacy of a Moslem group is much in evidence. The attitudes of Anglo-India are also introduced early: the Club members are part of an Army of Occupation, all of them British and in exile, and a former nurse opines that the kindest thing one can do to a native patient is to let him die. Mrs. Moore, a visitor, replies with an embarrassing rejoinder, "How if he went to heaven?" which does not disconcert the nurse who says that he can go where he likes so long as he doesn't come near her because all Indians give her the creeps. The so-called "Bridge Party" arranged by the Collector in order to satisfy the visitors' desire to know the real India excludes more than it can accommodate -- the lower middle class of India and the circles even beyond these, "people who wore nothing but a loincloth, people who wore not even that, and spent their lives in knocking two sticks together before a scarlet doll – humanity grading and drifting beyond the educated vision, until no earthly invitation can embrace it". Forster remarks wryly that perhaps all invitations must proceed from heaven. Even the missionaries are no longer important, Christian proselytization has lost its muscle.

What is crucial, however, is that the despair is both social and spiritual: the lack of any real communication between individuals and groups evokes the immense and indifferent emptiness:

> Some kites hovered overhead, impartial over the kites passed the mass of a vulture, and with an impartiality exceeding all, the sky, not deeply colored but translucent, poured light from its whole circumference. It seemed unlikely that the series stopped here. Beyond the sky must not there be something that overarches all the skies, more impartial even than they? Beyond which again ...

Even the so-called incident in one of the Marabar caves is to some extent caused by a conversational gaffe when Adela asks Aziz whether he has one wife or more than one, a question which shocks Aziz so much that he leaves her and plunges at random into one of the caves in order to recover his balance, thereby losing sight of his guest.

The menu of Anglo-India typifies the isolation of exiles as it is cooked by servants who do not understand it: "Julienne soup full of bullety bottled peas with the cutlets, trifle, sardines on toast." It is the deep unwillingness to adapt which makes Mrs. Moore disappointed in her son's official manner, the self-satisfied lilt of his voice and his undeveloped heart: "One touch of regret -- not the canny substitute but the true regret from the heart -- would have made him a different man, and the British Empire a different institution".

India has the effect on Mrs. Moore of unsettling her Christian religion which now seems to her puny and talkative because she senses that outside the arch there is another arch, and beyond the remotest echo a silence.

The cultural misunderstandings which inhibit communication are not confined to the whites: Aziz cannot distinguish between Fielding's casual remark suggesting that Post-Impressionism is an obscure matter and snooty Mrs. Turton's "Why, they speak English" and thus discloses the chip on his shoulder.

Godbole seems the most promising candidate for the East-West encounter: he seems to have transcended the distinction but his achievement is seen best in the third section of the novel. The Moslem Aziz is like the Christian in that he reduces the cosmic vision to what is humanly manageable: to poetry, the need for brotherhood, the importance of the emotions, the sense of tradition. Godbole's, however, is the song of the unknown bird. He can cope with diversity, he can compromise between destiny and desire, he can see religion as play and merriment.

India is a mystery and a muddle; nothing is identifiable, not even the green bird which Ronny and Adela see, nor the hazy animal, whether buffalo or hyena or even a ghost, which interrupts their car ride with the Nawab Bahadur. The caves are full of echoes which can cause neuroses in most people: only Godbole is immune because he considers his religion an even higher arch than what the caves project. For Mrs. Moore, the echoes are life-defeating and traumatic:

> There are some exquisite echoes in India; there is the whisper round the dome at Bijapur; there are the long, solid sentences that voyage through the air at Mandu, and return unbroken to their creator. The echo in a Marabar cave is not like these, it is entirely devoid of distinction. Whatever is said, the same monotonous noise replies, and

quivers up and down the walls unless it is absorbed into the roof. "Boom" is the sound as far as the human alphabet can express it, or "bou-oum" or "ou-boum", -- utterly dull. Hope, politeness, the blowing of a nose, the squeak of a boot, all produce "boum". Even the striking of a match starts a little worm coiling, which is too small to complete a circle but is eternally watchful. And if several people talk at once, an overlapping howling noise begins, echoes generate echoes, and the cave is stuffed with a snake composed of small snakes, which writhe independently.

The experience undermines Mrs. Moore's hold on life; she is told by the echo that pathos, piety, courage exist along with filth, and that though everything exists nothing has value.

If one had spoken vileness in that place, or quoted lofty poetry, the comment would have been the same – "ou-boum". If one had spoken with the tongues of angels and pleaded for all the unhappiness and misunderstanding in the world, past, present and to come, for all the misery men must undergo whatever their opinion or position, and however much they dodge or bluff -- it would amount to the same, the serpent would descend and return to the ceiling. Devils are of the North, and poems can be written about them, but no one could romanticise the Marabar because it robbed infinity and eternity of their vastness, the only quality that accommodates them to mankind.

So paralyzing is the experience that Mrs. Moore loses interest in her God, doesn't want to write to her children and becomes indifferent to the fate of her friend Aziz, on whose behalf she refrains from testifying at his trial. What had spoken to her from the caves was something very old and very small, before time and space, something snub-nosed, ungenerous -- the undying worm itself.

The outcome of the trial introduces a new strain on Aziz's friendship for Fielding, the well-meaning, heroic but rather dull school teacher who has to carry alone on his shoulders the pleasanter side of the British Raj. Fielding's rational analyses of the differences between Adela and Mrs. Moore do not impress Aziz, who asks him if emotion is measured like a sack of potatoes, so much per pound. Adela's withdrawal of her accusation does not impress the Indians because they felt her heart was not in it, and any action not colored by emotion is limited and sterile. Fielding's successful persuasion of Aziz which makes him drop the demand of twenty thousand rupees as compensation, later leads him to suspect that Fielding maneuvered this deal in order to obtain a larger dowry when he marries Adela. The rapidity with which he believes that this has in fact taken place is Forster's way of showing that the Indian character is not disposed to weigh objective evidence and is swept away by suspicion based on exaggerated emotion.

Even Fielding is affected by the echo: he realizes, though never fully in his consciousness, that it belongs to a universe he has missed or rejected. His wife Stella is on to something but even Fielding has an intimation that perhaps it is Hinduism which will ultimately vindicate religious faith. Aziz asks Fielding why he wants him to be a religious poet when he himself was an atheist:

> "There is something in religion that may not be true, but has not yet been sung."
> "Explain in detail".
> "Something that the Hindus have perhaps found".

It is Hinduism to which we must now turn to find the answer that the European liberal agnosticism has failed to understand in the muddledom and mystery of India. I don't believe, as some critics do, that the third section *The Temple* entirely roots out the profound sense of human and cosmic negation evoked in the part called *Caves*; however, it is a brave and sympathetic account which is not itself entirely negated by the vision of nothingness and the relative failure of the closest cross-cultural relationship in the novel, that of Aziz and Fielding.

The conflict, the despair and the transcendence: that a man like E. M. Forster with his attenuated liberalism in retreat should have been able to encounter the actualities of a very different civilization is a remarkable achievement, denied to more "religious" prophets like D.H. Lawrence: he saw above all that the ragged edges could provide the base for the cosmic dance. Despite the crudity of the props and the music, the worshippers attain a radiant expression, trans-personal, universal. The decrepit and tasteless paraphernalia do not rob the moment of its grandeur: God is love. The vision is all-embracing.

> All sorrow was annihilated, not only for Indians, but for foreigners, birds, caves, railways and the stars; all became joy, all laughter; there had never been disease, nor doubt, misunderstanding, cruelty, fear.

The unknown was ravished; merriment is part of the Divine Game. Even Aziz is willing to be friends again with Fielding and because of his tender memories of Mrs. Moore is willing to befriend her children, Stella and Ralph. "I am an Indian at last", he says. The ceremony includes even the lowest castes, the unclean sweepers have to play their tune, because they stand for the spot of filth without which the spirit cannot cohere, reminding one of the punkah-wallah at the courthouse who had the strength and beauty that sometimes flowers among the low-caste Indians.

When that strange race nears the dust and is condemned as untouchable, then nature remembers the physical perfection she accomplished elsewhere, and throws out a god -- not many, but one here and there, to prove to society how little its categories impress her.

Hinduism though indeterminate -- how would one locate the heart of a cloud? -- is supremely real: the visit to Mau convinces Stella Fielding that the caves have been wiped out, even Fielding thinks their union has been blessed. There is a change in Fielding -- he had thrown in his lot with Anglo-India as a devoted functionary of the Imperial education system. But his desire to continue his friendship with Aziz is genuine though he realizes that he may no longer be willing to act his former heroic role.

In their final ride together, their friendship cannot overcome either history or nature:

"Why can't we be friends now?" said the other, holding him affectionately. "It's what I want. It's what you want". But the horses didn't want it -- they swerved apart; the earth didn't want it, sending up rocks through which riders must pass single file; the temples, the tank, the jail, the palace, the birds, the carrion, the Guest House, that came into view as they issued from the gap and saw Mau beneath; they didn't want it, they said in their hundred voices, "No, not yet", and the sky said, "No, not there."

This powerful dramatic presentation of a fundamental pessimism about human relationships should not be taken as Forster's final word: its place in the total economy of the novel must be recognized but it must at least be balanced with Godbole's mystical sense of communication with Mrs. Moore:

He had, with increasing vividness, again seen Mrs. Moore, and round her faintly clinging forms of trouble. He was a Brahmin, she Christian, but it made no difference, it made no difference whether she was a trick of his memory or a telepathic appeal. It was his duty, as it was his desire, to place himself in the position of the God and to love her, and to place himself in her position and to say to the God, "Come, come, come, come". This was all he could do. How inadequate! But each according to his own capacities, and he knew that his own were small. "One old Englishwoman and one little, little wasp", he thought, as he stepped out of the temple into the grey of a pouring wet morning. "It does not seem much, still it is more than I am myself."

Forster is essentially a celebrant of the Mediterranean norm as is seen in Fielding's reflections in the last chapter of *Caves*, a key passage because it is placed just before the final section *Temple*:

The buildings of Venice, like the mountains of Crete and the fields of Egypt, stood in the right place, whereas in poor India everything was placed wrong. He had forgotten the beauty of form among idol temples and lumpy hills; indeed, without form, how can there be beauty? Form stammered here and there in a mosque, became rigid through nervousness even, but oh these Italian churches! San Giorgio standing on the island which could scarcely have risen from the waves without it, the Salute holding the entrance of a canal which, but for it, would not be the Grand Canal! In the old undergraduate days he had wrapped himself up in the many-colored blanket of St. Mark's, but something more precious than mosaics and marbles was offered to him now: the harmony between the works of man and the earth that upholds them, the civilization that has escaped muddle, the spirit in a reasonable form, with flesh and blood subsisting. Writing picture post-cards to his Indian friends, he felt that all of them would miss the joys he experienced now, the joys of form, and that this constituted a serious barrier. They would see the sumptuousness of Venice, not its shape, and though Venice was not Europe, it was part of the Mediterranean harmony. The Mediterranean is the human norm. When men leave that exquisite lake, whether through the Bosphorus or the Pillars of Hercules, they approach the monstrous and the extraordinary; and the southern exit leads to the strangest experience of all.

He could however enter into another world though his values were devastated in consequence, but it is his capacity for understatement, his liberal European sense of moderation that makes his endorsement of self-transcendance all the more compelling, all the more rare, worth-while and credible as a literary and personal testament.

Foster's treatment of personal relationships has been extensively documented and analyzed by his critics; less so, however, is the emotional chiaroscuro of his delineation of individual character with its subtle alterations in response to environment and circumstance. Early in the novel, after Mrs. Moore's meeting with Aziz in the mosque and her subsequent conversation with her son, Ralph, she muses as follows:

> In the light of her son's comment she reconsidered the scene at the mosque, to see whose impression was correct. Yes, it could be worked into quite an unpleasant scene. The doctor had begun by bullying her, had said Mrs. Callendar was nice, and then – finding the ground safe -- had changed; he had alternatively whined over his grievances and patronized her, had run a dozen ways in a single sentence, had been unreliable, inquisitive, vain. Yes, it was all true, but how false as a summary of the man; the essential life of him had been slain.

> Going to hang up her cloak, she found that the tip of the peg was occupied by a small wasp. She had known this wasp or his relatives by day; they were not as English wasps, but had long, yellow legs which hung down behind when they flew. Perhaps he mistook the peg for a branch -- no Indian animal has a sense of an interior. Bats, rats, birds, insects will as soon nest inside a house as out; it is to them a normal growth of the eternal jungle, which alternatively produces houses trees, houses trees. There he clung, asleep, while jackals in the plain bayed their desires and mingled with the percussion of drums.

> "Pretty dear," said Ms. Moore to the wasp. He did not wake, but her voice floated out, to swell the night's uneasiness.

Mrs. Moore realizes that out of simplification comes not just unfairness but evil, and the mysterious, "poetic" encounter with a wasp seen as non-human as a jackal, and as indifferent to human dear or human music, causes an unidentifiable but extreme disquiet. Mrs. Moore's increasing alienation from the Christian God and the etiolation of His significance is movingly dramatized:

> Mrs. Moore felt she had made a mistake in mentioning God, but she found him increasingly difficult to avoid as she grew older, and he had been constantly in her thoughts since she entered India, though oddly enough he satisfied her less. She must needs pronounce his name

frequently, as the greatest she knew, yet she had never found it less
efficacious. Outside the arch there seemed always an arch, beyond the
remotest echo a silence.

Christianity itself is the most satirized religion in the book; not only
do the caves add nothing to the sense of good and evil, but an
anthropomorphic religion like Christianity cannot countenance them in
any way; what transpires in the caves has an eerie, preternatural beauty,
which neither human speech, nor human vision, can accommodate:

> Nothing, nothing attaches to them, and their reputation -- for they
> have one -- does not depend upon human speech. It is as if the
> surrounding plain or the passing birds have taken upon themselves to
> exclaim "extraordinary," and the word has taken root in the air, and
> been inhaled by mankind.

> They are dark caves. Even when they open toward the sun, very
> little light penetrates down the entrance tunnel into the circular
> chamber. There is little to see, and no eye to see it, until the visitor
> arrives for his five minutes, and strikes a match. Immediately another
> flame rises in the depths of the rock and moves towards the surface like
> an imprisoned spirit: the walls of the circular chamber have been most
> marvelously polished. The two flames approach and strike to unite, but
> cannot, because one of them breathes air, the other, stone. A mirror
> inlaid with lovely colors divides the lovers, delicate stars of pink and
> grey interpose, exquisite nebulae, shadings fainter than the tail of a
> comet or the midday moon, all the evanescent life of the granite, only
> here visible. Fists and fingers thrust above the advancing soil -- here at
> last is their skin, finer than any covering acquired by the animals,
> smoother than windless water, more voluptuous than love. The radiance
> increases, the flames touch one another, kiss, expire. The cave is dark
> again, like all the caves.

A gentler, but nevertheless satiric tone is adopted toward the well-
meaning Christian missionaries, old Mr. Graysford and young Mr.
Sorley, who lived out beyond the slaughterhouses, travelled third class
on the railway, never went up to the club and who assiduously preached
that in the Father's house were many mansions, that the Divine
hospitality could include monkeys and even jackals and offer all
mammals their collateral share of bliss in Heaven. They, however,
stopped short at the wasps: "No, no, that is going too far. We must
exclude someone from our gathering, or we shall be left with nothing."

Even with minor figures like the missionaries, Foster's insight into human perception or sensibility is exceptional. It is even more marked when it comes to the major characters. What makes Aziz more than a stereotypical Indian Moslem, are, among other things, his genuinely confused cogitations on love and religion when thinking of his dead wife:

> She had gone, there was no one like her, and what is that uniqueness but love? He amused himself, he forgot her at times: but at other times he felt that he had sent all the beauty and joy of the world into Paradise, and he meditated suicide. Would he meet her beyond the tomb? Is there such a meeting place? Though orthodox, he did not know God's unity indubitably and indubitably announced, but on all other points he wavered like the average Christian; his belief in the life to come would pale to a hope, vanish, reappear, all in a single sentence or a dozen heart-beats, so that the corpuscles of his blood rather than he seemed to decide which opinion he should hold, and for how long. It was so with all his opinions. Nothing stayed, nothing passed that did not return; the circulation was ceaseless and kept him young, and he mourned his wife the more because he mourned her seldom.

Or, the quick and volatile change in mood, when initially offended by Fielding's rejoinder to Aziz's mention of Post-Impressionism, which merely displays, if any, Fielding's own disinterest in high falutin art terminology or criticism, when Aziz realizes that Fielding is essentially a man of good intent:

> The remark suggested that he, an obscure Indian, had no right to have heard of Post-Impressionism -- a privilege reserved for the Ruling Race, that he said stuffily, "I do not consider Mrs. Moore my friend, I only met her accidentally in my mosque", and was adding "a single meeting is too short to make a friend," but before he could finish the stiffness vanished from it, because he felt Fielding's fundamental good will.

Aziz has a nostalgia for a shadowy past, but this does enrich his character, and so he dreams,

> "We punish no one, no one," he repeated, "and in the evening we will give a great banquet with a nautch and lovely girls shall shine on every side of the tank with fireworks in their hands, and all shall be feasting and happiness until the next day, when there shall be justice as

before -- fifty rupees, a hundred, a thousand -- till peace comes. Ah,
why didn't we live in that time?"

Even Godbole, who could well have been caricatured as the
prototypical Hindu Brahmin, shows a serene disregard for the
contradictions in life and the cosmos: when the severely agitated
Fielding pointedly asks Godbole for his own personal opinion on the
weighty matter of Aziz's innocence or guilt, Godbole replies in a way
most exasperating to Fielding, that nonetheless issues from a rigid logic
and an enshrined metaphysic:

> "I am informed that an evil action was performed in the Marabar
> Hills, and that a highly esteemed English lady is now seriously ill in
> consequence. My answer to that is this: that action was performed by
> Dr. Aziz." He stopped and sucked in his thin cheeks. "It was performed
> by the guide." He stopped again. "It was performed by you.' Now he
> had an air of daring and of coyness. "It was performed by me." He
> looked shyly down the sleeve of his own coat. "And by my students. It
> was performed by the lady herself. When evil occurs, it expresses the
> whole of the universe. Similarly when good occurs . . . Good and evil
> are different, as their names imply. But, in my own humble opinion,
> they are both of them aspects of my Lord. He is present in the one,
> absent in the other, and the difference between presence and absence is
> great, as great as my feeble mind can grasp. Yet absence implies
> presence, absence is not non-existence, and we are therefore entitled to
> repeat, 'Come, come, come come.'"

This is as metaphysical, if you wish, as the definition of God, in the
Indian philosophical tradition from Shankara, in negative terms ("Neti,
neti") or even of the concept of evil as the absence of good in the
theology of St. Thomas Aquinas.

My conclusion would be that critics of the novel have not pondered
enough on its nature as a classic of cross-cultural literature, a genre
which has its own revelations and opacities, and to its important theme
of the collision of religions, especially the role played by Hinduism,
which only in a structural sense is relegated to the smallest third part of
the book. What Godbole and Hinduism stand for is not negated by the
relative failure of the reconciliation between Fielding and Aziz in their
last ride together; we must remember that even Aziz decides to spend
the rest of his days in a Hindu environment, and though he recalled his
dearly beloved Emperor Babur who found in Hinduism "no good fruit,

no fresh water or witty conversation, not even a friend", Aziz himself was content to settle for a compromise:

> The promontory was covered with lofty trees, and the fruit-bats were unhooking from the boughs and making kissing sounds as they grazed the surface of the tank; hanging upside down all day, they had grown thirsty. The signs of the contented Indian evening multiplied; frogs on all sides, cow-dung burning eternally; a flock of belated hornbills overhead, looking like winged skeletons as they flapped across the gloaming. There was death in the air but not sadness; a compromise had been made between destiny and desire, and even the heart of man acquiesced.

Fielding himself thinks that if any religion may, possibly, provide an answer to the human predicament, it would be Hinduism; his wife Stella, he says, is on to "something"; she believes that "the Marabar has been wiped out," and that in the language of theology their own union has been blessed, because of their passage to India.

Foster himself, subtle and tentative an artist as he was, seems to believe that humanity can endure its sense of death in the air, so long as there is no sadness.

The novel is not a static mosaic of differently colored tiles set in separate groups; though the perspectives are distinguishable, they develop in their interaction. Mrs. Moore's Christianity crumbles before the experience of India but she retains enough decency to disbelieve the story of Aziz's rape. However, she does not have the courage to testify on Aziz's behalf and this is not merely because she does not want to repudiate Adela or disgrace her son and the British clan. Her death while at sea is almost a suicide.

Adela herself undergoes a hallucination but is strong enough to speak the truth in court, although her action alienates her from her intended, and the rest of the British community.

Aziz, mercurial, a believer in love and personal relationships, retains his humanity despite the vilification to which he is subject.

Godbole the Hindu has a vision of the cosmos which can deal with the real world, with mystery and muddledom, because for him it is the truth which matters, a truth which even obviates the need for grammar: God is love is the same as God si love.

The different viewpoints form not only a nexus but tend towards a nisus, a search for a significance which is more valid than any of the component elements: the Forsterian liberalism, the value of personal relationships, the Christian or Moslem faiths, the sense of an ultimate emptiness seem in conflict and collision to reach out to the Hindu acceptance of life as religiousness. Perhaps Forster did not know enough of the real Hinduism but it is amazing that a man of his background could have been drawn to the most tempting, almost Circean seduction any religion could offer: Hinduism seems to him nearly indestructible. Bull-doze one dogma, it re-emerges in another form because it does not rest on any rigid underpinnings: mutability and *maya* are its pillars: it can both enrich and denude all human efforts at completion, fixity or fullness.

CHAPTER VIII

GEORGE ORWELLS' *BURMESE DAYS*

It is one of the theories in this book that where the locale or setting impinges on the action, modifies or even generates it, especially when the novel deals with the realities of cross-cultural contact, the relative success or failure of the work depends on the degree to which its physical, cultural and moral geography is integrated into the total statement. This would apply not merely to the novel's provenance as an example of the cross-cultural encounter but also to its success as a work of art. It would follow that an important measure of levels of fulfillment or failure is the power to recreate and use the context in this process of artistic integration; this is a yardstick that is rarely is applied in criticism.

George Orwell's *Burmese Days* is an excellent locus for the application of this principle. It is a fine novel, not unworthy of comparison with Forster's *A Passage to India*, though considerably inferior. Orwell was born in India and spent the years 1922 to 1927 as a member of the Imperial Police Force in Burma, a far longer time than Forster's two visits to India, though his second visit lasted six months. Orwell, therefore, spent enough time in Burma to observe it at first-hand and undoubtedly his picture of it is very impressive, but he fails to get under the skin of its culture as successfully as Kipling or Forster in the case of India, Leonard Woolf with Sri Lanka, or Anthony Burgess with Malaya. Though the physical setting of Burma, its intense heat and light, its dust and damp are vividly captured, Orwell's sense of the culture of Burma is deficient, one-sided and clichetic. Unlike in Forster, there is no attempt made to present the interaction of cultural groups. While in Forster there are quite a few characters seen in the round-- Aziz, Godbole, Fielding, Mrs. Moore, Adela--in Orwell only the protagonist Flory is multi-dimensional. The others are caricatures, and though some of them--U Po Kyin, Lieutenant Verall, Dr. Veraswami, Elizabeth, for example--are etched with remarkable skill, they do not undergo any change or development of character. The language is geared to a Western audience, and attempts made to use Burmese English or transliterations or modifications of local languages meet with little success. Imperialism, though a potent force in the novel, is too crudely imagined and is the subject more of stereotypical attitudes and routine debate than a significant agent in the unravelling of the plot. Finally, the story of Flory runs on its own steam and is relatively independent of the colonial context in which it is encapsulated. The treatment of Flory--what he is, how he changes, or rather oscillates between ideal and performance, and what becomes of him--are rendered powerfully enough to merit a serious treatment of this novel but other issues to which space is devoted are either skirted or side-tracked. *Burmese Days* is therefore a good example of the cross-cultural encounter for an examination of the strengths and pitfalls of such enterprises in the novel.

I shall comment on these aspects in order to draw them out more fully and enforce my judgements with more conviction. The very title "Burmese Days" suggests a casualness of approach very different from the reverberations of a "Passage to India". The title "Burmese Days" is misleading; the action is not confined to a few days. Besides, the connotations of a traveller describing days spent in a foreign country, at best a belletristic endeavor, militate against the professedly earnest intentions of the novel. The tone of a tourist or even a sojourner, a cicerone pointing out elements of scene, life and society in Burma to an uninitiated reader, is often disabling. But the pieces of natural description are not always touristy or casual: they are often linked to inner states of great sensitivity and importance. It is not merely the accuracy of physical notation which is remarkable, as in the following description of a typical Burmese market:

> There were pomelos hanging on strings like green moons, red bananas, baskets of heliotrope-colored prawns the size of lobsters, brittle, dried fish tied in bundles, crimson chilis, ducks split open and

cured like hams, green coconuts, the larvae of the rhinoceros beetle, sections of sugar cane, dates, lacquered sandals, check silk longyis, aphrodisiacs in the form of large, soap-like pills, glazed earthenware jars four feet high, Chinese sweetmeats made of garlic and sugar, green and white cigars, purple brinjals, persimmon-seed necklaces, chickens cheeping in wicker cages, brass Buddhas, heart-shaped beetle leaves, bottles of Kruschen salts, switches of false hair, red clay cooking pots, steel shoes for bullocks, papier-mache marionettes, strips of alligator hide with magical properties.

There are important moments where the natural scene provokes a peace-inducing vision accompanied by a poignant sense of the need to share the experience with a loved one: the protagonist's loneliness can only be overcome by a togetherness in the face of the excruciating loveliness:

Here a peepul tree grew, a great buttressed thing six feet thick, woven of innumerable strands of wood, like a wooden cable twisted by a giant. The roots of the tree made a natural cavern, under which the clear greenish water bubbled. Above and all round dense foliage shut out the light turning the place into a green grotto walled with leaves ... There was stirring high up in the peepul tree, and a bubbling noise like pots boiling. A flock of green pigeons were up there, eating the berries. Flory gazed up into the great green dome of the tree, trying to distinguish the birds; they were invisible, they matched the leaves so perfectly, and yet the whole tree was alive with them, shimmering, as though the ghosts of birds were shaking it ... A pang went through Flory. Alone, alone, the bitterness of being alone! So often like this, in lonely places in the forest, he would come upon something--bird, flower, tree--beautiful beyond all words, if there had been a soul with whom to share it. Beauty is meaningless unless it is shared. If he had one person, just one, to have his loneliness!

There are religious overtones: the use of words and phrases like "green grotto," "great green dome," "soul" by a master of the direct statement and the unadorned style would suggest that Orwell was trying deliberately to evoke a sense of the numinous which Flory could recognize but which in order to be worthwhile and satisfying had to be shared with another human being in an abiding personal relationship. Even his commerce with the native Burmans acquires a respectful character: this is how he addresses the man from whom he inquires how to find his way: "Come here, if you please, O venerable and learned sir! We have lost our way.   Stop a moment, O great builder of pagodas!"

But the portrayal of Burmese culture is often abstract and banal. Nor can one miss an ambivalence even when the culture is being flattered because the adulation is accompanied by an ambiguity which denigrates what it praises:

> "Just look at that girl's movements--look at that strange, bent-forward pose like a marionette, and the way her arms twist from the elbow like a cobra rising to strike. It's grotesque, it's even ugly, with a sort of willful ugliness. And there's something sinister in it too. There's a touch of the diabolical in all Mongols. And yet when you look closely, what art, what centuries of culture you can see behind it! Every movement that girl makes has been studied and handed down through innumerable generations. Whenever you look closely at the art of these Eastern peoples you can see that--a civilization stretching back and back, practically the same, into times when we were dressed in woad. In some way that I can't define to you, the whole life and spirit of Burma is summed up in the way that girl twists her arms. When you see her you can see the rice fields, the villages under the teak trees, the pagodas, the priests in their yellow robes, the buffaloes swimming the rivers in the early morning..."

The celebrated high culture sits oddly and uncomfortably atop a milieu that can only be seen as primitive, even barbaric as in the case of the Burmese doctor who by applying some poisonous concoction of crushed leaves succeeds in blinding a wounded boy; Mandalay is described as a disagreeable town, "dusty and intolerably hot, and it is said to have five main products all beginning with P, namely, pagodas, pariahs, pigs, priests and prostitutes." One of the important Burmans, U Po Kyin, is seen as a crocodile in human shape; even when the high ideal of Buddhist vegetarianism is at issue, U Po Kyin uses a specious argument for eating fish, for his wife's benefit:

> "Am I to blame if somebody else chooses to commit murder? The fisherman catches the fish and he is damned for it. But we are damned for eating the fish? Certainly not. Why not eat the fish once it is dead? You should study the scriptures more carefully, my dear Kin Kin."

What is left of Burmese religion and culture, except the nondescript pagodas which even U Po Kyin hopes to build before he dies in order to be reborn in some other shape than a rat or a frog:

Probably his good works would take the form of building pagodas. Four pagodas, five, six seven--the priests would tell him how many--with carved stonework, gilt umbrellas and little bells that tinkled in the wind, every tinkle a prayer. And he would return to the earth in male human shape--for a woman ranks at about the same level as a rat or a frog--or at worst as some dignified beast such as an elephant.

Imperialism, or the colonial adventure, which seems to be an obsessive concern is treated at the level of a high school debate: even in his brilliant essay "Shooting an Elephant" the dehumanizing of colonial power though powerfully rendered is marred, in my opinion, by the frequent references to the Burmese as yellow: the predicament of the official who behaves the way he does merely to sustain an image is also colored by an implied sense that somehow people other than white are inferior. The discourse between Flory and the Indian doctor Veeraswami is trite and doesn't progress beyond a facile counterpointing of the most obvious attitudes:

> Flory: "My dear doctor, how can you make out that we are in this country except to steal? It's so simple. The official holds the Burman down while the official goes through his pockets."

Veeraswami's response is that of the brown sahib totally deaf to his own culture and idolizing the foreign intrusion:

> "My friend, my friend, you are forgetting the Oriental character. How is it possible to have developed us, with our apathy and superstition? At least you have brought to us law and order. The unswerving British Justice and the Pax Britannica."
> "Pox Britannica, doctor, Pox Britannica is its proper name..."

The argument is puerile: a safety valve for two people who have to live with a lie. Flory himself had a bitter hatred of imperialism but he views with sympathy the futility of the imperialist adventurer, an unenviable life, "a poor bargain to spend thirty years, ill-paid, in an alien country, and then come home with a wrecked life and a pineapple backside from sitting in cane chairs, to settle down as the bore of some second-rate Club." The pukka sahib is as much a victim, as the colonizer. The problem with the book is that though imperialism is the context, the personal situation of Flory derived as in the naturalistic

novel from the forces of heredity and environment runs away with the
story: the need to excoriate imperialism seems the result of a
compulsion to exorcise a personal, even private demon. Orwell shows
no real love for the Burmese: the best character portrayal, apart from
the more minor but vicious delineation of Verall, is that of U Po Kyin,
a savage Dickensian-style portrayal of an unmitigated villain who is so
grotesque as to be even comic. In order to really penetrate Oriental
civilizations, one has to empathize with the religious tradition which
accords at many points with the specifics of meaningful social living:
otherwise you are left with the heat and the dust and the human
disaster. Orwell had no gift for this: he lacked Myers' knowledge,
Kipling's imaginative insight into the spiritual basis of an alien culture,
or even Forster's humility before mystery and transcendence. What for
me at least is most fascinating in this novel is the importance of the
sense of place, the application of what Orwell himself once said, "in all
the novels about the East, the scenery is the real subject matter." This is
what makes *Burmese Days* an important text of the cross-cultural
experience, though in many ways the novel could be seen as an
interesting failure.

Of the other characters, Veeraswami, though given many pages, is
the dull, educated Indian superior to the primitive Burmese natives:

> "These villagers--dirty, ignorant savages! Even to get them to come
> to hospital is all we can do, and they will die of gangrene or carry a
> tumor as large as a melon rather than face the knife. And such
> medicines as their own so-called doctors give to them! Herbs gathered
> under the new moon, tigers' whiskers, rhinoceros horn, urine,
> menstrual blood! How men can drink such compounds is disgusting."

So much for the traditional medicine, the Burmese ayurveda, the
time-honored pharmacopoeia! The contours of Veeraswami's mind are
mainly essays of the Emerson-Carlyle-Stevenson type and his thinking
illustrates the noted Indian tendency to see moral and cosmic meaning
in whatever he reads. Veeraswami remains a pasteboard figure, a useful
audience for Flory's diatribes against imperialism.

The other members of the British "set" are even worse caricatures.
Mrs. Lackersteen, wary of her husband's alcoholism and ambitions for
her niece, has her own nightmares of rape, the classic form of the
colonial encounter at its starkest (Forster's *Passage to India*, Paul
Scott's *The Raj Quartet):*

To her mind the words 'sedition,' 'Naturalism,' 'rebellion,' 'Home Rule,' conveyed one thing and one only, and that was a picture of herself being raped by a procession of jet-black coolies with rolling white eyeballs.

The trigger-happy Westfall mourns the fact that in eleven years he has not fired his gun and killed a man; Ellis is nearly deranged with hate for the native and even reprimands the butler for his improved English because natives can only be kept in their place if they did not progress beyond pidgin.

Macgregor the Deputy Commissioner runs true to type--dull, a club bore who wants peace at any price.

Elizabeth herself is too much of a stereotype to evoke much interest; her crude values, her philistinism, her excitement over violence—she felt almost an adoration for Flory now that she had seen how he could shoot--do not specially distinguish her except for the near Lawrentian oneness of sensuality and violence. The dead pigeon in her hand excites her sexually:

> She could hardly give it up, the feel of it so ravished her. She could have kissed it, hugged it to her breast. All the men, Flory and Ko S'la and the beaters smiled at one another to see her fondling the dead bird. Reluctantly, she gave it to Ko S'la to put in the bag. She was conscious of an extraordinary desire to fling her arms round Flory's neck and kiss him; and in some way it was the killing of the pigeon that made her feel this.

What is surprising is that Flory cannot see any of this and this imperceptiveness is an index of his sense of futility and despair: his amazing lack of discernment is not just that of the crazed lover. No one is shocked to hear that at the end of the story she marries Macgregor and becomes a memsahib with an exhaustive knowledge of the Civil List, a capacity to give charming dinner parties, and a knowledge of how to put servants in their place.

We are left with few other minor characters though the presentation of Verall and the Eurasians is a masterpiece of pungent delineation. Verall is a rabbit, "but a tough and martial rabbit." He takes no interest in Indians and his contempt for them shows in his swear words in Urdu which are all he cares to learn of the language. His social snobbery justifies in his own eyes his cynical treatment of women and his unmitigated scorn for the country in which he works. Though one feels Elizabeth deserved the contemptuous dalliance she receives from him, Orwell cannot help exposing the class prejudice he himself had to put up with, particularly as a poor boy at Eton.

The Eurasians are a pathetic lot: willing, nay eager to foreswear their native heritage and behave like Europeans they claim prickly heat as a privilege, "very prevalent disease among we Europeans."

The satiric treatment uses animal imagery to an extent that is disconcerting and suggestive of a bias against the human race as itself debased: though the plaudits and diatribes are distributed with an even hand between Europeans and natives, one cannot help but feel that the dice are loaded against the non-European. Though Maxwell is called a carthorse colt, and Mrs. Lackersteen is serpentine and Macgregor a turtle, the more damaging comparisons are for the non-whites: various people have eyes like dogs, the Chinese trader's baby is like a large yellow frog, Ma Kin has a simian face, peasant women have mare-like buttocks, school boys emit "hyena-like laughter," U Po Kyin is saurian. The Swiftian import of this is acceptable in a more generally anti-human vision but excessive in the portrayal of an imperialistic situation, neither welcomed nor accepted by an innocent Burman people. Apart from the animal imagery, there is a consistently derogatory tone in the way local people and objects are described. Ba Sein is a person with a "curiously smooth face that recalled a coffee blancmange," Ma Hla May is a doll, grotesque and queer, U Po Kyin eats with greasy fingers, Veeraswami's boots are clumsy and his library unappetizing, the Mali is a "lymphatic, half-witted Hindu youth," flowers are "oppressive to the eyes," Burmese music is a "fearful pandemonium ... a squeal of pipes, a rattle like castanets, and the hoarse thump of drums, above which a man's voice was brassily squalling."

We are left with the protagonist Flory, who is the center of the book: his life and fortunes need not be described in too great detail because already a lot has been said, and much implied. Flory is bedevilled by his birthmark, but it is not a rich symbol in the way it is in one of Hawthorne's stories with that title. Whenever Flory feels guilty or embarrassed the birthmark takes on a palpable life but the attempt to give it an allegorical quality, "it has begun in his mother's womb, when chance put the blue birthmark on his cheek," and persisted as a damning disfigurement till his death, "with death, the birthmark had faded immediately, so that it was no more than a faint grey stain," does not succeed, because Flory's predicament could be explained in more naturalistic terms.

Flory's character is not the product of his life in Burma, though it exacerbated his despair: his early life, he "left school a barbarous young lout," his lack of filial love or gratitude, the debauchery in Rangoon, the life in the jungle camp all sow the seeds and take their toll. However, one of the book's positives is the way he acclimatizes himself to Burma:

> His body grew attuned to the strange rhythms of the tropical seasons. Every year from February to May the sun glared in the sky like an angry god, then suddenly the monsoon blew westward, first in sharp squalls, then in a heavy ceaseless downpour that drenched everything until neither one's clothes, one's bed nor even one's food ever seemed to be dry. It was still hot, with a stuffy, vaporous heat. The lower jungle paths turned into morasses, and the paddy fields were great wastes of stagnant water with a stale, mousy smell. Books and boots were mildewed. Naked Burmans in yard-wide hats of palm-leaf ploughed the paddy fields, driving their buffaloes through knee-deep water. Later, the women and children planted the green seedlings of paddy, dabbing each plant into the mud with little three-pronged forks. Through July and August there was hardly a pause in the rain. Then one night, high overhead, one heard a squawking of invisible birds. The snipe were flying southward from Central Asia. The rains tailed off, ending in October. The fields dried up, the paddy ripened, the Burmese children played hopscotch with gonyin seeds and flew kites in the cool winds. It was the beginning of the short winter, when Upper Burma seemed haunted by the ghost of England. Wild flowers sprang into bloom everywhere, not quite the same as the English ones, but very like them--honeysuckle in thick bushes, field roses smelling of peardrops, even violets in dark places of the forest. The sun circled low in the sky, and the nights and early mornings were bitterly cold, with white mists that poured through the valleys like the steam of enormous kettles. One went shooting after duck and snipe. There were snipe in countless myriads, geese in flocks that rose from the jeel with a roar like a goods train crossing an iron bridge. The ripening paddy, breast-high and yellow, looked like wheat. The Burmans went to their work with muffled heads and their arms clasped across their breasts, their faces yellow and pinched with the cold. In the morning one marched through misty incongruous wildernesses, clearings of drenched, almost English grass and naked trees where monkeys squatted in the upper branches, waiting for the sun. At night coming back to camp through the cold lanes, one met herds of buffaloes which the boys were driving home

with their huge horns looming through the mist like crescents. One had three blankets on one's bed and game pies instead of the eternal chicken. After dinner one sat on a log by the vast camp-fire drinking beer and talking about shooting. The flames danced like red holly, casting a circle of light at the edge of which servants and coolies squatted, too shy to intrude on the white men and yet edging up to the fire like dogs. As one lay in bed one could hear the dew dripping from the trees like large but gentle rain. It was a good life while one was young and need not think about the future or the past.

On his return to Burma from his interrupted attempt to travel to England he realizes that he is indeed glad to be back, that "every particle of his body was compounded of Burmese soil," and that "he had sent deep roots, perhaps his deepest into a foreign country." But what is most important in him is the craving for an authentic life, a need to find someone who would share his life in Burma. He has to lead a secret life because he does not have the courage to violate the Ten Precepts of the pukka sahib: he does not want to get mixed up in the campaign against his friend Dr. Veeraswami and he throws away the anonymous letter about him soon before a manifestation of nature which echoes his real hopes:

> A cool breath of wind blew up the hill. It was one of those momentary winds that blow sometimes in the cold weather in Burma, coming from nowhere, filling one with thirst and with nostalgia for cold sea pools, embraces of mermaids, waterfalls, eaves of ice. It rustled through the wide domes of the gold mohur trees, and fluttered the fragments of the anonymous letter that Flory had thrown over the gate half an hour earlier.

Elizabeth gives him new hope and a new courage even though she is an entirely unconscious conduit of these emotions: in fact what is difficult to believe is that even though crazed with love and loneliness he fails utterly to see that his efforts to introduce her to Burmese culture and customs leave her completely cold and even hostile. But the effect of Elizabeth's entry into his life revivifies him, he even decides to sponsor Veeraswami's application for membership in the club, and repudiates his mistress, Ma Hla May. He lives in the hope that Elizabeth would share his life and alleviate the pain of exile. Despite the vicissitudes of his relationship he continues to nurture his dream till the very end:

When they were married! When they were married! What fun they would have together in this alien yet kindly land! He saw Elizabeth in his camp, greeting him as he came home tired from work and Ko S'la hurried from the tent with a bottle of beer; he saw her walking in the forest with him, watching the hornbills in the peepul trees and picking nameless flowers, and in the marshy grazing grounds, tramping through the cold-weather mist after snipe and teal. He saw his home as she would remake it. He saw his drawing room, sluttish and bachelor-like no longer, with new furniture from Rangoon, and a bowl of pink balsams like rosebuds on the table, and books and water colors and a black piano. Above all the piano! His mind lingered upon the piano--symbol, perhaps he was unmusical, of the civilized and settled life. He was delivered far even from the sub-life of the past decade--the debaucheries, the lies, the pain of exile and solitude, the dealings with whores and moneylenders and pukka sahibs.

But the dream is predictably dissipated and Flory takes his own life.

George Orwell's *Burmese Days* is then an excellent novel and a valid text for my examination of this type of literature. However, as I said at the beginning of this essay it is almost a locus classicus for considering the strengths and weaknesses of this kind of artistic endeavor. Edmund Wilson in a 1946 essay said it was "illuminating as a picture of Burma and distinguished as a work of literature." He also pointed out that though it is not a tour de force in the manner of Forster's *A Passage to India*, Orwell's book is "saturated" with his subject. Orwell was after all born in Bengal and served in the Burmese police. His setting is not the exotic backdrop used by Somerset Maugham in his stories of the East and the Pacific: Orwell was deeply concerned about the reality of Burma. The problem, however, is that he has not yet perfected a form, so nearly adequate to his intentions, as he was able to achieve in *Animal Farm* and *1984*. Orwell's talent was rare--he was an artist with a strong political and social commitment. He had unusual personal integrity for a writer and wanted to forge a medium which was direct and transparent enough to embody and communicate a political credo. When he does succeed he is unique: personal "wholeness." even holiness is not what one always associates with an artist. There is little in him of that affectation, the theorizing, the bravado that disfigures even great writers like Thomas Mann: Orwell was a simple man with the simple courage of his convictions. He had to wait till after *Burmese Days,* important as it is, to achieve that rarity in modern literature: the spectacle of a totally honest artist for whom the truth as he saw it was more important than a concern for his genius or his artistic achievement.

CHAPTER IX

ARMCHAIR INDIA: L. H. MYERS'
THE NEAR AND THE FAR

L. H. Myers' *The Near and the Far* was published in 1940 at a time when the reading public was pre-occupied with the Second World War. Yet, the academic, critical and popular neglect, except for a brief blossom of enthusiastic acclaim after its publication, of this tetralogy, which can be reckoned a masterpiece considering the dearth of novels in this century which merit this description, is one of the curiosities of literary history and taste.

True, the tetralogy belongs to what may be called the "novel of ideas", a class of fiction which appeals to only a minority of readers. Even the acknowledged master of the form, Dostoevsky, senses a need to limit the degree to which his characters live in and for their philosophies -- and the elaboration with which they discuss them. Thomas Mann, as in *The Magic Mountain*, takes the same pains, albeit in his own less impressive way, to avoid turning his people into a mere debating society or congress of ideologies. In the English language, novels of ideas are generally in a minor stream – Johnson's *Rasselas*, Peacock's comic novelettes such as *Crotchet Castle*, Pater's *Marius the Epicurean.*

Myers' *The Near and the Far* belongs in fact, though at some distance, with certain modern works which are chiefly continental in origin: one is Herman Broch's *Virgil*, an attempted prose symphony of the poet's life, times, work, intellectual interests and creative ancestry.

Another example is *The Man Without Personality* by Robert Musil, an attempt to analyze the early twentieth-century European soul in its major manifestations. Myers shares with these writers a contemplative style of exposition and narration, the employment of thoughtful characters who are as articulate as they are thoughtful, and a disinterest in well-made plot.

What makes Myers special in this company is his willingness to spread his own discursive, analytical eloquence among all his characters, as if in a highly cultivated and sophisticated dialogue or colloquium. This intellectual habit reinforces the impression that the work is an elaborate playing-out of a platonic tension between appearance and reality. But, unlike Mann or Musil, though like Broch or the Hesse of *Siddharta,* he has projected this intellectual drama onto an exotic historical past, Akbar's India, and done this in a way that does not offend or violate our sense of the place, the time and the multiple creeds involved. This Asian setting, while it allies the work with Forster's *Passage to India,* is developed in a fictional form that unlike Forster's, is less modern than even George Eliot's or Flaubert's. It is almost eighteenth-century in its narrative techniques -- like a novella of Voltaire spelled out at un-Gaelic length, and perhaps related to Montesquieu's *Persian Letters.* Apart from a few notices in *Scrutiny* which included pioneeringly suggestive, though perfunctory, pieces by D.W. Harding, the only extended critical work I have been able to find is G. H. Bantock's "L. H. Myers: A Critical Study." This is a highly useful and painstaking exploration because it provides not only good criticism but also a biographical sketch which is helpful, since Myers, shortly before he committed suicide, had his autobiography burnt and asked his friends to suppress all his letters. So far as I know, no biography of Myers has been written and he has been the subject only of a few doctoral theses, an unusual state of affairs considering the scarcity these days of subjects for this kind of enterprise.

Bantock's book, however, is seriously occluded in insight because he does not seem to be familiar with the Eastern modes of thought in which Myers was so saturated and the religious modes of being to which he was so well attuned. Bantock cannot help but consider Myers' preoccupations exclusively in a context of Western philosophical notions of the importance of personal relationships, as found, say, in E. M. Forster or in European notions of personalism: he does not quite see that despite Myers' own debt to the philosopher John MacMurray or Martin Buber, there is an Oriental, and more specifically

Indian, cast to his concerns as a thinker and a novelist which bear directly upon his sense of the purpose of life and therefore on how life has to be lived. Though Myers has many other subsidiary interests, his main focus is on the individual's path to spiritual perfection and his corollary need for the right relation to the world around him.

The title of this essay, "Armchair India," may give the impression either of a dilettantish tone or that the novel has been artificially distanced from contemporary reality, or even that India has been chosen in order to provide an exotically fabulous setting or for some other merely artistic convenience. This is certainly not what I had in mind: I am not using the words "Armchair India" in the way the phrase "parlour Bolshevik" has been used to describe some Marxist theoreticians who, far removed from the quotidian concerns of the class-struggle, plan revolutions in their sitting-rooms. No, the phrase is intended to draw attention to the disinterested contemplation by Myers of spiritual and ethical problems in a distinctive, recollected and meditative mode which seems to me one of the hallmarks of Myers as an artist.

Perhaps one cannot do better than to quote from his own Preface to *The Near and the Far* (May, 1940):

> This is not a historical novel, although the action is placed in the time of Akbar the Great Mogul (who was a contemporary of Queen Elizabeth's), nor is it an attempt to portray Oriental modes of living and thinking. I have done what I liked with history and geography as well as with manners and customs. Facts have been used when they were useful, and ignored or distorted when they were inconvenient. Few of my characters bear the names of real people, and of these the only person drawn with any regard for historical truth is the Emperor.
>
> In choosing sixteenth-century India as a setting, my object was to carry the reader out of our familiar world into one where I could without doing violence to his sense of reality--give prominence to certain chosen aspects of human life, and illustrate their significance. It has certainly not been my intention to set aside the social and ethical problems that force themselves upon us at the present time. On the contrary, my hope has been that we might view them better from the distant vantage-ground of an imaginary world.

Despite this equivocal disclaimer, it is quite evident that Myers was close to Oriental modes of living and thinking, that he had done considerable research on India, and had frequented the highways and byways of the religions and philosophies of that sub-continent, not for idle scholarship, but from a compulsive interest in them in order to ascertain how far they accorded with his deepest interests and what answers they provided for his metaphysical and ethical concerns. It is also quite remarkable that for a man who had not visited India, he has an amazing sense of the variegated landscape of the country, as can be seen in numerous passages of natural description. Having discovered the fact that Myers had travelled as far as Ceylon though I have been unable to determine the length of his stay, I think his visit there had given him a sense of the adjacent and similar landscape of India as well as helped him to acquire his fine perception of the subtle philosophy of Hinayana Buddhism, the predominant religion of Sri Lanka, which he embodies in one of his masterly creations, Rajah Amar. However, even if it were found that he had done extensive research into sixteenth-century India and its main philosophies, it must be emphasized that his principal concerns in the novel are contemporary and in an immediate way relevant to the condition of contemporary England and Europe. Perhaps one of the reasons why this novel has not achieved anything like the fame, or notoriety if you will, of Joyce's *Ulysses,* is that it displays no major technical novelty: it has no avant-gardish literary radicalism which can be mistaken at a simplistic level for an intellectual, political, or social radicalism as was the case with the early admiration of *Ulysses,* or even of T. S. Eliot's *The Waste Land. The Near and the Far* is a straightforward novel in the Victorian sense despite its use of indirect narration, flashbacks, interpolated diaries, and an epistolary journal. But I think it would be reasonable to assert that as a single work it is better than the best of Virginia Woolf and compares favorably with the novels of Conrad or D. H. Lawrence, who though they are certainly the more gifted artists, did not themselves attempt a multi-volumed unit of such ambition and amplitude.

When properly understood, Myers has to be unpopular because his work cannot be accommodated within the intellectual panaceas or systems that helped to sustain his contemporaries: even the liberal humanism of a Forster, a buffetted and battered thing as it was, cannot withstand Myers' sense of evil, his recognition that the trivial was not just a diminution of human possibility but an active embodiment of a malignant reality. Myers could not give even two cheers for democracy: still less could he accept the scientific or technocratic world-view which could satisfy the conscience of a C. P. Snow or the political liberalism, the revolutionary Marxism and the left-wing socialism into which so many promising writers of our century have been enmeshed. Even the "religious" writers and readers would have found Myers difficult to absorb; he was weighing over too many religions and philosophies in his mind simultaneously to suit the narrow and competing orthodoxies that wanted exclusive promotion for their own dogma. Even those intellectuals with eclectic religious views of life like, say, Huxley, or Isherwood, would have been disconcerted by Myers' belief that the search for individual perfection or holiness was an inadequate ideal by itself and that spiritual achievement had to be accompanied by a humble commitment to one's fellow man exemplified by a lifetime of simple, practical tasks devoted to sustaining the underprivileged and the poor.

Of course, one has to face the criticism of Myers that he is a philosophical novelist, that he was too much given to abstract speculation and the cerebral communication of ideas, that his art did not absorb his thought into a novelistic whole composed of concrete specifics of words, character and situation. While this angle of criticism, from a narrow view of the relation between art and philosophy, is largely valid, I would exempt *The Near and the Far* from it and particularly, the first three sections published as *The Root and the Flower* which are as dense in aesthetic texture as any reader could expect. Besides, there are some aesthetic difficulties in this kind of criticism. I would not describe his literary style as "cerebral" but rather as marked by cool, poised, expository, even analytic detachment which modifies the writing even when his feelings are noticeably engaged. The distance he deliberately places between himself as author and the narrative may give the impression that he is not an artist but rather a complex theoretician of thought and feeling: this would be a wrong conclusion because his style is what he *is* as an artist and what he could best achieve. It is true that he does not, except at rare moments, attempt the exploratory-poetic mode of composition, where the writer shows an inwardness with the imagistic and metaphorical dynamism of language, where he allows words almost to develop an autochthonous life of their own. But this mode itself is not without its dangers, and is not always to be recommended; nor does he indulge in varieties of expression to accommodate the diverse characters. Despite this uniformity of style in which all his characters seem to express themselves alike, Myers does not insist on his authorial presence. He does not indulge in jagged tortuosities of expression, impressionistic effusions or outpourings designed to highlight the author's own attitudes, a habit which disfigures the work of even such masters of the novel as D. H. Lawrence. That Myers is free of these qualities does not mean his style lacks novelty and surprise. His cool, seemingly understated, unimpassioned tone often communicates with remarkable power.

Myers was attempting a different mode of writing: a blending of an analytic approach to ideas with the feelings they generate, an exploration of the way one's ethical and philosophical principles modify character and action.

One has to look for European parallels as this is not a familiar method for accomplishing artistic goals in British fiction. I do not rank him with Dostoevsky or Thomas Mann, but the impassioned energy with which they charge their ideas is not very different from Myers' own excitement over the articulation and discussion of the philosophical and ethical principles which agitate him. If *The Near and the Far* cannot be described as a novel, the only recourse is to enlarge the scope and use of the word: we should not worry too much about what a novel should or should not contain so long as the vehicle seems suited to the writer's literary purposes. Myers is one of those exceptions in the history of the English novel: he is a bridge between the novel of sentiment or senatin and the kind of novel where the characters reflect on their experience and seek to discover their motives for action and relate them to a philosophical understanding of what to them is a desirable way of life.

It is not my intention to discover the reasons why Myers has not achieved wider recognition and acceptance but a further discussion of his main interests will probably disclose some of them. It may well be that the reception of his masterpiece was affected by its publication during the war when the interests of the common reader were directed elsewhere than toward the ramifications of a polity and statecraft set in sixteenth-century India: then, when the war was over, his British and European reading public may have found these concerns even more remote. But this cannot be a total explanation, and the completed understanding which is not my purpose here would need a deeper pondering of the beliefs which Myers held and propounded with resolute firmness.

It is not always a good critical procedure to extrapolate a novelist's beliefs and philosophical views but in the case of Myers it may well be necessary and is certainly useful to list some of them in a prefatory way since they play a crucial role in the fiction and are highly uncommon. First of all, he believed in something which is unfashionable in this century: that there is real evil. He never tries to "sociologize" or "'psychologize" it away. Though the language he uses to define the concept of evil, by employing such value-laden distinctions as between the "fastidious" and the "trivial," may appear to be a concession to the tastes of the twentieth century, there is a clear difference between Forster's loathing of vulgarity and Myers' condemnation of the trivial: out of triviality for Myers comes evil, even the diabolic. He did not glorify the instinctual or natural life, as D. H. Lawrence often did: for Lawrence the instinctual could be at variance with the mental or spiritual with sorry consequences for both but the instinctual was a good in itself. It is not surprising that Lawrence had no sense of sin. Myers did not separate the natural from the moral, and the human: a totally instinctual character like Gunevati has links with devil worship, a penchant for petty ambitions and a capacity to wreak grave harm on herself and others. Animism and the life of the body are not separable from total human growth; each human being in Myers' world is judged in terms of the total human potential: life lived according to nature is not absolved from the need to face, and master the challenges of human civilization, which is also a natural goal for humankind.

Another of Myers' untypical interests is his belief in the importance of sound personal relationships as in Forster, but unlike Forster, Myers sought to establish them in a spiritual sub-stratum: people can come together only as persons who, on the basis of perfect candor about the principles on which they conduct their lives, seek a common ground which they share and on which they build a true communion. This is associated with Myers' demand that people should reflect on their motives for action and consciously attempt to build their lives on a bedrock of commitment to values that have been intellectually grasped and emotionally absorbed. It is no doubt a tall order for the majority of mankind and it is difficult to exempt him from the charge of a forbidding elitism, one that is even more exclusive than fancied superiorities derived from ingrained cultural or social stratification.

Another of his interests is the perfectibility of human character, his belief that human beings can and ought to strive for perfection and that the exceptional ones can even reach it. There are so many opinions in our time about what constitutes perfection and contrary views about whether the several goals and paths towards them are even worth pursuing. It is not likely that Myers' conviction in this matter would attract many contemporary readers of fiction. Because he did not belong to an institutional religion or a particular faith and did not espouse a set of dogmas, Myers was deprived of the constituency of readers such an affiliation would have provided him. Heaven and hell had no definable place in his scheme of things; this, and his sense of evil, not as diminution of human personality but as radical distortion, always potentially inherent in the relation between instinct and spirit, would not have attracted much empathy from his largely Christian or post-Christian readership. The absence of dogma does not mean that Myers did not advocate strongly-held beliefs or opinions: he was much agitated by the challenges presented by the world of action and the considerations which have to be weighed before one could legitimately contemplate a life of withdrawal. A spiritually enlightened person is not absolved from the permanent need to resist evil: the holiness which is achieved in solitude must spill over into the world of social and political activity. Myers was a communist of sorts in his later years, although not a devotee of intellectual Marxism, since dialectical materialism could not have accommodated his religious needs. Rather, his communism was a sincere, if naive, response to a humanist impulse. The setting he chose was more the Tolstoyan variety where the interaction of classes resides in the network of moral connections between the aristocrats or the rich landowner and the peasant. Myers displays no recognition of the industrial proletariat, apart from the obvious reason that his novel is set in sixteenth-century India: his mind did not encompass political change in terms of the confrontation between modern strongly polarized social classes. One of the positive directions of *The Pool of Vishnu*, the last novel in the tetralogy, is the vision of a society where aristocrats share their wealth and their lives with the peasantry and thereby hope to attain true human brotherhood.

It is not surprising that in a novel of such length it would be very difficult to disentangle the many strands of narrative and thematic interest--even to separate the main lives of progression is a task of some magnitude. I have neither the space nor the skill. *The Root and the Flower*, composed of its three parts, *The Near and the Far*, *Prince Jali* and *Rajah Amar*, is a dense, rich and variegated tapestry woven into such an intricate pattern that it would be critical murder to dissect it into its different components. It is a mark of the lesser artistic quality of *The Pool of Vishnu* that such an undertaking may be attempted in respect of that book with less disadvantage. Nor is it rewarding to look at the themes and the characters in separation; there is so much growth and change that theme and character can only be examined as they are embedded in the cross-stitch of narrative.

It is possible, however, at an elementary and simplistic level, to consider the characters in isolation as representing, or embodying, different philosophies or points of view: Rajah Amar as a Hinayana Buddhist, Ranee Sita as a Christian, Hari as an honest hedonist, Smith as a humanist, Gokal and the Guru as Hindus of highly differing persuasions, Gunevati as the instinctual life, Prince Daniyal as the amoral aesthete, and Mabun Das as Machiavellian statecraft, Sheik Mobarek as Islamic fundamentalism, and so on--but all these labels are disabling. To take just two examples, Gunevati is not merely a representative of a vital instinctual life: hers is a naturalism, unredeemed by grace and hence liable to slide into sorcery and diabolism, capable of wreaking evil on herself and society.   Prince Daniyal's aestheticism is without a religious sense: hence his so-called love of beauty is meretricious, corrupt and corrupting.

The best course for me is to embark on a peripatetic, if hurried, journey through the novel following as far as possible its own sequence in order to draw attention to the main contours of Myers' vision, especially those which the few critics of Myers have inadequately emphasized.

Before going through the book in the light of my intention, it is worth stating that the action has a "public" character. Akbar the Great Mogul is Emperor and the succession to the throne is hotly contested by his two sons, Salim and Daniyal. The main characters of the story have to make up their minds whom to support and this lends an atmosphere of momentous world forces impinging on private lives, a dimension absent from the many contemporary novels which deal largely with apolitical concerns, with personal relationships and the like.

The main thread of the story is the growth, and "education" in the Henry Adams sense, of Prince Jali, son of Rajah Amar: the novel begins with Jali standing on the balcony of one of the Imperial palaces, being used to accomodate the princely visitors to Akbar's Durbag.

> He clung to the truth of appearances as something equal to the truth of what underlay them. There were two deserts: one that was a glory for the eye, another that it was weariness to trudge. Deep in his heart he cherished the belief that some day the near and the far would meet.

We are here introduced to the theme of Appearance versus Reality: the near is the world of becoming, of flux and change; the far is the inner world of personal identity, of spiritual illumination. Jali's progress is from the one to the other: once he achieves spiritual growth, he is better able to live in the world of appearance.

In the same balcony scene, Jali notices a small, wiry plant growing in a crack in the masonry below, perhaps nourished by rain water in a gutter running beneath it. He also sees a snake moving cautiously along the gutter, indifferent to the plant till a breeze makes one of its twigs touch the snake's head. The snake seems angry, "about to explode," when a strong gust makes the twigs thrash down upon its head. The snake lunges against the plant, loses its balance and falls on a roof below. The snake is writhing in agony.

I have summarized this scene as it is a typical instance of the multi-layered, symbolic meanings to be found in Myers' treatment of incident. It is not profitable to stress literal equivalences--the plant as the tree of life, frail and irresolute, the serpent as the principle of evil, the gutter as the process of life, the gust of wind as the irruption of fate-but it is worth mentioning that there are recognizable parallels in Hindu religious literature. It is sufficient to recognize Myers' sense of the mysteries that environ human life, mysteries which have to be reckoned with if one is to progress along the path towards enlightenment.

> His chin upon his drawn-up knees, he stared into the obscurity. The world unquestionably, was a place of mystery and terror. This was revealed in the writhing of the crippled snake, in the jaunty waving of the innocent plant in the wind, in the bright-eyes intentness of the hovering kite, in the terrible numerousness of living beings, both animal and human, all separate, all alone, all threatened by evil in ambush.

Jali's father, Rajah Amar, is a committed Buddhist with an intense, if narrow, belief in spiritual Perfection:

> Many years of study and meditation had at last brought the Rajah to the belief that he had grasped--and even in a certain sense rediscovered-the doctrine of Buddha in its authentic purity. Whole-hearted in his rejection of God, the Soul and Immortality, he had a profound contempt for all corruptions of the original teaching. He condemned the Mahayana as a whole; in his opinion, by shifting the emphasis from

self-discipline to altruism, it had entirely falsified Gautama's word. Such a concession to human sentiment was disastrous; the truth, in order to be the truth, must be accepted in its entirety. No man could help his fellow save by the force and his example, save by the spectacle of his achieved holiness.

Amar's somewhat anti-human pursuit of the Hinayana ideal of mendicancy and meditation is set against the differing views of the other protagonists; it also has to face major ordeals in the course of the action. Gokal, as Brahmin philosopher, lays his finger on the nature of Amar's quest in a conversation with Sita, Amar's wife, a conversation which shows how deftly Myers can handle philosophical concepts of great subtlety in a language which is untechnical but nimble enough to encompass a wide range of nuances of sensibility.

"Amar has love in his heart," continued Gokal speaking low and urgently, "but he believes that love should be indistinguishable from compassion, and that compassion should be exercised through the understanding rather than through emotions."

"You can read many of my thoughts," said Sita. "Don't you then also know that I shall never be able to accept Amar's view of life?" "I, myself, do not accept it," answered Gokal after a moment's pause, "neither do I reject it entirely. I think you of the western world should consider carefully whether you have not made an error in idealising the will to live life. The enrichment of life! The intensification of life! The prolongation of life into eternity! Does this obsession have any heartfelt meaning behind it? Do these notions have a coherent ideal at their core? Buddhism says no! and awaits in silence until the intoxication is over, until the commotion has died down."

The distinction between Buddhist compassion and what Christians call "caritas" or "love" embraces intricate refinement of thought: I recall an excellent philosophical treatise by a French Catholic theologian, Henri de Lubac, who in his book *Aspects of Buddhism* devotes several pages to this distinction. What is important to remember is that the novelist has an inward understanding of Amar's religious predilection: Myers' sympathy for diverse and often contradictory spiritual attitudes can be seen in the language he uses to describe them, as for example in these words from Amar himself:

"If there were a Creator Him would I passionately adore; but just as the empty firmament extends illimitably beyond the clouds and colors of our earthly sky, so over and above even the purest hopes and longings of man's heart there spreads the calm of truth. My face I turn upwards, and whether the sky be down; out of that emptiness there comes no voice, no breath--no, but into that emptiness I enter and with it I become reconciled."

Or even in the opposed Christian view, espoused by Sita for whom in the Hopkinsian sense the world is clothed with the garment of God and is charged with His grandeur, while it must also accommodate the empty spaces of Pascal:

"And the stars, they terrify me. Love is the only fire at which we can warm ourselves when the great spaces look down on us, and the empty coldness of them settles upon us. Up here, under the huge, snowy mountains, I feel remote from the ordinary kindliness of life. Yesterday I walked to the edge of the valley and looked down into the pearly distance towards the plains, and I thought that nothing could match the loveliness of the earth except an exquisite love in the hearts of men."

For Sita, eternity is an intensification of the here and now in an ennobled and redeemed reality; for Amar the world is *Maya* and "in Nirvana all human lives and loves are lost: but the love of human beings for one another is the last of the fetters that men are called upon to cast off."

Even though I claim that Myers, almost unique among novelists, can seize upon the refined differences among such religions as Hinduism, Buddhism, Christianity and Islam and reverse the distances between the world religions and the philosophies of humanism, materialism or even the practice of superstition and devil worship, I do not wish to imply that he neglects the cultural soil from which values spring. On the contrary, he constantly relates the value-systems to the man, the moment and the milieu. In a discussion with Gokal, this is how Amar characterizes Emperor Akbar:

"I agree," said the Rajah, "and I should even hesitate to call him abnormal. He strikes me as being the average man, but raised to a higher power of manhood. One cannot point to any faults or virtues in the average man which he does not possess. He is sensual, a lover of wine and women, boastful, often cruel, avaricious, cunning, hypocritical and a colossal egoist. He is also an impassioned advocate of abstinence and self-control, humble before God, occasionally generous, simple in his affectations, shrewd and credulous in equal degree and unsparing of toil, in the interests of his Throne and Empire, His Majesty is the plain man, I say, raised to a higher power ... I am not one of those who make it a grievance that he is great in his own fashion instead of in theirs; although, of course, it is hard for some amongst us, who are men of ancient tradition and culture, to accommodate ourselves to a civilization essentially materialistic. After all, he is more than half a Mongol, and the Mongols are a people of prodigious vitality, but, they remain, broadly speaking, barbarians. Civilization based on tradition, based on generations of gentlemen, is a virtue.

Or, take the way Myers relates the fanaticism of Islam to cultural geography, a comment not without relevance to the cruel upsurge of contemporary Islamic fundamentalism:

"In Fazul I recognized a product of the desert--that place where only brave men can live, and they only by matching its austerity with the austerity of their lives. I know enough of the desert to realize what the first twenty-five years of Fazul's life must have been like. I know those wastes of harsh sand, rough gravel, and sharp stones, scorched and bleached by day, swept by chilling winds at night. It is out of this desolation, out of this poverty-stricken and yet splendid aridity, that there springs, like the frankincense tree, an unequalled faith in God. From nowhere else upon the earth does a fragrance of such sweetness and purity arise. How can one describe a passion that is as taintless as that air, steely in strength, and incandescent like the desert sun? When I look into Fazul's face I see a patch of desert ground, a surface hardened by endurance, trodden by every hardship. A gracious thing it is not; nor is the level look of those eyes other than repellent. That face is an iron door behind which the worship of Allah flames."

Not only is Amar's Buddhism beset by soul-testing ordeals to which I shall revert briefly later on, Gokal's Hinduism itself founders on the rock of his sexual and instinctual desires: the religion which prides itself on containing the whole of reality has to suffer the natural shocks that flesh has inherited.

Gokal does try to idealize his infatuation for the beautiful though mindless Gunevati, unaware that a human being without a mind is not merely reduced but deformed by that condition: Gokal rhapsodizes that while thought crystallizes into patterns of merely formal complexity, the instincts with all the richness of their irrationality belong to creativity and that there is nothing better than animal instinct embroidered over with the arabesques of the imagination. The euphoria however is short-lived: it cannot cope with the profound pessimism of an earlier realization:

> "Let me talk to myself then in solitude--an old fool addressing an old fool. Gokal, you are reckoned a wise man and a learned, but all that you have learned is the simplest and most ancient lesson in the world; it is better to laugh and weep like a child than to follow the wisdom of the wisest. You have travelled down the river of time with a swiftness that you did not see, and the years have carried you unaware into the waste lands of regret. All your life your eyes have been fastened upon the invisible; never did you look up at the fruit trees in the spring, or at the young girls blossoming beside you the full year around. You have studied and pondered--to no profit, gaining nothing but the respect of the simple, who, in reality, are wiser than you. So here, in the end, stands Gokal, with a round back and a round belly and a crushing load of regret."

Amar's spiritual quest has to encounter several traps: very early in the novel, he oscillates between the tranquillity which for him is at the end of all desire and a tenderness towards his earthly and human connections, especially when he thinks of his wife and son. When he visits his aging father, he is disconcerted by the fact that Prince Daniyal who has set up camp near his father's house does not pay his father the courtesy of a visit: Amar's pride is hurt and he does not want to humiliate himself by soliciting a visit from the Prince. However, he feels he is in the sorry predicament of having to choose between being a bad Buddhist or an inhuman son. It is left to Hari who, despite difficulties of his own with Daniyal, sets out to risk being snubbed in order to promote such a visit and thus assuage the chagrin of an old man whose vanity has been deeply hurt. The *inhuman* aspect of Buddhist spirituality is convincingly captured: the poison of self-preoccupation, of spiritual hypochondria is seen as a close neighbor of deliverance from the self. However, Amar's spontaneous, almost instinctual fineness is quick to judge Prince Daniyal:

> All he knew was that in the presence of the Prince he got an immediate impression of vulgarity--or of something, at any rate, which for want of a better word had to be called vulgarity. It was a pity no

other term would fit, because the defect was reflected so shadowily on the external man; it was a defect of spirit--something that betrayed itself primarily to the moral sense.

What leads Amar into trouble not only in his future activities but in terms of his own self-knowledge is his disinclination to take sides, let alone join the crusade against evil. Myers the novelist is strongly attracted to Amar because he seems to share with him more than with any other character some aspects of his own temperament--a fastidiousness of spirit and a power of fine intellectual discrimination. This is why Amar is the spokesman for the critique of humanism; his percipient rejoinder to Smith who praises Buddhism for foregoing speculation on metaphysical or cosmological subjects and the Greeks for living wisely and happily, "shut in from the abyss" is as follows:

> The Greeks cultivated a little of civilization, they evolved a small but exquisite culture, at the price of ignoring the immensities in the midst of which men live. But to ignore metaphysical problems is not to abolish them; and in a sense it may be said that every man who thinks at all is, willy-nilly, a metaphysician ... The Greek liked to think of himself as a member of a city community, but his city was, none the less, a point upon the wandering earth, and the earth is a point in the universe, and every part of the universe partakes of the metaphysical mystery of its being.

Smith cannot see that Amar's Buddhism through denying God, the soul and immortality was born out of Hinduism which is not anthropomorphic in the way Sita's Christianity was:

> Even for Sita man is at the centre of the universe; God, in the last analysis, is postulated by her as necessary to man. She cannot understand the Indian way of placing the Absolute at the centre, and regarding the whole history of mankind from first to last as nothing but a ripple upon the surface of that Supreme Mind.

Amar's climactic test, nevertheless, occurs in his tragic encounter with Daniyal but before we consider that meeting, it would be useful to comment, however briefly, on the progress of his son, Prince Jali, whose growing awareness of the true nature of the Pleasaunce of the Arts, the camp established by Daniyal, is the principal source of the novelist's attitude towards Daniyal himself. Besides, Jali's growth is the main threat in the novel and the chief connecting link between *The*

Root and the Flower and *The Pool of Vishnu*: to trace his development would therefore be to undertake no less than a running commentary on the entire work, a task which neither space nor inclination permit. However, I shall use Jali's insights with a ruthless brevity in order to comment on the roles of Hari, Gunevati and Daniyal; interrupt this commentary to return to Amar, and finally resume the thread of Jali's growth in *The Pool of Vishnu* in his interactions with Rajah Bhoj and Lakshmi, Mohan and Damayanti, and of course the Guru. In a work of such amplitude and complexity as the *The Near and the Far*, one has to settle for such limited and limiting critical procedures as one can handle.

Hari, Jali's uncle, is one of the most attractive personalities in the novel. He is courageous, robust and his instincts are decent. He is without mean-spiritedness, calculation and intrigue and though a hedonist, his hedonism is not of the vulgar materialist kind since he believes in a hierarchy of values even in the world of pleasure. His candor and impishness save him from self-righteousness: he accepts the importance of love and of religious ideals though he cannot find his way among them.

> Hinduism in general, however, appealed to him as the broadest and most elastic of all religious systems. He was attracted by its independence of dogma, the smallness of its demands upon blind faith. But these attractions also constituted its weakness, lending point to the criticism made by Amar that Hinduism was not a religion but simply religiousness itself. Upon the spiritual substance it imposed no form, to the urge it gave no certain direction; and although among the uneducated it borrowed shape from the myth, superstitions and customs, with which the common mind was already richly stocked, in an unencumbered intelligence it remained fluid and colorless, as rarified, indeed, as any brain-spun metaphysics.

Though Hari does not have a specific religious affiliation, his human willingness to sacrifice himself for the sake of others, as when he persuades Daniyal to visit Amar's father, has a religious or at least a strongly moral tendency. He can distinguish his flirtations, and even his affair with Lalita, from his true love for Sita.

> Waiting for her at the corner of the house, Hari was conscious only of an immense, unhoped-for happiness; and he said to himself: 'What is this? What is this?' His feelings sharpened into a sense of agonizing

sweetness; his being was invaded by an anguish that was delicious and seemed to play not upon the nerves of the flesh, not upon the machinery of the brain, but upon the substance of the very soul. ...When he asked himself whether his present disposition was likely to be enduring he could not see the smallest shadow of a doubt. Time might work its changes upon the substance of his love, but that love was firmly rooted, and he would carry it, for good or ill, down to the grave.

Hari, who as I said earlier, is along with Sita, one of the few highly empathetic persons in the novel because of his humanism, is without abstraction and religious striving; Sita's Christianity also serves the completion of profoundly humanist impulses. But Myers cannot let the matter rest at that: even though Hari can sense the smell of the religious unlike Smith and can perhaps agree with Amar about the distinction between the aesthetic and spiritual faculties whereby the spiritual is the arbiter of greatness in life and art, he remains a prisoner of the human world. Hari's ideals and way of life cannot protect him from the abyss, which is not merely the void but the strong reality of the wind of fear as he explains to the Guru in *The Pool of Vishnu*.

What do *you* know of Fear? There are things that are terrible, there are things that are horrible; but what of them? There is torture and death; but what are they? Nothing. I tell you there is Terror beyond the Terrible, there is Horror beyond the Horrible. There is Fear-in-itself. Do you think that Fear needs any support, any cause? No! Fear stands all alone. The things to be feared are limited, but Fear is without limits. If happiness can be beyond all telling, how much more unspeakable is Fear? Fear is the well into which you sink alone. It is the solitary dark--where all coinage, and all love, and all hope are dead. They are of reality, but Fear is of unreality--which has no bounds, no law. It is without the mercy of madness in which you can fling your life away. In time, not madness you can find the courage of despair. But Fear is the cold madness that keeps you still. Fear, I tell you, is Spirit, conquered: it is the living, living, living. ...His voice died away.

It is Hari who gives Jali his first strategy for living: he tells him that the way to escape a pursuing tiger is to turn oneself into one, in short, to pretend to oneself that one is like others and to come to terms with *Maya* by accepting the world of appearance. The choice as Jali sees it is between seeing and being; since what was graspable was not spirit, it must be the "illusory" world: if you lived in and for reality you would dwindle and fade, if you cultivated appearance you would wax fat and grow strong. Jali's spiritual growth was from this complete antithesis of Hindu thought into true enlightenment but the road was long, risky and hazardous.

Gunevati is the first opportunity and the first temptation: she was to initiate Jali in adolescence to his first sexual experience. That Myers is not a Puritan, that he has a Lawrentian sense of the creative dynamism of the instinctual life is seen in this description of how Gunevati first appears to Jali:

> In and about the temple doorway Gunevati drifted, loitering, halting, and going on again, her lovely body as lazy as a water-weed swaying in a stream. Overhead the sun's eye glared intolerably and the weight of noon lay upon her like the heavy waters of a deep sea. It seemed to Jali that in her dreamy dawdlings she was at one with the unhurried earth: she was like a lotus unfolding upon a mere, she was an evening cloud, she was a down-fluttering leaf, and she was the slow yawn of the golden tiger drowsy in a cave. And the present moment--usually as sharp as a knife-edge ripping between the past and the future--the present moment, as he watched her, expanded into a great lake of peace.

Jali contrasts his own alienation from nature by saying that his loneliness must be quite unknown to Gunevati: "for, assuredly, in a single moment she could establish contact with anyone in the world; and when she was by herself she enjoyed the watchful and interested company of at least a hundred gods."

At this stage in Jali's awareness Gunevati stands nearer to the heart of things than his parents: sex and religion are at the center of her consciousness and she is firmly established on life's bedrock. But soon he realizes that there is no poetry in her soul or even a touch of romance, and her subsequent ensnaring of Gokal shows him how her apparent self-sufficiency in the body does her no moral credit, as it is but natural to her. It does not shield her from becoming an instrument of positive evil; she is after all a Vamachari, a Follower of the Left-Hand Way.   For Jali himself, spiritual growth has to weather the experience of sex as well as the evil that is inherent in life.

Jali is to meet Gunevati again in Daniyal's camp: she has become the object of Prince Salim's interest, has been kidnapped by his men but recaptured by Daniyal's cohorts and taken to the Pleasaunce of the

Arts. Jali's cousin, Ali, apparently in a homosexual liaison with Daniyal, introduces Jali to the camp. Initially, he is impressed by its inverted orthodoxy, entranced by its golden tree, silvered doves, scarlet macaws, green parakeets, snowy-white pelicans, Venetian-style houses, and above all, the inhabitants:

> Here you might come across people of every variety--except one, the commonplace. Dull, conventional people--people who were not lit by the divine spark, had no chance of gaining admission here. Daniyal had thrown away the shackles of ordinary prejudices and cant. Originality of mind, intellectual merit, poetic fire, these alone counted with him; and on this basis all were equal. Here you might meet Princes of the moot ancient line hobnobbing with poets, acrobats and artists. Much, however, as Daniyal honored superiority of the mind, he was not--you could see it for yourself--an intellectual snot. Pedantry bored him; he liked to be amused; the art which he recognized as Art had to be for ever young and new and gay.

The emphasis on novelty and originality, the disdain for the sedate, the conventional and the bourgeois was very much a part of the forward-looking ethos of Myers' time; however, his criticism, though relevant, was somewhat unfair to the Bloomsbury set as there were in contemporary England targetable groups far worse than this distinguished, if self-regarding, segment of a society which of itself was not yet the elite: the social envy of the outsider spoils the genuine distaste of the intellectuals, such as the contributors to *Scrutiny* who used Myers in their condemnation of Bloomsbury. However this may be, the type that is exposed deserves the exposure, as in this comment by Jali:

> He came to comprehend that the pleasure which the Camp took in regarding itself as scandalous was actually the chief source of its inspiration, its principal well-spring of energy. It was true that, for the appreciation of the finer shades of their own meanness and malice, Daniyal's friends had to look to themselves and be their own audience-- they had to depend upon the clack of their own tongues; upon their own giggles and shrieks, for the applause due to any particularly subtle stroke in the game; but broadly speaking, what sustained them, what carried them along and inspired their activities, was the belief that they were attracting the attention of an outraged outside world. The Camp was withdrawn because it had to be, moreover, the idea that they were sufficient unto themselves was very necessary to them; but it was

nothing else than the truth, that they depended basically upon a solid shockable world of decorum and common sense. They had to believe that a great ox-like eye was fixed upon them in horror. Without this their lives lost their point.

Jali's growing recognition that Daniyal and his set were meretricious, life-denying and evil prepares the way for his father's realization that he is called upon to fight and even extirpate the evil he counters: it will not do to withdraw from the world till one has fulfilled one's role in the realm of action. It is Gokal who tried to convince Amar that Daniyal is not merely aesthetic and trivial but also wicked; his wickedness consists of the desire to mock God through the suffering he inflicts on good people: the malignancy is almost motiveless as far as the persons are concerned but becomes diabolic in that it is an offense offered to the Creator, a humiliation done to Goodness itself. Amar is not altogether won over. The aestheticism of Daniyal is likely to come under the influence of Smith's advocacy of justice and altruism which since it proceeds only from a humanist urge will tend to draw its energy from "envy, real jealousy and disguised self-interest;" the love of mankind, when it is separated from a religious consciousness, is a hatred of God. Amar merely wants to pay his respects to Daniyal but the meeting takes such a form that he is inexorably provoked into taking a drastic step.   Gunevati is also present: however mindless and superstitious she may be, she is distinguished from the personalities of the court who suspire only on the impressions they create among themselves, whose polished intercourse is singularly boring because it is cut off even from the instinctual life with which Gunevati is in close connectedness. She is now dumb as her tongue has been cut off; a white cat is yawning and stretching itself on her lap, suggesting that despite the horrible brutality she has suffered she is still closer to the world of nature than Daniyal and his associates. Daniyal enters, juggling with three colored balls.

> The cat now came running across the floor, and, on reaching Daniyal, rubbed itself against his legs, causing him to miss one of the coloured balls. Then it threw itself down on the ground in front of him, lying on its back, and with a mew invited him to play with it. But Daniyal had frowned when the ball dropped, and now, lifting the sole of his right foot, he placed it on the cat's head. Then with a swift and smiling glance at his spectators he slowly pressed his foot down. One after another the bones in the cat's head could be heard to crack, and,

when this sound came, the Prince's eyes glanced for one smiling second into those of Gunevati. The cat's paws were beating in the air; its little body rose stiffly in an arc and then collapsed in spasms; a little pool of blood spread out upon the floor.

Very slowly Gunevati slipped off her seat and lay upon the ground prostrate.

Daniyal's wanton cruelty was no doubt a warning to Gunevati as well as an intended provocation of Amar who if he did walk into the trap would be made a victim. Amar can no longer control himself:

Suddenly, with a movement of great swiftness, Amar's hand went to the hilt of his short sword, and the blade was half out of its scabbard before the negro, who had stationed himself behind him, and was watching his every movement with ready alertness, brought down a metal elephant-goad on the top of his head. The Rajah crumpled to the ground.

Amar recovers from the assault but becomes permanently blind. He feels that the moment for his withdrawal from the world has come and joins a group of mendicant pilgrims who are heading south. He hopes eventually to reach Ceylon where he would live as a Buddhist monk. Gokal wants to have another conversation with Amar and goes in search of him. Meanwhile, Amar's

spirit was moving along the road of his choice, and yet something was happening that he did not understand. It had no place in his philosophy. The self with which he communed was becoming something other than him. It was becoming as God. He did not attempt to understand. Understanding would come to him later.

Myers seems to imply that the Buddhist Nirvana is a positive state although it can only be described in negative terms, as the extreme of nullity in relation to what the mind can conceive or the heart ponder. Gokal sees Amar but does not go up to speak to him. The novelist's comment says it best:

For half an hour or more, until the sun dipped beneath the horizon, Gokal remained there. Then in the sudden tropical dark he moved

furtively away. He stumbled through the palm-grove; he knocked
against the tree-trunks; he did not know what he was doing. Tears were
running down his face, but he did not know that either. Somewhere in
his heart there was thankfulness, for he had seen enough to be sure that
Amar had found peace.

So ends a great friendship and one of the finest portrayals of a
religious sensibility in English literature: we take our leave of Amar,
convinced of his authenticity as a person and a literary creation. One
has only to compare it with the characterization of Ramasamy in Raja
Rao's *The Serpent and the Rope* to realize how perilous is the task of
presenting a religious nature and a spiritual quest in fiction.

Quite early in *The Pool of Vishnu*, some of the main characters in
The Root and the Flower disappear from the active scene; the loose
ends are tied up and new characters are introduced. Rajah Amar
becomes a beggar, withdrawn from the world of action; little is heard of
Sita or Gokal after Part I when Gokal looks on the reassuring
countenance of Amar from a distance; Gunevati has been thrown to the
mad elephant. The important characters who remain in the story are Jali
and Hari. Hari is as vivid as ever, but he is disposed of rather
perfunctorily in Part 7 when he is stabbed in the back by his enemies. It
will not do for Myers to develop his relationship with Sita as Hari is
chronically impervious to spiritual change and the novelist requires
more explicit models to carry the burden of his message. *The Pool of
Vishnu* is a less successful work of art and therefore an inadequate
sequel to the earlier trilogy. There are many reasons for this: to begin
with, Myers sensing that this was the culmination of his work, wanted
to make his ethical concerns and values clearer to the reader. There is
also a problem of structure: the main presence in the novel is the Guru
who comes between the novelist and the reader, constantly interpreting
the action and the characters, while in *The Root and the Flower*, the
main personalities are shown directly involved in the action, the events
speak for themselves, there is a dramatic interrelation between
character and incident. The world of political intrigue is diminished in
scope and importance because the question of the succession to Akbar,
the need to take sides in regard to Salim and Daniyal, is no longer
pressing. Consequently the sense of the play or major world forces is
missing, the action is scaled down. The manipulations of Mabun Das
and Sheik Mobarek which gave the earlier trilogy almost a Stendhalian
quality are absent. In *The Root and the Flower,* even a "noble"

character like Hari is dragged into the world of political alignment and choice; he recognizes that unless Mabun Das, however cynical and amoral the means he uses to secure his ends, succeeds in his endeavors, the way of life of such as Amar, Gokal and himself are threatened: Hari is persuaded to accede to perjury because "one's own private and personal distaste for perjury was not an impressively weighty factor in the opposite balance" when considerations of great moment for the body-politic were at issue. But most important of all is that the Guru has already transcended "the fury and the mire of human veins" and is therefore the spokesman of a simplified and less challenging ideal, a Hinduism onto which has been grafted a neo-Christian personalism derived from Martin Buber and John MacMurray, a philosophy which had a vogue at that time. It also accorded well with the Communism to which Myers had been converted, a Tolystoyan socialism which emphasized a more equitable sharing of man's worldly goods. It is devoid of a tragic vision. The Guru himself is already an enlightened man, he is not exposed to the turbulence that is part of Hari's life nor can he succumb to the sexual temptation which overcame Gokal. He has gone beyond the world of *Maya* Jali himself, while he continues to grow in spiritual awareness, is the passive recipient of the Guru's wisdom: even Mohan and Damayanti whose relationship proceeds through travail into a mature union are constantly guided by the Guru. *The Root and the Flower* is a tragic novel; and tragedy has to do with the clash between the transcendental and an active principle of evil where the human suffers a defeat even if the moral order is rehabilitated. Rajah Amar is a tragic hero though he seems to have achieved peace in his withdrawal from the world.

Sex, in the sense of the almost autonomous life of the body, is also missing in *The Pool of Vishnu*. So is superstition, the hoary world of animistic religion which is the base of rarefied metaphysical systems. Gokal, though he is poisoned by her, learnt from Gunevati: even an intellectual like Rajah Amar is cured of his fever by taking the pills which the yogi, priest of the underground, gives him: the yogi's comment is apposite:

> "The true religion," the yogi broke in, "is that which has run like a vein of gold through the history of this country from the earliest times. Underneath all the shams and inventions of false shame, pedantry, and hypocrisy, there has lived amongst us Hindus the ancient verity that Sexuality and Religion are one. You, Rajah are an ascetic, and it may

pain you to listen to these words; nevertheless in your asceticism you recognize the truth. Chastity is a noble way of recognizing the divinity of Sex. But there are other ways."

The Guru though he expresses himself in subtle language tends to be repetitive as though Myers wanted his reader to be in no doubt about the philosophical and ethical values he wanted to impart. The prose is often abstract, and sometimes slips to the level of a journalistic tract.

When all this is said, *The Pool of Vishnu* is a remarkable novel and would have a higher standing if it were not judged purely as a sequel to the earlier trilogy. There are several dramatic moments; an excellent exposure of the world of Bhoj and Lakshmi, who though they are not evil in the ways of Daniyal and his court, disclose a quality of self-centered and devastating boredom; and the Mohan-Damayanti relationship is a rare and refreshing study of successful love which has blossomed to communion despite the clash of separate wills and selfhoods as they learn to share a common spiritual purpose under the wise guidance of a religious master. In many ways, *The Pool of Vishnu* does complement *The Root and the Flower*. Though it would be convenient to summarize the Guru's philosophy in one place, I do not propose to do this as it would destroy the sense in which the Guru's opinions and insights issue from particular incidents, and would also offend against the integrity of the novel. It would also exaggerate the novel's main problem which is that the Guru intervenes between the novelist and the characters-in-action. At the risk therefore of scattering the skein of the Guru's thought, I will follow the novel's own progression.

The first exchanges are with Hari who is in sore need of the Guru's help. When Hari asks him how he has become such an enlightened being, the Guru replies:

"Hari Khan, my life has been--and still is--like the peeling of an onion. One skin after another of self-deception and pretence do I strip off. In the process my eyes water and my vanity smarts."

But the Guru's past is only reported--the novel does not deal with a continuing struggle as he has already mastered the temptations of pride and false humility. When Hari says that he is reluctant to bare his heart to Sita, to confide in her all his doubts and hesitations, the Guru enunciates one of the main principles of his philosophy of life:

It seems to me that half the trouble that arises between human beings is caused by lack of candor. A man imagines that he is the other's superior--not in intelligence, not in fineness of feeling, not in anything that he can name--and yet in *something* which makes it his right, or even his duty, to treat the other as less than his equal. He assumes responsibilities that he ought to share, he makes concealments, he will not ask of the other what he asks of himself, or apply to the other the same standards. The man who says to himself that the other wouldn't understand, or couldn't bear to face the truth, or would be made too angry by it, is really being protective not of the other but of himself.

The Guru stresses the value of true communication between person and person, and this is precisely what Hari can never achieve, even in such an intimate relationship as he has with Sita. His main fault is self-dramatization, an ingrained habit of posturing, an attempt to put on masks in order to cope better with the social world: consequently he is what he seems in his delirious dream, in a pyramid unable to find the center and unable to reach others who are in other passages of the same pyramid. Always wanting to produce an effect, dressing himself up, and presenting different faces to the world, Hari can never become an integral character or a candidate for salvation, even though he belongs with the spiritual elite in the novel: despite the Guru's best efforts, he fails with Hari who even at the moment of his death can only say,

"O life, what a business! But I didn't want this. No, it came to me. I didn't want it.

But Hari is the Guru's only failure: he succeeds remarkably well with Jali, with Mohan and Damayanti and, still more surprisingly, even with Akbar. Jali is introduced to still another world when he stays at the Palace of Rajah Bhoj. The Palace, like all other palaces, was set apart from the "swarming populace" but this

> dark ancient building was shouldered by the poor, whose squalid hovels clung, like swallows' nests, to its thick, frowning walls. The crowd, however, if near, was very far from making itself felt. Not a sound could come through those isolating depths of stone; and if you cared to remember that an outside world existed, that consciousness only heightened your sense of privileged seclusion.

Even though this description contains an intimation of something deeply amiss, Jali's first reaction, as usual, is highly favorable. He is impressed by the courteous formality of Bhoj and the refined taste, social graces, and the seemingly tranquil self-possession of his wife, Ranee Lakshmi. But the contrast between the Palace and the Guru's dell soon begins to disquiet him: Bhoj and Lakshmi do not hold the Guru in high regard, nor do they have much time for Mohan and Damayanti, to both of whom Jali is strongly drawn. Soon Jali was to be awakened and see Bhoj and Lakshmi for what they really were. To get on with them, Jali realizes, you have to accept their values and their valuation of themselves; their apparent serenity and ease hid deeper strains and tensions: they were the prisoners of their own social standards and, worse, did not recognize themselves as slaves of their values.

> A woman like Lakshmi was concerned to keep up appearances every instant of the day--and not only for the benefit of others but to satisfy her own private self-esteem. With every movement, every intonation, and--so far as possible--with every thought and emotion she was applying tiny brush-strokes to a never-finished portrait of herself. At this moment, most probably, she was lying with her women friends grouped about her, in seeming negligence and ease upon her couch. Every muscle apparently relaxed, she would be speaking lazily, and even, possibly yawning. But, actually, at no time was she further from real spontaneity than in moments such as these. For she was presenting a picture not of what she was but of what she longed to be. The deep, unacknowledged craving of her heart was that the strain, the calculation, might not be there. And her unconfessed shame was this: the constant presence of effort, the constant absence of ordinary ease of mind.

Jali realizes that Lakshmi spent all her effort in dressing up "the poor, neglected substance of her spirit in fine clothes." Beneath "her lovely modulated animation" was a "devastating boredom."

As for Bhoj, Jali sees him as the upholder of the status-quo, with a deep appreciation of his own worth:

> Bhoj thinks that for all time there should be a few very wise and rich and cultured men (like himself) at the top of society, and progressively less wisdom, and less wealth, and less culture as you go down the social scale. He would not have society arranged differently for anything in the world.

The apparent self-discipline and public-spiritedness is only a cloak for the suffocated intelligence of the heart. Jali comes to realize that the enemy of friendship is money. For the same reason, Mohan cannot stomach conversations with Bhoj on social reform.

> With gentle, tireless persistence Bhoj would explain that money did not make for happiness, that the poor did not know how to use money, that leisure was no use to them either, that if you enriched them they would soon become poor again, that it was not merely the privilege but the duty of the chosen few to preserve the culture, the graces of life, which in them alone were embodied, and, finally, that just as Providence had ordained that there should be clever people and stupid people, industrious people and lazy people, so it was in the nature of things that there should be princes and paupers.

One of the important episodes in this novel is the exchange between the Guru and Sheik Mobarek: this confrontation is all the more important as the Sheik is the Guru's philosophical enemy unlike some of the characters who are responsive to the Guru's ideals. Besides, Mobarek gives a good account of himself, and it is to Myers' credit that he can present both sides of the dialectical picture with great effectiveness. The dialogue recalls to mind the famous story of *The Grand Inquisitor* in Dostoevsky's *The Brothers Karamazov*: of course, the Dostoevsky narrative is by far the greater piece of art, in the power of cultural and moral confrontation and the range of mental adventure, but which English novelist can handle at so high a level of poise, such a weighty intellectual debate? Some excerpts are in order because they are more cogent in this author's own formulations than they would be in my paraphrase:

> Mobarek: "Beware of creating confusion, Guru, where no confusion need exist! The State determines men's temporal duties and looks after their temporal welfare. Their spiritual welfare is safe in the hands of those appointed to guard it. If in my life I have been of any service to my fellow men it is in this: that, after studying the great religion of the West, I introduced into this land the idea of the Church. The Church is an institution by means of which man can satisfy--in the religious sphere--his desire for order, his respect for tradition, his craving for continuity." A faint glow had risen to Mobarek's sunken cheeks and in his eyes there had awoken a frosty light. "Church and State! On these I base the whole edifice of Society, Civilization, Culture. It is for you, like everybody else, to find your place within that frame."

The Guru: "I neither reject nor ignore--it is not in my power to ignore--any voice, either living or dead, that speaks words that strike into me as true. When from among the dead someone addresses me and I enter into relation with him, then it is as though a friend walked by my side. But what is this body of authority of which you speak? It is a mound of corpses..."

Mobarek: "Your theories are but an extension of your personal vanity. You seek to glorify human nature because your own nature is human. But such individualism is not merely anarchic, it is impious. In attempting to exonerate the individual at the expense of society, you forget that it is in Society--in its traditions, its institutions--nay, in its very structure--that we discern most clearly the guiding hand of God. If Society is imperfect it is because its members are imperfect; but some are less imperfect than others, and it is right--as it is also inevitable-- that the higher creature should discharge the higher function..."

The Guru: "...There is no greatness at the end of your road--only despair. Spirit, which must stream through the individual man, if he is to preserve a sane and living soul, must stream through society as well. Every civilization, every culture, that has ever existed has owed its life to this. When the stream tarries the body politic stiffens into a prison-house; forms and institutions become manacles, and the State turns into a monstrous slave-driver. Demoniac forces have taken control. With the leaders there is only a semblance of leadership. As a monster the State moves on to a ruinous destiny. The leaders will tell you that they are acting under divine inspiration, or that they are obeying inexorable laws; and always they will dangle before the multitude the vulgar emblems of an impossible glory. But there is death in their hearts. Your priests, too, will pretend to enclose the Spirit in Churches. But those churches will be empty. Spirit is waiting in the market-place--waiting for the re-awakened, and re-awakening man."

The re-awakened and re-awakening man in the novel is Jali who is able under the Guru's counsel, to recognize the qualitative distinction between Bhoj and Lakshmi on the one hand, and Mohan and Damayanti on the other. I will first deal with Jali, while accepting the Mohan-Damayanti relationship as the contrasting positive: in any event this relationship is almost a story within a story, though the Guru's involvement is crucial, and it would be more convenient to comment on it in my conclusion to this essay.

Jali's enlightenment does not happen till he is ready to absorb the Guru's wisdom, and here the symbolism of the pool of Vishnu plays an important part:

> Beneath was an oblong pool about fifty feet in length with a stone-flagged path running round it. A large figure of Vishnu, outstretched as if in sleep, lay in the water, the head with its aureole of hooded cobra just rising above the surface. Calm and beautiful was the face of stone that looked up into the evening sky. The place breathed out repose. Neither the ripples running over the water, nor the waving of the ferns, nor the swaying of the convolvuluses on the wall disturbed the scene's tranquillity.

The crux of the realization is that Vishnu has been lying in that pool for hundreds of years. He had been there long before Buddha was born. This comment establishes the fact that it is in an adaptation of the Hindu religion that Myers would like to present his final, comprehensive conception of life:

> ...With an intensity unknown to him ever before he was aware of the world around him--branch-entangled gleamings left behind by the sun, a cool upwelling from the low-hung moon, small bird-sounds, leafy silences, scents--now cold, now warm--breathed up from the water and the stone. All this he felt, all this he *was*. *Tat tvam asi.*

Jali at the end of the novel is an awakened being but ready to reconcile the world of spirit and the world of action: unlike his father who wanted to abandon prematurely the human world of obligations, *Realpolitick* and love. He can now accept and live by the final advice of the Guru given in three trenchant and aphoristic pieces of wisdom.

> "One must cling to the memory. One must remember and one must act. The knowledge gained in communion, and ripened in solitude, must pour its life into the world through action. Thus only will you and the world about you live."

> "One must. All communion is through the Centre. When the relation of man with man is not through the Centre, it corrupts and destroys itself. This you already know."
> "You know that Spirit is the world's master. You know that you are not the slave of mechanical fate, but the master of divine destiny. You

know that there is a divine meaning in the life of the world--in the life of men, of you, and of me."

Between the Guru and Jali there was a presence which looked forth from the face of Vishnu, and Jali's spirit could also go forth, with the Guru's into freedom—"to mix in the black leafiness of the trees, and mount to the growing light of the stars, and sail in the dusky, placid air. And it looked down upon the sleeping god in the pool." Since now Jali can completely expose his heart to the Guru's piercing gaze, Jali can understand the Hindu intimation of the oneness of all life, which includes even the squirrel: man's difference from other created beings, the greatness and melancholy of his estate is that he can ask the question, "What are we?"

Jali takes his farewell of Mohan and Damayanti and of the Guru who has only a few weeks left to live; the good-bye has a symbolic setting:

> At the gate he looked round at the scene for the sake of a last memory. The two [the Guru and Damayanti were now again in the same position as before. He looked down at Vishnu and up at the passing clouds. The clouds, he thought, were gone in a breath, and human beings in only a few breaths more. Only Vishnu remained.

I have left the Mohan-Damayanti relationship to the last because it is here that Myers tries to reconcile human love based on a religious sense of life with the need to relate with one's fellowmen, an undertaking that another great master of the science of love, D. H. Lawrence could never successfully accomplish. I do not deny that Lawrence is the more accomplished novelist but if one accepts Myers' own criteria, what does being the greater genius ultimately matter? Both Mohan and Damayanti experience the clash of wills, a familiar Lawrentian theme; Damayanti herself has to establish a right relation with her father but with Mohan she proceeds to a more complete union than any envisaged by Lawrence. To my mind, it is not altogether convincing as art but I salute the endeavor. The use of the concept of transubstantiation to underpin the profound change in their relationship is no less than brilliant:

> For what had happened was not the passage from one emotion to another, but a change of the being upon which emotions play. As in a critical illness there is a moment when the body says: "I'm changed,"

so now each felt that an old self had died and that life would henceforth be lived with a self that was different. And in this change there was something a little sad. There was at least nothing of the elation, the exaltation, that had attended their reconciliations in the past. In this change of being something had been given up; but each had given up the same thing; each was weary with the same weariness, consoled with the same consolation, and above all thankful with the same thankfulness.

This is so unique in English fiction as to be worth emphasis. The practical solution preferred by Mohan in terms of polity is not altogether sensible: one wonders, for example, about the ethics of Mohan's divesting himself of his suzerainty when he knows full well that it would only transfer unfettered power to his brother, the mediocre conservative. Would it not have been better if Mohan continued to exercise extended jurisdiction over a much larger population than to be dependent on his brother's largesse? However, the final state of the love relationship is worth the enterprise, because it is so unique in literature. One can express one's hesitation only when comparing it with the greatest art: I am reminded of the conclusion of Tolstoy's *Anna Karenina* and Levin's more human and realistic expectations, a state of mind which I myself would rather settle for, as one cannot live a quotidian life in the world, even if one has had a mystical vision, without the profounder Tolstoyan realism: let Levin have the final word:

This new feeling has not changed me, has not made me happy and enlightened all of a sudden, as I had dreamed, just like the feeling for my child. There was no surprise in this either. Faith--or not faith--I don't know what it is--but this feeling has come just as imperceptibly through suffering, and has taken firm root in my soul.

I shall go on in the same way, losing my temper with Ivan the coachman, falling into angry discussions, expressing my opinions tactlessly; there will be still the same wall between the holy of holies of my soul and other people, even my wife; I shall go on scolding her for my own terror, and being remorseful for it; I shall still be as unable to understand with my reason why I pray, and I shall still go on praying; but life now, my whole life apart from anything that can happen to me, every minute of it is no more meaningless, as it was before, but it has the positive meaning of goodness, which I have the power to put into it.

CHAPTER X

ANTHONY BURGESS: *THE MALAYAN TRILOGY (THE LONG DAY WANES)*

This novel has two titles--*The Malayan Trilogy* in the original British publication and *The Long Day Wanes*, the more interesting and revelatory title of the American edition. Burgess is many things to many people, readers and critics alike: his prolific output from novellas to novels of Victorian length make it easy for discrimination to be blunted and distinctions to be blurred. But I think the future will find this novel one of the best in an expanding oeuvre.

Our scene in my own book has shifted from India to Sri Lanka, back to India, then to Burma, returned to historical India with contemporary relevances, and we are now in Malaysia. Enough has been said in previous chapters about my scope and purposes to obviate the need for lengthy and detailed treatment; it is sufficient now to consider in a more succinct fashion only the special or novel features of our texts.

The first difference is Burgess' serio-comic tone: he does not want to surrender to an altogether grave endeavor. His Victor Crabbe, whose name itself has suggestions of both crustaceans and fruits, makes Orwell's Flory seem almost maudlin, though the tragedies that overtake them both are worthy of an earnest demeanor. Besides, Burgess is a comic genius: he would sacrifice a major portion of his talent if he were to diminish his comic gift.

There are at least two types of artist among the manifold varieties: the one whose talent cannot encompass his experience and the other whose skills sprint far ahead of his capacity to regulate and mould the multifarious realities he would like to chase. Burgess belongs clearly to the latter category. His problem is prolixity.

There are few writers in English with equal linguistic gifts; it is not an accident that he is an admirer of Joyce. But the same debility, the same inability to corral linguistic exuberance, afflicts Burgess except when he has, as Joyce had in *A Portrait of the Artist As a Young Man* and in the short stories, a subject and a setting which is specific and concrete. If only he had the reverence for the unknown Forster knew or the earnest sense of commitment which distinguishes Orwell, what an incomparably great novelist he would have been! But we have to take our profits with our losses, and for what Burgess has done, we must be truly grateful.

Burgess' achievement is not an East-West encounter of significance. It is a mix and not a mixture, rather like the difference between a Malayan or Thai curry and its Indian counterpart. His subject is not cultural collision or integration but rather a cultural mélange, a hodge-podge where many ingredients collide or float lazily on the surface. This may have something to do with both his vision and his setting, but it is the setting I want to emphasize. He has no contact with the weighted religious and philosophical traditions which Myers essays to dissect and absorb: he does not bring to his material the shock Forster feels when his liberal European background shivers and stumbles before the age-old anomalies and mysteries of India. The written literary traditions of Malaysia are meager: the Hinduism is that of ex-patriates, bent to accommodate worldly success; and Islam in South Asia does not have its pristine breathings from the desert.

Misperceptions in cultural understanding flock Burgess' comedy. The non-whites see the whites as actors in a play. In the kedai in the single street of Gila, the natives watch Nabby Adams crack his head against a hanging oil-lamp and bring their infants to be blessed by Fenella Crabbe. They delight in the rough passage of incomprehensible languages and are corrupted not by Communist indoctrination but by wrist-watches, cigarettes, lipstick and brassieres. What Crabbe is implementing in the classroom is spreading in the jungle, more effectively because of the lure of the Westernization contained in the goodies of the consumerist society. Nabby Adams's comment "we ought to have taken the bloody hat round" could not have been more apropos. The satiric treatment of the anthropologist's approach to local cultures is acid in its exposé:

Fenella's first flush of *Golden Bough* enthusiasm was mitigated a little by this. But, still, aboriginal dancing... The monograph droned on, "The culture-pattern of the *orang darat* is necessarily limited. The jungle houses them and feeds them and provides them with an anthropomorphic pantheon of the kind which is familiar to us from our observations of primitive life in the Congo, the Amazon and other centres--where a rudimentary civilization seems to have been arrested at what may be termed the "Bamboo Level". Morality is simple, government patriarchical, and the practice of the arts confined to primitive and unhandy ornamentation of weapons and cooking utensils... In the dance, however, the *orang darat* has achieved a considerable standard of rhythmic complexity and a high order of agility..."

Even among the characters who interact because of social or economic connections, the incomprehension of each other's culture is acutely comic:

Three languages rapped, fumbled or oozed all the while. At these sessions Nabby Adams spoke only Urdu and English, Alladad Khan only Urdu and Malay, the Crabbes only English and a little Malay. And so it was always, "What did you say then?", "What did he say?", "What did all that mean?" Sometimes they would go to the cinema and, tortured by bugs, watch a long Hindustani film about Baghdad, magic horses that talked and flew, genies in bottles, sword-play, sundered love. Alladad Khan would translate the Hindustani into Malay and Nabby Adams, before he slept, would forget himself and translate the Hindustani into Urdu. Or perhaps they would go to an American film and Fenella Crabbe would translate the American into Malay and Nabby Adams would, before he slept, translate what he understood of it into Urdu.

Even among the Europeans the distances between their interests seem unbridgeable. Here we have Crabbe talking with Hardman who marries a Malay widow, gives up his religion and even tries to abandon altogether the European way of life. It is Crabbe who, though he feels he has something more to contribute to Malaya than to his native country, recalls the Western-world:

"But think of European architecture, and the art galleries, and London on a wet day, river fog, the country in autumn, pubs decorated for Christmas, book-shops, a live symphony orchestra..."

"The exile's dream of home," grinned Hardman. "My dear Victor, what a sea-change. Is this our old ruthless dialectician, our hard-as-nails pillar of pure reason? You must be getting fat, you know."

"God," thought Crabbe, "I'm talking like Fenella. What devil made me do that?"

"There speaks the old Empire-builder," said Hardman. 'You're a bit late, old man. You've only got to the third drama of the cycle. After the grubbing for Rhinegold come the thundering hoofs. And then Rhodes and Raffles, Siegfrieds in armour and bad verse. And always this ghastly 'What do they know of England?' Why did you come out here?"

"I told you before," said Crabbe wearily.

"I know. You spouted some nonsense about heliotropism and applying for a job when you were tight. How about the metaphysical level, the level of ideas? I mean, knowing you, unless you've changed all that much..."

"Well" Crabbe puffed at a cigarette that was damp with the night air, "I suppose part of me thought that England was all television and strikes and nobody giving a damn about culture. I thought they needed me more out here."

"They didn't need you. They needed somebody else, and only long enough to teach them how to manage a strike and erect a television transmitter. And that's not your line, Victor."

The characters have extremely divergent views of what constitutes the East and a cocksureness that their views are the only right ones. For Flaherty, Palestine where he did a stint in the Police is the East, and he is sure the others wouldn't know the "bloody East if they saw it." He feels the need to preserve his own cultural roots by associating with them in the Club and the Sergeant's Mess, unlike Nabby Adams, who frequents kedais with his non-white corporal, running up bills in native pubs.

Burgess' view is that colonialism has failed spectacularly:

> The history of the state differs little from that of its great neighbors, Johore and Pahang. A prince of Malacca settled on its river at the time of the Portuguese invasions. He had known the old days of quiet and leisure, the silken girls bringing sherbet, the long, subtle theological debates with visiting Islamic philosophers. The Portuguese, sweating in trunk-hose, brought a niggling concern with commerce and the salvation of pagan souls. Francis Xavier preached about the love of an alien God, tried to fracture the indivisible numen and establish a crude

triune structure, set up schools where dreary hymns were sung, and finally condoned the rack and the thumbscrew.

The British were not more effective in welding a nation:

> The work of governing Lanchap has been carried out quietly and with moderate efficiency by the British Advisers--mostly colorless, uxorious men with a taste for fishing or collecting matchboxes or writing competent monographs on the more accessible Malay village customs.

Even the buildings in the school where Crabbe taught are a hodge-podge and the seductions of the mass-media and American technology are more than a match both for the local cultures and the British import:

> The many buildings of the school represent a whole museum of colonial architecture, ranging from the original *attap* huts, through stucco palladian, to broiling Corbusier glass-houses on high stilts. All subjects have always been taught in English, and the occidental bias in the curriculum has made many of the alumni despise their own rich cultures, leading them, deracinated, to a yearning for the farthest west of all. Thus, the myths of cinema and syndicated cartoon have served to unite the diverse races far more than the clump of the cricket-ball and the clipped rebukes and laudations of their masters.

Nowhere is the tension of adapting to an alien culture more pronounced than in Crabbe's wife Fenella who finds she has no one to talk to, there is mildew on the shoes, sweat-rot in the armpits of dresses, one meets scabby children, spitting pot-bellied shopkeepers, terrorists, burglars, scorpions, flying-beetles. "What is there to like?", she wails, dreaming of a nice little lunch at that Italian place in Dean Street, or the French film at the Curzon or Studio One. She cannot but think that such an Elizabethan play of adultery and jealousy as *A Woman Killed With Kindness* had reflected a civilization a thousand times more complex.

The book has many voices--Punjabi, Sikh, Tamil, Chinese, Malay, Eurasian, English, Australian, even American. It is to Burgess' credit that his ear is so sensitive that he can recapture the intonations of such widely different races. But it is the cultural chaos which everyone inhabits that is the predominant impression:

Crabbe looked at the 'No Spitting' notice on the wall and his head swam with the absurdity of four languages telling people not to spit, all on the same notice. A thin Chinese bathing girl beckoned from a calendar. From behind her, in the swimming open kitchen, came the noise of painful expectoration.

True enough it is British imperialism in disintegration and withdrawal that Burgess portrays and it is natural that the expatriates encounter major problems. But even a Catholic priest like Father Laforgue modifies his beliefs by falsifying the doctrine of the Trinity in a polytheistic parish, reduces his faith to a few essentials while assiduously studying the philosophy of Confucius in Chinese. He is utterly deracinated from his native culture:

France meant nothing to him. Europeans had sometimes invited him to dinner and given him stuffed aubergines and onion soup and Nuits St. Georges and what they said was good coffee. They had gushed about Normandy and the Cote d'Or and little places on the Left Bank. They had played him records of French cabaret music. They had evinced, in their curious French mixed with Malay (both were foreign languages, both occupied the same compartment, they were bound to get mixed), a nostalgia for France which amused him slightly, bored him much, flattered him not at all.

For a Frenchman especially he has come to a sorry pass: he has changed radically, holding fast only to his thaumaturgical functions of forgiving sins, turning bread and wine into God and saving a dying child from Limbo. Such a complete sloughing off of one's heritage can only strike the reader as pitiful, if not disastrous.

But even when Burgess deals with the natives he cannot but be satiric of their philosophies and traditions. Even the venerable tradition of Taoism is the butt and job of ridicule:

The Noah of China, Emperor Yu, walked along the banks of the Yellow River one day after the Great Flood. He saw a tortoise rising from the river with a strange pattern on its back. Miraculously, this pattern resolved itself in his eyes into the "Magic Square," the ideal arrangement of the yin-yang digits. Out of this came a plan for reconstructing the world and devising the perfect system of government.

The characters themselves are eccentric and often disagreeable. Che Normah the wealthy Malay widow is gross, crude and insatiable in her sexual appetite. Hardman her husband is a possession to be jealously guarded from the danger of relapsing into Catholicism, a prospect which drives her to irate violence.

> Soon she brought to the door-step a plate of cold curried beef, fiery pepper-choked fibres, and forked it in delicately. Then, unaware of irony, she hummed "One Fine Day" while picking her teeth. "A man, a little man, is approaching across the padang." She did not know the words.

> Before twelve-thirty the court recessed. She saw her betrothed come out, talking to a white-suited Tamil, making forensic gestures, his brief under his arm. Then she saw him prepare to move off and then someone come on to the scene up left, and accost him gently. The storms began to stir in her eyes, for, despite everything, she was still a daughter of Islam, and the man that Rupert Hardman was talking to was just the man he should not be talking to. She banged her fist on the empty curry plate and it cracked in two.

Alladad Khan, Nabby Adams' assistant, is saved from domestic bullying by his wife's brother when he marries a Margaret Tam outside his clan and reveals himself as one of the shoddy ikons that the Prophet himself had denounced, but despite this and his own promotion to Sergeant all Alladad has to look forward to is the flat in the Police Barracks, "and in it a long-nosed wife with cannibal teeth, a baby, a bed, chappatis hissing and jumping on the stove." Or there is this description of Abdul Kadir, a caustic account of the indeterminate nature of the Malay:

> He was a mixture of Arab, Chinese, and Dutch, with a mere formal sprinkling of Malay floating, like those red peppers, on the surface. His friends, complacently pitying this eccentric product of miscegenation, would forget the foreign bodies in their own blood. Haji Zainal Abidin would cease to be mainly Afghan; Che Abdullah no longer spoke the Siamese he had sucked from his mother; little Hussein forgot that his father was a Bugis. When they talked about Malay self-determination, they really meant that Islam should frighten the Chinese with visions of hell; but perhaps they did not even mean that. They themselves were too fond of the bottle to be good Moslems; they even kissed women and ate doubtful meat. They did not really know what they wanted.

began to sweat after it. "When we British finally leave there's going to be hell. And we're leaving pretty fast."

Ironically enough, the only unity that is envisaged in the book is when three British soldiers of the Royal Barsets wearing drainpipe trousers, serge waisted jacket and boot-lace tie encounter Malay youths in a similar costume. "Cor," one of the soldiers said, "Teds 'ere too. Oo'd have thought we'd meet nigger Teds?" The sodality of Teddy boys is the only hope for Malaya:

> But there now started a sodality that was to prove more fruitful in promoting interracial harmony than any of Crabbe's vague dreams. Wandering down the street one night, the seven of them, they came across a Tamil youth in Edwardian costume. "Wotcher, Sambo," said the corporal. "You doin' anythin'?" And later there were two Chinese boys who joined the gang, and one of these, whose name was Philip Aloysius Tan, swiftly became the gang-leader. The corporal was good-humoured about it, glad to see it: after all, the days of British rule were over.

In this setting it is not difficult to see why Victor Crabbe must appear a cranky idealist and his life must end in tragic failure. He has endured misfortune, never recovered from the accidental death of his first wife which he believed he caused, married an unsuitable woman he could not love, maimed as his love was from the start, indulged in casual sex with the local prostitute Rahimah and with the hilarious caricature, Mrs. Talbot: this is too great a handicap to be surmounted by his penchant for doing good.

My friend Michael Duffet has suggested to me that the title of the trilogy in its American edition, *The Long Day Wanes,* is from Tennyson's *Ulysses:*

> The long day wanes; the slow moon climbs;
> the deep moans round with many voices.
> Come my friends, 'Tis not too late to seek a newer world.

In a paper for a project which I directed, he says

> It is surprising that, amid the plethora of references the critics I have mentioned have spotted, they have not identified this.   It is astonishingly apt. Quite apart from the obvious applicability of the first phrase to the waning of the long day of British colonialism, there is

both the appropriateness of the "many voices" of Malay, Chinese, Tamil, Urdu and Eurasian in the trilogy and finally, and most significantly, I think, the intense optimism of the final line. One feels that, despite the detached, cynical, comic mark, it represents the true tone of Burgess' voice which we have noticed in those serious compassionate peepings-through of his involved, concerned humanity.

While congratulating him on spotting the quotation and making this comment, and while not denying Burgess's involved humanity and compassion, I cannot help but conclude that these qualities do not negate the deep-seated pessimism, however sweetened by hilarity and humor, which is the ground-swell of this remarkably sad book. And, lest I have been misunderstood, I would like to affirm that the blame, if any, for the cross-cultural mix, rather than mixture, which Anthony Burgess makes of Malaya cannot be laid at his door. Some of the main cultural groups are exiles from their original environments and Burgess made an honest attempt to fabricate a pattern, such as it was, from what he saw.

CHAPTER XI

PAUL SCOTT'S *STAYING ON*: THE POIGNANT AFTERMATH OF IMPERIALISM

If Burgess' *The Malayan Trilogy* deals with the Empire near the time of its dissolution, Scott's *Staying On* is set in its aftermath. Because of the wide popular success of the recent television series *The Jewel in the Crown* based on Scott's *The Raj Quartet*, *Staying On* may appear more like a coda to the massive symphony of its predecessor rather than as an autonomous novel in its own right.

But, oddly enough, despite the grand ambition of its title, suggestive of a weighty subject, *The Raj Quartet* does not have the artistic unity or even the close cross-cultural examination of character, motive and event which distinguish its epilogue, *Staying On.* The journeying back and forth in time, the cross-references, the fractured story-line, the historical quest meant to be given flesh and blood by the portrayal of individuals in interaction, the counterpointing and circular modes of the narrative, are all present in greater or less degree in all his novels but the aesthetic effect is more successful in a work of more modest compass, such as *Staying On*, than in such a grand undertaking as *The Raj Quartet*. Besides, reading the four long novels in one stretch is a strain because of its vast panorama, meandering narration and soap-operatic techniques: what remains in the memory of *The Raj Quartet* are the spectacular insights into the inner and outer spaces of individual lives, not always subsumed under a unified organic vision.

We first encounter the main characters of *Staying On*, Tusker and Lucy Smalley, in the earlier *The Towers of Silence:*

> Most stations had their Smalleys; a number of stations had at some time or another had these Smalleys. Because they looked nondescript and unambitious they provoked no envy and hardly any suspicion. In Pankot, where they had been since the end of 1941, they arrived at parties harmoniously together and then put distance between them as if to distribute their humdrum selves in as many parts of the room as possible. Leaving, they did go arm-in-arm, giving the impression that by playing their separate parts in communal endeavor something integral to their private lives and mutual affection had been maintained. The Smalleys were slight bores but very useful people.

There are so many links between *Staying On* and *The Raj Quartet* -- echoes, memories, deliberate reminiscences -- that it would be in order to consider it a sequel and even to assert that a reading of the earlier work is essential to its total understanding. An old acquaintance Phoebe Blackshaw sends Lucy a newspaper cutting of an obituary notice relating to Lt. Col. Layton, father of Sarah and Susan, important characters in the earlier novels, and Lucy responds with a long letter giving all her news. Minnie, who had been little Edward's ayah in *The Day of the Scorpion,* is now a maid at Smith's Hotel. Towards the very end of the novel Lucy recalls in an imaginary conversation with an expected visitor from England the incident from *The Towers of Silence* when the Smalleys were stranded after a party because there was no one to give them a lift home. Tusker spends a lot of his time in this novel reading, annotating and quarrelling with a book, "A Short History of Pankot" by Edgar Maybrick, a character in *The Towers.*

However, *Staying On* can be read on its own terms and for its own sake. This is because it is a domestic drama of two aging people in an alien world with drastically reduced comforts. It does not tempt you to ponder the future of post-colonial India though it does tell you what it may be like. The general concerns issue from concrete human situations; the characters are unheroic, making it easier for the reader to identify himself with them. Besides, the problem of old age is common to all cultures even if attitudes tend to be culture-specific: consequently, the theme is universal.

The characterization, even apart from Lucy and Tusker Smalley, is very deftly done. Mrs. Lila Bhoolabhoy though a caricature is an when I practiced, Joseph kept watch to run and warn me, just in case you took it into your head to visit and see nobody had run away with the Church." They laughed. Joseph had know, too, then. Only he had not known.

"It must have cost a great deal of money," was all he could say, but trying to look pleased, as happy for himself as they seemed to expect him to be.

Susy said, "Father Sebastian is on a Grants committee for things like this."

"And not everybody," the priest said, "is interested only in money these days. It was much a labour of love. Brother John said it was not technically difficult. He and his assistant soon had it fixed up. At Whitsun we hope he will come up again and give a recital."

"He played so beautifully," Susy said. "Oh, I felt such a nincompoop in comparison. His Bach was out of this world. Miles better than poor old Mr. Maybrick's, who taught me when I was quite a little girl and could hardly reach."

I too am quite out of this world, Mr. Bhoolabhoy thought; and thought it again as he typed, "Yours very Sincerely,"

I am no longer needed here. I do not know about organs. I cannot play organs. I take other people's word for it when they say organs are U.S. I inquire gently year after year about restoring organs and say to people please may we not do something about this organ. But the only organ I know anything about is the one that has contributed to all my difficulties and does not need restoring but having cloth put over it.

The pun on the word "organ" relieves the desperation of Frank Bhoolabhoy's attitude but does not alter it.

Of the other characters Ibrahim is very important both for himself and for illustrating another element in the dependency nexus: the man-servant relationship is a paradigm of the domination-subservience pattern of most colonial encounters but as the master grows older and more feeble, the servant is a dominating personality in his own right. Ibrahim sees his employers in the same lights, even though he is proud to continue as the servant of a white sahib and his mem-sahib:

Years younger than both he felt for them what an indulgent, often exasperated but affectionate parent might feel for demanding and

impressive figure both in size and delineation. Waddling about like a galleon, she is called Ownership as opposed to her husband Frank who is only Management. Her sexual climaxes are gigantic but her husband is able to cope because, though a small man, he has an immense sexual appetite. The humorous aspect of this can be seen in the way the novelist treats Lila's unpredictable Monday night desire which depended on her fortunes at the evening's games of bridge:

This tended to depend on how much she had won. More often than not she came home up on the evening in which case Mr. Bhoolabhoy had to be prepared to be up to things too. He had to be similarly prepared if she had lost so much in the day-long bridge session that she was feeling unloved and unwanted in an unkind and swindling world. He found this rather touching and on such occasions, after their combined and gigantic climax, they often had a little weep together and exchanged protestations of their beholdenness one to the other and of their resolve to be beholden forever. (Her breakeven nights could be very dull.) Too often, though, the combination of money lost, midnight snack, violent intercourse and tears of relief and love, led next day to Mrs. Bhollabhoy's further prostration.

Her insatiable desire is perhaps not confined to her husband; there is some doubt to what extent her lawyer, accountant and financial adviser Pandey enjoyed more than just Mrs. Bhoolabhoy's professional confidence.

Frank Bhoolabhoy is clearly faithless. He accuses himself of lewd and lustful thought when he observes Suzy Williams' neat little bottom as she stands on tiptoe to arrange flowers. He is not above making a pass even at Lucy Tusker, a lady of faded charm. But his clear case of adultery is with the nautch-girl Hot Chichanya who keeps an illustrated edition of the *Kama Sutra* by her bedside in order to titillate her lovers if they showed signs of flagging desire. He even buys a novel type of underpants, learns new sex positions such as the double-lotus, but cannot bear to contemplate what would happen to him if he tried this new technique with his wife: weight and gravity alone would have broken every bone in his back and legs before the connection had been achieved, or he would have been smothered. His love-life is only an interlude in an existence branded by suffering:

When she woke life would be difficult. It would be wiser to extricate himself before she did so. He had a technique for this which he used occasionally in the middle of the night to return to his own room without waking her. Mostly she chucked him out with no ceremony. She preferred to sleep alone and he had learned from experience that the morning glory of Mrs. Bhoolabhoy's conjugal contentment (a rare bloom) withered rapidly if she did not find herself alone, even if she had not personally dismissed him because incapable of doing so (poleaxed, he liked to think, by a particularly passionate five-star performance on his part).

Bhoolabhoy is a tragic figure only in a lesser key than Tusker Smalley: he becomes more increasingly aware that as Management he is only part of the fixture and fittings, he cannot even save his friend Tusker from the doom that is awaiting him. The business deals are outside his scope and ken: his wife treats him like a ventriloquist's dummy in the crook of her great arm. She wants to buy into the consortium and, besides anticipated reconnaissances into the vast territory of her flesh, he is only the caretaker of a development site. Even in the church where he has expected to fulfill himself, decisions are made without his knowledge. The organ in the church has been resuscitated without his knowledge. He is being side-tracked.

He should have been told about the organ. Yes. For years he had gone on and on about the organ. He had once tried himself to raise the money for its restoration. Mr. Thomas himself knew this. Susy knew it. The sudden pealing of the organ yesterday which should have been a job had been a shattering blow to his self-esteem. "We wanted it to be a surprise for you, Francis," Father Sebastian said. "A little reward for all your past endeavours." *Past* endeavours? "How kind," he replied. And looked from one to the other and noted their smiles. Smiles of pity? Gradually the explanation of the organ's otherwise miraculous resurrection had been unfolded. Father Sebastian had had a look at it. He knew something about organs. He suspected that things were not so bad as they had been allowed to seem. (Allowed?) He also knew of an expert technician, in Calcutta. The man had come up. He had stayed with Susy. Mr. Thomas had let him into the church with the spare key. Within ten days he had worked the miracle and for days afterwards Susy had been practicing.

"We wanted to surprise you," she said, echoing Father Sebastian. "But, oh, goodness, what we didn't have to get up to. We thought you'd catch us at it any time. During day time Mr. Thomas' kids kept watch with orders to divert you if you put in an appearance while one of them went to warn Brother John in the organ loft. And at night   t

unreasonable children whom it was more sensible to appease than cross.

Ibrahim makes the best comment in the novel of Tusker's predicament, he describes him as a man who knew he'd left it too long to go to Mecca. He loved his master because he was a real sahib unlike a counterfeit like Dr. Mitra. Even his relationship with Lucy though a more complicated one needs the considerable finesse born of a long association:

Being the first day of the month it was also accounts day for Memsahib and pay-day for Ibrahim. When Tusker had gone, accompanied by Bloxsaw, Ibrahim waited in the kitchen for the familiar sounds of Lucy-Mem opening her escritoire, then the drawer in which the metal cash-box was kept. Hearing both sounds he put the kettle on to Smalley.

She had a poor vicarage childhood and had been a secretary before marrying Tusker, both handicaps in the competitive world of Anglo-India. She also had an unerring sense for saying the right thing at the wrong time. She was a dogsbody for the superior ladies, a useful adjunct who was never given a say in deciding what was to be done. Tusker was a plodder who always chose the less demanding job throughout his career. What is amazing, however, is that these commonplace people show in their old age unsuspected capacities for mutual affection and sensitivity. It is like a renaissance in old age. They are poor in India though not so poor as they would have been if they returned to England. They are the victims of Indian capitalism, typified by Mrs. Bhoolabhoy who wants to buy into a consortium for which she trades Smith's Hotel and the annex rented by the Smalleys. It is as vicious a capitalism as anywhere in the world. In addition, the Smalleys are aging and Lucy particularly has to worry about her income and a lonely widowhood. It is indeed a rare act of courage for a novelist to draw his protagonists from such humdrum characters. Tusker Smalley is a willing work-horse of the British Raj, an old, irascible, and undemonstrative man. Lucy Smalley is an aging woman, who lives a half-life in her fantasies derived from childhood memory and the films she habitually sees. Because of her lowly origins her compatriots never treat her quite as a Memsahib and never permit her to assume the manner appropriate to the sobriquet. The two, however, reach a communion which is denied to the panjandrums who played more important parts in the administration of the subcontinent.

Towards the conclusion of the novel Lucy receives a love letter from Tusker explaining what he has provided for her in the event of his death -- meager provision but all told a loving testament. The book ends with one of the most moving valedictions I have read in a long time:

> --but now, until the end, I shall be alone, whatever I am doing, here as I feared, amid the alien corn, waking, sleeping, alone for ever and ever and I cannot bear it but mustn't cry and must, must get over it but don't for the moment see how, so with my eyes shut, Tusker, I hold out my hand, and beg you, Tusker, beg, beg you to take it and take me with you. How can you not, Tusker? Oh, Tusker, while you yourself go home?

Lucy and Tusker Smalley have been arm in arm, throne by throne, and now hope to be urn in urn. The humor of "throne by throne," their separate but interconnected loos without a partition, only adds to the tears at the heart of things, of a woman stranded amid the alien corn:

> Perhaps the self-same song that found a path
> Through the sad heart of Ruth when, sick for home,
> She stood in tears amid the alien corn.

There is a profound eschatological note to the novel, a pervasive aura of the ultimate realities, a melancholy sense of "last things." The book itself begins with the reported death of one of the two main characters -- Tusker Smalley -- but the comedic note is also a struck at the same time because at the precise moment when Tusker died, his wife Lucy was having her hair blue-rinsed and set at her hairdresser's in the Seraglio Room, an appellation suggestive ironically of both a Sultan's palace and a harem, of the new glass and concrete hotel. A good example of this eschatological concern is the introduction of the figure of the *mali* Joseph, the substitute gardener. He is in pitiful circumstances, half-way between life and death when Mr. Bhoolabhoy revives him with a chappatti and a cup of tea. We encounter him in the churchyard clearing the graves of grass and weeds with an old pair of clippers. Joseph is not exactly Death, the Grim Reaper, mowing down human lives with his scythe. But it is not an accident that we meet

Joseph often in the churchyard to which he repairs, when he is free and when he is not so free.

When Lucy makes a visit to the church and she hears the sound "snick-snick" it is not "the rhythmic sound of the coppersmith bird beating out its endless saucepans in the smithy of the great pineclad hills in which Pankot rested two thousand feet or more above sea level;" nor is it the sound that her father made cutting the hedge to the accompaniment of another sound "click-click" which was the sound the twins made playing cricket on the vicarage lawn. It was the sound of Joseph with his shears.

> *Snick-snick*
> She left the lychgate and set out on the path through the churchyard but suddenly stood arrested -- not by the sound which, coming again, was clearly that made by a pair of shears, but by the appearance of the graves. A lot of grass had been trimmed and many of the headstones cleaned. Whoever was responsible for this was obviously even now at work, but invisible.

The preoccupation with the churchyard and its graves, the description of Joseph as "invisible" are not idle references but meant clearly to generate a whiff of mortality.

In a later scene, Bhoolabhoy is in church repenting of his sins to the punctuation of the sound "snick-snick" till the sound suggests the bulldozers he fears will soon raze the Smalley residence:

> (p) *Snick-snick*
> The sound, so soft, scarcely a sound but just audible in this place that seemed this morning no more than an echoing chamber for noises of temporal activity outside, suddenly impinged on Mr. Bhoolabhoy's outer ear. The hairs on the back of his neck stirred, thousands of tiny antennae programmed to tune in to signals of approaching disaster.

> (Cr)*Snick-snick*
> Mr. Bhoolobhoy stumbled to his feet. The demolition gang had already arrived and begun work on the churchyard. He staggered along the pew making for the south door and reaching it opened and thrust himself forward and out almost into the arm of Mrs. Smalley who uttered a little cry like that of a ghost on its way to a haunting.

The intimations of mortality are unmistakable.

The last time we hear the same sound is when both Lucy and Mr. Bhoolabhoy are talking to each other:

> *Snick-snick-snick-snick*
> This time the sound was near at hand. Both turned their attention to its likely source which was now revealed. Round the bend of the path came Joseph, making slow but steady progress, sideways, and on his hunkers, rather like a Russian dancer in slow motion, but also because of the sharp claws of the shears that seemed an essential part of him, like a large landcrab, foraging. He was cutting the edges of the grass. "Why, *mali*! It's you" Lucy said. The young man glanced up and then unwinding himself came to a standing position. Holding the shears to a side in one hand he gave a grave salutation with the other: Mr. Bhoolabhoy was already making for him; making *at* him it looked, and shouting at him in Hindi. The *mali* stood his ground but cast his eyes down.

Joseph is now far away from the half-dead boy with a pair of tired clippers: he can stand his ground, he is both grim and menacing, and his salutation is grave, an intended, sardonic pun. Of course, Mr. Bhoolabhoy tries to play down the sombre significance; he tells Lucy that Joseph is a simple boy who tries to read the names on the gravestones in order to pray correctly for the souls of the departed. Of course, also as often happens in life, the snick-snick is soon overtaken by the click-click of the paid photographer who has been commissioned to take pictures of the church: the reminders of mortality are soon overwhelmed.

The true home is after death, and the way Scott has developed his symbolism out of seemingly trivial details and incidents shows us how careful he is as an artist. He has written a novel of great human import about two characters who are as mediocre as can be found, a revelation to us who feel superior to the ordinary and the everyday, and an attestation of the unsuspected and magical virtues of the conventional. It is also an ideal text of the East-West encounter because it deals not with the grandiose clash of cultures but with the intimate exchanges which constitute the most worthwhile and meaningful concordance of human beings reaching out to each other across the voids that separate not just races and nations but men and women from one another.

CHAPTER XIIA

THE PHILOSOPHICAL MEETING OF EAST AND WEST: THE CONTRIBUTION OF ANANDA COOMARASWAMY

Very few of us particularly, in today's world, lumbered as it is with discreteness and irrelevance, are blessed with the synoptic genius, let alone that unremitting attention to the things of the mind and the spirit, which characterized the life of Ananda Coomaraswamy. Being clearly not one of this few, I have always felt when reading him like the beggar at the feast, greedy but unable to savor, let alone digest, the many delights at this rich table of traditional knowledge and wisdom. The feast is God's plenty, as Dryden said of Chaucer's *The Canterbury Tales*.

Even though Coomaraswamy has not yet received as much recognition as his work so clearly merits, he has from time to time been praised in extravagant terms. In India, among the cognoscenti, he is a monumental figure, a star in the constellation of culture heroes. One does not have the right to expect from politicians, prime ministers or heads of state powers of sound judgment about intellectual matters. However, it is gratifying to find that Indira Gandhi--or at least her ghost writer--once ranked him with Tagore in the Indian Pantheon, and that the first prime minister of independent Sri Lanka--or at least his ghost writer--once said of him that to Coomaraswamy as to no other man Sri Lanka owed the stimulus for the revival in modern times of its cultural and spiritual heritage. Radhakrishnan, philosopher and president of

India, said of him, "Among those who are responsible not only for the Indian Renaissance but for a new Renaissance in the world, Coomaraswamy holds a pre-eminent position." He counted among his admirers in the West T. S. Eliot, Eric Gill, and Aldous Huxley, who praised him for that extraordinary combination of vast learning and penetrating insight which gave him his unique importance as a mediator between East and West. Genetically and in cast of mind he was a blend of East and West: he considered it his role to discover and expound the tradition which was common, at its deepest layers, to both Eastern and Western art, metaphysics and religion.

One of the reasons why he has not been as influential in the academic world as he should be is the fact that his learning and centrality of approach obliterate and straddle over currently established boundaries between academic disciplines, such as aesthetics, art criticism, history of art, metaphysics, philosophy, theology, and so on. Coomaraswamy was not concerned with being an academician or even making a contribution to one or more of several fields of knowledge. Increasingly over the years he was trying to relate all his interests to the central question of what is man that God should be mindful of him, and what is God that man should desire to know him. This blurring of boundaries is naturally resisted by those for whom the prevalence of distinct areas of study is a requirement for the display of specialized excellence, if not for mere survival among the coteries of Academe. I may here mention the case of a graduate student in an American university whose thesis proposal for a doctorate on Coomaraswamy as a philosopher was rejected on the ground that Coomaraswamy was neither in the mainstream of philosophy nor an original philosopher, as though it were more important to be different, unique and even eccentric rather than to build on foundations, so long as they were sound, and to extend the frontiers of knowledge as long as the knowledge remained valid. This incident would not have surprised Coomaraswamy, as he went out of his way to disclaim originality while displaying it in its real sense of "going back to the beginning" for the rediscovery and application to modern times of the traditional knowledge. The charge that Coomaraswamy is not in the mainstream would perhaps have amused Coomaraswamy as in all his endeavors he was concerned only with the "mainstream," in the way he understood it.

Another reason for the scant attention paid to Coomaraswamy in academic circles is that he is so much better than the scholars at their own games--his deep knowledge of many languages, Eastern and Western, classical and modern, and his inveterate habit of burdening his lines and encrusting his footnotes with the most thorough and recondite references, in order to prove his argument beyond all possible doubt, is likely to dismay all but the dedicated seeker of knowledge.

In his earlier writings it may seem, on a superficial reading, that he was an Asian post-colonial nationalist protesting against the slavish imitation (in India and Ceylon) of the Western way of life. He thought it wholly impossible for an Asian woman to look anything but vulgar in European dress, or anything but a lady in her own. He complained of the way Asian homes were filled with ugly and useless furniture and ornaments utterly unsuited to local needs, and pitiful even as specimens of the worst that European traders could produce. But he was wise enough to realize that what was happening in Asia was only a part of what was happening all over the world. He protested against "the continual destruction of national character and individuality and art by the pressure of what is called in bitter unconscious irony, the civilizing factor." What he was really objecting to, however, was the imitation in the East of the debased elements of Western culture. What he was protesting against was the vulgarity and commercialism of the industrialized world.

His objection to the industrialized world was not based on a naive primitivism like that of some modern conservative political parties: it derives from one of the first principles of his philosophy, which is that there is no distinction between the fine and the applied arts, "that beauty and utility are indivisible in the object, and that nothing useless can properly be called beautiful." For Coomaraswamy, as for Aquinas, art was the principle of manufacture; he therefore deplored the production of art solely for profit under conditions determined by the money-values of the marketplace. What Coomaraswamy wanted for the Asians was simply that they should absorb what was best in the Western tradition while retaining what was best in their own inheritance. He pleaded that Asians should meet the wave of culture on equal terms and that they should be masters of the art of life, instead of the slaves of civilization.

Coomaraswamy, therefore, was not a believer in a simple polarity between Eastern spirituality and Western materialism: he predicted, in fact, writing as early as 1918, that in the future it was the East which would become materialistic and the West more spiritual. Since this is a neglected aspect of Coomaraswamy's vision of the future, almost totally ignored in the East as it does not accord well with the narrow chauvinisms that now rage over so many of the countries in the Eastern half of the world, an extended quotation would not be out of place:

> And we may expect that Europe, having sunk into industrial competition first, will be the first to emerge...In the meantime the decay of Asia proceeds, partly of internal necessity, because at the present moment the social change from cooperation to competition is spoken of as progress, and because it seems to promise the ultimate recovery of political power...the rapid degradation of Asia is thus an evil portent for the future of humanity and for the future of that Western social idealism of which the beginnings are already recognizable. If, either in ignorance or in contempt of Asia, constructive European thought omits to seek the cooperation of Eastern philosophers, there will come a time when Europe will not be able to fight Industrialism, because this enemy will be entrenched in Asia ... for if Asia be not with Europe, she will be against her, and there may arise a terrible conflict, economic or even armed, between an idealistic Europe and a materialistic Asia.

It is not difficult in 1999 to imagine such a future. Coomaraswamy's main intuition was the Hindu sense of the unity of all life--material and spiritual, political, social and cultural. In numerous places throughout his works he eloquently expounded his view that the recognition of this unity was the highest good and the uttermost freedom. For him, Hinduism was not a place-bound, time-bound, or culture-bound religion; it was religiousness itself. He saw all the world religions as *Philosophia perennis,* not as Leibnitz first used the phrase but in the sense that all spirituality had a common ground in an immanent and transcendent God. For him, tradition chooses the human being wherever he happens to be born, but since it is the innate potentiality and privilege of human life to discover the Godhead within, the tradition into which one happens to be born is not important in the ultimate sense, though it could hamper and stunt the fulfillment of one's full potential. Coomaraswamy could, therefore, derive as much sustenance from the Gospel, especially according to John, as from the Vedanta, as much support from Meister Eckhart whom, with the possible exception of Dante, he considered the greatest of all Europeans. He was a spiritual snob in the best signification one can give the word "snob." He would settle for no less than St. John of the Cross or the Sufi mystic poet Jalal-uddin Rumi. "The astrolabe of the mysteries of God is love."

Coomaraswamy's aesthetics--he himself preferred to call his theory of art or expression a *Rhetoric*--was based not just on a religious view of the Universe, or the poetic sense that the world was charged with the beauty and grandeur of God, but on a strict metaphysical system which for him was the foundation of a normal or traditional civilization, a foundation he found common to the Indian, the classical and the mediaeval Western traditions as well as to the so-called folk culture, or the "primitive mentality" of ancient and still surviving cultures. This system derived from a primordial wisdom which of its very nature could not be supplanted by modern science or knowledge. The work of art therefore was a support of contemplation. But what saved Coomaraswamy from a mere archaism was his insistence that he was returning to first principles; and the fact that these principles had been enunciated earlier by Plato and in the *Bhagavad Gita* or had been universally accepted in past ages did not necessarily destroy their validity in the present. He was also able to meet the charge of elitism by responding on two fronts: first, art for him has layers of significance which need not lie open to all capacities to the same extent so long as the core of symbolic meaning is shared by all; second, the artist for him is not a special kind of man, but every man is a special kind of artist. Coomaraswamy was thus able to give a democratic dimension to art while retaining the need for discrimination--he could say that no man had a right to any social status unless he was an artist. He believed in the anonymity and impersonality of art as opposed to the sentimentality, and the obsession with personality which disfigured the art of his time. But Coomaraswamy was no narrow traditionalist who dreamed of a possible return to the Middle Ages: he once said that "the vitality of a tradition persists only so long as it is fed by intensity of imagination."

Though one may disagree with Coomaraswamy's formulations of some theoretical concepts in aesthetics--and I shall make some comments later on in this connection--and seriously wonder how useful his preoccupation with such questions is to the critic *qua* critic, one cannot gainsay the fact that he was conspicuously endowed with the faculty of discrimination and judgment and blessed with *taste,* an inborn aptitude for which there is no acquired or learned substitute. The rare possession of this faculty, though it is often accompanied by egregious lapses in particular judgments, such lapses seemingly almost a necessary concomitant, is what distinguishes Samuel Johnson, Matthew Arnold, F. R. Leavis, or Wyndham Lewis from the hordes of critics in the history of literary criticism, many of whom are perhaps more correct in detail but rarely reveal that innate and inward sense of what makes for life, and what for death, in the products of art and literature.

One of Coomaraswamy's touchstones for the greatness of a work of art was *Samvega,* or aesthetic shock, the capacity of a work of art to shake one's being to its roots. He says in one of his essays that he was completely dissolved and broken up when he listened to the Gregorian chant and comments that this could not have been a mere aesthetic emotion but "the shock of conviction that only an intellectual art can deliver, the body-blow that is delivered by any perfect and therefore convincing statement of truth." Comparing Blake's line from *The Tiger* "Did He who made the lamb make Thee?" with Joyce Kilmer's line "Only God can make a tree," Coomaraswamy says: "In the question 'Did He who made the lamb make Thee?' there is an incomparably harder blow than there is in 'Only God can make a tree,' which could as well have been said of a flea or a cutworm."

Of course there are limitations in his work, as there are bound to be in the work of any writer of such an ambitious scope. His Brahmin sociology was unhistorical and oversimplified; the same could be said of his admiration for medieval Christendom, the historical realities of which he seems to have ignored. But Coomaraswamy's greatness does not lie in his having been a mere historian or a mere sociologist. He did not defend the caste system as an ideal ordering of society: his argument was that differences based on caste were no worse than differences based on wealth. If he seemed to prefer the caste system of India it was only because he found that in such a society man was not separated from man as much as in modern industrial culture. "A Western professor and a navvy do not understand each other half as well as a Brahmin and a Sudra." He approved of cultures in terms of the quality of the intellectual ideals which were dominant at the centers of power. He judged cultures in terms of these ideals. Much as he admired the ancient arts of Sri Lanka and what remained of the traditional way of life, he left the country after a few years as he could not breathe freely in its then uncongenial cultural climate, dominated as it was by the rootless and culturally confused elites who were the leaders of opinion at that time. When in England, he sympathized with the school of William Morris and lamented the divorce of work from culture.

We have gone so far as to divorce work from culture, and to think of culture as something to be acquired in hours of leisure; but there can be only a hothouse and unreal culture where work itself is not its means; if culture does not show itself in all we make we are not cultured.

In the United States he lived for thirty years and seems to have found the best environment, such as it was, for his life's vocation. But the religious man and critic of society that he was, he could not help but deplore the way commerce was settling on every tree. His incidental remarks on education are of interest to teachers, not just in the West but the world over. He once remarked that it would take at least ten years to outgrow even a Harvard education. Today with our emphasis on equality in education (whatever that may mean) we must beware that such an emphasis does not distort the relationship between teacher and pupil and leave us with a state of affairs where the student feels the only difference between him and the teacher is that the teacher has somehow "made it." The teacher to be effective must after all be given some recognition at least because he has had more time to read, and perhaps think more deeply than the student about the subject he has chosen to teach!

While my view of Coomaraswamy's oeuvre is highly laudatory, and I have a keen sense of its current relevance, it would be well to comment on some of his critical concepts, as they constitute the most vulnerable portion of his intellectual equipment. Coomaraswamy's theories, whether it is his adoption of the concept of imitation from Plato or the theory of *katharsis* from Aristotle, are vulnerably exposed to modern criticism, though there are notable modifications and refinements in his interpretations, as for example when he defines katharsis as a "standing aside" of the spiritual from the natural self due to a purifying or purification from the passions. I do not want to consider these particular concepts in any detail, but it is worth saying at the outset that his view of the fundamental identity of all the arts, whether music, poetry, architecture, sculpture or pottery, can only be accepted without major disputes and qualifications at a very high and therefore forbidding level of generality. An aesthetic which feels it has to subsume all the arts under a single umbrella has necessarily to be too abstract to be of use in the actual appreciation of particular works of art executed in such different material as pigment, clay, vibrant air or wood. Further, his antipathy to naturalism, his depreciation of the artist's engagement with the sensuous surfaces of things does lead to a loss of concreteness and a shrinkage of artistic scope. The ways in which William Carlos Williams' remark, "There are no ideas except in things," or Mallarme's aphorism, "Poetry is not written with ideas; it is written with words," may be seen as at least partially true, would tend to escape the net of Coomaraswamy's theorizing.

His notion of form likewise tends to leave out of account the dense recalcitrance of nature. The emphasis on the archctypal image, the immaterial form, the intelligible pattern, which is imposed on the appropriate material substance, while giving the proper importance to the intellectual operation in art tends to offend against its organic wholeness: Coomaraswamy in this respect is pre-Coleridgean, and perhaps I can best define my meaning by quoting this passage from Coleridge:

> The form is mechanic, when on any given material we impress a predetermined form, not necessarily arising out of the properties of the material,...the organic form on the other hand, is innate, it shapes, as it develops, itself from within, and the fullness of its development is one and the same with the perfection of its outward form. Such as the life is, such is the form.

Coomaraswamy's frequent statements on the relation between idea and artifact require to be completed by a sense of the active interplay between idea and form suggested by the following from Paul Valery:

> But poetry insists upon or suggests a quite different "universe": a universe of reciprocal relations, analogous to the universe of sounds in which musical thought has its birth and movement. In this poetic universe resonance gets the better of causality, and the "form" far from vanishing into its effect, is ordered back by it. The idea reclaims its voice.

A theory of form should have an integral relation to beauty and ugliness alike: a painting by Cezanne, *Wuthering Heights* or *Little Dorrit* should all have a place in the order to the good and the beautiful. I am not saying that Coomaraswamy would dispute this but he does seem to stick too closely to Platonic, Aristotelean and Indian formulations. Coomaraswamy seems to go along with the view that since the eternal and intelligible models are supersensual and invisible, they must be known in contemplation; contemplation is certainly necessary for the production of a work of art but one cannot discount observation which is surely a prerequisite in this world where knowledge is perdurably related to sensory perception.

Coomaraswamy's theory of intention, which should be a *locus classicus* on this subject, admirably exposes some of the errors in statements made by Messrs. Monroe C. Beardsley and W. K. Wimsatt, but one is not altogether comfortable with Coomaraswamy's version nor the stage at which he leaves the problem. When he says, for example, that the artist must know what he wants to do before he sets about his task, he seems to simplify the quotation from St. Thomas Aquinas on which he sets much store: "The artist works through the word conceived in his mind, and through the love of his will regarding some object." It would be quite in order to say that an artist knows fully what he wants to do only when he has completed his task. The essential point about "the word conceived in the mind," the interior or mental word, is that it is mental, and not realized in words. A disparity may be felt by the artist between intention and product without his being able to correct it. The end (*telos*) may draw the artist to create before it is intelligible, and in some cases (as in mystical poetry) without its ever becoming intelligible at all. Coomaraswamy does not sufficiently realize that the work of art defines itself in the process of creation, the poem in the process of writing. He does often stress that poetic language is not merely indicative but also expressive but he does not investigate the seminal difference between the poetic and other uses of language. While in referential prose the medium is relatively neutral for the communication of thought, in poetry the medium is alive, there is interaction and reciprocity between thought and the word. It often happens that the word gets hold of the inchoate or incipient thought, sometimes altering it beyond all recognition. This has an important bearing on the critical procedure of judging a work of art according to its intention. It is worthwhile delaying somewhat with this subject as what is involved is not merely a critical method but the nature of artistic creativity.

In criticizing a poem one has a right to object if one notes an internal discrepancy between what the poet wants to do and what he is really doing; but since the discovery of what he wants to do has also to be made from the poem itself (we have no other evidence), the judgment is not as between intention versus result, concept versus product, forma versus figura, or art in the artist versus artifact, but as between art in the artist as revealed in the work of art versus the work of art itself. One does not judge according to intention unless by "intention" one means

which will best mirror the experience that belongs to my inner world. I have to make the reader read the words as I want him to read them. I have to see that the words evoke in him the same inner world of being, the same silence. Words then are not merely signs of ideas, nor even tools of interaction between human beings; in the context of poetic language a word becomes a gateway or a barrier towards the communication of silence. The word may well be a barrier: if he who reads my poem is unaccustomed to the same silence he will not understand me; or if he is sensitive to words but still misinterprets me, I have failed as a poet; I do not understand the way words work.

Let us consider the comparable situation of two lovers: when they speak to each other, it is important they understand each other--they may, following the advice of Pascal, *En amour un silence vaut mieux qu'un langage* prefer the language of silence; but if through weakness of spirit or the immaturity of their love they decide to use words, they should attempt through words to proceed to each other's silence. The problem of language is thus seen as the problem of otherness: another person living in another world of silence attempts to join me in my own. To understand the word, one must understand the wordless; to comprehend language, one must reach what is not language. Both the lover and the poet have to scatter the silence.

A complete theory of verbal meaning, even if one neglects poetry and the exchanges of lovers, has to pay heed to the separation and the congress between the interior word and the sound uttered by the voice.

Of course, the inadequacies in Coomaraswamy's theory of form, of intention in art, of poetic meaning, can be found even more conspicuously in Plato or Aristotle or some Indian philosophers; and it may seem niggardly on my part to have spent so much time on them when there is so much to be learnt from the wealth and distinctiveness of his contribution to art, philosophy and religion, so much to be admired in his freshly creative reinterpretations of the *philosophia perennis* and his courageous stand against the mainstream of modern thought. For preeminently it has been Coomaraswamy who has been the spokesman of the traditional philosophy in the twentieth century. But it is just as well to subject him to criticism if we are to prevent his becoming a dead cult, a fossil like many of the ancients before him; this is surely one of the ways of keeping his abundant insights in current circulation. Coomaraswamy himself would have agreed with some of the formulations in this essay; one of his major disadvantages was that he was isolated and neglected in the intellectual discourse and conversation of his time. In his essay *The Nature of Buddhist Art* he uses a form of words to describe his theory of inspiration which, if separated from its context of divine revelation would fit very well with the theory of form I have tried to adumbrate in earlier paragraphs.

> All that can be thought of as prior to formulation is without form and not in any likeness; the meaning and its vehicle can only be thought of as having been co-created. And this implies that whatever validity attaches to the meaning attaches also to the symbols in which it is expressed; if the latter are in any way less inevitable than the former, the intended meaning will not have been conveyed, but betrayed.

This is as good a statement taken by itself as any one can find of the organic theory of form, whether for sacred or profane art.

I would like to take leave of Coomaraswamy by saluting him for an aspect of his genius which is often obscured by his phenomenal erudition and the density of this thought: I refer to his prose style. The possession of a good style is one of the clearest signs of largeness of mind. In one of his early essays "The Status of Indian Women" he speaks of the love of man and woman as a "momentary experience of timeless freedom" and prefers arranged marriages on the ground that "where there is no expectation, there can be no disappointment." This wry comment does not in any way damage his belief that in an arranged marriage there is a greater likelihood that love may find a congenial setting in cultural and spiritual continuity and consonance. His polemical style is often enlivened by sophistication and wit: his philosophical exposition gains its cogency and lucidity by an impressive concordance of thought and word. However intricate the reasoning, his meaning is always clear to the reader who is willing to make the effort. His late treatise *Hinduism and Buddhism* is a masterpiece of succinct, trenchant, expository philosophical prose worthy of comparison with the best work of the great philosophers: it is also in my view the best short account of these two great world religions that has so far been written. Even if in the years to come his scholarship is superseded and his particular judgements seem more and more controversial, Coomaraswamy's style as a distinguished instrument of a personally charged, mental ratiocination will remain an example of unageing intellect.

Besides, Ananda Coomaraswamy is an example, par excellence, of the East-West encounter at its most fundamental level; even if the intellectual ambition seems too awesome, too partial, even somewhat unhistorical at this stage in the history of the world, it draws our attention to the most significant congruity in the tradition of human, universal wholeness, and therefore merits our respect.

CHAPTER XIIB

COOMARASWAMY AND THE MODERN POPULAR ARTS

1. STYLE AND STATUS

The diamond and pearl of Coomaraswamy's thought and style--diamond for sharp discrimination, pearl for delicacy of tone--are reminders of pre-World War I literary managers. The supple articulation of judgement and taste is based, however, on a notion of fixed and pre-ordained values that has passed from the scene almost as definitely as the Edwardian greytopper. Very few of the better-educated Western readers under the age of fifty, except for specialists, have heard much more than the name of this remarkable scholar and high-minded connoisseur of the arts. He who was acclaimed to be one of the foremost interpreters of India to the West, has now for most Western readers the aura of the esoteric.

The proof of this is that so little notice was taken in the United States of his 1977 centenary. Despite the small but steady sales of some of his titles in the last twenty years the periodicals made little mention of his memorial year. This was true not only of general-interest periodicals but also of periodicals specializing in intellectual affairs, the arts, Oriental studies, and religion. So much for the man who organized and annotated the great Oriental collection in the Boston Fine Arts Museum. So much for a man whose learning was so cosmopolitan and engaging. The oversight seems so provincial that it challenges us to reflect on its possible conditions and causes.

Was the neglect occasioned in part by massive shifts in intellectual fashion in the United States? For a quarter of a century now the United States has been saturated with a new wave of interest in the Oriental-- and much of this has been on a level of cheap and vulgar popularization that would have caused Coomaraswamy to wince. His focus was classical in its tone; the more recent focus is romantic and even self-indulgent.

Was the neglect occasioned in part by the nature of his specialty-- the arts of India, Sri Lanka, Indonesia, Southeast Asia? As the United States was withdrawing its interest from Vietnam, it was increasing its affirmative political and cultural relations with China. The most dramatic art event of the mid-1970's was the series of exhibitions in the United States of superb funerary art from China. In the meantime, relations with India had moved into a so-so stage. All this may have shifted attention away from Coomaraswamy. American interest in alien cultures is all too human in its slavery to fads and to shifts in foreign policy.

Was it occasioned in part by Coomaraswamy's concentration on a certain long-past historical period? His greatest work elucidates the plastic and visual art of Southeast Asia's "Middle Ages". Society was then organized around sacred kingship; everyday life was organized around the tilling of the soil and the production of artifacts and artistic objects crafted by hand and by hand-powered tools. But the love-affair of the United States with the medieval was going strong one hundred years ago -- as evidenced for example in its Victorian architectural fashions. Today it is limited to the academic few and to the readers who enjoy getting stoned on Tolkien's patented Hobbit-mixture of mead and moonshine.

Had it to do with his manner of writing? Most of his pages are pellucid; but his works are often encrusted with notes that testify to his deep scholarship. They overwhelm the reader with his erudition. Moreover, Coomaraswamy never wrote any "popularizations" of his scholarly work -- not even "high popularizations". He talks most of the time to a very small group of scholarly peers who work in disciplines related to his own. Others can easily feel like outsiders.

By contrast, the art historian Bernard Berenson, a Carnegie of the art industry, generally laid down the law about his subjects without much reference to the laborious sifting by which he had arrived at his re-cast conclusions about the authenticity and the merit of the works he was discussing.

Had it to do with Coomaraswamy's successful effort to avoid becoming the object of a cult of personality? He discouraged most attempts to elevate him as an "individual" and a "genius" and even discouraged potential biographers. His refusal to engage in the public relations of culture, which has become a major modern industry, may have had its effects for the time being on his fame.

Finally, had it to do with the nature of his following? Did he do his work so well that he hardly left any room for a young successor to distinguish himself in the same field? True, he was made the focus, in spite of himself, of a certain cultism by a band of his admirers, especially in India and Britain; and this may influence his standing. Some of these followers, such as Marco Pallis, for example, seem to be engaged in a total devotion to his works and attitudes and sometimes appear to be rather slavish in their insistence that it is they who are the true expounders of his canon. This may have had the effect of defining him as a sort of antiquarian and fogey and may encourage younger readers to believe that they will find nothing of relevance to the aesthetic problems of modern times in his work--nothing relevant, that is, except his spurning of modern art.

Isn't it possible that these latter views have the effect of reducing his true stature? Why are we compelled to pin him down so much to his practical criticisms, his taste, his methodology? His methods are, in fact, with respect to certain questions of iconography and symbolism, of pre-industrial social organization, of the sacred and the profane, and of language, plainly dated. They could not help but be. He had no choice but to work from the best thinking on these topics that happened to be available to him at the time. It is not only that fashions of thought have changed since then but that some of his approaches to symbolic and linguistic matters have been undercut by more recent theorizing.

2. TASTE AND PRINCIPLES

This essay takes the position that we should at least try to bypass these more obsolete factors in Coomaraswamy in order to learn from his more basic intuitions, to try to spell out his principles rather than his taste, to follow up his orientations rather than his pronouncements. The materials that provide the test-case for this approach are the artifacts of the modern popular culture that Coomaraswamy generally averted his gaze from. And the test questions are these:

Isn't it possible that his spurning of modern popular artifacts was based in part on his having acquired from historians of his time an inadequate theory of the development of mass-production out of the previous craft stage of industry?

What permeates and dictates the contemporary image of technology is not the image of technology as it has existed throughout human history but specifically the technology of the Industrial Revolution, based on science. But the root meaning of the word technology remains as "art and craft"--from its first Greek denotations. This definition was gradually specialized to cover discussion of the applied arts only, then expanded to cover a huge arena of ideas and processes, in addition to tools and materials, finally broadening out to constitute every means or activity by which man seeks to change or manipulate his environment, a definition which, of course, continues to include the arts. Ancient Egypt, China, and the Middle East mastered the resources of their territories through traditions of technological theory and skill. The medieval period in Europe saw a blossoming of technological invention more creative than in any previous period.

Isn't it possible that his perception of the modern culture as completely secular and secularizing is, by our late twentieth-century views, over-stated?

Philosopher Susan Sontag, in her essay, "On Style," has pointed to the futility of attempting to disassociate the "sacred" from the "profane" in modern life. This follows upon a whole generation of work by anthropologists such as Malinowski, historians of religion such as Eliade, cultural anthropologists such as Clifford Geertz, as a result of which late nineteenth-century ideas about the sharp cleavage between the sacred and the profane have been altered beyond recognition. Moreover, a factor of great importance, as Coomaraswamy himself has suggested, is the sharing of larger mythic forms by human consciousness in general. These even in their most avowedly secular forms, can have, as Jung has shown, the most intense religious meaning.

Isn't it possible that his attack on the cultural dislocation of art objects by the museum and the cult of individualistic expression is an attack that actually encourages us to withdraw some of our attention from such cultism -- and to pay more attention to our modern popular arts?

Finally, isn't it possible that, if he is correct in arguing that the "intention" of the artist and the "uses" of the art work are suffering neglect, it might be appropriate to look at those works, the works of popular culture, in which the "intentions" and the "uses" are always and everywhere in discussion?

These concepts are the bread and butter of everyday conversation and argument about movies, advertising art, the detective novel, science fiction.

The conversation, of course, occurs sometimes at a high level and sometimes at a low. The judgements made of "intentions" or "uses" sometimes identify them as cheap, banal, and base and sometimes identify them as praiseworthy, creative, and life-enhancing. But the discussion is continuing, is crucial, and is worthy of closer attention and discrimination.

I suggest, therefore, that if I can brush aside some of the historically accidental factors in Coomaraswamy's approach to craft and art, I may find that some of his intuitions and principles provide remarkably helpful initial guides in exploring aspects of modern life that he spurned in its details.

3. THE RELEVANCE OF COOMARASWAMY

I have already suggested, but would like to further underline, the idea that there is a continuing crisis in the appreciation and criticism of the modern popular arts. A responsive and responsible vocabulary of criticism is already being developed for jazz and movies. In other areas, the work has only just begun. In the United States, for example, criticism of TV has so far failed to attain integrity and richness of application. In actual social fact, viewers in the United States get one of their few chances to see how banal and cheap the homegrown TV drama is only when an import shows up from Great Britain.

In the course of his writings on a wide spectrum of subjects in the field, Coomaraswamy's attention dwelt on three quadrants of a four-part pattern: ancient art of the people (via craftsmen); ancient elite art for religious purposes by specialized craftsmen and/or scholars and priests; and modern museum and gallery art (the elite arts of post-Renaissance individualism). The component naturally following these, the modern popular arts, is curiously absent from his repertoire of history and criticism, except by implication. These exist in the profane world of modernity which had, for Coomaraswamy, renounced both the original craft and religious impulses of art as a fundamental human expression, and were beyond redemption or hope. Thus, Coomaraswamy would appear at first to have no connection as a critic with the mass-mediated popular culture of the advanced technological and secular culture of the United States. Yet the effort to explore this "non-connection" may prove rewarding.

Some of the critical concerns of Coomaraswamy have direct parallels, if not immediate application, in the field of popular culture study. They include: artistic intention, the relations between the artist and his audience, the dislocation of the art object in the elite world of gallery and museum; the dislocation of the artist in his removal from the world formerly shared by both himself and his audience; the problems posed by the conversion of traditional craftmanship into more advanced forms of technology; the accessibility of the art form to commonly-shared popular understandings and concepts; and the network of communications between artist, art form, and audience.

Coomaraswamy quite appropriately conceived these themes in terms of discontinuities between the traditional (studies bound in time and space) and the modern arts, largely, the discontinuities produced by the branching off of traditional arts into two divergent paths: 1) that of the mass-produced object of utilitarian nature; and 2) the elite arts of the avant-garde schools of painting, the plastic arts, and of literature. By taking this path, Coomaraswamy failed to take into consideration a third pathway of artistic development: that of the modern popular arts, which themselves derive in part from the traditional arts, and come forward as an extension (with certain modifications) of the styles he writes about as related religious and mythic concerns. If Coomaraswamy had not been alienated from these as a result of their strange appearance in the guise of modern, mass-produced, and secular symbols, he might have been able to extend his commentaries further and with more efficacy to comment on modern times and modern culture.

The most pertinent notion of Coomaraswamy's relevance can be given in his critical attitude towards one of the conventions of modern elitist art--the "cult of the museum." This cult, he pointed out, separates art from life and puts it on a specially-designed pedestal--which actually acts as a "prison" of culture--the museum (and by implication, the gallery). Art is quickly defined out of the mainstream of culture to become specialized and rarified, untouchable, inaccessible. The alienation of cultural artifacts from their cultural milieu was for him a preposterous and criminal act.

On the other hand, and following Coomaraswamy's lead, contemporary works of popular art in the cinema, the advertising arts, formula fiction (with its classic rudiments of character type and plot), popular music of all kinds, bred from grass-roots inventiveness joined with technology, the comic strip--all these forms can be considered within the context of works of art arising out of and continuing more traditional pre-industrial popular arts.

John Kouwenhoven, in *The Arts in Modern American Civilization,* says that the major and most worthy art tradition within what Charles Beard called the "technological civilization" of America is the modern vernacular tradition rooted in science and technology. As the sole major world power born into industrial technology, America has offered a new strain of arts, "revealing more clearly on the whole than the arts of any other people" the nature and meaning of modern civilization as a whole.

It would not, I think, be flying in the face of Coomaraswamy's deeper views if one were to look to see better modern mass arts, which in some cases might share aspirations and even merits with the pre-industrial popular arts whose best products he was prone to admire. For one thing, it is becoming more and more recognized that many of these modern products are being produced by teams which resembled medieval guilds rather than the atelier and the studio. Again, many of the artifacts had the disingenuous virtue of avoiding the claim that audiences had to reach up to them through an intervening hierarchy of curators and critics. And they avoided the claim that they deserve attention simply because they are the self-expressions of geniuses above the crowd. Further, when one does venture comments and judgements upon them, one did not find them fortified against dispraise, as the fine arts were, ancient or modern, that had an intellectual, cultural and financial vested interest in them. Along such lines, one might conduct a critical excursion into the modern popular culture that Coomaraswamy felt he had no time to bother with, on the idea that some of his principles, if not his applied taste, might be the ground of finding virture in some of them.

Since Coomaraswamy's principles were so beautifully the basis of his taste, this might seem a presumptuous thing to do--as if, had Coomaraswamy been pressed with a question about Chaplin's creativity as a mime, in connection with Coomaraswamy's genius in analyzing the body movements or mudra of Indian dance, he would have been compelled to see some great things in the film comedian. Yet such a gratuitous extension of his thought is not, surely, unfair to him. His concentration almost entirely on the Medieval art of the East and West was inspired not only by his deep admiration for it and the society that produced it, but also his superbly modest strategy of concentrating his one lifetime on what he knew and loved best. My conjecture is that if he had had the time and interest to acquaint himself with some modern "science fiction" he might well have agreed that some of it, as some of its proponents say, has an inventive and even mythical imagination that allies it with great Indian tales in the Ocean of Story. And that some of the animal figures of popular draughtmanship, story, and film in America not only have some of their ancestry in the creatures of the *Panchatrantra*, as well as Aesop, but also, in some instances, are evoked with a skill that would have pleased the story-tellers and limners of old.

In any event, Coomaraswamy's emphasis on the questions of "uses" of art is strikingly in harmony with the direction being taken by the more sophisticated students of modern popular culture; and his emphasis on "intention" is a reminder to such students that this concept cannot be ignored in the practice of criticism. Disregard of this point has led to certain claustral and thinned-out effects in modern literary criticism, which sometimes seems these days to be reduced to indulgence in a cryptic game. If the same impulse were to dominate criticism of the popular arts, the chance of developing a useful critical vocabulary would be in peril. With Coomaraswamy's guidance, that danger can perhaps be averted.

CHAPTER XIII

RABINDRANATH TAGORE: THE POETRY IN ENGLISH

After writing this essay I was able to read the Penguin New Classics *Rabindranath Tagore*: *Selected Poems,* edited and translated by William Radice. It is more an informative and scholarly account rather than a fresh critical assessment. Unfortunately, except for drawing my attention to some orthodox poems, skillfully translated by Mr. Radice, such as *Earth* and *In the Eyes of a Peacock,* it does little to modify my own evaluation of Tagore's poetry in English. One must not neglect Tagore's contribution as a writer of impassioned English prose: since this is not one of my concerns in this essay, a single quotation from the second lecture in *Nationalism* must suffice:

> I know my voice is too feeble to raise itself above the uproar of this bustling time, and it is easy for any street urchin to fling against me the epithet of "unpractical". It will stick to my coattail, never to be washed away, effectively excluding me from the consideration of all respectable persons. I know what a risk one runs from the vigorously athletic crowds in being styled an idealist in these days, when thrones have lost their dignity and prophets have become an anachronism, when the sound that drowns all voices is the noise of the market-place. Yet when, one day, standing on the outskirts of Yokohama town, bristling with its display of modern miscellanies, I watched the sunset in your southern sea, and saw its peace and majesty among your pine-clad hills, -- with the great Fujiyama growing faint against the golden

horizon, like a god overcome with his own radiance, -- the music of
eternity welled up through the evening silence, and I felt that the sky
and the earth and the lyrics of the dawn and the dayfall are with the
poets and idealists, and not with the marketmen robustly contemptuous
of all sentiment, -- that, after the forgetfulness of his own divinity, man
will remember again that heaven is always in touch with his world,
which can never be abandoned for good to the hounding wolves of the
modern era, scenting human blood and howling to the skies.

It is impossible to ignore Tagore in a discussion of Indian poetry in
English, both as precursor and influence. He also wrote directly in
English and was indeed a deliberate true mediator between East and
West. Just on the basis of his poems in English he received for a time
wide acclaim in England and Europe: on this slim evidence he was
even awarded the Nobel Prize. But his real setting was Bengal, his true
voice was Bengali: his main thrust is to assay universal themes and
preoccupations rather than mirror the East-West axis. Unlike the highly
over-rated Sri Aurobindo or the minor Sarojini Naidu, his poems have a
genuine if small merit in English. His relevance to my subject is that he
did try to present his Indianness to the Western reader and to adapt
Western ideas, mainly social and political, to the Indian climate of
opinion. As for religious cross-fertilization, his own Hinduism,
accommodating as it was of the heterodox, was wide enough to
encompass his interests.

Notable among his enthusiastic supporters were W. B. Yeats and
Ezra Pound, and it was the former's high praise for Tagore's
translations of his own work into English in the collection entitled
Gitanjali which led to Tagore's winning the Nobel Prize. However,
these enthusiasms were short-lived. Yeats, who described *Gitanjali* as
follows in his Preface

I have carried the manuscript of these translations about with me for
days, reading it in railway trains, or on the top of omnibuses and in
restaurants, and I have often had to close it lest some stranger would
see how much it moved me. These lyrics, which are in the original, my
Indians tell me, full of subtlety of rhythm, of untranslatable delicacies
of color, of metrical invention--display in their thought a world I have
dreamed of all my life long. The work of a supreme culture, they yet
appear as much the growth of the common soil as the grass and the
rushes. A tradition, where poetry and religion are the same thing, has

passed through the centuries, gathering from learned and unlearned
metaphor and emotion, and carried back to the multitude the thought of
the scholar and the noble

was in later years to modify his encomium and even to say that
Tagore did not know English. The context is worth quoting, as
illustrating one of the problems of translated literature and of the cross-
cultural reception of alien art. In a letter to William Rothenstein, Yeats
says:

> Damn Tagore. We got out three good books, Sturge Moore and I,
> and then, because he thought it more important to see and know
> English than to be a great poet, he brought out sentimental rubbish and
> wrecked his reputation. Tagore does not know English, no Indian
> knows English. Nobody can write with music and style in a language
> not learned in childhood and ever since the language of his thought. I
> shall return to the question of Tagore but not yet--I shall return to it
> because he has published, in recent years , and in English, prose books
> of great beauty, and these books have been ignored because of the
> eclipse of his reputation as a poet.

Rabindranath Tagore has the reputation of being India's greatest
poet of this century. But his fame is of an entirely different kind from
the literary reputations of such poets as, say, Paul Valery in France or
T. S. Eliot in England. I have heard it said that Tagore's poems are
recited and his songs are sung by the common man in Bengal and even
in the rest of India: they are said to have passed into the life of the
people in the way Dante's poetry is said to have become a part of the
mind of the Italy of his time. Even if this were true, it is not in itself a
matter for satisfaction. Whether or not what is best in poetry has ever
vitally affected the masses in any country at any time is an uncertain
matter: at any rate no one in America or Europe today expects (or
should expect) that a poet would exert this kind of influence over his
people: poetry has become a cult of highbrowland and is nourished in
art societies and literary discussion groups while what passes into the
lives of the people are the daily papers, Hollywood films, soap opera,
the comic strip and other similar purveyors of triviality. But even
among literary circles in the West, Tagore does not enjoy a vogue that
is in any way comparable to the esteem in which he is held in India.
The adulation of Tagore's work on its first introduction to the West was
largely due to the literati and persons of religious persuasion who were

interested in the Orient and saw him as an ally in the fight against nineteenth--century scientific rationalism and modern materialism of every description.

The swing of the pendulum in Ezra Pound's response to Tagore is even more interesting as an example of the cultural dichotomy between East and West; it deserves to be a *locus classicus* in the consideration of the literature of cross-cultural contact and in the acceptance by one culture of the imaginative work of an alien civilization. In a letter to Harriet Monroe, dated September 24, 1912, Pound says:

> Also I'll try to get some of the poems of the very great Bengali poet, Rabindranath Tagore. They are going to be the sensation of the winter ... W.B. Y -- is doing the introduction to them. They are translated by the author into very beautiful English prose, with mastery of cadence.

Hardly seven months later on April 22, 1913, Pound writes to the same person as follows:

> God knows I didn't ask for the job of correcting Tagore. He asked me to. Also it will be very difficult for his defenders in London if he takes to printing anything except his best work. As a religious teacher he is superfluous. We've got Lao Tse. And his (Tagore's) philosophy hasn't much in it for a man who has 'felt the pangs' or been pestered with Western civilization. I don't mean quite that, but he isn't either Villon or Leopardi, and the modern demands just a dash of their insight. So long as he sticks to poetry he can be defended on stylistic grounds against those who disagree with his content. And there's no use his repeating the Vedas and other stuff that has been translated. In his original Bengali he has the novelty of rime and rhythm and of expression, but in a prose translation it is just more theosophy. Of course if he wants to set a lower level than that which I am trying to set in my translations from Kabir, I can't help it. It's his own affair.

Tagore's poetry, however, was not the sole cause of his tremendous influence in India; his interests were varied and his talents versatile. Poet, playwright, novelist, critic, philosopher, political and social theorist, composer, painter, educationist and patriot, indeed a many-sided personality and capable of wide and far-reaching influence. It is beyond my powers to deal with the varied aspects of his life and work: but I do not think I limit my interest unfairly if I confine myself to his poems. Outside his own country Tagore is known primarily as a poet and perhaps therein will lie his enduring fame: and in any event poetry is still among the completest acts of human utterance and the supreme modes of knowledge available to man. But there is a more serious limitation in my equipment: my knowledge of Tagore is restricted to the poems available in translation, even when the translations are by the poet himself. One need not expatiate here on the insurmountable distance between an original poem and a translation, but in this instance the difference is enhanced because many of his poems are also songs: the music is wedded to the language in such a way that the melody is not externally fastened on to the words nor the words chosen to fit a preconceived tone. Words and music are indissoluble: they stem from the same creative source and, in an almost simultaneous creative act, form one body. Very often in his translated poetry one comes across suggestions of an experience more resonant and profound than that conveyed by the words. The medium appears to be at fault: even in his good translations, an otherwise adequate rendering is disfigured by an occasional inapposite image or spurious phrase. These blemishes often resemble the defects and inadequacies to be found in the modes of poetic expression in English with which Tagore was most familiar-- Shelley, the 'romantic' writers of the Victorian age and the aesthetes of the end of the century. It must also be remembered that only a fraction of Tagore's poetry is available in translation. When we remember that his published verse and plays amount to 150,000 lines (Milton's English verse and few poets today can equal him in bulk, is less than 18,000 lines), we will realize how imperfect an estimate of Tagore we can form if we have read him only in translation. But the translations of Tagore are his own and one should consider them not as translations from one language to another but as re-creations, as English poems in their own right: and I think it can be claimed for Tagore that he will survive as a minor poet in English, that some of his poems are of permanent if minor interest as poems written in the English language.

Even among those who read Tagore only in English it will be observed that the best known poems are his weaker and more sentimental work while the poems I intend to discuss are not widely known or appreciated. Such poems as 'Languor is upon your heart and the Slumber is still on your eyes' from *Gitanjali* or 'You are the evening cloud floating in the sky of my dreams' from *The Gardener* are typical of the mushiness of feeling and expression in which he often indulged himself and of the "endless mist of vague sweetness" in which it was so easy for him to squander his poetic gift. Apart from these sentimental pieces so popular among Tagore's admirers, another set of poems often quoted and anthologized are those which abound in abstract moralizing--what emerges from them is cerebral rumination, conveyed in prosy rhythms and unliving language. Even the well known

> Where the mind is without fear and the head is held high;
> Where knowledge is free;
> Where the world has not been broken up into fragments by narrow domestic walls;
> Where words come out from the depth of truth;
> Where tireless striving stretches its arms towards perfection;
> Where the clear stream of reason has not lost its way into the dreary desert sand of dead habit;
> Where the mind is led forward by thee into ever-widening thought and action
> --Into that heaven of freedom, my Father, let my country awake.

is mere generalized rhetoric and does not become poetry. Tagore is essentially a religious poet and at his best a personally apprehended truth finds satisfying expression in felicitous language and subtlety of cadence. To appreciate fully his religious verse one must bring to the poetry a mind unhampered by prejudices regarding his subject matter: God was for the poet not only the One, Absolute, Indivisible, Reality: He was also a Person with whom the poet had a direct friendship, human and other. The Soul and God are often seen as I and Thou.

> The great pageant of thee and me has overspread the sky. With the tune of thee and me all the air is vibrant, and all ages pass with the hiding and seeking of thee and me.

The paradox of God seen as immanent in Nature and at the same time utterly transcendent in Himself is the subject of "Thou art the sky and thou art the nest as well" from *Gitanjali*: the feeling is defined in terms of the two images of the nest and the sky. In spite of the somewhat conventional diction the poetic idea seems legitimate or at least nearly so.

> But there, where spreads the infinite sky for the soul to take her flight in, reigns the stainless white radiance. There is no day nor night, nor form nor color, and never, never a word.

Tagore's poetry has been blamed for its lack of thought; as a censure of his successful poems this is unjust while as an explanation of his failures it is misleading. His unsuccessful poems fail not because they are wanting in thought but since the images and phrases, unoriginal and often prolix, give the impression of having been assembled rather slickly: it is merely that they do not issue from the complete intelligence which is necessary for successful poetic creation.

But even Tagore's better work has I think suffered due to some prevailing expectations whereby we tend to associate 'thinking' in verse with intellectual complications of idea and metaphor, with learned references to current thought; the good poet, we believe, should in his poetry display an ability to handle ideas or at least disclose a sophistication in the ideas current in his time. This is linked with the wider demand we make from the poet that he should in some sense reflect the age in which he lives. There are few heresies more harmful than this last; even the influential criticism of T. S. Eliot has not completely escaped it despite the reservations he introduces when discussing this question. Obviously the poet is never a mere recording artist of the sense of his age: if the age is base and corrupt, if the climate of ideas in a particular generation be shoddy, do we ask of the poet that his work mirror this corruption and triviality? Poetry no doubt will be related to the age in which it is written; the work of some poets will be more redolent of their times than that of others: but the particular historical period has, or should have, no determining power.

Merely to have expressed the consciousness of his age and presented the image of man as he appeared in a particular time is not what is finally valuable in the work of a poet; if what is of significance is the intrinsic merit of the work, this consists not so much in what the poet derived from his age as in what, of himself, he gave to it. It is to the poet's credit that he knows the thought of his age, but thinking in poetry is not the business of making poetry out of ideas--neither the inclusion in one's verse of ideas, current or otherwise, nor even their use as motive or occasion for the expression of related feelings. Poetry is the product of mind functioning at its fullest potential, and if the thought can be siphoned off as a separate element, it is invariably a sign that it has not been fully integrated into the poetic rendition. It is in this sense that we say, to adapt a remark by Middleton Murry, that six great lines of Shakespeare are as much a flight of the mind as the best science or philosophy, and more. Poetry for Tagore is the fruit of a contemplative art, however rooted in the sensuous world it may be.

The best of Tagore's religious poems show the presence of thought, the kind of thinking is an innate and inseparable aspect of a more total poetic experience, often the product of a meditative cast of mind. In some of his religious poems the feeling is not adequately described by the words "meditative" or "devotional"; the situation that is unfolded is more directly and dramatically personal. In "Where dost thou stand behind them all, my lover, hiding thyself in the shadows?" the poet addresses God in the accents of a lover speaking to his beloved, complaining of the loved one who chooses to hide himself.

Where dost thou stand behind them all, my lover, hiding thyself in the shadows? They push thee and pass thee by on the dusty road, taking thee for naught. I wait here weary hours spreading my offerings for thee, while passers-by come and take my flowers, one by one, and my basket is nearly empty.

The morning time is past, and the noon. In the shade of evening my eyes are drowsy with sleep. Men going home glance at me and smile and fill me with shame. I sit like a beggar maid, drawing my skirt over my face, and when they ask me what it is I want, I drop my eyes and answer them not.

Oh, how, indeed, could I tell them that for thee I wait, and that thou hast promised to come? How could I utter for shame that I keep for my dowry this poverty? Ah, I hug this pride in the secret of my heart.

I sit on the grass and gaze upon the sky and dream of the sudden splendour of thy coming--all the lights ablaze, golden pinions flying over thy car, and they at the roadside standing agape, when they see thee come down from thy seat to raise me from the dust, and set at thy side this ragged beggar girl a-tremble with shame and pride, like a creeper in a summer breeze.

But time glides on and still no sound of the wheels of thy chariot. Many a procession passes by with noise and shouts and glamour of glory. Is it only thou who wouldst stand in the shadow silent and behind them all? And only I who would wait and weep and wear out my heart in vain longing?

Tagore's religion was not an asceticism that was in any way anti-human; growth in the love of God did not mean a spurning of human joys and a forsaking of the world. His path did not resemble the austere journey of those who in order to look on God feel obliged to turn aside from the human world and shut their eyes on the visible beauty of His creation. For Tagore, religion gave man a sense of supernatural purpose and transfigured the world, bestowing on it a supernal dignity.

In the series of poems in *Gitanjali* where he speaks of the end of his life, the poet is ready for his death and welcomes it but the world he leaves is not presented as a vale of tears from which he is only too glad to depart. The quotations below are not among his best lines, but they are suitable illustration:

A summons has come and I am ready for my journey.
Even so, in death the same unknown will appear as ever known to me.
And because I love this life, I know I shall love death as well.
When I go from hence let this be my parting word, that what I have seen is unsurpassable.

Tagore has written many poems of nature but it is not natural description for its own sake that primarily interests him. The blade of grass quivering with life, the splash of fish in the water, the chatter of the sparrows, the buffalo lazing in the cool mud, the waterfall leaping over the boulders, the dense forest, the rain-swept villages by the riverside--the poet conveys through them his sense of the one life in all nature. Often, however, the images from nature help to define a different mood as in the following where the poet communicates his sense of the weary loneliness that comes to a man, abandoned and alone at the end of his life:

I spent my day on the scorching hot dust of the road.
Now in the cool of the evening, I knock at the door of the inn. It is deserted and in ruins.
A grim ashath tree spreads its hungry clutching roots through the gaping fissures of the wall.
They spread their mats in the courtyard in the dim light of the early moon, and sat and talked of strange lands.
They woke refreshed in the morning when birds made them glad, and friendly flowers nodded their heads at them from the wayside.
But no lighted lamp awaited me when I came here.
The black smudges of smoke left by many a forgotten evening lamp stare, like blind eyes, from the wall.
Fireflies flit in the bush near the dried-up pond, and bamboo branches fling their shadows on the grass-grown path.
I am the guest of no one at the end of my day.
The long night is before me, and I am tired.

Some of Tagore's love poems are among his best work in English and they exhibit considerable variety of situation and treatment. In the

following poem from *The Gardener,* the relationship of two lovers
acquires a special quality because they belong to the same village:
their togetherness is enriched by local attachments held in common.
The composition is deft, and the poem shows a charming purity of
feeling. It is refreshing too, because so much love poetry is concerned
with oppositions within love almost as though no true love can exist
without them.

> The yellow bird sings in their tree and makes my heart dance with
> gladness.
> We both live in the same village, and that is our one piece of joy.
> Her pair of pet lambs come to graze in the shade of our garden trees.
> If they stray into our barley field, I take them up in my arms.
> The name of our village is Khanjana, and Anjana they call our river.
> My name is known to all the village, and her name is Ranjana.
> Only one field lies between us.
> Bees that have hived in our grove go seek honey in theirs.
> Flowers launched from their landing-stairs come floating by the
> stream, where we bathe.
> Baskets of dry kusm flowers come from their fields to our market
> The name of our village is Khanjana, and Anjana they call our river.
> My name is known to all the village and her name is Ranjana.
> The lane that winds to their house is fragrant in the spring with mango
> flowers.
> When their linseed is ripe for harvest the hemp is in bloom in our field.
> The stars that smile on their cottage send us the same twinkling look.
> The rain that floods their tank makes glad our *Kadam* forest.
> The name of our village is Khajana, and Anjana they call our river.
> My name is known to all the village, and her name is Ranjana.

"On the slope of a desolate river" from *Gitanjali* is more complex
both in sentiment and execution. The experience is dramatized; the
speaker, who appeals to the woman he loves that she return his love,
views with a poignant sense of waste the way she expends her
substance on other purposes.

> On the slope of the desolate river among tall grasses I asked her,
> "Maiden, where do you go, shading your lamp with your mantle? My
> house is all dark and lonesome--lend me your light!". She raised her
> dark eyes for a moment and looked at my face through the dusk. "I
> have come to the river," she said, "to float my lamp on the stream when

the daylight wanes in the west." I stood alone among tall grasses and watched the timid flame of her lamp uselessly drifting in the tide.

In the silence of gathering night I asked her, "Maiden, your lights are all lit--then where do you go with your lamp? My house is all dark and lonesome--lend me your light." She raised her dark eyes on my face and stood for a moment doubtful. "I have come," she said at last, "to dedicate my lamp to the sky." I stood and watched her light uselessly burning in the void.

In the moonless gloom of midnight I asked her, "Maiden, what is your quest, holding the lamp near your heart? My house is all dark and lonesome--lend me your light." She stopped for a minute and thought and gazed at my face in the dark. "I have brought my lamp" she said, "to join the carnival of lamps." I stood and watched her little lamp uselessly lost among lights.

"In the dusky path of a dream" is another of Tagore's memorable love poems; whether the phrase 'mine in a former life' is to be taken in a literal or figurative sense, the situation in the poem is clearly one of two lovers who had drifted apart and are now unable to come together. The feeling is restrained; the language is almost bare; there is careful choice of detail; the sense of privation is movingly evoked:

In the dusky path of a dream I went to seek the love who was mine in a
former life
Her house stood at the end of a desolate street.
In the evening breeze her pet peacock sat drowning on its perch,
and the pigeons were silent in their corner.
She set her lamp down by the portal and stood before me.
She raised her large eyes to my face and mutely asked, "Are you well,
my friend?"
I tried to answer, but our language had been lost and forgotten.
I thought and thought; our names would not come to my mind.
Tears shone in her eyes. She held up her right hand to touch me. I took
it and stood silent.
Our lamp had flickered in the evening breeze and died.

Tagore's religion did not make him gloss over the ills that attend human living: it did not induce in him a complacent view of suffering. It is untrue to say of him that his religion was a 'romantic' withdrawal from the world or that he peddled simple solutions for the disharmonies in human existence. His poems do not always express a sense of joyous certainty in an eternal life where all our questions are answered and doubts resolved. One of his poems from *The Fugitive* treats of a boy of seven who tries to come to terms with the fact of his mother's death; the immediate awareness of loss is not mitigated by the consolation of a hereafter; in the face of grief heaven appears remote and unreal.

> His father took him in his arms and the boy asked him, 'Where is mother?'
> 'In heaven', answered his father, pointing to the sky. At night the father groaned in slumber, weary with grief. The boy woke up from sleep, felt with his hands the emptiness in the bed, and stole out to the open terrace. The boy raised his eyes to the sky and long gazed in silence. His bewildered mind sent abroad into the night the question, "Where is heaven?"
> No answer came: and the stars seemed like the burning tears of that ignorant darkness.

The image of "burning tears" in the last line is a blemish: but if this is an example of the many poems of Tagore that are spoilt by occasional lapses in expression, it is also an illustration of the variety of attitudes and feelings that inform Tagore's art, a fact not appreciated by those who complain of the monotony and narrowness of his sensibility.

Tagore's reputation in Europe has suffered a considerable decline in recent years. During the second decade of this century, the years following the Nobel Prize award, Tagore's fame in European countries was widespread and his books sold extremely well. The reasons for the rise and fall of a poet's popularity with the general reader are not always easy to ascertain -- but it is worthy of notice that the poetry which W. B. Yeats esteemed so highly and to which he paid such a fine tribute in his introduction to *Gitanjali* and the poet whom Ezra Pound compared with Dante

> He has sung of all the three things which Dante thought "fitting to be sung of, in the noblest possible manner," to wit, love, war and holiness. I have nothing but pity for the reader who is unable to see that their piety is the poetic piety of Dante, and that it is very beautiful.

is now hardly read in England or in Europe. I am not qualified to assess Tagore's rank as a poet for I do not know his work in his own language, but one can see that his poems in English are extremely uneven in quality. Very often his poetry does not appear to be the product of an inner compulsion of mind; his rhythms, which Pound praised as the kind that come to a man who after years of word-arranging would shun cacophony almost unwittingly, often reveal an uniformity of cadence and are wanting in novelty and surprise. We have already noted his heavy dependence on the hackneyed idiom of Victorian romantic poetry. But it is an easy task, and one that calls for no discrimination in a critic, to dismiss a poet altogether by considering only his weaker verse: Tennyson or Arnold, Swinburne or Rossetti, Hardy or Browning--who among these poets will survive such treatment? Even Wordsworth wrote a large amount of poor verse, and Hardy is a great poet not because of the size of his output but on the strength of a few poems which constitute so distinguished an achievement as to rank with the finest in the language. It was almost a habit with nineteenth century poets to write in bulk and inevitably much of it is mere versifying. I am far from claiming for Rabindranath Tagore a status similar to that of the best English poets; but his English verse has to be judged in relation to the Romantic tradition with which it is unmistakably connected; and we should extend to it at least the discriminating charity with which we now view the poets of nineteenth-century England. Perhaps the decline of Tagore's reputation in England is a part of the general disfavor into which the romanticism of the last century has fallen but to succumb to literary fashions is to disclose a time-bound mentality in criticism. If we describe modern English poetry as 'unromantic' in contradistinction to nineteenth-century poetry, we merely simplify the main issues: for unless we limit the term to describe a particular set of literary habits, romanticism is a spiritual condition that cannot be isolated as a nineteenth-century disease. If a naive belief in human progress and a desire to withdraw into a comforting dreamworld are romantic, there is much that is irrational and exaggerated in the cult of the lost generation, the fetish of the uprooted or dispossessed individual that has defaced a considerable portion of modern literature: if we wish to absolve fully Joyce, Lawrence, Yeats, Eliot and Pound from the charge of romanticism, we merely narrow the meanings of words and refuse to see romanticism as the deep-seated disorder that it really is.

Much of the poetry of T. S. Eliot which is now widely and readily accepted will perhaps date as easily as most nineteenth--century verse since its popularity to my mind depends on certain superficial notions of poetic excellence current at the present time.

The early poetry of Eliot is more popular than the *Four Quartets* largely because the readers of Eliot have a greater sense of community with Prufrock and Sweeney in whom they recognize their own *accidie* and boredom: it is easier to experience the tedium of living than find one's way in the world of the *Quartets*. T. S. Eliot himself, particularly in his early poetry is not entirely free from responsibility for the attitude of his readers: one is not always sure how to respond to his characters because the satiric tone is sometimes wobbly and the judging of his characters is not made in relation to an unambiguous moral order.

One must not therefore attach a simple and unambiguous value to the reputation a poet has among the general reader. One of the reasons why Tagore is unacceptable to the modern reader is perhaps the sense of quiet that underlies his poetry and the mood of recollection that it so often reveals. Today we set a high premium on poetry that is taut with conflict or pitched on a violent key: and we look for these qualities in our normal human experiences. We have all been infected by the nervous turbulence that passes for love in the films we see; in our religion, too, we approve of a degree of spiritual bravado: we tend to prefer the poetry of Donne to that of Herbert.

Some of Tagore's countrymen claim even for his English verse a significance comparable to that of the best English poetry of our time: this of course is to exaggerate, and to make a totally unnecessary claim. Obviously the English poetry of Tagore does not rank, for example, with that of his admirer W. B. Yeats, who, at least to my mind, is the greatest English poet since Wordsworth. However partial one may be to Tagore, it is not easy to select more than a few of his poems for praise, and there too, one has to qualify one's admiration. I cannot find a single poem in his translated work that bears comparison with the major art of Herbert, Blake or Hopkins. Even when his poetry, having shed its usual mistiness, achieves a simple effectiveness of diction it is often a limp nudity of statement rather than an austere style issuing from an intense poetic discipline. But it would be unfair to dismiss his poetry, as one dismisses the bulk of Georgian verse, by describing his world as unreal, or equivocal or downright chicane: Tagore's translated poetry reveals distinctively Eastern modes of thought and feeling, and a genuine, if limited, personal sensibility. Whatever the serious defects of his expression in English one can recognize that his attitudes, sanctioned by a traditional culture, have a sanity that is not often found in modern European literature.

The poetry is an affirmation of *bhakti,* of the love of man and God: Tagore could look forward towards a time when all the antinomies in human life would be resolved in an enduring harmony, when all doubts

would vanish in silence as the Boatman, who in the following lines I
take to be an analogue of God himself, reaches the shore:

> The Boatman is out crossing the wild sea at night.
> The mast is aching because of its full sails filled with the violent wind.
> The waves dash their heads against the dark unseen, and the Boatman is
> out crossing the wild sea.
> The Boatman is out, I know not for what tryst, startling the night with
> the sudden white of his sails.
> What is the quest that makes his boat care not for storm or darkness.
> It is long since the Boatman sailed.
> It will be long before the day breaks and he knocks at the door.
> The drums will not be beaten and none will know.
> Only light shall fill the house, blessed shall be the dust, and the heart
> glad.
> All doubts shall vanish in silence when the Boatman comes to the
> shore.

CHAPTER XIV

INDIAN POETRY IN ENGLISH:
A SAMPLER

The main problem of writing about Indian poetry in English after Rabindranath Tagore is that while there is a plethora of singing birds, the more interesting of them can only offer about half-a-dozen poems each to merit inclusion in a worthwhile anthology.

Although the really great poems of any poet, with the exceptions of such as Shakespeare or Pushkin, represent only a fraction of the total ouevre, with the leading Indians it is a matter of a fraction of a fraction. Thomas Hardy wrote many poems, a majority of which have only a paper modesty, but he wrote a fistful of outstanding poems, which alone make him qualify as one of the world's masters. Indian poets, on the other hand, do best in anthologies because only a few poems from an already slim output entitle them for recognition as worth discussing. Therefore it is not possible for me to write on Indian poetry in English the way I have written on the Indian novel.

Of course, from the more specific point of view of the cross-cultural encounter, the poetry represents a more inward and intimate level of interaction, where the nuances of human interchange are more sensitively recorded. For this reason it is invaluable. The themes, too, abound: the physical Indian scene--the heat, dust and snowdrift, monsoon and drought, desert and tropical flamboyance--the different pace of life, the other-worldly religions, minimizing if not altogether negating, the riches of the lay world, the impact of

Modernization and Westernization, the emancipation of women, gradual yet traumatic, the strong pull and presence of family, and of the extended family, the poverty straddling conspicuous wealth and ostentatious consumption, the racial arrogance and compensatory pride of country: these are but some, there is God's plenty.

Writing in a language which, though spoken by many, is still cut off from traditions, sometimes stagnant, sometimes evolving over centuries, presents its own problems. Even in the United States, where the language was used by native speakers of English, it took quite a while for the art of letters to acquire a self-sustaining national quality. In India, where the connotations of the English vocabulary are thin, they will become denser, but we have to wait. The language is used efficiently in many areas of communication and interchange where it enjoys pre-eminence, such as law, journalism, commerce and administration, but the creative use has to compete with local languages enjoying historically continuous, established traditions and large audiences.

Besides, there is a preciosity associated with the language of a ruling elite, a self-consciousness about forging a language which is the most important gateway to the centers of power in one's own country as well as the outside world, while at the same time it does separate, even sunder, the writer from the teeming populace. This can have a devastating effect on the lyric poem, let alone making it unthinkable to imagine an Indian Chaucer or Shakespeare in the English tongue.

Of course, there are also the potent and ancillary problems of treating local events, situations and sensibility in a foreign or learned language. I say this despite the achievement in prose of R.K. Narayan, Nirad Chaudhri or Anita Desai. But India is populous, the use of English is growing (unlike, for example, in Sri Lanka or Burma, two countries which are more in need of international involvement), and we can look forward in the future to the distinct and compelling presence of Indian literature in English.

Of the poets I consider good I would name Nissim Ezekiel, Kamala Das, A.K. Ramanujan, R. Parthasarathy, Shiv Kumar, Jayanta Mahapatra, Arvind Merhotra, Gieve Patel, Keki Daruwalla, and Arun Kolatkar. The best of their poems rank with the best that is being written in other English speaking countries, but considering the total body of their work, only Ezekiel, Ramanujan, Parthasarathy, perhaps Mahapatra and certainly Kolatkar have written poetry with thematic sequences such as would lend them to some measure of extended treatment.

My modus operandi, then, would be to mention some of the poems I favor linking them with the most cursory comment on the poets' interests and techniques, before I proceed to a more detailed consideration of *Jejuri,* a poetic sequence by Arun Kolatkar.

The doyen -- the dean of the poetic corps -- of modern Indian poetry in English is Nissim Ezekiel. He is a BeneIsrael Jew, an almost forgotten tribe with Indian residence over centuries. Ezekiel is a native user of English but this advantage is offset by his being an outsider in a double sense, first by being a member of an incompletely assimilated ethnic group with a religion, historically and obdurately resistant to conversion, and second, by electing to write in a minority language with impoverished resources both because of its distance from the mainstream of Indian life and letters and its isolation from the countries where English is the main language. Paradoxically, this isolation leads sometimes to an almost chauvinistic fervor which disfigures the otherwise brilliant, occasional reviews he has written of V.S. Naipaul, Ruth Prawer Jabhwala and Kamala Markandaya.

Ezekiel has a good command of rhythm, his words are slim in connotation, he does not strive for the exploratory, metaphorical density of the normally acclaimed English poets but his cold, analytical style can encompass unusually impassioned reverberations as in "Night of the Scorpion." I can do no more than provide a sampler in his case as well as in that of the others: I would recommend "Philosopher;" "Poet, Lover, Birdwatcher;" "The Visitor" among others: a single quotation must do, though Ezekiel does often face "the final formula of light"

Poet, Lover, Birdwatcher
To force the pace and never to be still
Is not the way of those who study birds
Or women. The best poets wait for words.
The hunt is not an exercise of will
But patient love relaxing on a hill
To note the movement of a timid wing;
Until the one who knows that she is loved
No longer waits but risks surrendering--
In this the poet finds his moral proved,
Who never spoke before his spirit moved.

The slow movement seems, somehow, to say much more.
To watch the rarer birds, you have to go
Along deserted lanes and where the rivers flow
In silence near the source, or by a shore
Remote and thorny like the heart's dark floor.
And there the women slowly turn around,
Not only flesh and bone but myths of light
With darkness at the core, and sense is found
By poets lost in crooked, restless flight,
The deaf can hear, the blind recover sight.

Ramanujan, a master of poetic syntax, celebrates the Indian family and the extended family: essentially a poet of memory and recollection, though with a clinical, ironic detachment, he is the one poet who can rarely be faulted in his use of English words or prosody. A few lines from "Love Poem for a Wife"

Really what keeps us apart
at the end of years is unshared
childhood. You cannot, for instance,
meet my father. He is some years
dead. Neither can I meet yours:
he has lately lost his temper and mellowed ....
Probably only the Egyptians had it right;
their kings had sisters for queens
to continue the incests
of childhood into marriage.
Or we should do as well-meaning
Hindus did,
betroth us before birth,
forestalling separate horoscopes
and mothers' first periods,
and wed us-in the oral cradle
and carry marriage back into
the namelessness of childhoods.
can be complemented with this uncharacteristic mood.
For me a perfectly ordinary
day at the office, only a red lorry
past the window at two;
a sailor with a chest tattoo.
A walk before dark with my daughter to mark
another cross on the papaya tree;
dinner, coffee, bedtime story
of dog, bone and shadow. A bullock cart

in an Eskimo dream. But I wake with a start
to hear my wife cry her heart
out as it from a crater
in hell: she hates me, I hate her,
I'm a filthy rat and a satyr.

Kamala Das is a feminist, honest in convention-bound India about her sexual urges and her need for fulfillment: I represent her with a single poem:

The Looking Glass

Getting a man to love you is easy
Only be honest about your wants as Woman.
Stand nude before the glass with him
So that he sees himself the stronger one
And believes it so, and you so much more
Softer, younger, lovelier .... Admit your
Admiration. Notice the perfection
Of his limbs, his eyes reddening under
The shower, the shy walk across the bathroom floor,
Dropping towels, and the jerky way he
Urinates. All the fond details that make
Him male and your only man. Gift him all,
Gift him what makes you woman, the scent of
Long hair, the musk of seat between the breasts,
The warm shock of menstrual blood, and all your
 Endless female hungers. Oh yes, getting
A man to love is easy, but living
Without him afterwards may have to be
Faced. A living without life when you move
Around, meeting strangers, with your eyes that
Gave up their search, with ears that hear only
His last voice calling out your name and your
Body which once under his touch has gleamed
Like burnished brass, now drab and destitute.

Merhotra, original, a puzzler is well exemplified in *The Sale,* a poem which has to be savored in its entirety because it has a truly metaphysical wit and complexity.

1

It's yours for the price, and these
old bits have character too.
Today they may not be available.
Naturally I can't press you
to buy them, and were I not leaving--
you hear the sun choking with an eclipse--
I would never have thought of selling.
You may take your time though, and
satisfy yourself. Yes, this is Europe,
that America. This scarecrow Asia,
that groin Africa and amputated
Australia. These five, I don't have more.
Maybe another egg-laying island remains
in the sea. You remember in my letter
I wrote of forests? They're wrapped
in leaves and there should be
no trouble in carrying them.
This skull contains the rivers.
Of that I'm sorry. Had you come
yesterday I might have given you two.
I shall take another look. Yes, I do
have a mummy somewhere; only last
night the pyramids came,
and knocked at my gate for a long time.

2

Would you mind if I showed you
a few more things now yours
Be careful, one river is still wet
and slippery; its waters continue to
run like footprints. Well, this is a
brick and we call that string.
This microscope contains the margins
of a poem. I have a map left, drawn
by migrating birds.
Come into the attic.
That's not a doll - it's the
photograph of a brain walking
on sand and in the next one
it's wearing an oasis-like crown.
I must also show you a tiger's skin
which once hid a palace.
On one roof you'll see
the antelope's horns, on another--the falling wind. These round

things are bangles and that long one
a gun. This cave is the inside
of a boot. And here
carved wheels turn through stone.

3

I wish you had asked me earlier.
The paintings have been bought
by a broken mirror
but I think I can lead you
to a crack in the wall.
I've a skeleton too.
It's full of butterflies
who at dawn will carry away
the crown.
I've also a wheel-chair to show you;
it belonged to my uncle
and one day the hook
which hangs from the sky
touched him. If you open the
cupboard you'll see his memory
on the upper shelves and two books
now yours.
Ruskin's Lectures on Art and
A Short History of English Literature by Legouis.
I'll take another minute.
Can you climb this ladder?
Well, that's the sun and moon
and with this candle you can
work the clouds. I'm sorry I was
short of space
and had to pack the Great Bear
in this clock. Oh them,
let them not worry you.
They're only fisherman and king
who will sail soon as one's bait
is ready and the other's dominion.

Mahapatra a good, consistent poet who rarely rises to intensity
may be examined in the short *A Missing Person:*
In the darkened room

a woman cannot find her reflection in the mirror
waiting as usual at the edge of sleep.
In her hands she holds the oil lamp
whose drunken yellow flames
know where her lonely body hides.

Daruwalla, whom I do not quote, may be sampled in "Death of a
Bird," a moving echoing poem. Gieve Patel, a humane, activist man
of medicine may be seen in poems like "On Killing a Tree" or
"Servants." R. Parthasarathy's entire sequence "Rough Passage" is
important, he has excellent imagistic skill, even if his images rise and
evaporate within single lines. Though a fine poet, I find his moaning
about his need to write in Tamil in order to define himself as a man,
somewhat artificial: I am a Tamil myself and an unpublished poet but
except for occasional use of words like "aiyo" for alas, or "ouch", and
of words like "Kadavul" for God, I have no disquietudes about using
English: I dream in it. Human experience is surely more important
than fussing about linguistic media.

I would like to conclude this sampler with a poem by Shiv Kapoor
who besides excellent translations from that great poet Faiz Ahmad
Faiz, has also written fine poems of his own.

Indian Women

In this triple-baked continent
women don't etch angry eyebrows
on mud walls.
Patiently they sit
like empty pitchers
on the mouth of the village well
pleating hope in each braid
of their Mississippi-long hair
looking deep into the water's mirror
for the moisture in their eyes
with zodiac doodlings on the sands
they guard their tattooed thighs
waiting for their men's return
till even the shadows
roll up their contours
and are gone
beyond the hills.

CHAPTER XV

GOING TO THE SHRINE: IN *JEJURI* KOLATKAR IS PILGRIM TO BOTH PAST AND PRESENT

Arun Kolatkar is an Indian poet whose mother tongue is Marathi, a language spoken in Western India, principally in the state of Maharashtra, which includes the city of Bombay. Speakers of Marathi number about 45 million. Kolatkar writes poetry in Marathi as well as in English. As he did not learn English until he was fifteen years old, English for him is very much a second language. Nevertheless, his collection of poems entitled *Jejuri* won the Commonwealth Poetry Prize for 1977, a prize for which he had to compete with poets from all over the British Commonwealth for many of whom English is a native language. Despite this success, Kolatkar is still little known, even in the Commonwealth. It would not be an exaggeration to state that he is unknown in America. This is indeed regrettable in view of the fact that modern Indian poetry in English, including Kolatkar's *Jejuri,* often shows a highly individual absorption of American influences ranging from T. S. Eliot to e.e. cummings.

The subject of Kolatkar's sequence of poems is religion, and in the matter of the relation between religion and culture, Kolatkar's attitude is very different from treatments of the same theme in modern Europe and America. The difference is not ideological; it arises out of an

entirely distinct climate of sensibility. As we shall see, Kolatkar's
poetic mind, enlivened though it may be by irony, irreverence, even
insouciance, remains paradoxically a combination of the sardonic, the
negatively dark and even the joyous: it represents in the final analysis a
modern adjustment to an accepted tradition. Unlike some Western
work, it is not a floundering for, nor an attempt to construct something
in a godless universe.

The poems describe a visit to a traditional place of pilgrimage. The
poet joins the pilgrimage, but is different from the other pilgrims in that
he does not share the same religious attitude. His approach may be
better described as a search whereby he comes to terms with the place
and with himself. He is ironic about the place of pilgrimage as well as
the religious experience itself, but it would be a mistake to think that
his attitude denigrates or is altogether dismissive of religious realities.

The first poem, "The Bus", sets the scene. The poet, along with the
other pilgrims, boards the bus. So far, *Jejuri* is merely a destination.
The imagery has a surreal quality. The reader is involved in the journey
by use of the word "you"; the bus journey does not indicate the
direction, as the bus is enclosed and the only light comes through an
eyelet in the tarpaulin, shooting only at the glasses of an old man sitting
opposite who is also a passenger/pilgrim. When the reader-poet gets off
the bus, he retains his individuality and has not been swallowed up
within the world of the bus, symbolized by the old man's head:

> Your own divided face in a pair of glasses
> On an old man's nose
> is all the countryside you get to see....
> At the end of the bumpy ride
> with your own face on either side
> when you get off the bus
> You don't step inside the old man's head.

In the next poem, "The Priest", the same surreal mode is used to
communicate the poet's attitude towards the subject of the poem.
Comparisons between the sun falling on the priest's cheek and a pat
from the village barber, or between the bus and a purring cat, while
being unusual, stop short within that range of fantasy which does not
dissolve the comic and satiric intention. The ironic mode helps to
define the character of the priest, warts and all. His anticipation of good

fortune with the arrival of the bus demonstrates that religion is the priest's livelihood:

The bus goes round in a circle
Stops inside the bus station and stands
purring softly in front of the priest.
A catgrin on its face
and a live, ready to eat pilgrim
held between its teeth.

"Heart of Ruin" is about a ruined temple, now inhabited by the god Maruti, a bitch and her puppies, and a dung beetle. The refrain "maybe he likes a temple better this way", varying only in the use of the personal pronoun and applying as it does to the god himself and to the animals, expresses in its hesitation an ambivalent attitude: although the temple is no longer a place of worship, it has nevertheless become the house of god, a place that is equally well-served by his non-human creatures.

"Water Supply", where the movement of the lines recalls Eliot's well-known comparison of the fog to a cat in "The Love Song of J. Alfred Prufrock", results in a totally original effect -- a picture of dereliction in an Indian setting where the plumbing is weird and water taps are often dry. It will not be an exaggeration to relate the broken water tap to the drying up of traditional religion in the world of *Jejuri*. Though the language is conversational, the word-order and syntax are idiosyncratic: words and images are chosen not for their dense connotation but because they stand for a direct and bare concreteness.

This method of comparison is well demonstrated in the next poem, "The Door", where the fallen door is like a dangling martyr, "a flayed man of muscles who can not find his way back to an anatomy book", and a "local drunk". In the conclusion the poet, in a mood of witty fancy, asserts that the door would have walked out long, long ago,

if it weren't for
that pair of shorts
left to dry upon its shoulders.

"A Low Temple" presents the kind of temple which keeps its gods in the dark. It is illuminated by lighting a match, but what is actually seen is fleeting and deceptive -- and whether a hidden goddess has eight arms or eighteen does not, anyway, seem important to the priest.

The skeptical visitor responds by coming back out into the light of the sun, lighting up his cigarette as though the match serves him better this way. The indifference of the priest to the true nature of the goddess seems to be matched by that of the children who play on the back of the twenty-foot stone tortoise. In the following poem, "The Pattern", the tortoise-slab appears again, used by old men as a checkerboard, the lines of which are later smudged by the feet of children playing on it.

The character Manohar, in the poem of the same name, looks for a temple but finds a calf inside which makes him conclude that it is just a cowshed. Manohar would seem to be the poet himself trying to come to terms with the ruined enterprise that the religion of *Jejuri* represents. The beggarwoman in the following poem "The Old Woman" has the same sense of futility and justifies it by referring to the miserable and deadening environment: "What else can an old woman do/on hills as wretched as these?" The cracks around her eyes match the cracked hills and the cracked temples. The poet humorously describes the old woman as reducing the visitor to near insignificance:

> And as you look on,
> the cracks that begin around her eyes
> spread beyond her skin.
> And the hills crack.
> And the temples crack.
> And the sky falls
> with a plateglass clatter
> around the shatter proof crone
> who stands alone.
> And you are reduced
> to so much small change
> in her hand.

The short poem "Chaitanya", which follows, associates the creative energy of the god with mute stones:

> he popped a stone
> in his mouth
> and spat out gods.

In "Hills" the demons Khandoba killed were turned into hills where "cactus thrust/up through ribs of rock". In the following "The Priest's Son", the poet asks a young boy whether he believes in the legend of

Khandoba. The boy "looks uncomfortable" and is saved from his embarrassment (and from revealing his skepticism) by the quick appearance of a butterfly, a symbol of natural life among these infertile hills. The image is continued in "The Butterfly", with the apparition of the insect as transitory, disappearing as quickly as it appeared:

> just a pinch of yellow
> it opens before it closes
> and closes before it o
>
> where is it.

Unlike *Jejuri*, and in contrast to the ancient but no longer enduring spiritual significance of the shrine, the butterfly exists only in the moment:

> It has no future.
> It is pinned down to no past.
> It's a pun on the present.

Blending the images of stones and gods, the poet is now able to hypothesize about the nature of the divine in *Jejuri*:

> what is god
> and what is stone
> the dividing line
> if it exists
> is very thin
> at *Jejuri*
> and every other stone
> is god or his cousin.

The next and longer poem, "Ajamil and the Tigers", is a mature and intelligent rationale for the need of sacrifice and compromise, with the poet writing a powerful and witty fable to illustrate the need for political manipulation in order to survive and be content. Ajamil the shepherd realizes that he can have peace with the tigers only if he allows them to eat some of his sheep, that a full stomach is the best guarantee of an enduring treaty and a "common bond". The succinct narration -- almost staccato when necessary -- with its effective

dialogue and the conversational but ordered rhythms, contributes to the
success of one of the best poems in this sequence:

> Ajamil cut them loose
> and asked them all to stay for dinner.
> It was an offer the tigers couldn't refuse.
> And after the lamb chops and the roast,
> when Ajamil proposed
> they sign a long term friendship treaty,
> all the tigers roared,
> "We couldn't agree with you more".
> And swore they would be good friends all their lives
> as they put down the forks and the knives.
>
> Ajamil signed a pact
> with the tiger people and sent them back,
> Laden with gifts of sheep, leather jackets and balls of wool.
> Ajamil wasn't a fool.
> Like all good shepherds he knew
> that even tigers have got to eat some time.
> A good shepherd sees to it they do.
> He is free to play a flute all day
> as well fed tigers and fat sheep drink from the same pond
> with a full stomach for a common bond.

The two succeeding poems, "A Song for a Vaghya" and "A Song
for a Murli" are spoken by a man and a woman respectively -- Vaghya
in the first poem is a first-born male child given away by the parents to
serve god; and Murli is a first-born female who is dedicated to the
temple and often becomes a prostitute. The poems are ironically
poignant: Vaghya recognizes that if he cannot beg he must steal and
that if his instrument has only one string, it does not matter because he
only knows a one-word song:

> God is the word
> and I know it backwards.
> I know it as fangs
> inside my flanks.
> But I also know it
> as a lamb
> between my teeth,
> as a taste of blood
> upon my tongue.

And this is the only song
I've always sung.

The sense of his role as a sacrificial victim and the cruelty of that
sacrifice is strikingly conveyed. The irony of Murli in the second poem
as performing both the role of protectress and prostitute is typical:

you dare not ride off with it
don't you see khandoba's brand on its flank
you horse thief

look
that's his name
tattooed just below the left collar bone
keep your hands off khandoba's woman
you old lecher
let's see the color of your money first

The imaginative problem in this poem is one of vision -- you need
the light of the moon in order to see the god's mark on the hill. Murli
needs the moon's light so as to identify the thief, but as a prostitute,
using him, she also needs it to see the color of his money.

The small poem, "The Reservoir", uses the imagery of drought to
indicate that the great architectural feats of the ancient rulers are now
without any possibilities of life. The springs of the spiritual life have
also run dry. In "A Little Pile of Stones" the poet is telling a young
woman, a devotee, how to find happiness. The devotee is instructed
that she can learn from the stones a lesson which may lead her to
happiness. "Makarand", the poem which follows, is a rejection by the
poet of the temptation to pray: rather than take his shirt off he would
smoke in the courtyard, preferring its freedom in the same way as he
preferred to be outside in the sun with a cigarette at the conclusion of
"A Low Temple".

"The Temple Rat", in which a rat seems to be as much at home in
the temple as the god himself, brilliantly describes the creature's
journey from the "longer middle prong" to the sanctum behind the big
temple drum. Kolatkar's characteristic use of images which are related
to action, as well as his use of line divisions to indicate pace of
movement, are very well illustrated in this poem; and some of the
imagery is startling -- the rat is like a "thick gob of black blood". The
animal is indifferent to the wedding ceremony which is taking place

and Kolatkar contrasts the lifeless gods with this living, however unpleasant, specimen from the animal world.

In "A Kind of Cross" and "The Cupboard", the sense of religion as disintegrating and obsolete is continued. In the first poem, the poet identifies religion with suffering, with the temple as a place of torture. The ironic parallel of a Christian cross reinforces the effect created by the "strange instrument of torture", once an instrument for the slaughtering of the bull calf, but now a useless relic. In "The Cupboard" the dilapidated state of the shrine is further emphasized. The precariousness, insecurity, and the shabbily inorganic nature of the cupboard is suggested by the mention of linear or metallic objects -- rectangles, set squares, trapeziums, jagged slivers. The irony is directed not only against the "golden gods", but against a dominant media which has buried them under vapid editorials, recipes for eternal youth, and the usual stock-in-trade of Indian newspapers -- used here to plaster and hold together the cracked and broken glass of the cupboard itself.

"Yeshwant Rao" is one of the better poems in what is, in any case, a remarkably good collection or sequence. The poet prefers a "second class god" to the more powerful and mainstream ones. The strong rhetorical tone of the following stanzas show the poet proceeding beyond irony to a more intense and bitter statement even though the concluding lines are playful in tone:

> I've known gods
> prettier faced
> or straighter laced.
> Gods who soak you for your gold.
> Gods who soak you for your soul.
> Gods who make you walk
> on a bed of burning coal.
> Gods who put a child inside your wife.
> Or a knife inside your enemy.
> Gods who tell you how to live your life,
> double your money
> or triple your land holdings.
> Gods who can barely suppress a smile
> as you crawl a mile for them.
> Gods who will see you drown
> if you won't buy them a new crown.
> And although I'm sure they're all to be praised,
> They're either too symmetrical

or too theatrical for my taste....
Yeshwant Rao
does nothing spectacular.
He doesn't promise you the earth
or book your seat on the next rocket to heaven.
But if any bones are broken,
you know he'll mend them.
He'll make you whole in body
and hope your spirit will look after itself.
He is merely a kind of bone setter.
The only thing is,
as he himself has no heads, hands and feet,
he happens to understand you a little better.

The emphasis is on ordinary values, with Yeshwant Rao the "bone-setter" being more practical and more congenial to the worshipper's need for solutions to immediate problems.

Kolatkar writes savagely in "The Blue Horse", where a cabaret act arranged by a priest is presented as a picture of despair and futility. The performers, such as they are, are described as "God's own children/making music": the temple is present again. Just as the priest in "A Low Temple" had insisted on seeing an *eight-* (rather than eighteen-) armed goddess, so, here, he remarks on a *white* horse painted on the wall, "Looks blue to me".

"Between *Jejuri* and the Railway Station" is a highly innovative experiment. The poet is now ready to leave *Jejuri* ("this little temple town", and there is a monotonous listing of the town's sixty-three priests inside their sixty-three houses, the three hundred pillars and so on, which is interrupted by the sixty-fourth house which belongs to the temple dancer. (The priest's son, perhaps of the earlier poem of the same name, "would rather not talk about" the dancer's skill -- in the same way that he earlier evaded a question by the poet.) The pilgrimage is thoroughly reduced in significance:

You've left the town behind
with a coconut in your hand,
a priest's visiting card in your pocket
and a few questions knocking about in your head.

Into this empty mood breaks a vision -- the only visionary experience in the sequence -- of a dozen cocks and hens in a harvest dance. Again, as in a number of earlier poems, it is the animals (here the fowl) which seem to have any vitality. The typographical arrangement of "up" and "down" conveys both the joyousness of the dance as well as its topsy-turvy nature.

The concluding poem, "The Railway Station", is divided into six short sections which are rendered in a wittily surreal mode. Both the temple and railway station seem to be ensconced in a state of unliving timelessness. The railway station, which should be a link with the world outside this nearly fossilized place of pilgrimage, does not offer any prospect of escape into a more meaningful human world. The station has acquired some of the temple's remoteness from the concerns of everyday. The indicator, which should point to something or reveal something, points to nothing: it is described in a mock-religious way as a wooden saint who gives no clue when the next train is due. A sense of nothingness is expressed:

> the clockface adds its numerals
> the total is zero.

The station dog is described as a "pilgrim" doing penance for the last three hundred years; the young waiter at the tea stall is described as a "novice" who has taken a vow of silence. The religious imagery is persistent: the waiter exorcises you, sprinkles dishwater in your face, performs ablutions and ceremonies; the booking clerk believes in the "doctrine" of the next train and the two-headed station master belongs to a "sect" that rejects every timetable. Words such as "apocryphal", "ritual", "sect", "doctrine" each emphasize the religious connotations. A typical humor predominates, however -- through, for example, the way the station-master cannot be bothered with such pedestrian matters as timetables. The poet is also satiric about the religious exegesis which tries to make out that everything is implicit in the original text, all wisdom in the *Vedas:*

> all timetables ever published
> along with all timetables yet to be published
> are simultaneously valid
> at any given time and on any given track
> insofar as all the timetables were inherent
> in the one printed
> when the track was laid.

The fifth section, entitled "vows", portrays the poet-protagonist as a person willing to make any sacrifice in order to find out the time the train is due. The criticism of the traditional Indian bureaucracy wherein the station master is the most important civil servant in Jejuri, is based on the common experience of the ruler and servant relationship, whereby the public official is not the public servant but someone who must be propitiated:

> slaughter a goat before the clock
> smash a coconut on the railway track
> smear the indicator with the blood of a cock
> bathe the station master in milk
> and promise you will give
> a solid gold toy train to the booking clerk
> if only someone would tell you
> when the next train is due.

The sixth and concluding vignette, called "The Setting Sun", is not, however, altogether ironic. There seems to be a sense that the sun is "touching upon the horizon/at a point where the rails" appear to meet is symbolic of a fulfilled or fulfillable prophecy; but it is not altogether a hopeful ending because the image of the wheel is also suggestive of the train, and therefore of the unrewarding railway station. The setting sun symbolizes the end of a journey. What has been discovered in the search is not clear.

It is difficult to say at this stage whether Arun Kolatkar will develop into a great poet in the English language. One does not even know if he will write any more poems in English. But it is important to recognize both the achievement and potential manifested in *Jejuri*. Obviously, not all the poems in the sequence are of the same order of excellence, and I have preferred not to dwell on the inadequacies or the occasional failures of tone. But the exuberant fertility of this poet's inventiveness in a language, which while being at the same time Indianized and highly individual, is clearly the end product of a tongue which now seems to belong not only to the countries which produced Milton and Mark Twain but also to that latecomer on the stage of English literature, the vast and populous subcontinent of India.

CHAPTER XVI

THE INDIAN NOVEL IN ENGLISH

This chapter is not a survey of the Indian novel in English nor does it seek to uncover all the problems of writing in a foreign or adopted language. Writing in an alien language is, by definition, a cross-cultural endeavor. But the choice of a language is but one of the facets of a complex situation.

Though it is the first or adopted language of some millions and the language of administration and commerce, English in India seems somewhat overawed, even overwhelmed by the numerically superior and traditionally confident speakers and writers of ancient literary local languages. The problems are inherent in interpreting old local cultures in a language of an alien corn.

The strong resistance of local languages and traditions when compared to the weaker resistance of local languages and dialects in the Caribbean and some African countries seems at least in part to account for a more daring creativity in the use of English by such writers as Chiva Achebe, Wole Soyinka or Derek Walcott at least till recent times. The presence of literary languages is not by itself an unmitigated calamity: witness the case of Nirad Chaudri, who was able to forge a personal idiom and cadence out of a book-learned English, without benefit of a current and contemporary community of English users and speakers.

What is stupid about much critical discussion of these problems is that it misses the fact that the most crucial element is the talent of the individual artist: however much you may explain Achebe's or Soyinka's superiority in terms of a context of situation, you have to finally reckon with their artistic gifts.

My chapter, therefore, is rather an attempt to discuss the East-West encounter in broad terms and the directions Indian writing in English is likely to take in the future. Of course this discussion must include the Indian uses of the English language and Indian responses to Western ideas and their adaptation to an Indian climate of sensibility.

My critical procedure is not to attempt generalizations on theoretical problems and hypotheses, but rather to select whom I consider the more important writers and comment on their literary merits while I discuss their illustrative relevance to my more general concerns.

But I have another, more intractable problem: the question of modernity. Anita Desai, an excellent novelist, and Arun Joshi, a lesser artist but supremely illustrative, bid fair to join a select group of Indian novelists in English who seem to embody the forward points of the modern Indian mind, and can therefore be described as authentically modern. The difficulty lies in the attempt to define, or at least suggest, what I mean by modernity as distinct from being merely contemporaneous. One is aware of the hidden dangers lying in wait on such an ambition; it was T. S. Eliot who once characterized the attempt to define the word "modern" as a blackboard exercise to be erased as soon as it is completed. "Existential modernity" is a carry-all term if it is made to cover Kafka, Sartre, Camus, Gunter Grass and John Fowles, but there is a specific aura that surrounds these writers and it is my belief that some Third World writers share this sensibility. In order to demonstrate this it is essential to travel from the earlier to the later novelists and hope that my meaning will be clearer at the end of my journey.

The three established novelists, the elders, as it were, of the Indian novel in English are Mulk Raj Anand, Raja Rao and R.K. Narayan. They do not exemplify the quality of modernism I am groping towards: they are certainly contemporary but are unsympathetic to existential modernism. R.K. Narayan, for example, refused to read Salman Rushdie. But to understand and discriminate, it is essential to consider their contribution, without succumbing to the egregious error that to be possessed of this quality of modernity is itself a criterion of artistic worth.

As I have said, writing in a foreign language is itself a cross-cultural enterprise: Anand, therefore, warrants consideration as a precursor and an example. His works exhibit considerable range. There is the early *Untouchable*: contemporary in its concerns, and even "modern" in its day. The frequent banality of its prose, and the simplistic, propagandist nature of its motivation is more than redeemed by the honesty of its social passion and the courage of its humanitarianism. There is also such work as *Death of a Hero* which I had the misfortune to read recently – a straightforward tale of political heroism and martyrdom, which, though better in both its comparatively unvarnished style and the quality of its attitudes than the average pulp fiction of the Western world, is still a long way from be coming a work of art. At the risk of being unfair to Anand's other work, I quote from *Death of a Hero* the better to contrast it, for example, with the prose of, say, Anita Desai. Hagbool, the hero, is here mouthing the following "unspoken" words at that climactic point in the novel when he is being charged with treason:

> "Truth has no voice", he began by chewing the words in the bitter froth of his mouth to himself, so that his lips did not open and no voice could be heard. "Only lies flourish for a while.... I have no face. I have no speech. I cannot move you. This land, which gave birth to me, this land is like a poem to me - how shall I explain my love for it to you? From out of the valleys there has risen for centuries the anguish of torture ... And we were trying to emerge from the oppression to liberate our mother, because we know her each aching caress.. And you have come and fouled her and wounded her! How could any of us stand by and not protest against your cruelty..."

Anand is personally a fine and large-hearted man, and I have the privilege of knowing him. He is a serious and committed writer. He was also, being a product of two cultures, an interpreter of the East to the West while espousing a passionately progressive attitude, derived from the West, to social and economic oppression in India. But it is not difficult to demonstrate that he does not share the anxieties of late twentieth-century Western man; his work does not carry the onus of the kind of modernity I find in Anita Desai or Arun Joshi, a quality I find a vexing matter to define.

However, I do not like to take my leave of Anand with a quotation from one of his weakest efforts. There are other novels in his *oeuvre*, notably *The Private Life of an Indian Prince*, which are more complex in range and sophistication than the early successes, *Untouchable*, *Coolie* and *Two Leaves and a Bud*.

Nor do I want to slight these early novels, which are solid achievements for all their weaknesses. *Untouchable* observes the unities of classical drama and the protagonist is a credible human being, drawn from the lowest caste of society. This ability to enter into

the minds of people in the "lowest depths" was an original contribution
to the Indian novel not just in English but in any of the indigenous
languages. Equally original in *Untouchable* is the use by Anand of a
Western ideology, Marxist humanism, which gives form to his literary
interests, not in the manner of an external imposition but as a system of
beliefs felt on the pulse. When Bakha's sister Sohini goes to the caste-
well in the hope of getting some water through the pity of one of the
users of the well, Anand records her need in terms that are not
doctrinaire:

> How a round base can be adjusted on a round top, how a sphere can
> rest on a sphere is a problem that may be of interest to those who think
> like Euclid or Archimedes. It never occurred to Sohini to ask herself
> anything like this as she balanced her pitcher on her head as she went to
> and from her one-roomed home to the steps of the castewell where she
> counted on the chance of some gentleman taking pity on her and giving
> her the water she needed.

The conclusion of the book is an admirable example of the merger
of East and West, not as diametrically opposed and opposing entities
but as a coming together to form a new consciousness. Bakha's sense
of self-worth, based on a change of heart not only within himself but in
Indian society itself in the future, if it were to model itself on Gandhian
principles, joins with the introduction of the flush system and modern
plumbing to make the caste of untouchable obsolete.

Coolie, Anand's second novel, does not observe the unities of time,
place and action: it is rather a picaresque novel, except that unlike in
Fielding the protagonist's adventures are invariably unpleasant and life-
defeating rather than fortunate. We trace the history of Munoo, a strong
boy with a keen appetite for life, ravaged and weakened by a series of
misfortunes till he is finally snuffed out. From an unhappy life with his
uncle and aunt in his village, he becomes a servant at a bank sub-
accountant's home and is exposed to further maltreatment. Sponsored
by a benefactor he escapes to the city of Daulatpur where he works
with some measure of satisfaction at Cat Killer's Lane till his patron's
business collapses. He then enters the Bombay underworld, treated with
a Dickensian *saeva indignatio*. He spends his final days as a rickshaw
puller for Mrs. Mainwaring in Simla, where he dies of consumption.

For a book of unrelieved gloom, it does hold the interest of the
reader largely because of the deep human sympathy it evokes.

Two Leaves and a Bud is a novel of plantation life which does treat of the interaction between British and Indians, though this interaction does not go beyond the limited intercourse of master and slave. It has its black coolies, its kancranis or recruiters of labor, its moneylenders, traders and middlemen, its British planters and official bureaucracy, and its tiger hunt. In fact, Anand's mouthpiece in the novel is a humane English doctor, John de la Havre, an outspoken critic both in conversation and in his journal of the attitudes of the British ruling class:

> Why didn't it occur to anyone -- the simple obvious thing that people don't need to read Marx to realize here? The black coolies clear the forests, plant the fields and garner the harvest, while all the money-grabbing, slave-driving soulless managers and directors draw their salaries and dividends and build up monopolies...

The doctor has a reciprocal love-relationship with Barbara, the daughter of the English Estate Superintendent Charles Croft-Cooke but her love cannot withstand the pressures of the local British community which ostracizes John de la Havre for his unorthodox views, considered subversive of the system. The novel has its villain too, Reggie Hunt, a psychologically maladjusted sadist.

The main character is Gangu, an older man than either Munoo or Bakha, with a family of his own, transplanted from his native habitat and subjected to cruelties of all kinds.
He is still able to meditate as follows:

> The Tibetans stood mute, immutable, their small eyes lowered under the darkness of their brains, even as they bent their vision to its invisible blanks of Nirvans, in the temples of their villages, accepting the gifts that God showered upon them.
> Gangu looked across them through the dark layers of his own bitterness and tried to penetrate into the fastnesses, and beyond them to the villages, where the tense insistence of their loins had driven the plough deep, deep into the earth, where they had sprinkled the seed and waited for the rain from heaven to irrigate their furrows, where they had watched the opening of the buds and gazed at the flowering of the crop into fruit, with smiles as broad as the rays of the Himalayan sun. He knew the meaning of their toil, he had known the beauty of that magic which was in the hard-yielding earth, he knew the love with which men spent themselves so that they could reap the fruit at the end, he know the agony of having to part with that fruit, and the disillusion

consequent upon selling it or bartering it to a hard, un-understanding, hard-hearted, mean bania or city broker. He yearned toward the Tibetans, and bursting with indignation and remorse at their suffering, and his own, wallowed in the wells of a music that made him dumb with its turbulence.

Though somewhat overwritten, this is effective writing, unlike other passages such as Gangu's daughter Leila's attempt to extricate herself from the grip of a python which seems to have been introduced to overload the misery, as though there weren't enough human pythons to deal with.

Private Life of an Indian Prince is a more complex and ambitious novel than the earlier ones we have so far discussed. It was written as therapy for his own condition caused by his love for a hill-woman which led in turn to a divorce from his wife. He found, however, on his return to India to marry his beloved that she had run away with a Frenchman. The trauma caused by this experience colors this novel and gives it an uncommon degree of personal engagement. There is also a probing of character as in the so-called "psychological" novel. The prince, Victor, is almost a case-history: some readers may find the prince too debauched, too craven in his infatuation, too much of a caricature in a world of political and moral change. However, the development of psychotic tendencies into total madness is convincingly done. An important technical device is the role played by Dr. Shankar, personal physician, father-confessor, and chronicler of Victor's disintegration: his Western, scientific training is set against the odd combination of Eastern spirituality and oppressive, inhumane materialism which princely rule in a changing India seems to represent.

The writing, though at times finely controlled, often tends to be over-emphatic and "arty", a fault far too common with Indian writers of English who, because they write in a foreign language, seem to want to draw attention to themselves by wearing elaborate clothes and walking on tiptoe. Of course there are notable exceptions, such as R. K. Narayan and Anita Desai.

Mulk Raj Anand is no mere ideologue and even though his Marxism is derived from the West, his novels are unmistakably Indian in subject-matter, setting and atmosphere. Nor is he a naturalist in the Western sense; he calls himself an expressionist who draws on fantasy and the sub-conscious. Even though he rejects Hindu traditionalism, he adopts the tone and method of the moral fable. As he says in the following excerpts from his letters:

> I rely on my subconscious life a great deal ... and allow my fantasy to play havoc with facts. I believe all of us Indians are expressionists, that is to say, we enact a body-soul drama in everything we write...
>
> Critics around me conceive of literary realism as the description of the world as it is. I was born a Hindu and, therefore, I have never taken appearance for reality... I wished to write about human beings who were not known or recognized as human at all, or admitted into society-such as the outcastes ... by going below the surface to the various hells made by man for man with an occasional glimpse of heaven as the 'desire image.' I have never been objective, as the realists claim to be. And my aim is not negative, merely to shock but to stimulate consciousness at all levels.
>
> There was no tradition in the Indian novel for this. And being of the thirties, I was mistaken for a proletarian writer, a social realist. This is nonsense... I do not believe in the Scientific novel or documentary. I never abandoned human beings in order to pursue a theory... I admit that this has led to a certain formlessness, but look for the fantasies in the labyrinthine depths of degradation and you will find them there. Perhaps much better than in Kipling... I wanted to create in *Coolie* a boy in all humaneness, as against the fantastic Kim.

Mulk Raj Anand then is a good example of the penetration of the East by the West. He is a writer who can adapt the borrowed, Western ideology of Marxism and the social attitudes, both humanitarian and Gandhian; he is *au fait* with modern psychiatry and the psychology of madness and can incorporate them in an Indian situation of the love between an Indian prince and a hill-woman. Though his sympathies still lie with the downtrodden in this princely state and the rest of India, Anand *is* artist enough to movingly evoke and sympathetically capture the mental turmoil of a prince with an impoverished sense of reality, being inexorably stripped of both throne and reason.

This seems as good a place as any to list some of the varied approaches to the use of the English language by Indian writers, bearing in mind that the methods chosen are determined primarily by the author's purposes and point of view.

In the Indianizing process of the English language there is first of all the case of Mulk Raj Anand, which is basically the use of standard English, apart from the liberal sprinkling of literal translations of Indian words, phrases, terms of speech, even oaths and curses and the transliteration of Indian words and phrases. Since the use of English speech by workers and peasants, except for the commonest borrowings in the local spoken language, itself calls for a suspension of disbelief, the question whether this practice mutes such suspension and ministers to verisimilitude or even realism is certainly a moot one. Unlike some critical pundits, mostly Indian, I have no objection to this practice: the question simply is whether it works, whether it is integrated or a needless superimposition. Anand's shortcomings are not traceable to this technique.

At a rather opposite extreme is the unique case of G.V. Desani's *All About H. Hatterr*, a literary sport, a "coterie pleasure" as Anthony Burgess so aptly described it. It is clearly a creation of a language within a language, composed of Babu, Shakespearian archaisms, Indian colloquialisms, English slang and other elements all in various forms of distortion, which, however, never descends into meaninglessness or mumbo-jumbo. But this work cannot breed successors, and I do not give this hilariously comic novel sufficient space in this book because it does not seem to grow out of either a British or an Indian tradition. Another reason is that the dialogue is aptly treated by Dr. Dinshaw Burjorjee in his little known article entitled "The Dialogue" in G.V. Desani's *All About H. Hatterr* published, I believe, in the journal *World Literature in English*. There is nothing I can add to Burjorjee's critical and painstaking exegesis of this novel.

Another atypical example is the prose of Nirad C. Chaudri, who developed a highly individual style out of his reading and study of English literature, which is a compound of Johnsonian weight and seriousness with a Macaulayan or late Victorian cadence. Chaudri had a love-hate relationship to his own country (more hate than love, it turns out, as a counterweight to the adulation of the motherland among Indians in the context of the struggle for independence) along with a profound empathy for English civilization, to be distinguished, however, from a rapport with Anglo-India. His *Autobiography of an Unknown Indian* is a masterpiece in its own right in this genre, apart from being a classic of the cross-cultural encounter. I pay scant attention to it, as Chaudri is not a novelist and hence outside the scope of this chapter but I cannot refrain from quoting an extract which not only shows the integration in his rich sensibility of Western thoughts and attitudes but is an example of his nimble style when exploring a philosophical exposition, without recourse to his almost habitual anger:

I think there is even in the highest and most characteristic teaching of Hinduism (apart from the layer on layer of infinitely varied primitiveness which constitutes its buried foundation), something impelling a Hindu towards the simpler in preference to the more complex, towards the unemerged in preference to the emergent, and towards the general in preference to the particular. According to some of the noblest teaching of Hinduism, the manifest universe is an illusion, the ultimate reality attribute-less, and man's supreme happiness lies in putting an end to the cycle of births and deaths, or, in other words, to eliminating precisely those particular forms possessing sensible attributes which confer qualities and values on reality, and clothe it with attractiveness for us. With such a philosophical background it is not surprising that a Hindu should tend to ignore distinctions. To me, however, Hinduism appears to be swimming against the current. Although its penchant for the undifferentiated and the attributeless is undoubtedly due to its anxiety to bite on the rock of truth and reality lying underneath the flux of changes, I would still say that in actual fact it is retrograde and out of sympathy with reality. For I believe in change and hold all reality to be a process, a process which is justifying itself, as well as making itself more significant, by becoming more particular and differentiated and by endowing itself with even more new values.

This is an example of expository prose, as written by any outstanding practitioner in the English language. To conclude this typology of the Indianizing of the English language, I would like to refer briefly to the prose style of four Indian writers, R.K. Narayan, Kamala Markandaya, Anita Desai and Raja Rao, before I consider their fictions, beginning with the last named.

R.K. Narayan, Kamala Markandaya and Anita Desai inhabit as it were the middle-ground of the spectrum: they use variations of standard English and I would like to dispose of their linguistic contributions before I consider their work and move on to their standing as examples of cross-cultural literature. I will conclude with Arun Joshi as a good illustration of the ancillary problems of "modernism" which continue to vex me.

R.K. Narayan uses the language of the bilingual Indian middle-class, the idiom of the English language newspapers, the jargon of law and the administration, but what a supple use he makes of these restricting founts can only be shown by an examination of his work. Kamala Markandaya employs Standard English but in her later novels, perhaps due to being browbeaten by Indian critics of her alienation she resorts to staccato expression, truncated sentences and sentence fragments in order to inject a note of originality. This attempt is largely a failure, though in the treatment of character in action she has truly changed and matured. It is almost a crime for an Indian writer in English to establish a foreign domicile: Nissim Ezekiel, a fine poet, though a narrow chauvinist, put it well:

> Confiscate my passport, Lord,
> I don't want to go abroad.
> Let me find my song
> Where I belong.

Anita Desai is an altogether different type: she is a fine writer, and except for the search for unusual words and phrases in her early work, she uses Standard English to explore realms of perceptions and sensibility in the manner of a Virginia Woolf, though at her best she is superior to Woolf.

Raja Rao -- and here I move from mere consideration of prose style to assessment of content and significance -- is a good point of transition. His originality and claims to creative achievement rest on *Kanthapura,* an early novel, which is a real, if limited, success. The success -- and even a species of "modernity"--consists in his being able to forge an English idiom, which accommodates itself, in its diction as well as its movement, to rhythms, forms of thought, patterns of sensibility, and turns of phrase which are unmistakably Indian, and particularly of his own mother tongue, Kannada. The advent of the rains is described as follows:

> The rains have come, the fine, firstfooting rains that skip over the bronze mountains, tip-toe the crops, and leaping into the valleys, go splashing and wind-swung, a winnowed pour, and the coconuts and the betel nuts and the cardamon plants choke with it and hiss back. And there, there it comes over the Bebbur Hill and the Kanthur Hill and begins to paw upon the tiles, and the cattle come running home, their ears stretched back, and the drover lurches behind some bel tree or pipal tree, and people leave their querns and rush to the courtyard, and turning towards the Kenchamma Temple, send forth a prayer, saying, "There, the rains have come, Kenchamma; may our houses be white as silver," and the lightning flashes and the thunder stirs the tiles, and children rush to the gutterslabs to sail paper-boats down to Kashi....

It is not a requirement for an Indian writing in English that he should adapt himself to, or incorporate stylistic habits of a particular Indian language--R.K. Narayan does quite well in terms of his own purposes without displaying much of this skill. However, it is undeniable that this ability bestows on the language a special power of concreteness and a closeness to the Indian scene. The creative adaptation of his mother tongue gives Rao's English an innovative flavor, reminiscent of some of the West African and Caribbean writers, a skill not often found in Indian writers of English. It is seen not only in Rao's descriptions such as "Everybody saw that Narsamma was growing thin as a bamboo and shrivelled like a banana bark" or his literal rendering of a Kannada phrase into "Stitch up your mouth, do you hear?" where the more conventional writer would have used "Shut your mouth," but also in several longer passages such as this account of Moorthy entering the temple:

> And the beating of the clothes sank into his ears, and the sunshine sank into his mind, and his limbs sank down into the earth, and there a dark burning light in the heart of the sanctum, and many men with beards and besmeared with holy ashes stood beside the idol, silent, their lips gently moving, and he, too, entered the temple like a sparrow, and he sat on the handle of a candelabra, and as he looked fearfully at the holy, floods suddenly swept in from all the doorways of the temple, beating, whirling, floods, dark and bright, and he quietly sank into them and floated away like child Krishna on the pipal leaf.

When Raja Rao tries his hand at a novel of broader canvas treating the meeting of East and West as in *The Serpent and the Rope*, he foregoes this technique and substitutes for it long passages of abstract rumination and phony eloquence, with disastrous results. To my mind, this novel is an example of how the literature of cross-cultural contact should not be written: there is no interpenetration of East and West, rather a simple juxtaposition resulting in interminable talk, often at cross-purposes, and philosophical encounters which are frequently nonsensical. The abstract intellectual discussions with their unsubtle differentiations have little connection with the movement of the narrative, except to obfuscate, or to give implausible excuses for the protagonist's failure to commit himself either in marriage, love or responsible action.

The glorification of things Indian and the uncritical egoism of
Rama, made worse by the fact that he is also the narrator of the story,
lead to acutely embarrassing moments for the reader:

> I was too much of a Brahmin to be unfamiliar with anything, such is
> the pride of caste and race, and lying by Madeleine it was she who
> remarked, "Look at this pale skin beside your golden one. Oh, to be
> born in a country where tradition is so alive," she once said, "that even
> the skin of her men is like some royal satin, softened and given a new
> shine through the rubbing of ages." I, however, being so different,
> never really noted any difference. To me difference was inborn--like
> my being the eldest son of my father, or like my grandfather being the
> Eight-Pillared House Ramakrishnayya, and you had just to mention his
> name anywhere in Mysore State, even to the Maharaja, and you were
> offered a seat, a wash, and a meal, and a coconut-and-shawl adieu.

In an age when the notion of white supremacy has many adherents,
the contrast of pale with golden skin is amusingly compensatory. Even
a simple exercise like Rama's draping a sari on Madeleine ends in
high-falutin mumbo-jumbo:

> As she undressed I could see the contours of her beautiful body, so
> simple, so erect, so unopened, I tried to dress her, and she let me do it,
> for she wanted to be touched by me, to be held by me, to know, the
> knowing that has made knowing a single presence.

And so it goes on till he takes a bath and concludes, "A clean body
seems full of wisdom!"

Where in the world of modern literature, or in the world itself, can
one find a conversation such as the following between Rama and
Savitri, who are destined later on in the novel to become more intimate,
though the intimacy is never made explicit because of the philosophical
hocus-pocus in which it is shrouded?

> "Therefore, what is Truth?" I asked....
> "Is-ness is the Truth," she answered.
> "And Is-ness is what?"
> "Who asks that question?"
> "Myself."
> "Who?"
> "I."
> "Of whom?"

"No one."

"Then 'I am' is."

Rather, 'I am' am."

"Tautology!" she laughed.

"Savitri says Savitri is Savitri."

"And you say Savitri is what?" she begged.

"I."

"And the moon and the silence seemed to
acknowledge that only the 'I' shone."

"There is no Savitri," I continued after a while.

"No, there isn't. That I know."

"There is nothing," I persisted.

"Yes," she said. "Except that in the
seeing of the seeing there's a seer."

"And the seer sees what?"

"Nothing," she answered.

"When the I is, and where the Nothing is,
what is the Nothing but the 'I'?"

"So when I see that tree, in that moonlight,
that cypress, that pine tree, I see I--I
see I--I see I."

"Yes."

"That is the truth," she said, as we
turned and walked back to the village.

Even adolescent undergraduates excited by their introduction to philosophy would not carry on in this manner except in a guying or jocular spirit: when Savitri beseeches Rama to marry him, this is how he meditates:

> You can marry when you are one. That is, you can marry when there is no one to marry another. The real marriage is like 00, not like 010. When the ego is dead is marriage true...It was not lands and rivers that separated us, it was Time itself. It was myself. When the becoming was stopped I would wed Savitri. If the becoming stopped would there be a wedding?

Even on that crucial occasion when Savitri visits Rama at his sick bed and offers to leave her husband for him, this is how Raja Rao records the dialogue:

"My love, my love," she would say, putting her lips against mine, "How I wish I could suck the sorrow out of these twists," and she would lay her head against mine and try to feel me.

"You know I don't love you," she said one day. "That I know," I said. "For if you did, all would be Brindavan."

"Then why don't you play on the flute, and I leave the cattle and the children and that man called my husband?"

"Don't say, 'that man called my husband.' He is your husband, and you are mine."

"Of course he is. Alas he is."

"Pratap is a very fine person, Savitri. As a husband one needs nothing better."

"But then where is Brindavan?"

"Where there is Krishna."

"And who is Krishnam?"

"I, when I am not Rama. Where the mind is not," I continued, "Nor the body, there is his home, Brindavan, and there he shines, Lord Murare."

"Then why this sin of Radha?"

"Because Krishna is not Krishna yet. And when he is Krishna there is no Radha as Radha, but Radha is himself. That is the paradox, Savitri, the mortal paradox of man." "And the paradox is the fever, Lord. What would I not give that this fever should go, this fever that is me ... Lord, take me, and let me forget the world."

"Savitri, who can take whom? I once told Madeleine, there where we take there is no love, and there where we love there is no taking. You can but take yourself."

It should be clear now that there is something radically false and crippling about Rao's attempt to portray an Indianness against a Western world-view; if all reality is illusion, and the true reality is the oneness of Atman and Brahman, you cannot deal with the world of phenomena; you must, as in true Hindu thought, grant at least a limited value to the world of sense perception, to the quotidian course of human action and behaviour, to the moral world of man. You cannot write a novel, not make its central character a liberated soul, particularly such a soul as does not hesitate to sleep with the wife of a friend.

I know that Raja Rao has written other books since: short stories, novellas *The Cat and Shakespeare*, and *Comrade Kirillov, The Chess Master and His Moves*, seven hundred and thirty-five pages long and intended as the first volume of a trilogy! The last-named, hailed by his acolytes and adulators as a masterpiece has not, though written in

English, appeared in the West. I am not surprised that Western publishers don't want to bother with a book of such inordinate length when they are not sure that it can be marketed. I can record the fact that a cursory reading of Raja Rao's later work has shown a sad decline from the creative, innovative prose of *Kanthapura* into a bloodless and inert medium, characterized by a posturing ineffectuality. One cannot sustain philosophical debate unless one has the suppleness, vibrancy and passion of a Dostoevsky, or the range and novelistic craft of a Tolstoy. Raja Rao wants to be both a seer and a modern novelist but one cannot write a modern novel unless one has experienced the unease, the spiritual confusion and the rudderless turbulence of modern life. Despite his later work, my comments on Rao seem to me valid.

I have spent some time on Anand and Raja Rao in order to establish more clearly the special quality of modernism I have in mind but I think this distinction will be even more firmly demonstrated if I consider, however briefly, the case of Narayan, a much finer novelist than Anand or Rao and in some ways far more germane to my purpose. However, if you compare, say, Narayan's *The Vendor of Sweets* with Joshi's *The Last Labyrinth*, you will see how different their fictional worlds are as regards the question of "modernity".

Narayan treats a world which is pre-industrial and pre-capitalist in the modern sense. He deals with agricultural or pastoral family capitalism, his characters are of the middle class, neither so rich as to flaunt their luxury nor so poor as to feel the pangs of destitution. They do not have a strong craving for upward social mobility as they are pretty well content with the time-sanctioned, occupationally derived hierarchies of life; whatever anxieties and ambitions they display have to contend with a strong undertow of traditional sanctions and pieties which are not only social but based on a sense of cosmic order. Narayan no doubt selects his world, it is a slice of the larger reality of India, but it is this selectiveness which gives him his strength. It is a world he himself knows. What business there is, is small and small-town; it is not a world which has disappeared; it is still very real in modern India though the expansion of multinational corporations and of local business continues to erode its base. I would not want to deny Narayan even in 1999 the appendage of "modernist" but the protagonist of *The Vendor of Sweets,* Jagan, who is confused by modernization and resists the machine intended to mass-produce fiction which his son wants to import from America, is indeed very different from a Som Bhaskar, the hero of Joshi's *The Last Labyrinth,* expert in a world of industrial capitalism, of companies and mergers, of stock-watering and proficient in the predatory seizures of other people's shares in order to build his business empire. Jagan himself in Narayan's novel, though a Gandhian, is not averse to cheating the tax department; he would siphon off some of his daily income and maintain two sets of books:

> He made an entry in a small notebook, and then more elaborate entries in a ledger which could be inspected by anyone. In his small notebook he entered only the cash that came in after six o'clock, out of the smaller jug. This cash was in an independent category; he viewed it as free cash, whatever that might mean, a sort of immaculate conception, self-generated, arising out of itself and entitled to survive without reference to any tax.

But when the time is ripe, and he is ready, Jagan can take the road of renunciation (although with his checkbook, just in case!) and leave the world for the next generation because his own life has reached as final a form as it is possible for him on this earth or at least in his own life-span. Bhaskar, on the other hand, is an agnostic; he is not nourished by the wellsprings of a shared moral and religious tradition; at the end of the book he remains confused, ambivalent about life's meaning and still an isolated seeker. What is impressive about Jagan, however, is his remarkable sense of identity; buttressed as he is by his personal and social relationships, his sense of being a person in his town, his moral values shared by the community around him, he can weather the cataclysmic shocks of his son's strange habits brought from the West, such as his living openly with a mistress masquerading (such, anyway, would it seem) as a wife, and his cynical desire to exploit a new-fangled fiction writing machine for profit. What is persistent in Narayan's world is the feeling that even though the old man withdraws from life, his son will also in due time shed his corruption as he himself matures according to the moral and spiritual ethos he has to share and the compulsions he has to serve.

Besides, Narayan is a comic writer: his art has its ancestors and contemporaries in British fiction. It is not surprising that Graham Greene said of him "since the death of Evelyn Waugh, Narayan is the novelist I most admire in the English language." Apart from the fact that his medium is English, his sensibility and technique have been influenced by his reading of English literature. But this is not to minimize his Indianness; in fact, the East-West confrontation is the

source and occasion for comic wit.   Above all, even   in his more
humorous passages, Narayan stresses the continuity of Indian life
persisting through generations rather than a violent disruption caused
by an intruding culture.   The following from *Man-Eater of Malgudi*,
despite its somewhat grotesque comic mode, shows Narayan's sense of
the extended family and its relevance to the Indian tradition:

> A rattan easy chair on which my grandfather used to lie in the
> courtyard, watching the sky, was claimed by my second uncle whose
> wife had started all the furor about the property. She also claimed a
> pair of rosewood benches, which shone with a natural polish and a
> timber wooden chair that used to be known as the bugproof chair. My
> father's third brother, as a compensation for letting us go, claimed a
> wooded almirah as his own and a "leg" harmonium operated by a
> pedal...Our grandfather had lent a hundred rupees to a local dramatic
> troupe and attached their harmonium as their only movable property
> after a court decree, lugged it home and kept it in a corner of our hall.
> He died before he could sell and realize its value, and his successors
> took the presence of the harmonium in the corner of the hall for granted
> until this moment of partition.

Sometimes the comic verve in Narayan is too broad, and serves
merely an intention to entertain, though the fun is generated with
considerable skill, as in this report of the Chairman's speech at a
meeting of the Historical Association from *The Bachelor of Arts*:

> After his cheering and stamping had subsided, Ragavachar rose, put on
> his spectacles, and began, "Ladies and gentlemen, I am not going to
> presume to introduce to you the lecturer of this evening. I do not
> propose to stand between you and the lecturer. I shall take only a few
> minutes, perhaps only a few seconds, to enlighten you on a few facts
> concerning our association... " He then filled the hall with his voice for
> a full forty minutes. The audience gathered from his speech that an
> Historical Association represented his faith in life; it was a vision
> which guided him in all his activities. The audience also understood
> that darkness prevailed in the minds of over ninety per cent of human
> beings, and that he expected the association to serve the noble end of
> dispelling this darkness. Great controversial fires were raging over very
> vital matters in Indian History. And what did they find around them?
> The public went about their business as if nothing was happening. How
> could one expect these fires to be extinguished if the great public did
> not show an intelligent appreciation of the situation and lend a helping
> hand? To quote an instance: everybody learnt in the secondary school

history book that Sirajudowlla locked some of the East Indian company people in a very small room, and allowed them to die of suffocation. This was the well-known Black Hole of Calcutta. There were superhistorians who appeared at a later stage in one's education and said that there had been neither Black nor Hole nor Calcutta. He was not going to indicate his own views on the question. But he only wished to convey to the minds of the audience, to the public at large, to all intelligent humanity in general, what a state of bloody feud existed in the realm of Indian History. True History was neither fiction nor philosophy. It was a hardy science. And to place Indian History there an Association was indispensable. If he were asked what the country needed most urgently, he would not say Self-Government or Economic Independence, but a clarified, purified Indian History. After this he repeated that he would not stand between the lecturer and his audience, and, calling upon Professor Brown to deliver the Inaugural Address, sat down.

In the nineteen-eighties, Narayan published a collection of short stories, *Malgudi Days* and three novels, *A Tiger for Malgudi, Talkative Man*, and *The World of Nagaraj*. They only endorse my comments on his earliest work, except that there is a divagation into the fabulous when a tiger tells the story of its life in *A Tiger for Malgudi*, and a tendency towards the formulaic as in the use of intruder and an intrusion to muddy the waters of an otherwise placid environment, in both *Talkative Man* and *The World of Nagaraj*. I hope Narayan is alert to these dangers because undue concentration on trivia for its own sake can lead to boredom and formulae or set techniques can be deadening. However, both these works have the characteristic wry, affectionate, befuddled wit which proceeds from an inner calm, rare in modern literature.

Malgudi Days shows that Narayan is equally a master of short story belonging in the select circle of Guy de Maupassant, Somerset Maugham and V.S. Pritchett. Each story has its bends and twists and at least one major turn; a day in the life of an astrologer who recognizes his old enemy and uses his astrological gifts to send him packing, and gets rid of him forever; the town postman whose activities extend beyond the delivery of mail to arranging an important marriage; the pick-pocket who wants to put back in his victim's pocket a balloon which was intended for a motherless boy but is apprehended in the attempt because he is gifted with only "one-way deftness." These characters are unforgettable. Even *A Tiger for Malgudi*, though an autobiography of a tiger, is full of human drama: the animadversions on other animals are fascinating:

> Every time I passed below a tree I would hear a cynical cackle and hoot and if I looked up I'd see the loving couple, the owl and her mate. One would say to the other, "When the King passes, what should one do?" There would be some answer to that. "If you don't?" "Then he will nip off your head." "Yes--only if he could carry his mighty bulk up a tree-trunk..."

However, the main focus is on a quadruped's view of the activities and behavior of bipeds, ranging from mercenary entrepreneurs, Indian Style, to a genuine holy man who affirms his beliefs in rebirth, which is the goal of all men.

Narayan can proceed from this inspection of the gritty and cross-grained surfaces of life to plumbing more serious layers of implication; he does not deliberately plumb too deep for he does not want to strike the veins of tragedy; his temper naturally shies away from the tragic essence and the tragic mode. Narayan is a fine artist and knows how best to function within the self-chosen limitations of his world.

Between the "elders" and Anita Desai, who is an unusually fine novelist according to the best standards, regardless of her being a woman, an Indian or a writer who deals with cross-cultural realities, there is the important figure of Kamala Markandaya, to whom we must now give our brief attention. Her novels need not be explored in depth because she is not a significant innovator in language or technique but yet remains an impressive figure on account of the quality and range of her output.

Her first novel, *Nectar in a Sieve,* was a popular success. It is still durable. Her concerns here are similar to those of Mulk Raj Anand: the novel deals with the grinding destitution of a poor rural family further crippled by the march of the twin forces of modernization and urbanization, seen here as more malevolent than beneficial. The novel's sympathetic treatment of the "lower depths" and its record of the patience, hardihood and courage of the poor beset by one misfortune after another, are truly heart-wrenching. As the main character Rukmani says:

> The home my husband had built for me with his own hands... In it we had lain together, and our children had been born. This hut with all its memories was to be taken from us, for it stood on land that belonged

to another. And the land itself by which we lived. It is a cruel thing, I thought. They do not know what they do to us.

Markandaya's output since *Nectar in a Sieve* has been uneven, to say the least. One can group her work under such simple classifications as excellent, good, fair and bad. Some of her novels one would not reread unless one had an assignment to honor, such as writing an essay on The Indian Novel in English. Her novels do not have the consistency of far greater writers like Jane Austen or George Eliot: one does not reread some of her fiction the way one repeatedly picks up Emily Bronte's *Wuthering Heights*, that inexhaustible read, to limit oneself to women writers only. Most noticeably, and disconcertingly, in her later work, she resorts to all the errors composition teachers try to correct in Freshman English or Expository Writing courses: sentence fragments, overuse of commas, shifts of tenses, dangling participles and the like. These blemishes are due perhaps to an increasing confidence as a writer enabling her to take undue liberties with the language, or to the intimidation caused by critics who carp at her living in England, her so-called slavish use of Standard English and her inability to create a specially Indian use of English. Even in an otherwise confident deployment of her linguistic resources to record important themes and moods, one is put off by the syntax and the movement, as, for example in this extract from a late novel, *Shalimar*:

At times like these Rikki felt the division between them, between one man and another; their minds, their reach and sway, the reality of the distance between himself and Tully. Distance? Notes of incredulity sounded as well. Distance between them chipping at marble in the poolroom together, sharing the light, and emotions? Where was the reality, what was vapor? Presently he had to lay down the chisel and simply sit, wondering, looking full-face at Tully. "What is it, Rikki?" Absorbed though he was, Tully could ignore the glance. It would be opaque, he could tell even without looking up. Absinthe gone cloudy, after additives."Distance," said Rikki. "There are oceans between us," he said flatly. Tully, not being born yesterday, had to admit it. But, oddly, he found he had to work at it to believe in the solid admission. For was there an ocean? Really? Actually? His incredulity echoed Rikki's. For there were times, long serene stretches in which they were within touching distance, when they touched. He was aware, then, of things going on, at levels not subject to corruption, from which rose

feelings of authoritative clarity: a quality of simply being that washed
over them like water or light, and merged them into one landscape.

Of her other novels, I would rank *The Nowhere Man* the best as it is
a complex portrayal of an Indian family settled in England, living at
peace with the neighbors, though still able to provoke cultural criticism
along with apathy and indifference, and even to incite in the lunatic
fringe violent hate which leads to destruction and death. It is a rich
novel of cross-cultural confrontation: the protagonist is treated as a
social leper, he also becomes a real leper, a victim of the disease of
leprosy. It is one of the most harrowing presentations of the ugly face
of racism I have read in literature, comparable to fiction written by
American blacks. I deal with this novel rather skimpily but it must be
read by any student of the clash of cultures.

The remaining body of her work comprises good to middling
novels, all of which have interesting elements, such as *Some Inner
Fury*, *A Handful of Rice*, *The Coffee Dams*, *The Golden Honeycomb*,
and *Shalimar* as well clear failures such as *Possession* and *Two Virgins*.
Her second novel, *Some Inner Fury*, deserves attention both for the
cross-cultural problems it raises and its creation of interesting
characters: it treats of the aborted love affair between an Indian woman,
Mira, and a personable Englishman, Richard, of Roshan, a rich Indian
woman who is dedicated to sedition, of an adopted brother Govind, also
a revolutionary with a doomed love for the attractive, married Premala,
who helps a confused missionary, Hickey. The characterization is rich
and varied. Particularly impressive is the character or Premala, who is
transformed by suffering into a heroic condition of being:

> Excitement had sent the colour to her cheeks, and there was something
> else, less evanescent about her too -- a glow, a serenity which had not been
> there since she came to live in this city. Yet it was a serenity of a different
> order-finer, more tempered, as if the dross had been taken from its Virgin
> gold in some unknown fiery crucible -- a serenity that does not come, save
> on the far side of suffering.

The novel ends with unanswered questions: did Govind kill Kit,
Premala's husband, did Hickey perjure when he said he saw Govind
throw the knife at Kit, did Mira perjure when she claimed she had
clasped Govind's hands so that he could not have killed Kit? But the
answers are not so important as the questions generated by the human

entanglements and the political confrontations set in the context of the "Quit India" movement.

Her third novel, *A Silence of Desire,* is about Dandekar and his wife Sarojini, who has a seemingly incurable illness which she takes to a Swami for a spiritual cure. The Swami, intent on spiritual possession, draws Sarojini away from her husband. Dandekar fights tooth and nail to get rid of the Swami and finally has him exiled from the town by the use of unethical methods. Dandekar, however, is able to justify his actions to the Dwarf, the Swami's grotesque and macabre *vademecum*:

> I wanted these things (i.e. the silver and gold) and I fought for them because they meant a good deal to me. That is a fragment of the truth. But I fought also for other things -- my wife, my children, and there are the other fragments of which even you must be aware. You told me once why you came here: that your mind may not grow as warped as your body. Remember that, as I shall always remember all my life those who are here, the derelict.

The attitude to the Swami is ambivalent: he took Dandekar's wife away from him but gave her back to him. Sarojini, meanwhile, is cured of her illness, not by faithhealing but by scientific medical treatment.

The next, *Possession,* is a failure: it spans India, England and America, and is the story of a rich English culture-vulture, Caroline Bell, who wants to "possess" a young Indian boy with artistic talent who had a special relationship with his own spiritual guru in India. She fails, but the contrasts are too simple: colonialism is supplanted by possession based on the power of wealth, which is equally a dismal failure.

A Handful of Rice returns to the Indian poor. It is a poignant but unequal story. *The Coffee Dams* is a more complex work: the ex-colonials the British have a contract to build a dam across a turbulent river in the Indian highlands. The team is led by a dedicated martinet, an Englishman by the name of Howard Clinton. While Clinton is absorbed in his work, his wife Helen is drawn to a technician who was once a member of a local tribe. The novel has a tragic ending with the deaths of both the technician and Howard himself. Apart from the clash of English pragmatism and Indian tradition the stress falls on the instinctual needs which are crushed by Western civilization. *The Virgins,* about which the less said the better, is a pretentious story written primarily for a Western audience with stereotyped characters (one of the virgins makes a speciality out of masturbation). The prose is flat, the references are needlessly exotic, and the conclusion predictable. A good sample of the language is the following:

> Aunt Alamelu had some Amrutanjan. She unknotted her bundle and took out the jar and rubbed the balm into Saroja's temples. Saroja wanted to be cool more than anything, whereas the balm made her burn, being invaluable for chest complaints but she bore it because she knew her aunt meant well.

When the other "Virgin" Lalitha, who went to the city in search of a movie career, was seduced by the producer, and had an abortion, returns to her village, all she can say is that her appearance in a film would depend on "finding the necessary backing, it is not easy in a philistine city which prefers to keep to rutted commercial paths."

The last two novels of Kamala Markandaya which I have read, *The Golden Honeycomb* and *Shalimar*, are well worth reading, despite the clumsiness to which I have earlier referred. *The Golden Honeycomb*, as the title suggests, combines the fragilities, as well as the splendor, of the princely states of India before Independence. The work must have entailed considerable research as evidenced by the superb evocation of the Durbar. The young prince's *bildungsroman* is very effectively done, the characterization of the British resident, Sir Arthur Copeland and of the Brahmin Dewass are nearly faultless. *Shalimar* is equally successful: Markandaya holds the scales evenly between British and Indian, promising a vital partnership, a balanced collaboration between the former rulers and the newly independent state, which is heartening, though the relationship between Tully, the kindhearted Englishman, and Rikki, the sixteen year old Indian fisher-boy, does not altogether escape the sentimental; a hoped-for end, not a present reality.

Even in her earliest novel, *Cry the Peacock*, Anita Desai shows promise of becoming the best novelist to appear on the Indian scene since R.K. Narayan. She is already adept at chronicling and charting the inner lives of her characters while relating them to the outer environment. We can see the movement of her interests and style in the direction of an "inferiority" of art, a concern with the psychological growth and change of her characters while she evokes mood, atmosphere and sense of place.

The art at its best is personal and poetic; there is no striving for an Indianization of the English language. She uses language in a way that is "exploratorily" creative, searching for metaphors and symbols to give her prose its density of suggestion. She seems indebted, if at all, to D.H. Lawrence and Virginia Woolf.

The novel is carefully orchestrated, with its structured transition from third-person narration to narrative in the first person and back again to a concluding section in the third person. The main defect is overwriting: she is unsure of the links she creates between the psyche and external nature; some of the nature "notes" are tiresomely repetitive. Another is an unfortunate penchant for using unfamiliar words like crepitation, tenebrific, opsimaths, synocete, styptic, fulvous, oneirodynia and oneiric, a habit she mercifully sheds after this novel. But to truly appreciate her originality and her "creative" use of language, a somewhat lengthy quotation is needed:

"Do you not hear the peacocks call in the wilds? Are they not blood-chilling, their cries of pain? 'Pia, pia,' they cry; 'Lover, lover. Mia, Mia-- I die, I die.' Go into the jungles before the monsoons come -- at the time when the first clouds cross the horizon, black as the kohl in your grave eyes. How they love the rain -- these peacocks. They spread out their splendid tails and begin to dance, but, like Shiva's their dance of joy is the dance of death, and they dance, knowing that they and their lovers are all to die, perhaps even before the monsoons come to an end. Is it not agony for them? How they stamp their feet and beat their beaks against the rocks! They will even grasp the snakes that live on the sands there, and break their bodies to bits on the stones, to ease their own pain. Have you seen peacocks make love, child? Before they mate, they fight. They will rip each other's breasts to strips and fall, bleeding with their beaks open, and panting. When they have exhausted themselves in battle, they will mate. Peacocks are wise. The hundred eyes upon their tails have seen the truth of life and death, and know them to be one. Living, they are aware of death. Dying, they are in love with life. 'Lover, lover', you will hear them cry in the forest when the rain-clouds come, 'Lover, I die..' And the rain-clouds emerged again from the horizon that was eternally pregnant with promise at one end, and at its opposite pole, was an eternally hungry and open grave. In the shadows, I saw peacocks dancing, the thousand eyes upon their shimmering feathers gazing steadfastly, unwinkingly upon the final truth, Death? I heard their cry and echoed it. I felt their thirst as they gazed at the rainclouds, their passion as they hunted for their mates.

With them I trembled and panted and paced the burning rocks. Agony, agony, the mortal agony of their cry for lover and for death."

When she was a child, Maya, the main character has been told by a soothsayer that there would be a death in the family after she had borne a certain number of children. Maya assumes that it would be her lot to die. Her husband, Gautame, a latter-day Karenin, pooh-poohs the prediction. He is a cool, detached, pompous, somewhat insensitive lawyer. Maya's gradual descent into madness, the neurological intensities which shape and fuel her attitudes to her husband, lead to her dawning conviction that she may not be the one destined to die, and that Gautame does not necessarily have to be the survivor. The apocalyptic mood leads to murder and the final suicide.

What is remarkable about this early novel is that the psychological probing, the introspective analysis of states of thought and feeling are paralleled closely by events in nature, intense, varied and menacing.

Anita Desai's development does not follow an even course and it is therefore unnecessary to pay the same degree of attention to each of her novels. Her next work of fiction, *Voices in the City,* is not so accomplished, being less well organized, even though it has a more pronounced social context. Nirode, one of the main figures, encounters some implausible experiences and the attempt to see both his mother and the city of Calcutta as symbolic of Kali, the Goddess of Death, is somewhat extravagant.

Her next novel, *Bye Bye Blackbird,* attempts a story set in an altogether lower key. Its locale is England and it is a balanced and successful statement of the East-West encounter. It is undeniably slight in comparison but the ironic transformations of character are deftly portrayed. Adit, who seems initially well acclimatized in England, supercilious about his Indian past and proud of his new country, becomes sorely disillusioned and returns home while Dev, who at the beginning finds England obnoxious, decides to stay on as he finds his new country more and more congenial. There is no cross-cultural bias or stridency here: there is, on the other hand, a restraint of approach, and manner: the scales are held evenly. Even Adit's English wife Sarah, though embarrassed to be Mrs. Sen in white company, is strongly drawn towards India.

Its successor, *Where Shall We Go This Summer,* essays the intensities of *Cry the Peacock* and *Voices in the City,* but it is a disappointment. It deals with the need to break away in middle age from the stifling restrictions of a conventional life and find new realities under conditions of freedom but the conclusion is an untragic one as the original impulsions which provoked the flight remain unresolved. The natural setting, however, as often is the case with Desai, comes alive.

This novel is succeeded by *Fire on the Mountain*, a clear triumph, perhaps the best and most unified of her work. The book is about Nanda Kaul, the ex-wife of a prominent man, a Vice-Chancellor, who in her hey-day led a busy social life, took care of children and grandchildren, lorded it over servants galore and has now come in her old age to seek an earned tranquility in a solitude that will give her in time a deserved Nirvana. She chooses to live in a rather inaccessible villa on the foothills of the Himalayas, looking up to the majestic snows above her and the panorama of the dusty plains beneath. She is old, and wants desperately to be left alone. Into this solitude comes the postman with an intrusive letter from her daughter announcing the bad news that great-granddaughter Raka was coming to spend the summer with her to recuperate from a serious illness. Nanda is terror-stricken but old habits of taking care of her progeny die hard, especially if she is not given an option.

What Nanda wants is well suggested by the Hopkins poem which the novelist quotes: it is called "Heaven-haven: A Nun takes the Veil," a title Desai does not use, though it aptly indicates the kind of vocation Nanda is seeking.

> I have desired to go
> Where springs not fail,
> To fields where flies no sharp and sided hail
> And a few lilies blow.
> And I have asked to be
> Where no storms come,
> Where the green swell is in the havens dumb,
> And out of the swing of the sea.

Nanda meets her match, and more than her match in Raka, who is as avid for solitude as she is. Raka wants neither friendship nor familiarity though they live under the same roof. The girl wants to explore and "inhabit" the more forbidding, less travelled parts of the region and live entirely in order to commune with them.

Nanda realizes that Raka is most like her own self. Seeing Raka bend her head to study a pine cone in her fist, the eyelids slipping down like two massive shells and the short hair settled like a dusty cap over her scalp, Nanda Kaul saw that she was the finished perfected model of what Nanda Kaul herself was merely a brave, flawed experiment....Like an insect burrowing through the sandy loam and pine-needles of the hillsides, like her own great-grandmother, Raka wanted only one thing --to be left alone and pursue her own secret life amongst the rocks and pines of Kasauli.

As Nanda herself tells her, 'Raka, you really are a great-grandchild of mine, aren't you? You are more like me than any of my children or grandchildren. You are *exactly* like me, Raka?' In fact it is Nanda who capitulates to the need to establish a relationship with Raka:

> She could not tell why she wanted to bring Raka out into the open. It was not how she herself chose to live. She did not really wish to impose herself or her ways, on Raka, yet she could not leave her alone.

Raka is an incendiary, arsonistic child: her native element is fire. The novel is shot through with prefiguring of the end which engulfs them both in an extirpatory baptism of fire, uniting them both for ever.

> It was the ravaged, destroyed and barren spaces in Kasauli that drew her: the ravine where yellow snakes slept under grey rocks and agaves growing out of the dust and rubble, the skeletal pines that rattled in the wind, the wind-levelled hilltops and the seared remains of the safe, cozy, civilized world in which Raka had no part and to which she owed no attachment. Here she stood, in the blackened shell of a house that the next storm would bring down, looking down the ravine to the tawny plains that crackled in the heat, so much more intense after the rain, and where Chandigarh's lake lay like molten lead in a groove. She raised herself like onto the tips of her toes -- tall, tall as a pine -- stretched out her arms till she felt the yellow light strike a spark down her fingertips and along her arms till she was alight ablaze. Then she broke loose, raced out onto the hillside up the ridge, through the pines, in blazing silence. ''Cuck-oo - cuck-oo' sang the wild mad birds from nowhere.

This powerful presentment of Raka's "incendiary" nature can only foreshadow the end by fire.

The other intrusion into Nanda's life is the visit of her decrepit and impoverished friend, a ghost from earlier days of luxury and ease, Ila Das. Doomed to a half-life from her birth,

Strange to think there was an infant once who, when lisping the nanny-goat-and pinafore rhymes that western and westernized babies speak, curdled the blood of the adults who dandled her on their knees. But one could imagine – Nanda Kaul narrowed her eyes as she stared down at the bald white scalp, bent to the tasks of struggling uphill in the afternoon heat -- Ila Das as an infant in an afternoon frock of blue ribbons and white lace, screeching the most unimaginably horrid sounds that send shivers down the spines of guests and relatives invited to hear her recite her nursery rhymes.

Ila Das is a caricature but what a powerful caricature: it is no accident, in this novel pervaded by the symbolism of fire, that what is recalled is Ila Das, prancing on her tiptoes, to recite *The Boy Stood On The Burning Deck*.

When Ila Das visits her friend, she joins her in applauding past experiences and memories of a more luxurious and fuller life, a life that Nanda had deliberately abjured. But Nanda has not shed it altogether, she still wants to regale Raka with stories that are later acknowledged to be false. It is when she hears of Ila's murder and rape that she is compelled to face reality, the tissue of lies on which she had tried to erect her plans for her precarious future. This *anagnorisis*, the recognition, adds its note of pitiless poignancy to an already tragic situation. At the very end of the book, Raka seems to announce the fire she had herself caused in a note of glee, wonder and even intimacy as though she has on her own forged a relationship with her great-grandmother.

> There was a scratching at the window that turned to a tapping, then a drumming. 'Nani, Nani,' whispered Raka, shivering and crouching in the lily bed, peeping over the sill. 'Look, Nani, I have set the forest on fire. Look, Nani -- look, the forest is on fire.'

Her stories were all a lie, for Nanda Kaul. They had no bears or leopards, only overfed dogs and bad-tempered parrots. Her husband has been unfaithful with a life-long mistress, a teacher of mathematics. All her children were alien to her nature; her fantasies were merely tranquilizers.

This short novel, with its paucity of incident, is so well plotted that it seems to move, slowly but grippingly, yet inexorably to its conclusion, having brilliantly evoked a rich sense of an unusual setting, of remote mountains and plains, almost at World's end. For all its vivid, vibrant sense of locale, its concern with human pretensions leading to an aching need for withdrawal in solitude gives it the reverberations of a general predicament.

Though not as economical, spare and stark, *Clear Light of Day* is a worthy successor to *Fire on the Mountain*. It is more complex in its interests and its modes of organization.

It is a memory trip, a journey back in time to the last days of British India, Independence and Partition. The crackle of gun-fire is heard from the direction of Delhi but the concentration is on another kind of memory trip, a recall of the shared days of childhood and growing up, where everything changes and everything remains the same. Though the milieu is post-colonial India, no longer British versus Indian but Hindu versus Muslim, this conflict is only marginal: it consists solely of the relationship of one of the characters, Raja, who admires the Muslim, Hyder Ali, marries into his family and moves out of Delhi and the story itself. Though present as a character from time past he does not appear in the latter part of the book, and seems to be doing well in his new habitat: the only casualty, though he finds his own niche, is Hyder Ali who has to find a new home.

Clear Light of Day has the feel of Chekovian drama: it is one of the rare examples in fiction of the juxtaposition of the genteel and the turbulent, the submerged under a placid surface, that I have read.

As usual, Desai chooses felicitous epigrams: the lines from Emily Dickinson

Memory is a strange bell --
Jubilee and knell

show the mixed nature of remembrance, celebration and despair.
The quotation from T.S. Eliot

See, now they vanish,
The faces and places, with the self which, as
it could, loved them,
To become renewed, transfigured, in another
pattern.

points to the new, transfigured patterns that memory can create.

The novel is about the excavation of shared memories, sometimes pleasant but more often painful till the final realization by Bim, the

most interesting and dynamic character in the novel, that the buried
earth of shared memories is common to them all, that herself, her
brothers and her sister, that this earth provides her with roots still
growing and spreading, that it is this repository which is resource,
continuity and health.

> '*Time the destroyer is time the preserver*'. Its meaning seemed to
> fall out of the dark sky and settle upon her like a cloak, or like a great
> pair of feathered wings. She huddled in its comfort, its solace she saw
> before her eyes how one ancient school of music contained both Mulk,
> still an immature disciple, and his aged, exhausted guru with all the
> disillusionments and defeats of his long experience. With her inner eye
> she saw how her own house and its particular history linked and
> contained her as well as her whole family with all their separate
> histories and experiences not building them within some dead and
> airless cell but giving them the soil in which to send down their roots,
> and food to make them grow and spread, reach out to new experiences
> and new lives, but always drawing from the same soil, the same secret
> darkness. That soil contained all time, past and future, in it. It was dark
> with time, rich with time. It was where her deepest self lived, and the
> deepest selves of her sister and brothers and all those who shared that
> time with her.

The novel relies more on the evocation of moods rather than on the
piling of incidents and strives to bring into the clear light of day the
subterranean attachments, passions, distempers, entanglements,
ecstasies and phobias that bind together members of a family in the
process of maturation. The apt symbol is that of a well in which their
beloved cow was drowned. It is Bim who as always takes the initiative.

> When Tara came back, she took her firmly by the elbow and
> made her kneel beside her, then bent forward to peer through the
> weeds into the depth of the well. The water at the bottom was
> black, with an oily, green sheen. It was very still except when a
> small frog plopped in from a crack between the stones, making
> the girls start slightly. They narrowed their eyes and searched
> but no white and milky bone lifted out of it. The cow had never
> been hauled out. Although men had come with ropes and
> pulleys to help the gardener, it had proved impossible. She had
> been left to rot: that was what made the horror of it dense and
> intolerable. The girls stared, scarcely breathing, till their eyes

started out of their heads, but no ghostly ship of bones rode the still water. It must have sunk to the bottom and rooted itself in the mud, like a tree. There was nothing to see -- neither hoof nor horn nor one staring, glittering eye. The water had stagnated and blackened, closing over the bones like a new skin. But even the new skin was black now and although it stank, it gave away nothing. Nothing in their hands, the girls backed away on their knees till it was safe to stand, then turned and hurried away, through the grey thorns and over the midder heap, and finally butted their way through the hedge back into the garden, the familiar and permitted and legitimate part of the garden where they found Raja coolly sitting on a cane stool beside Aunt Mira, eating the slices of guava that she cut and peeled for him. Rushing forward with renewed fury, they screamed and jeered and raged at him. He stuck out his tongue at them for he had no idea that they were not screaming with rage at his escape from their clutching fingers and pinching nails but at the horror behind the hedge, the well that waited for them at the bottom of the garden, bottomless and black and stinking.

The traumatic nature of the children's experience when they peeped over the edge of the well in the forbidden bottom of the garden underscores its symbolic distance from the more licit sections where the girls could play their innocent and unthreatening games of hide-and-seek with their elder brother, Raja.

It is the return of Tara, the wife of a smooth diplomat and a successful mother, to her family home in the suburbs of Delhi that releases the substance of the novel. Her sister Bim now runs their rather cheerless and decadent household. Their parents are both dead and their much loved Aunt Mira, a pathetic but keenly etched character who had taken care of the children far more than their parents ever did, has succumbed to alcoholism. The elder brother, Raja, has long fled the family nest. The other brother Baba, retarded, perhaps autistic, continues to live at home unable to communicate except through a gramophone on which he plays ad nauseam the same popular, sentimental songs of a somewhat earlier time. Tara descends into the murky depths of childhood memory as though it was her native element, much to the chagrin of her socializing husband who resents having to spend any time at all in this atmosphere domesticity. But this return to *temps perdu* it is not so dominant as to remove the protagonists from a social setting: the description of the decadent abode of their neighbors is presented with sharp, humorous criticism of a seedy gentility:

> What attracted Tara was the contrast their house provided to her. Even externally here were such obvious differences -- at the Mirsas' no attempt was made, as at Tara's house, to 'keep up appearance.' They were as sure of their solid, middle class bourgeois position that it never occurred to them to prove it or substantiate it by curtains at the windows, carpets on the floors, solid pieces of furniture placed at regular intervals, plates that matched each other on the table, white uniforms for the house servants and other such appurtenances considered indispensable by Tara's parents. At the Mirsas' string beds might be carried into the drawing room for visiting relations, or else mats spread on the veranda floor when an influx of visitors grew so large that it overflowed. Meals were ordered in a haphazard way and when the family smelt something good cooking, they dipped impatiently into the cooking pots as soon as it was ready instead of waiting for the clock hands to move to the appointed hours. The chauffeur might be set to minding a fractious baby, driving it up to the gate and back for its amusement or dandling it on his lap and letting it spin the steering wheel, while the cook might be called out of the kitchen and set to massaging the grandmother's legs. Elaborate arrangements might be made for a prayer meeting on the lawn to please an elderly relative and then suddenly set aside so that the whole clan could go and see the latest film at the Regal.

But, obviously, the main mark of Anita Desai's distinction is a rare ability to evoke atmosphere by the suggestive use of seemingly unimportant items and objects which are repeated at different stages of the narrative. One example of this poetic method must suffice: take the reference to the snail which Tara spies flashing from under a pile of fallen rose petals -- a pearl or a silver ring -- and swoops upon it, excitedly sweeping aside the petals and uncovering a small, blanched snail. What had flashed was her childhood snail "slowly, resignedly making its way from under the flower up a clod of earth only to tumble off the top onto its side -- an eternal, miniature sisyphus." A grown woman, Tara was still child enough:

> Would she go down on her knees to scoop it up on a lead and watch it draw its albuminous trail, lift its tiny *antennae*, gaze about it with

protruding eyes, and then, the instant before the leaf and it slid downwards, draw itself into its pale pod?

The snail is at once a symbol of memory, surfacing and slipping down, as well as the nucleus of an uncertain future for the children waiting intensely for wondrous changes:

> They would wander about the garden, peering intently into the phosphorescent green tunnel of a furled banana leaf, or opening a canna lily pod and gazing at its inner compartments and the embedded pearly seeds or following the path of a silent snail, searching for a track that might lead somewhere, they had no idea where.

For the children the silent snail is not just a small, reticent creature.

Clear Light of Day was followed in 1984 by *In Custody,* which is also one of her finest novels. It should not be necessary to examine it in great detail as the sources of Anita Desai's strengths as a novelist should now be somewhat clearer. But one has to adduce it as a sign of her versatility because it is a wondrously different thing. It is also set in post-Partition India and in the background is the clash between Moslem and Hindu, Urdu and Hindi. The main character, Deven, is an impoverished college teacher of Hindi with a passionate love for Urdu poetry, married to a surly and frustrated woman, Sarla, whose sense of failure stems from her inability to acquire a refrigerator and to frequent the local cinema, two ambitions she had hoped to fulfil by marrying Deven. Murad, a so-called friend, a crude Muslim with undisguised contempt for Hindi as a language, raised on radishes and potatoes, commissions Deven to write an article for the magazine he edits on the work of Nur, an established poet in Urdu. Deven, a man weighted down by poverty, seeks refuge in the pursuit of poetry. Deven idolizes Nur and wants to warm his hands at the fire of art. He is himself a poet *manque.*

In Custody is also about the thin line that divides Art from Bohemia, and the laceration of laughter at what ceases to amuse. Nur is a poet emeritus, decaying in this neck of the woods and writing in a moribund language. He needs to fill the void of his spent genius with the titillations of a fading sexual drive and the adulation of sybarites and sycophants. He is obsessed with food and drink. His first wife is an ignorant if well-meaning woman while his second is an ex-prostitute, a feminist who thinks she is a poet in her own right, a leech who believes that she can thrive only by drawing out what is left of the old man's fire on to herself, rather like that type of American wife who flings her writer-husband's typewriter out of the window in order to get all his attention all to herself. Deven is prepared to worship this exhausted force in the name of poetry, even to pay his bills, but his project fails because of the bitter opposition from Nur's second wife and the old man's worsening senility.

Deven is left at the end unfulfilling and unfulfilled but he has the courage of his convictions: what else does he have but dreary and impoverished domesticity? Prisoner of poverty, acolyte of art, Deven will always remain in custody.

Anita Desai's most recently published novel, *Baumgartner's Bombay,* is about exile, not for reasons of economic advancement or for literary and cultural advantages, as in the case of Henry James, but as the outcome of sheer, existential, traumatic necessity. The theme of displacement has always been a major impulsion and challenge for literature, from as distant a time as examples in Homer and the case of Dante himself, though he was exiled only to another part of his own country. One of the basic, ultimate and primordial metaphors is the exile from Heaven. *Baumgartner's Bombay,* as an example of the crosscultural encounter, recalls, though in reverse, one of her earlier novels, *Bye-Bye Blackbird,* though the last-named does not go beyond the problems of adjustment and acclimatization confronted by Indians emigrating to England. *Baumgartner's Bombay,* however, is about a German Jew who has no choice, his life being in danger, but to flee the Nazis in Germany: when he is reasonably well settled in India, he is treated not as an accepted expatriate, not even as a fugitive Jew, but as a German, an enemy alien, and consigned to a detention camp, the most extreme condition of exile. While the book is in many ways a sad and melancholy story, even a poignant narrative, it is more pathetic than tragic because the protagonist though accepting everything is himself rejected, and especially because he is more sinned against than sinning, more acted upon than acting: his predicament is unheroic.

Baumgartner is exposed to a radical confusion of identities, both of personality and place: is the setting real, or is he real?

> Baumgartner on the steamship, travelling to Dacca. Baumgartner with his feet sweating in white canvas shoes, propped up on the rail, sitting in the shade of a straw hat and studying the bank in an attempt at separating the animate from the inanimate. The forest that was like a

shroud on the bank, ghostly and impenetrable. Crocodiles that slept like whitened stones, spattered by the excrement that rode them delicately. Bamboos that stirred, women who lowered brass pots into the muddy swirl from which a fish leapt suddenly -- but when he remembered them later, in a hotel room in a steaming city that rang with rickshaw bells, he wondered if it had not been all a mirage, a dream. If it had been a real scene, in a real land, then Baumgartner with his hat and shoes would have been too unlikely a visitor to be possible, a hallucination for those who watch from the shore. If he were real, then surely the scene, the setting was not. How could the two exist together in one land? The match was improbable beyond belief.

In India, as in his homeland, Germany, he is the quintessential *Firanghi der Jude,* the Jewish outsider. Even in his most intimate early relationship with his mother who sang songs of ineffable sweetness to him, the sweetness always ended in a quaver. In India, rejection was his lot. He was indigestible, inedible. Even the god spat him out, *"Raus,* Baumgartner, out. Not fit for consumption. German or Hindu, human or divine?" Even the painted hussy Lily who had time for him in days of yore cancelled an invitation her now rich husband had extended to him. Even at the funeral of his friend, Chimanlah, the others shrank away from the presence of a foreigner, a Firanghi who dared to participate in an intensely personal rite.

Baumgartner is exploited by nearly everyone: the self-righteous, mealy-mouthed Farrokh, proprietor of the Cafe de Paris, who knew him well but had a sense of colonialism in reverse, inveighing against white hippies, living off Indian generosity, is but one example. The crux of the matter is best stated by the author:

> Nothing, then, was what life dwindled down to, but Baumgartner found he enjoyed that nothing more than he had enjoyed anything. Perhaps enjoyment was too strong a word for such mild pleasures as he now knew--watching his cats devour a bag of fish he has brought them, dozing with one of them on his lap for company, strolling down to Lotte's for a drink -- but they suited him. He felt his life blur, turn grey, like a curtain wrapping him in its dusty felt. If he became aware, from time to time, that the world beyond the curtain was growing steadily more crowded, more clamorous, and the lives of others more hectic, more chaotic, then he felt only relief that his had never been part of the mainstream. Always, somehow, he had escaped the mainstream.

But escaping the mainstream is not the final remedy: it is indeed ironic that the denouement is caused by a German Aryan hippy, a drug addict, whom Baumgartner befriends, who kills him in order to steal the tarnished silver trophies, the only valuable objects he possessed, in order to find some money to buy more drugs: Baumgartner, who fled the Germans because of his Jewishness, meets his death at the casual hands of a member of the race who wanted him wiped out anyway.

The only real tenderness Baumgartner encounters is from the equally derelict Lotte, an expatriate German cabaret dancer whom he has known a long while in India. Even when soaked with gin, he would sleep with her in the same bed on a steamy Bombay afternoon, rub her rubbery red arms and nudge her thigh. She herself would nibble at his ear, taking genuine delight in his friendship, which outlasted his years in the detention camp. While this relationship is touching, and in many ways redeeming, it does not wipe out the pervasive sense of depression in which this novel leaves the reader; while it exhibits magnificently Desai's ability to evoke a vivid sense of place, especially here of the seamy side of Indian cities, the book has blemishes: an example is that it is interlaced with quotations of German songs and lullabies which are not very relevant. One cannot help but feel that the novel is directed at a European or Western audience, and that in some oblique way Anita Desai is saying "Goodbye to India." While I hoped this prognostication was not true because her Indianness is an important part of her creative impulse, here comes along her latest novel, *Journey to Ithaca,* rather pretentious alike in its title with epigraphs from Cavafy and Milan Kundera, certainly her worst novel to date. Of the main characters only Sophie is plausibly realized: Matteo her husband is plain deluded, if not plain stupid, and incredibly callous and selfish. Of the holy woman, known as the Mother, Sophie's judgement seems the sound one: "a monster spider who had spun this web to catch these silly flies," but a disaster as a credible fictioned character.

Sophie alone realizes that at the heart of the mystery of India is a dead child: so interlarded is Indian spirituality with gross materialism and ravenous entrepreneurship that it is difficult to separate the wheat from the chaff: the human squalor persists abundantly while religiosity seems to thrive on it with equal vigor. Even when the religious impulse may seem genuine, there is a spiritual aggressiveness, a flexing of a seemingly pious brawn, a muscular Hinduism which the novelist does not treat ironically enough. The language too harks back to the verbal infelicities of her first novel, *Cry the Peacock,* with its straining for effect in clichetic phrases like "feasting on beauty", where even the lowly crickets are heard "in audible ecstasy." I hope this novel does not betoken the beginning of the end of the career of a distinguished novelist.

My next choice of novelist is Arun Joshi. The reader may wonder why I devote so much space to him and give him special attention. He is unknown outside India: as far as I know, there hasn't been a British or American publication of any of his works. He is still relatively young, his style is still changing and developing, he is hardly to be considered as an accomplished novelist of the order of R.K. Narayan or Anita Desai. But he is a new phenomenon in Indian letters: he is illustrative of the strengths and weaknesses of Indian writing in English and he is a good resource for further considerations of the question of "modernity" which I raised earlier in this chapter. His four novels, *The Foreigner, The Strange Case of Billy Biswas, The Apprentice* and *The Last Labyrinth,* represent an original contribution to Indian fiction in English. Unfortunately, he was cut off in his prime.

The Foreigner would seem to have the right ingredients for a perfect "cross-cultural" novel. It moves, both in time and space, between America and India, Boston and New Delhi. Sindhi, the main character, is the son of an Indian father and an English mother, was raised by an Indian uncle in Kenya and came to the United States after a sojourn in London. He is the foreigner, *par excellence;* his American girlfriend, June, tells him as early as on the occasion of their second meeting:

> "There is something strange about you, you know. Something distant. I'd guess that when people are with you they don't feel like they're with a human being. Maybe it's an Indian characteristic, but I have a feeling you'd be a foreigner anywhere."

The foreignness becomes a kind of aloofness from human society and the aloofness in turn results in a deliberate cultivation of detachment. Even though he loves June, Sindhi dares not marry her:

> I said, "Marriage wouldn't help, June. We are alone, but you and I. This is the problem. And our aloneness must be removed from within. You can't send two persons through a ceremony and expect that their aloneness will disappear." "But everybody else gets married. Are they all fools?" "They are not fools. But they have the benefit of their delusions. Their delusions protect them from the lonely meaninglessness of their lives. It is different with me. I have no

delusions to bank upon. I can't marry you because I am incapable of
doing so. It would be like going deliberately mad. It is inevitable that
our delusions will break us up sooner or later." "Nothing is inevitable,"
June said vehemently. "I am happy you look at the world that way,
June. America has given that to you. The Statue of Liberty promises
you this optimism. But in my world there are no statues of liberty. In
my world many things are inevitable and what's more, most of them are
sad and painful. I can't come to your world. I have no escape, June. I
just have no escape."

Though Sindhi's predicament is a personal one, it is important to
note that cultural discontinuities make their own contribution. The
theme of the novel may be baldly summarized as a lesson in the nature
of true detachment. At the beginning *Sindhi* sees "detachment" as non-
involvement in human affairs and it is only when such an attitude leads
to disaster that he realizes the true nature of detachment.

"Detachment at that time had meant inaction. Now I had begun to
see the fallacy in it. Detachment consisted of right action and not-
escape from it. The gods had set a heavy price to teach me just that."

This realization -- the same as the doctrine of the *Bhagavad Gita* --
is the beginning and foundation of Sindhi's maturity.

Allied to the theme of detachment is the theme of guilt and moral
responsibility: Sindhi comes to feel that his deeds of commission and
omission caused the death of his friend Babu, who on hearing that his
wife June had once been Sindhi's girlfriend and had even slept with
Sindhi after their marriage, drives away in his car to meet his death;
caused also the death of June when she tried to abort her baby. Though
Sindhi's responsibility is not direct, he feels an unshakable pressure of
guilt.

Sindhi goes to Delhi and is persuaded to join Babu's father's firm.
While working there he realizes that Mr. Khemka is an avaricious,
pompous racketeer beneath the veneer of politeness and sympathy for
his fellow-men. The confrontation had to come. Sindhi explodes at
him:

"I have only been one of your victims. It is you who have swindled
those miserable wretches in rags who push carts on your streets and die
at twenty-five. It is you who have been telling lies and fabricating
documents just so that you could air-condition this ostentatious house
and throw gigantic parties for the horde of jackals who masquerade as
your friends."

When Mr. Khemka's business empire crashes, Sindhi is persuaded to rejoin the company in order to save it and thereby protect its employees: this humanitarian motive is the ground of Sindhi's decision. He realizes that true detachment lies in getting personally involved and that such an action would free him of his burden of responsibility:

> Still the old, nagging fear of getting involved with anything, anyone, was pushing through the mists of reason -- a line of reasoning that led to the inevitable conclusion that for me, detachment consisted in getting involved with the world.

Arun Joshi's style is a good instrument for his mode of narration; if somewhat clipped and jerky, it is free of padding or otiose language: the direct matter-of-factness accords well with the novelist's obvious sincerity. The following account of how June declines Sindhi's dinner invitation because she has decided to marry Babu is a good example:

> June picked up the phone. She sounded pleasantly surprised to hear my voice. "We though you had gone out somewhere," she said. We, indeed! I said I was very much in town, although I had been planning to go out. We chattered for a while. Then I said, "I want to see you, June." There was a silence. Perhaps she was thinking. "I was wondering if we could have dinner together tonight." "I'm sorry, Sindhi ... I will not be able to see you anymore, I mean not as I used to. Babu and I are getting married soon." There was a long pause. The pendulum had swung at last and I had been removed by its stroke. "Can't I see you just once?" "No, Sindhi, I am sorry." She sounded genuinely pained at having to say that. "All right," I said. I heard the click of the telephone as she hung up. I put down the receiver. Then pressing my face against the cold, hard metal of the telephone, I cried. I cried silently and hopelessly until a knock on the glass door indicated that I was wasting somebody's time.

Arun Joshi's first novel contains and anticipates the further development of his themes in the succeeding novels and therefore it is not necessary to dwell on them at length, though they well deserve more detailed treatment than I have space for. *The Strange Case of Billy Biswas* is a novel in which the main preoccupation is the modern quest for authentic self-hood, though intimations from the Hindu tradition modulate its modernity. Joshi's protagonists, even if they feel alienated from modern industrialized civilization are not Camusian outsiders: they have to take account of the pull of mystery and myth and the enveloping presence of living religion. Billy Biswas wants to find a more satisfying life outside the social whirl of the city; as an anthropologist, he is drawn towards the vitality he senses in primitive cultures. Even when living in New York, he chose Harlem as his domicile.

> I asked him why he had chosen to live in Harlem. That was the most human place he could find, he said. White America, he said, was much too civilized for him. His apartment was appalling. It was on the second floor of a tenement house that housed at least a dozen other families. It was situated in what must have been one of the worst slums of New York City.
>
> Such paint as still remained on the walls peeled day and night, flailing in pinch sized heaps of powder. The shutters hung loose; so did the mail boxes in the hall. Nearly all the glass in the front door had been knocked out (during a gun fight, I was later told) so that it had to be boarded up with cardboard pieces cut out of Heinz tomato soup. The stairs were cluttered with empty beer cans, newsprint, children and an occasional condom. At night you could hear the rats scampering among the garbage drums.

Though Joshi's style is often disfigured by the use of cliche, "gaping chasms of the mind," "the black mist of the unconscious," he can delineate as in the above quotation a vivid scene with great precision of detail.

Billy Biswas returns to India as a professor of Anthropology at Delhi University and on one of his expeditions with his students, he disappears to join a tribe, marries a tribal woman and fathers a tribal son, thus abandoning a devoted if conventional wife and family. What Billy is seeking is a society based on instinctual living, believing as he does that the true life of the instincts is superior to the spiritual torpor of the lives of "civilized" man. But this is not a simplistic tract on "civilized" versus "primitive"; Billy's disappearance has its highly venerated forerunners as in the decision by the Buddha to leave his family in search of spiritual enlightenment. Billy, however, in a moment of altruism in order to save his tribe from massacre, reappears in the outside world: society, including his wife and father obdurately want his return to their fold. The search for him leads to his death. Billy's tragedy was inevitable, society has to relentlessly hunt down the outsider as it cannot tolerate an endorsement of a way of life it cannot comprehend. In fact, incomprehension is of the essence. Billy's views strike at the core of modern society, leaving it hardly any choice but to extirpate the rebel:

> "I sometimes wonder whether civilization is anything more than the making and spending of money. What else does the civilized man do? And if there are those who are not busy' earning and spending -- the so-called thinkers and philosophers and men like that -- they are merely hired to find solutions, throw light, as they say, on complications caused by this making and spending of money. What need would there be of psychiatrists, research foundations, learned societies, great scholars, scientists, ministerial advisers, ambassadors, generals, had the world not initially been hung on this peg of money."

The Strange Case of Billy Biswas is for me the most moving of all Joshi's novels; and I think this has something to do with the attempt to portray a hero, and not an ordinary man laden with feelings of guilt over his own weakness or corruption: it has also something to do with its tragic conclusion. The last word about this man who lived in the sanctuary of the great god of the primitive world must belong to Dhunia, his admirer:

> "He is like rain on parched lands, like balm on a wound. These hills have not seen the like of him till the last of our kings passed away."

In *The Apprentice,* his third novel, Arun Joshi probes deeper into the ethical questions of guilt and responsibility than in *The Foreigner.* He has in *The Apprentice* an actual case of corruption which leads to grave harm caused to the innocent. Attention is focused not so much on the individual malfeasance but on a crime in civic life. This gives him the opportunity to dwell on the general degeneration of the person, the crassness and selfishness that canker the soul imperceptibly when a person is so trapped in the rat race and the chase after money and middle class social standards that he compromises all his values.

Ratan Rathor, the son of an impoverished political activist, has ambitions, at first, of following in the footsteps of his father who in his turn was a disciple of Gandhi. He sees his father being shot to death in a demonstration, and from that day he is determined to join the struggle for independence in which his father had taken so prominent a part. He goes to see Gandhi, but his enthusiasm flags apparently in the course of his efforts to meet the great man, and, instead, he borrows some money from his mother and goes to the city in search of a job. There, after undergoing much hardship, he finds a job as a clerk in a "department for war purchases," it being the time of the Sino-Indian border conflict.

From that time onwards, Ratan Rathor records the story of his gradual moral deterioration as his character gets fitted with the armor that will shield him from unnecessary pricks of conscience as he climbs on the backs of his less fortunate colleagues struggling to reach the top of the social ladder. In his words:

> I imagined the day when I would leave that horrible room, get into better rooms, then move into a house, get married, even have a car, perhaps, and be included among those whose destinies had a superiority of their own, independent of rain and sunshine.

He rises to the top of his profession, both by dint of hard work and innate intelligence, and also what he calls his docility and an obsequious servility that pleased his boss. In the process he betrays his colleagues, the poor clerks who agitate for higher wages, and thereby gets on the good side of the administration. The crowning sin that he now admits to himself to have committed is to have taken an enormous bribe shortly before the Chinese invasion. A man named Himmat Singh offers him the money in order to induce him to approve the quality a pile of military materials to be sent to the front. The materials are defective, and Ratan Rathor had rejected them at the beginning. But he takes the bribe in the end and "passes" them. The horrible consequences of this act are revealed to him only later.

In the meantime his degradation continues. He goes to office late, gives up his reading habits, keeps people waiting for hours to see him, particularly if they are unimportant, has become pompous, and has even begun visiting prostitutes. And the fear that his act of bribe-taking would be discovered constantly haunts him. His closest friend, and, perhaps the only friend he has, is a Brigadier whom he has not seen for a long time because he had been out on the front. Now he comes back after the war, but he is in a mental hospital, said to be in a state of shock. Ratan Rathor is not allowed to see him in the hospital, but finally he visits him in his home, and this is how he finds him:

> Through the glass of the window we could see the Brigadier in the verandah. He was rocking. Rocking. Rocking. What was the matter? I asked his wife again. She said they were not meant to disturb him. The two of us watched the sick man in silence. He was shaved and his hair was combed. His night suit was crisp and clean, his dressing gown elegant as ever. And yet it did not add up. Something, some priceless essence that I had known and recognized for forty years, had vanished. Presently I became aware that as he rocked the Brigadier muttered. And occasionally he laughed, the thin ghostly chuckle that was to him the war's parting gift. All at once, getting up abruptly, he started to pace the verandah. And I noticed then the strange wobble in his gait as though he were a ship on the high seas, a ship that had broken her rudder. His feet seemed to fall not on a straight line but at an angle so that every time he took a step he glided sideways until he reached a wall, turned about and glided back in the other direction. And all the while he continued to mutter under his breath.

It is the revelation of the causes of the Brigadier's madness that leads to Ratan Rathor's final breakdown. The faulty equipment that had been cleared by Ratan Rathor had been flown to the front to the Brigadier, several hundred men of his unit had died because the equipment failed, and the Brigadier stood accused of having deserted. The police get information that it was Ratan Rathor who had cleared the defective war materials, and question him. Ratan, however, puts up a bold front and denies everything. In the end the Brigadier commits suicide by blowing out his own brains.

The most important, though not by any means the most fortunate result of the contact of Asian culture with the culture of the West, is the clash of moral values and the confusion that this clash brought about. Ratan Rathor is a sensitive young man, the son of a father who lived and died for an ideal, but he is placed in an environment where the values he has been reared in do not seem to matter. The traditional ethic did not have a code that could guide a man in the sphere of modern civic life. On the first occasion when Ratan Rathor refuses a bribe of ten thousand rupees offered him by a contractor, he mentions the matter to his boss the Superintendent, the man to whom he owed the rise in his career. But the Superintendent, in characteristically evasive fashion, says things that only confuse the young man:

> "You know, Rathor, he said, nothing but God exists. You can be certain only of Him. Now, what do you make of such a reply, my friend? It leaves you puzzled, doesn't it? So did it puzzle me. I asked him what he means. He meant, he said, that there was no point in looking for truths aside from the truth of God. Money in the world always changed hands. God was only concerned with what one did with the money. Did a man, for example, use it for good purposes. Did that mean, I asked him, 'that I should have accepted the bribe?' He said I should not have. But the reason he gave was in everybody's knowledge, and since I could not change it I had no right to accept money for it. That was not to say, he added, that he advocated taking bribes. After that he calmed up. We went back to work. I was more perplexed than before. Did he mean that it was the way you used the money that God was watching and not how you got it? Was graft, in his eyes, the same as any money?..."

Arun Joshi opens up a new dimension for the Indo-Anglian novel, a context that shows how this literary form can be used for probing serious problems concerning human relations. His work is a relief from the light-heartedness of Narayan, the pompous rhetoric of Raja Rao, and the limited range of the propagandist writings of Mulk Raj Anand and Bhabani Bhattacharya. Arun Joshi is concerned with the moral implications of both decision and action as well as indecision and inaction. He tries to show that responsibility in civic life does not consist of mere adherence to a code of right and wrong, but must be subsumed under the broader principles of moral responsibility that govern the life of human beings in their relations with one another.

Joshi's most recent novel, *The Last Labyrinth,* is his most ambitious attempt yet, but also the most disappointing, though seeds are sown which could sprout in a future work in interesting, fruitful new directions. The problem seems to be that Joshi has not yet mastered the idiom that could accommodate this vaster ambition.

His hero, Som Bhaskar, is a millionaire several times over, has all he wants, is married to an extraordinary woman with all the virtues of traditional Indian womanhood, and has two delightful children. Yet he has a deep want, an existential need comparable to the *Angst* of Western existentialists but with a distinctively Indian flavor:

Beyond them all, audible only to my ear, a grey cry threshed the night air: I want. I want. I want. Through the light of my days and the disquiet of those sleepless hours beside my wife, within reach of the tranquilizers, I had sung the same strident song: I want. I want. I want.

Som Bhaskar is preoccupied with Death: he hears voices, he is bothered by unaccountable noises:

It is the voids of the world, more than its objects, that bother me. The voids and the empty spaces, within and without. First, it was only the voids without: empty mountain sides, stretches of oceans, beaches, unsown fields, alleys after dark, corridors of hospitals, the hum against the ear of a conch, caves, that was how it had probably started -- with the caves. I was home that summer. I was eighteen. I was alone in a cave at Ajanta. It wasn't one of the showpieces. I must have gone in for a break from the sun. It was cool inside and dark. Then the walls started to float in, trembling, shimmering, daubed here and there with colour. The colours were faint, as they are in dreams. I had stood there trying to make sense out of them. And then, as gradually as they had materialized, the walls dissolved into the darkness. I continued to stand there until I was cooler. The walls came and went in dizzy waves, the daubs of colour dancing before my eyes. The spasms of darkness grew steadily longer. Or, so it had seemed. Finally, I could not stand it any longer. When the wall disappeared once again I dashed out.

Lust for women is the common symptom of the search for the panacea to this desire, but it is always quickly satiated upon possession and he returns to his devoted and faithful wife, Geeta. That is, until he meets Anuradha. She is the wife (or mistress, one is never really sure which) of a decadent, bhang-smoking fellow industrialist, Aftab, whose company Som Bhaskar wishes to acquire. The desire to take over the company is rapidly replaced by an obsession with Anuradha. She, and her world of Aftab's strange labyrinthine house at Benares, Benares itself, and the whole air of physical corruption and moral decadence that surrounds that world become a focus for his phobias, fears and desires. It is first an obsession of love and lust. However, when Anuradha leaves him, after he has suffered another, massive heart attack that his friend says should have killed him, his insecurities are intensified and the obsession becomes one of hate. He resumes buying into Aftab's company, having suspended his purchases for Anuradha's sake (and virtually as a trade for her body), and then pursues his search for a block of shares all the way to a temple in the Himalayas.

There he finds the mysterious Gargi, a deaf-mute, daughter of a Sufi whose background is strange and miraculous, and is a part of Aftab's world. Gargi is one of the most mysterious characters of all in this novel of enigmas. At the temple, K., who has accompanied Som on his search, tells Gargi what Som did not know before. K. says that during Som's last attack he had given him up as dead when Anuradha visited. He gave Anuradha the news the there was no hope. Since then, Anuradha has intimated to K. that she had gone from Som's sickbed to Gargi to plead that she should save Som's life. At first, Gargi had refused to even acknowledge her power to do anything, but later charges Anuradha to give up Som entirely, and Som would live. So Som had recovered and Anuradha refused to see him any more. (The story echoes the story of Gargi's father, who had fallen ill and was denying the existence of God. His father was advised to give up what he most loved and his son's life would be spared, so he called on God to take his own life. The father died and the son recovered.)

So the issue is finally one of faith or belief in God, or miracles, or at best, in something beyond the material world. Som Bhaskar's skeptical mind cannot accept faith. He takes the shares which Gargi has in her charge and goes away vowing to have Anuradha as well. He visits Aftab's house seeking her. After an interview with Aftab, Anuradha comes out and pleads with Som to go away for his life's sake. When he returns the following morning, Aftab informs him that Anuradha has disappeared from the Janmasti celebration and cannot be found. Som Bhaskar has the police investigate but she is not found, and Som goes in real fear for his life, for Aftab, in his grief, has threatened him. The question of faith is, furthermore, unresolved, for Som cannot discover whether Anuradha's disappearance was the work of human interference or a mysterious disappearance engineered by God in fulfillment of the terms of a boon granting Som Bhaskar his life.

It can be seen that Joshi's exploration of the inner quest has become more complex with time. Billy Biswas was certainly a strange case, but his story is simply told as the record of an external narrator. Ratan Rathor reveals his tale to a much younger man as the unwinding confessions of a conscience tortured despite his acts of contrition each day at the temple. By this means the complexity of Rathor's guilt feelings is fully portrayed.

In *The Last Labyrinth* the structure is as labyrinthine as the central themes and the processes of Som Bhaskar's mind. Symbols are used in a far more sophisticated manner to explore the complex psychology of a mind that is tormented by the relationship between the material and the mystical. Yet despite this growing sophistication of treatment, Joshi's interest has always been in the alienated being, whether the individual be extraordinary, as was Billy Biswas, supremely ordinary like Ratan Rathor, or psychologically disturbed in the manner of Som Bhaskar.

In conclusion, I would like to say of Joshi that despite his modernism he was a product of the immemorial Indian culture. I knew him personally and in an unpublished article he gave me, it is clear how different he is from the atheistic intellectual of the Western world:

> And what about God? Does He exist? Can we do without Him? I know it has become old-fashioned to talk of God. But the question remains, because the same limitations that had prompted man to invent an Absolute in the first place, exist in him still. As long as good and evil remain in the world, so remains the idea of God. From what I can make out, men the world over have once again become aware how inadequate they are without faith in an Absolute. The absolutes we have tried to live by for more than the last one hundred years have proved far from satisfactory. I have a feeling that men, including writers, will be seen embarking on new expeditions in search of the Absolute. Man is infinite as is his environment. Infinite therefore are the ways in which the two interact. It is the privilege, if not the duty of the writer to be the chronicler of this interaction.

It is too early to assess Joshi's contribution to literature. It is clear that his prose style was still not variegated enough, rich or nimble enough, to encompass the serious themes he so surely wanted to deal with. He cannot match the style of R.K. Narayan or of Raja Rao at his best. He does not seem to be as at home in the English language as Nirad Chauduri, whose book-learned, even period flavor, still manages to give the impression of an original contribution to English prose. But in his concerns and novelistic temperament, Arun Joshi, if not great, was an important novelist at a very interesting stage in the development of Indian fiction in English.

CHAPTER XVII

LESSONS OF THE MASTER: RUTH PRAWER JHABVALA'S *SHARDS OF MEMORY*

This novel moves into and out of three continents and spans four generations of the Kopf family, which is touched profoundly by the ongoing influence of an enigmatic guru, called the Master. When the guru, clad in frock coat, cravat (with enormous diamond pin) and patent leather pumps, chokes on a succulent piece of meat, his mantle falls to Henry Kopf, a man destined to become the custodian of the Master's writings, the interpreter of his simplistic message, and his incarnation, if not his biological son.

The scene of the Master's death is uproariously comic, though laced with the wry irony that is one of the hallmarks of Ruth Prawer Jhabvala's talent. Some of her characters are pasteboard figures, stereotypes of one kind or another--for example, Kavi, a poet whose best effort is to intone such banal lines as "O Kavi, shipwrecked on the river of life in its surge to the ocean, why could you not steer your boat with more skill?" Edward Said, in his book *Orientalism,* has shown how the colonizer, in order to assuage his conscience, has to stereotype the colonized as stupid, ineffectual, devious and so on. Jhabvala, though not herself one of the colonizers, must have consumed enough AngloIndian fiction to exhibit, even if unconsciously, the imperialist vision.

For a writer who spent 25 years of her life in India, Jhabvala often displays a narcissistic disgust for her subject. Yet she is at her best when she writes about India. Her three most successful novels are *Travellers, Heat and Dust,* and *Three Continents,* where the collision of East and West ends in unmitigated disaster. Sometimes she drops to the level of the cultural anthropologist: in *The Householder,* when the young husband and wife of an arranged marriage are feeding sweetmeats to each other, the novelist, instead of stressing the burgeoning love between them, seems to be studying their feeding habits.

But elsewhere she is more surefooted, as when, in *Shards of Memory,* she describes what happens after a long lunch at the home of the kind of well-to-do Indian family with which she is familiar:

> The mother and daughter began to get ready for their daily outing; the mother was fat, the daughter scrawny, but all dressed alike in the daintiest white georgette and lace, with satin court shoes peeping from the embroidered hems of their saris. They piled into the family carriage to be driven to the Taj Mahal Hotel, where their little marble table was always reserved for them. It was on the first landing, so that while drinking their pineapple juice, they could watch people go up and down the red-carpeted marble staircase.

Jhabvala's main novelistic device is a literary variant of the flashback, but it is her own original technique. Her practice of writing screenplays, two of which have won her Academy Awards, no doubt carries over into her complex method: it is a matter of interweaving different times, places and persons, of intercuts and juxtapositions, of characters at different stages of their lives, sometimes narrating their own histories, at other times being narrated about and commented upon--an altogether fascinating modus operandi.

Her prose style is bare and unadorned; one often wishes that it could be enriched by colors, sights and sounds, but it is an excellent instrument for her purposes. It cuts out any fussiness or flak and admirably fits her many tones--wry, ironic, satiric, comic or even laudatory. Her plotting, too, is so deft that she holds the reader's attention.

Gurus like the Master abound in Jhabvala's fiction: They are almost an obsession. Even when she leaves the Indian scene, as in *In Search of Love and Beauty,* a guru emerges in the persona of a psychospiritual therapist. In *Shards of Memory* there are some acceptable characters, notably the kind, pragmatic Baby and her husband, Graeme, who, ironically enough, despite his apathy toward spiritual matters, seems to have been the only one to have gotten the Master's true message.

But the true nature of the Master--one of the more rounded characters of the novel-remains unresolved: was he an astute go-getter or a predatory charlatan? Jhabvala does not give a satisfactory answer to this question here or elsewhere in her fiction.

CHAPTER XVIII

THE CASE OF SALMAN RUSHDIE

I was plagued by many hesitations in planning this chapter on Salman Rushdie. I have called it a "case", not in the sense that he presents himself as a case study for diagnostic evaluation but because of the reverberations of his work as a literary, cultural, political and religious phenomenon. First of all, it seemed too early to attempt an - assessment of a still developing writer in mid-career: Rushdie is only fifty-one years old, and, as a publisher's blurb would say, at the height of his powers. We will note later on that there are important areas of human and artistic exploration which are nascent. It would be unfair to assume that they are forever closed or that he will not deal with them in future work.

Secondly, if you wish to properly "place" Salman Rushdie in a context or contexts without robbing him of his originality you have to see him as belonging to, and distinct from Indian literature in English, with its multiculturalism and its variegated mirrors of the clash of East and West. You must also see it as stemming from the older tradition of the English novel, especially the line of Sterne, Swift and Joyce. You have to see him in relation to the modern and post-modern novel in England and America. You have to reckon with the "influences" on his work of the novels of Gunter Grass and Thomas Pynchon, of the "magical realism" of Alejo Carpentier and Gabriel Garcia Marquez, the European novel as in Milan Kundera: in fact, you have to roam so far afield that your essay may well become a monograph in its own right that has to be published separately rather than as a chapter in a book, given as this book is to many themes, many preoccupations.

Thirdly, I did not feel I had the knowledge, skill, space or even the inclination to make extended analyses or judgements of his themes or his techniques of literary expression, especially since they are in a stage of constant change and development.

Already, at the time of writing, there is a new book which has only recently crossed the Atlantic, *Haroun and the Sea of Stories*, a product of his enforced seclusion. It is a departure in fabrication towards the fable and the fairytale, though profoundly akin in its methods and interests--the same creative genius, the same verbal brilliance, blending the bizarre with the day-to-day, the fantastic with the real, informs the work. Its real subject is Art versus Censorship, the compulsive need for politics and power to castrate the word, and the more robust compulsion of the word to prove that it is mightier. The book like all fairytales ends on a note of hope, a quality that distinguishes Rushdie from many other post-modernist surveyors of the human condition. Rushdie's technique as a story-teller, with his use of fluidity and metamorphoses is well described in this excerpt:

> So if the Water-Genie told Haroun about the Ocean of the Streams of Story, and even though he was full of a sense of helplessness and failure the magic of the Ocean began to have an effect on Haroun. He looked into the water and saw that it was made up of a thousand thousand thousand and one different currents, each one a different color, weaving in and out of one another like a liquid tapestry of breathtaking complexity; and if explained that these were the Streams of Story, that each colored strand represented and contained a single tale. Different parts of the Ocean contained different sorts of stories, and as all the stories that had ever been told and many that were still in the process of being invented could be found here, the Oceans of the Streams of Story was in fact the biggest library in the universe. And because the stories were held here in fluid form, they retained the ability to change, to become new versions of themselves, to join up with other stories and so become yet other stories; so that unlike a library of books, the Ocean of the Streams of Story was much more than a storeroom of yarns. It was not dead but alive.

It is a flawed work: the phantasmagoria is sometimes unbearable but the direction is promising.

One has also to note that Rushdie himself is likely to grow as an artist, encompassing even more central human concerns: he seems to be becoming consciously aware of what is lacking in his art, something which if he can acquire will certainly entitle him to a place in the pantheon of the greatest writers. His gifts are indisputable. In a recent interview with Gerald Marzorati, a perceptive admirer of Rushdie, published in *The New York Times Magazine*, Rushdie says:

> There is very little sex in my novels, very little stuff at all about the deep emotions. I've always been embarrassed by it, I suppose. But I've come to see that one of the things I have failed to do, at the center of my work is write about strong feeling, cathartic emotion, obsession.

It is good that he is reading the Brontés and Jane Austen, as what indeed is lacking in Rushdie is the capacity to evoke deep emotion, to create, except on rare occasions, an empathy for his characters and their struggles. If he had this ability, he could well join the ranks of Dickens and Tolstoy.

I also had a real problem deciding in which part of the book this chapter should fall: does Rushdie belong to the Third World, the First World or to the World itself? These categories are merely convenient, and often misleading. How can he be compared, for example, with another Indian, Vikram Seth, as in his remarkable novel in verse, *The Golden Gate*, very modern in its treatment of sexual "normality" and "deviance", of heterosexuals, homosexuals and bisexuals, and displaying expert prosodic craft? Or how does Rushdie compare with Kazuo Ishiguro, as in his masterpiece of understated intensity, *The Remains of the Day*, a work beside which Rushdie seems altogether loquacious? Neither Seth nor Ishiguro disclose the slightest trace of their countries of origin, unless one wants to argue, in the latter instance, that one needs a Japanese reverence for tradition to draw a convincing portrait of an English butler.

I decided to include Rushdie with the Third World writers because most of his major fictions, for the greatest part, have the Indian subcontinent as their setting. There are also significant ways in which he develops the corpus of Indian writing in English while at the same time extending the resources of the hospitable English tongue and the literary experience in English. In any event, in the case of an important writer, pigeonholing of a finicky kind, labelling the bottle and putting it on the shelf are a disservice and a distortion.

But there was no way I could have avoided Rushdie in the book: not only is he a signal example of the cross-cultural encounter set in an even later time than that of the post-colonial Paul Scott, he is one of the few who have taken pains to conceptualize the experience. He is in fact an intellectual theorist of this kind of reality.

In the novel in English he is an original representative of the postmodern, of what has come to be loosely categorized as "magical realism". Influenced though he is by such disparate writers as Gunter Grass, Thomas Pynchon, Milan Kundera and Gabriel Garcia Marquez, from three different continents of the world, he has preserved his own singularity, rowed his own catamaran. If there is a Global writer, it is Rushdie.

But he is also British in some important ways: he can be associatec with some of his near contemporaries, with writers like Martin Amis, Julian Barnes, William Boyd, Peter Ackroyd, Jeannette Winterson, as we will have occasion to comment later on in this essay.

As for the cross-cultural meetings and clashes, Rushdie has gone far beyond what is suggested by these phrases. His concern has travelled further than the interpretation of a foreign culture, so ably achieved by such a writer as Lafcadio Hearn. Rushdie's thrust is transformed into a cultural take-over, even a cosmic change: witness this vision of the tropicalization of England in the *Satanic Verses*, which is not merely an evocation of the country's diverse ethnic composition, and therefore needs to be quoted at some length:

> Gibreel Farishta floating on his cloud formed the opinion that the moral fuzziness of the English was meteorologically induced. 'When the day is not warmer than the night,' he reasoned, 'when the light is not brighter than the dark, when the land is not drier than the sea, then clearly a people will lose the power to make distinctions and commmence to see everything--from political parties to sexual partners to religious beliefs--as much the same, nothing-to-choose, give-or-take. What folly! For truth is extreme, it is so and not thus, it is him and not her; a partisan matter, not a spectator sport. It is, in brief, heated.' 'City,' he cried, and his voice rolled over the metropolis like thunder, 'I am going to tropicalize you.' Gibreel enumerated the benefits of the proposed metamorphosis of London into a tropical city: increased moral definition, institution of a national siesta, development of vivid and expansive patterns of behavior among the populace, higher-quality popular music, new birds in the trees (macaws, peacocks, cockatoos), new trees under the birds (coco-palms, tamarind, banyans with hanging

beards). Improved streetlife, outrageously colored flowers (magenta, vermillion, neon-green), spider-monkeys in the oaks. A new mass market for domestic air-conditioning units, ceiling fans, anti-mosquito coils and sprays. A coir and copra industry. Increased appeal of London as a centre for conferences, etc.; better cricketers; higher emphasis on ball-control among professional footballers, the traditional and soulless English commitment to 'high workrate' having been rendered obsolete by the heat. Religious fervor, political ferment, renewal of interest in the intelligentsia. No more British reserve; hot-water bottles to be banished forever, replaced in the foetid nights by the making of slow and odorous love. Emergence of new social values; friends to commence dropping in on one another without making appointments, closure of old folks' homes, emphasis on extended family.   Spicier food; the use of water as well as paper in English toilets; the joy of running fully dressed through the first rains of the monsoon.

 Disadvantages: cholera, typhoid, legionnaires' disease, cockroaches, dust, noise, a culture of excess.

 Standing upon the horizon, spreading his arms to fill the sky, Gibreel cried: 'Let it be.'

This is clearly not a statement about cultural clash or collision: it is a new syndrome of the aspirations and fantasies of the resident alien who wants to supplant his host culture with his culture of origin.

Bharati Mukherjee in her novel *Jasmine* refers to the first stage of cultural displacement in these words:

> We are the outcasts and deportees, strange pilgrims visiting outlandish shrines, landing at the end of tarmacs, ferried in old army trucks where we are roughly handled and taken to roped-off corners of waiting rooms where surly, barely wakened customs guards await their bribe. We are dressed in shreds of national costumes, out of season, the wilted plumage of intercontinental vagabondage.

But in an introduction to a collection of short stories, she exudes a new confidence, a progress to "the exuberance of immigration."

> I have joined imaginative forces with an anonymous, driven, underclass of semi-assimilated Indians with sentimental attachments to a distant homeland but no real desire for permanent return. I see my "immigrant" story replicated in a dozen American cities, and instead of seeing my Indianness as a fragile identity to be preserved against obliteration (or worse, a "visible" disfigurement to be hidden), I see it now as a set of fluid identities to be celebrated. I see myself as an

American writer in the tradition of other American writers whose
parents or grandparents had passed through Ellis Island. Indianness is
now a metaphor, a particular way of partially comprehending the
world. Though the characters in these stories are, or were, "Indian", I
see most of these as stories of broken identities and discarded
languages, and the will to bond oneself to a new community against the
ever-present fear of failure and betrayal.

Rushdie himself does not share the same confidence or even
aspiration but he faces squarely the problem of spending time present in
a foreign land while his past is "home". In a seminar of Indian Writing
in English held in London in 1982, Rushdie spoke of the confrontation
between memory and the current experience, which results in
fragmentation and the consequent need for a writer to stylize this
fragmentation: he advocated the need to escape from a ghetto mentality
while retaining his Indian inheritance and his personal past. What has
to be achieved in life as well as in art is a genuinely plural identity, not
the veneer which is unease and discomfort. In an earlier interview with
the same Gerald Marzorati published in *The New York Times Magazine*
of January 19, 1989, Rushdie says:

> In writing *The Satanic Verses*, I think I was writing for the first time
> from the whole of myself. The English part, the Indian part. The part of
> me that loves London, and the part that longs for Bombay... What is
> being expressed is a discomfort with a plural identity. And what I am
> saying to you--saying in the novel--is that we have got to come to terms
> with this. We are increasingly becoming a world of migrants, made up
> of bits and fragments from here, there. We are here. And we have never
> really left anywhere we have been.

The question is not of a loss of identity but of assuming a new
identity which is defined by living in a foreign land, an identity which
springs or has to spring from fragmentation and multiculturality.

Of course, since displacement, multiculturality and fragmentation
are some of the main features of the human condition in our time, they
are bound to appear in different forms, as we have noted in detail in
earlier parts of this book. They can range, to take some additional and
recent examples, from subtle undercurrents as in Naguib Mahfouz, the
Egyptian novelist (not so recent but only recently available in the West)
where the cross-cultural influences, however, are subsumed under the
ambition of defining a national psyche. There is the more direct

collision of cultures in Jamaica Kincaid's *Lucy* between her West Indian upbringing and her travails in the United States. Even in the last named, the cultural contrast develops into the main character's need to exorcise her past in order to achieve her womanhood. Nadine Gordimer, for example, though widely read and admired, has been pushed to the periphery of critical discourse because she deals with a world distant from, and alien to the West, and perhaps also because she treats reality too brutal to be borne. The clashes are more than cultural conflicts: the context is one of deep racial hatred and ethnic war. But it is more than a context: the brutal racial antagonism interanimates the human drama, just as in her latest novel, *My Son's Story*, the main character's erotic adulterous love radically alters his almost idyllic marriage and family and savages his son, savages him enough to make him a writer. The illicit love that Sonny the black protagonist shares with the white Hannah becomes a strong spur for Sonny's own political commitment and struggle.

The nature of the artistic approach and treatment can also vary with the differences in acceptance of the immigrant by the host culture. There are marked contrasts between the situations in Britain and the United States which can be illustrated, for example, by comparing Amy Tan's remarkable and poignant first novel *The Joy Luck Club* with, say, Hanif Kureishi's *The Buddha of Suburbia*—a hilarious, irreverent but moving novel. The pull of different civilizations in opposite directions and the effort to fabricate a balance, or at least a compromise, is almost a stock-in-trade of the more inventive novels of this century. But both the artist's strategy and equation depend on the social and political realities the immigrants encounter in specific contexts. In the United States, perhaps because of the long history of immigration, reasonably confident sub-cultures have been established despite the early ostracism, persecution and even lynching; in Britain, however, because of its more homogeneous society with its patterns of social dominance, the immigrant remains a half-caste. Amy Tan's Chinese characters can form a Joy Luck Club, their cross-cultural anxieties become generational problems which they share to a degree with the more settled groups of Americans. The Chinese feel they have a claim on America, that they have a distinct contribution to make. This is even more explicitly apparent in the non-fictional work of writers like Maxine Hong-Kingston whose *The Woman Warrior* and *China Men* express the role of memory and inheritance in the process of adaptation. I am not a literary weatherman but I can risk my reputation by predicting that Amy Tan's future novels will be as good, if not better than her first works; her gifts are clearly of that order of promise. Similarly, Richard Rodriguez of Mexican stock describes in *Aria: Memories of a Bilingual Childhood* the fierce oppositional pulls of home and the outside world of grocery store, gas station and school, his own clan and the others, *los gringos* and, above all, the contrast between the melodious intimacy of his native Spanish language and the guttural, abrasive, public English, movingly conveyed in such descriptions of his father's public efforts at conversation: "at one point his words slid together to form one word--sounds as confused as the threads of blue and green oil in the puddle next to my shoes."

But what distinguishes Amy Tan and Maxine Hong-Kingston is that, unlike Hani Kureishi, they feel they have earned the right to become part of the host society while Kureishi's narrator Karim Amir in Britain, despite his father's announced marriage to his mistress, Eva, is ambivalent about the future. There is hope, but it is dim:

> And so I sat in the center of this old city that I loved, which itself sat at the bottom of a tiny island. I was surrounded by people I loved, and I felt miserable and happy at the same time. I thought of what a mess everything had been, but that it wouldn't always be the same.

But what is most apropos to my theme in this book is Karim's remark, "the immigrant is the Everyman of the twentieth century." The Indian response is based on the real dilemma of wanting to acclimatize while retaining the old identity: his father's friend Anwar "died, mumbling about Bombay, about the beach, about the boys at the Cathedral school" while his father who never showed any interest in returning to India "wasn't proud of his past, but wasn't unproud of it, either."

Kureishi's attitudes resemble those of Salman Rushdie, except that Salman Rushdie seems to revel in hybridity and mongrelization: to quote him, "I am a bastard child of history. Perhaps we all are, black and brown and white, leaking into one another, as a character of mine once said, like flavors when you cook."

Above all, Rushdie dreaded the absolutism of the Pure.

To properly assess Rushdie's contribution to the novel, one has to relate him not merely to the comparatively new tradition of the Indo-Anglian novel but to the longer lineage of the novel in English, both in Britain and America. How, for example, does he rank with Jane

Austen, George Eliot, Charles Dickens, Joseph Conrad, Henry James and D.H. Lawrence? It is too early to say and it would be unfair to Rushdie to make such an attempt. F.R. Leavis, whose *The Great Tradition* was a heroic attempt to chart a line illustrating where the real greatness of the novel in English consists is still eminently valid in many respects but both his theory of the novel and his choice of candidates result in many exclusions: what is left out is as considerable as what is admitted. Of course, he does not deal with the American share--the work of Hawthorne, Melville, Mark Twain and Faulkner--in a substantial way. But what is more disabling is the failure to link the novel with the existing tradition represented by the Bible and the drama, especially the poetic drama of such as Shakespeare. This, I think, leads to his disposal of Emily Brontë's *Wuthering Heights* as a "sport" of genius in a footnote: this does scant justice to what is perhaps, in its poetic use of language and modes of organization, the greatest of the novels written in the nineteenth century. Leavis' theory of the novel also presents problems. A remark like the following: "when we examine the formal perfection of *Emma*, we find that it can be appreciated only in terms of the moral preoccupation that characterizes the novelist's peculiar interest in life" resembling, as it does, the following from Henry James's Preface to *The Portrait of a Lady*

> There is, I think, no more nutritive or suggestive truth in this connection than that of the perfect dependence of the "moral" sense of a work of art on the amount of felt life concerned in producing it. The question comes back thus, obviously, to the kind and degree of the artist's prime sensibility, which is the soil out of which his subject springs.

is an arresting critical *apercu* but because of its generality skirts more issues than it solves.

In any event, it would be a mistake to ignore the effect on the novel of pre-existing literary forms such as the prose of the Bible and the richly mixed form of the poetic drama. One cannot properly appreciate the origins of Bunyan's allegorical *The Pilgrim's Progress* or even that of the minor masterpiece, T.F. Powys' *Mr. Weston's Good Wine*. Without a sense of the Bible and Shakespearean poetic drama, one cannot appreciate Emily Brontë's *Wuthering Heights*, Hawthorne's *The Scarlet Letter*, Melville's *Moby Dick*, Mark Twain's *Huckleberry Finn*,

Finn, the prose of Charles Dickens, the style of D.H. Lawrence, the innovative language of James Joyce and the fictional purposes of William Faulkner. It would also be ungenerous to slight the originator Henry Fielding, the different lines represented by Sterne and Swift, particularly Sterne who has had more than his fair share of revenge for his critical belittlement by his influence on the more innovative, post-modernist novelists.

Traditional styles have persisted with modifications in such authors as Evelyn Waugh, Kingsley Amis, Angus Wilson and Muriel Spark and a mixture of styles, traditional and post-modernist, are to be found in William Golding and John Fowles. But before attempting to relate Rushdie to his older and near contemporaries, it would be well to begin by comparing him with V.S. Naipaul, a novelist of great critical and popular esteem; they both have a common Indian origin and are settled (how ironic a word in the case of Rushdie!) in their countries of adoption.

Such a comparison seems to be the best way of uncovering the bases of Rushdie's art, especially his satiric purposes.

Sir Vidiadhur Surajprasad Naipaul, knighted by the Queen, author of more than twenty books, often mentioned as worthy of the Nobel Prize, published by Andre Deutsch in a uniform edition, an honor rarely achieved by a writer before he is dead, has indeed come a long way for the grandson of an indentured Indian laborer from a remote outpost of Empire. However, when one considers his ouevre, there is only a small fraction that merits high praise, a slightly larger segment of uneven merit, of qualified failure or limited success, and the bulk which is badly disfigured by nihilism, blatant racism, sado-masochism and the unqualified celebration of Western ideals and civilization.

His work shows a progressive descent into bleakness and pessimism (if this is possible) except for the somewhat more reconciled, mellower tone of *The Enigma of Arrival*, even if written in a somewhat etiolated language, and the new mood of *India: A Million Mutinies Now*. Rushdie, on the other hand, despite the *saeva indignatio* of his satiric vein, appears almost buoyant. Naipaul does not embark on metaphysical debates in fiction nor does he, despite his own subliminal psychoses, engage in the overt cultivation of fantasy. His prose, too, although limpid for the most part and often elegant, can border on the anemic, while Rushdie's style in comparison can be called unruly, or even rambunctious. Of course, there are many differences between Rushdie and Naipaul. There is the obvious difference between a poor man whose ancestors moved from one third-world country to another and remained, despite their cross-cultural relationships and the creeping onset of modernization, very much a part of an ethnic group, and Rushdie, the scion of a wealthy Indian family who was able to buy his way into an English public school and a developed Western milieu. Rushdie had to learn how to eat kippers but Naipaul may not have even heard of them in his native Trinidad. Rushdie encountered a host culture which was dominant but not altogether alien; he had the luxury of choice: he could comfortably return, save for his own spiritual metamorphosis and his literary ambitions, to his country of origin. Naipaul had to win a merit scholarship to go to Oxford. In Trinidad, both the Indians and the Blacks could hang on to their old and distinct traditions for long periods. I am personally acquainted with a community of Indian Tamil indentured laborers who came to Sri Lanka in the last century, in the heyday of British Imperialism, who have retained till now much of their old way of life, although the hill country of Sri Lanka where they reside is an altered landscape.

Rushdie, though he is caustically satiric about the black segment of the British population, especially in *The Satanic Verses*, never allows his feelings to cascade over into racial hate. Naipaul, however, has never outgrown the anti-black feelings he developed while he lived in Trinidad: two cultures, the East Indian Hindu and the Black or Creole, living in close proximity but never merging, was a stubborn fact which influenced him deeply. The kindest he could be towards the blacks is perhaps the Englishman Bobby's attitude in *In a Free State*: "Sweet infantilism, almost without language: in language lay mockery and self-disgust." But even towards the Indians of his own skin-color living in his ancestral land he shows a marked revulsion; in his first book on India, *An Area of Darkness*, he is so shocked by the transformation of physique of Europe as it moved across Africa, Arabia and Asia that he determines to retain his own total humanity while repudiating a large portion of the human race. He shows no sense of the part played by European rapacity, deformation and colonialism in the disfigurement of colonized people; does he think the physique of Europe is his own?

> The physique of Europe had melted away first into that of Africa and then, through Semitic Arabia, into Aryan Asia. Men had been diminished and deformed; they begged and whined. Hysteria had been my reaction, and a brutality dictated by a new awareness of myself as a

whole human being and a determination touched with fear, to remain what I was.

While for Rushdie hybridity and miscegenation are sources of excitement, to Naipaul they are anathema.

A House for Mr. Biswas is Naipaul's masterpiece: it is also one of the best novels in English in our time. The reasons for its success are many but the most important is Naipaul's ability to evoke an empathy for his main character, the anti-hero Mr. Biswas, who wants to define himself as a writer, and even more significantly establish himself as an authentic person. Unfortunately, he is crippled by poverty, a forbidding milieu and an incapacity to reconcile his traditional values with the personal values he wants to develop in a changing world and a changing Trinidad. Mr. Biswas' struggles are played out against the backdrop of the travails of a country caught in a time of transition between the old feudalism and an inchoate capitalism, between a weakening tradition and the ineluctable onset of modernization. Mr. Biswas is doomed to fail because he does not have the imagination or the courage to understand and overcome the exigencies of his individual predicament.

Another reason for the novel's success is that Naipaul is very close to the social realities of Trinidad at that time; there is a strong sense of place and a convincing recreation of the texture of social life and manners. This is noteworthy because in his later novels, especially those with an African setting, he is content with an almost ersatz diorama of towns with native and mock-European segments, and the undifferentiated bush. In *A House for Mr. Biswas* he is able even to use dialect and the local versions of English with a flair of authenticity. It would be useful to illustrate this with a quotation:

> Mr. Biswas was about to say that he hadn't been fooled by Mungroo when Moti said, "He don't rob the rude and crude shopkeepers, people like himself. He frighten they give him a good dose of licks. No, he does look for nice people with nice soft heart, and is them he does rob. Mungroo see you, he think you look nice, and next day his wife come round for two cents this and three cents that and she forget that she ain't got no money, and if you could wait till next pay day. Well, you wrap up the goods in good strong paper-bag, you send she home happy, and you sit down and wait till next pay day. Next pay day Mungroo forget. His wife forget. They too busy killing chicken and buying rum to remember you. Two-three days later, eh-eh, wife suddenly remember

you. She bawling again. She want more trust. Don't tell me about Mungroo. I know him good. Man should be in jail, if anybody had the guts to throw him there.

A further reason why *A House for Mr. Biswas* is a powerful novel is that the protagonist is nearly a tragic hero whose fate has a mythic resonance. Like Rama in the Hindu epic *The Ramayana* Mr. Biswas has to fulfil his *dharma* or life's vocation; unlike Rama he has to reconcile it with his personal dharma, his own quest for meaning and salvation. The book is full of symbolic overtones; the family into which he marries, the Tulsis, is both a refuge and an abomination. It is not accidental but indeed quite germane that their house is called Hanuman House, recalling the monkey-god who helped Rama rescue his kidnapped wife, Sita. But in the case of Mr. Biswas, the house only serves to make him stray from the search for his own self-image and lead him inevitably to his disintegration.

But the novel by Naipaul which offers the best comparison to Rushdie's work is *The Mimic Men,* Naipaul's only other successful novel, though in my opinion only partially so. Both Naipaul and Rushdie share a political and satiric cast of mind but both the objects of the satire and the methods employed are of very different kinds.

Naipaul's satire is more an exposure -- brutal, pitiless, nihilistic--of peoples and cultures that he loathes. He has no sense of the ontological "otherness" of the Third World communities he sets out to portray. The satiric thrust is one-sided; *nothing Western,* especially if it is British, can be bad. Rushdie's satire, on the other hand, is more than double-edged, it is quadruple-edged, or more. In the first place, it is even-handed in its satirizing, even scorifying both the ex-colonized and colonized; the colonized, for the venal character of its leadership and the gullibility of the common people, the ex-colonized for their patronizing air and their treatment of expatriates from the Third World as second-class citizens. Rushdie's targets include the newly independent nations of India, Pakistan and later Bangladesh, with their corrupt and corrupting leaders, the brown sahibs adept at bamboozling the populace. The masses are like sheep confused by the rival pulls of modernization and their age-old, time-honored traditions, their minds jostled by the clash between their ancient myths and the beglamorized, escapist versions peddled by the Bombay cinema, the collision of a family, tribe and caste-bound culture with the impersonal, nuclear networks of the encroaching industrial age.

What I find most disquieting in Rushdie, and his major defect, is his dismissive, degrading attitude towards the common people. Despite his exultant stance on mongrelization, his celebration of "newness", "How does newness come into the world? How is it born? Of what fusions, translations, conjoinings is it made? How does it survive, extreme and dangerous as it is?"

Rushdie sees the people as moronic: in *Shame* his Baluchis copulate with sheep and the war of liberation, the struggle for the independence of Bangladesh, is demeaned, as in the following passage:

> The real trouble, however, started over in the East Wing, that festering swamp. Populated by whom? O savages, breeding, endlessly, jungle-bunnies good for nothing but growing jute and rice, knifing each other, cultivating traitors in their paddies. Perfidy of the East; proved by the Popular Front's failure to win a single seat there, while the riff-raff of the People's League, a regional party of bourgeois malcontents led by the well-known incompetent Sheikh Bismillah, gained so overwhelming a victory that they ended up with more Assembly seats than Harappa had won in the West. *Give people democracy and look what they do with it.* The West was in a state of shock, the sound of one Wing flapping, beset by the appalling notion of surrendering the government to a party of swamp aborigines, little dark men with their unpronounceable language of distorted vowels and slurred consonants, perhaps not foreigners exactly, but aliens without a doubt.

In *The Satanic Verses* the Jahilian Grandee requisitions the poet, Baal, to excoriate the poor with the "art of Metrical Slander"; among the followers of Mahound, the primary satirical targets are Salman the scribe who "improves" on the revelation, and later becomes a traitor to Mahound and the faith, Khalid the water-carrier and the slave, Bilal. Baal is scornful of the new religion: "A revolution of water-carriers, immigrants and slaves" he calls it and proclaims that such scum and riff-raff are hardly worthy of his talent.

This denigration of the common people is meant to be taken seriously because Baal cannot be altogether seen as an object of the writer's odium. He is no caricature; he even seems to speak for the author when he tells Mahound and the other accusers: "I am Baal", he announced, "I recognize no Jurisdiction except that of my muse; or, to be exact, my dozen Muses." It is also interesting to note that the renegade scribe Salman bears the same name as that of the author: Rushdie's repudiation of Islam is shown clearly in the matter of his namesake's substitution of words of his own for the revealed and hence sacrosanct language dictated by Mahound.

Rushdie's demeaning of the common people is not limited to historical figures; his treatment of the minor, some not so minor, Indian and Pakistani characters shows no redeeming features while the portrayal of the Afro-British figures has the quality of caricature. Dr. Uhuru Simba, the fat man named after the elephant in the Tarzan films is arrested for the Granny Ripper murders; the deejay Pinkwalla is introduced as follows:

> Our host speaks: ranter, toaster, deejay non-pareil -- the prancing Pinkwalla, his suit of lights blushing to the beat. -- Truly, he is exceptional, a seven-foot albino, his hair the palest rose, the whites of his eyes likewise, his features unmistakably Indian, the haughty nose, long thin lips, a face from a *hamza-nama* cloth. An Indian who has never seen India, East-India-man from the West Indies, white black man. A star.

How far is this from the celebration of hybridity recommended by Rushdie? A piece of grotesquerie, as bizarre as the hate-figure, Prime Minister Margaret Thatcher, whose wax effigy is melted down to the spectator's cheers and ecstacy:

> Attendants move towards the tableau of hate-figures, pounce upon the night's sacrificial offering, the one most often selected, if truth be told, at least three times a week. Her perma-waved coiffure, her pearls, her suit of blue. *Maggie-maggie-maggie,* bays the crowd. *Burn-burn-burn.* The doll, the *guy,* is strapped into the Hot Seat. Pinkwalla throws the switch. And O how prettily she melts, from the inside out, crumpling into formlessness.

The problem with this kind of satire, directed as it is at two diametrically opposed targets is that it tends to cancel itself out. The two employees of the London Underground, Uriah Moseley and Orphia Phillips, lusting for each other on elevator rides and in-between stops, *"Now walk backwards to the lift and just suck him right in there, and after that it's up and away we go,"* are other instances of the writer's mishaps, of satirical *contre-temps.*

Even in *Midnight's Children,* Rushdie's novel which is most free of the vilification of ordinary humans, the narrator's wife, Padma, often a sensible critic, even an amanuensis, has to be described as a dung-lotus, because of her illiteracy:

> Dung, that fertilizes and causes the crops to grow! Dung, which is patted into thin chapati-like cakes when still fresh and moist, and is sold to the village builders, who use it to secure and strengthen the walls of kachcha buildings made of mud! Dung, whose arrival from the nether end of cattle goes a long way towards explaining their divine and sacred status! Oh, yes, I was wrong. I admit I was prejudiced, no doubt because its unfortunate odors do have a way of offending my sensitive nose -- how wonderful, how ineffably lovely it must be to be named for the Purveyor of Dung!

The fruitful comparison between Rushdie and Naipaul can be extended beyond the question of their satirical techniques to a consideration of their different views of the post-colonial world, and even their philosophies of life. Naipaul's *The Mimic Men* tells of "headpieces filled with straw". The main character Ralph Singh sees his separation from the mother country in terms of sexual images, of narcissism and personal disintegration. Rushdie has no sexual hang-ups! Singh sees the transition from colonial subject to independence, both for himself and his country, in terms of biological and sexual situations: as a schoolboy he decides not to participate in a sports meet because maturation imposes a pain too difficult to be borne; he wants to be a baby again at his mother's breast "in a back veranda, all around a blue of dark bush", the bush representing the life from which he had been protected by the colonial power and the mother's breast the consolation offered by the mother country. Later the fledgling independent state wanted to nationalize Lord Stockwell's estate but Singh abandons the project and is seduced by Lord Stockwell's daughter, Lady Stella. A third incident relates to his encounter with a Spanish prostitute, which is almost pathological in its description: "the barest touch of a fingernail arching my areola" causes his "self to drop away". The former Imperialist power still has the capacity to castrate the former subject, even if as in *In A Free State*, the naked savage has a penis one foot long. *Guerrillas*, a novel highly praised in the West, is laced with sado-masochism and is to my mind almost pornographic: Jimmy Ahmed is a paste board figure with no language of his own, his mind stuffed with ideas and feelings acquired from the "liberal" segments of European powers, his only way of wreaking vengeance on his colonial male master is by the buggery, rape and finally murder of a

white 'progresssive' woman who wants to emancipate him. The lack of
a single successful love relationship in Naipaul's fiction does not
necessarily argue a condition of psychosis but his mental animus
strongly suggests such a diagnosis. Rushdie also does not create any
harmonious love-relationships but his comic verve makes him
wholesome in comparison. Rushdie does not repudiate intimacy with
the ferocity Naipaul shows, as in this passage from *The Mimic Men*:

> Intimacy: the word holds the horror. I would have stayed for ever at
> a woman's breasts, if they were full and had a hint of weight that
> required support. But there was the skin, there was the smell of skin.
> There were bumps and scratches, there were a dozen little things that
> could positively enrage me. I was capable of the act required, but
> frequently it was in the way I was capable of getting drunk or eating
> two dinners. Intimacy: it was violation and self-violation.

In *Guerrillas*, even the quality of Naipaul's prose suffers: it is
certainly not at his limpid best.

A Bend in the River carries the process of post-colonial disintegration
a stage further, though it is better written and structured than
Guerrillas. Naipaul believes that the Third World has little history, and
what little history it has has been written by Europeans. Without them,
there would be no 'past' for these countries, it would have been washed
away "like the scuff marks off fishermen on the beach". The past must
be trampled on, there was "only one civilization and one place --
London, or a place like it" and unless one adopts its values, there was
no alternative but reversion to the bush. Rushdie, on the other hand, has
an intimate knowledge of Islamic Sufism and of the old cultures of
India and Pakistan: he speaks of the barbarity of colonialism and has no
illusions of an ideal Western civilization.

Naipaul's autobiographical novel, *The Enigma of Arrival*, which
Rushdie describes, in a review recently collected in a book of essays,
Imaginary Homelands, as "very, very sad", is the most overt paean to
the Western way of life; in earlier books he did refer to the white man
as God but such remarks were placed in the mouths of his characters,
but here he limns an idyllic picture of the English countryside as the
landscape most attuned to human wants and satisfactions, the best
adapted to the human scale and the human condition. England offers
him a second childhood seen not nostalgically but as a present source
of wonder and joy, a "fulfillment of a child's dream of a safe house in

the wood". Though when living in Wiltshire he experiences illness, melancholy, explosions in his head, deaths in his family and intimations of his own end, the novelist sees England as the ultimate Eden, a feeling that would no doubt be most reassuring to a country and a people in decline, trying to relive an imperial past of manifest glory.

What is perhaps even more instructive in our extended comparison of Salman Rushdie with V.S. Naipaul are their very different literary techniques, their philosophies of life and their expectations about the future of man. I do not want to enter into a detailed comparison of styles: they are different kinds of artists. As Rushdie has shown in his collection, *Imaginary Homelands,* he can write both workmanlike and elegant prose: he could have written like Naipaul but he chose not to. Instead Rushdie chose a hyper-kinesthetic mode, abounding in verbal pyrotechnics, using an amalgram of Standard English, educated upper-class English of the Oxbridge variety, words borrowed from several languages, Indo-English, literal translations of Indian idoms and languages, post-Joycean extravagances, street patois, film hype, advertising lingo, billboard jargon, immigrant dialects and rhythms of intonation, in fact whatever was grist to his mill, in order to fabricate his mix of magic and realism, fact and fantasy. Naipaul stayed with classical limpidity and while at his best his prose is stylish and translucent, in his weaker efforts, most often identified with retrogressive attitudes, his writing becomes bloodless. In this sense Naipaul's strategies, though distinctive, remain within the conventional arena: this is not a dismissal, because extremely fine fiction has been written by Kingsley Amis, Margaret Drabble, William Golding, John Fowles, Anthony Burgess, Iris Murdoch, Muriel Spark and of course Graham Greene, and V.S. Prichett, to pick some names only from Britain. It only serves to demonstrate Rushdie's uniqueness and originality.

Of all the critical theorists I have read in recent times, I find Bakhtin's theories of diegesis and mimesis the most fruitful in an analysis of Rushdie's literary technique. I wish David Lodge, whose illuminating collection of essays on some modern writers, *After Bakhtin,* could have included a chapter on Rushdie. I would like to draw special attention to Bakhtin's sense of the primacy of language in the creative presentation of mimesis: it is here that the divide between Naipaul and Rushdie becomes most glaring: Naipaul in denying an authentic language to the speakers in his post-colonial societies impoverishes the reality of art as imitation while Rushdie exults in the "living dialogic threads" and weaves them into an intricately rich tapestry. I quote from Bakhtin's *Dialogic Imagination*:

"As a living, socio-ideological thing, as heteroglot opinion, language for the individual consciousness, lies on the borderline between oneself and the other."

It is this sense of the other which Naipaul ignores and Rushdie enthusiastically affirms.

To continue with Bakhtin:

> The word in language is half someone else's. It becomes one's own only when the speaker populates it with his own intention, his own accent, when he appropriates the word, adapting it to his own semantic and expressive intention. Prior to this moment of appropriations, the word does not exist in a neutral and impersonal language (it is not, after all, out of the dictionary that the speaker gets his words!), but, rather it exists in other people's mouths, in other people's contexts, serving other people's intentions: it is from there that one must take the word, and make it one's own.

This is germane to what Rushdie calls "reclamation". In defending *The Satanic Verses* he talks of the process of reclaiming language from one's opponents, turning insults into strengths. The devil can be an angel, black can be beautiful.

But where the divergence between Rushdie and Naipaul is most patent is in their views of man and his future. Though Naipaul's literary strategies are the accepted ones, his view of man is that he is a rootless and unanchored creature. Though he has been compared with Conrad, he does not share Conrad's metaphysical sense of evil. The evil Naipaul treats is socio-political in origin: his deficiency is his lack of the sense of 'otherness' in other people and at the same time a failure to identify himself with the teeming human beings around him. It is not merely a case of being negative about the future of the Third World but being messianic about Western culture: no condemnation of colonialism but rather a wholesale endorsement of Western values and Western development as the acme of human progress towards the millenium.

In a recent address given at the Manhattan Institute in New York, Naipaul defines Universal Civilization as that which gave him the idea of the writing vocation and enabled him to practice his vocation as a writer, "the civilization that enabled me to make that journey from the periphery to the center"; going from the periphery to the center means for example, his discovery of the Christian precept, "Do unto others as you would have others do unto you." How oddly limited, and limiting in its first part, as Ananda Coomaraswamy whose essay, "The Bugbear of Literacy", demonstrates, and how commonplace in the second!

Rushdie's vision for the future is at once more realistic, more modest: he thinks the ghetto mentality is the most dangerous pitfall, "the elephant trap", immigrants and exiles should exult in cultural transplantation and all human beings should be like Corde in Saul Bellow's *The Dean's December* who imagines that the dog is barking in protest against the limit of dog experience and that its rage and its desire is everyone's: "for God's, sake, open the universe a little more!" Rushdie's is forever opening out into newness and metamorphosis.

While the extended comparison with Naipaul has helped me to define Rushdie's singularity, it is important to "place" him in the context of the new fiction in Britain, the fiction of his new and even younger contemporaries. Attention has been given almost exclusively to the "influence" on Rushdie of post-modernism and magical realism, of the likes of Gunter Grass, Milan Kundera, Italo Calvino, Thomas Pynchon, and of course *El Realismo magical* as exemplified by Gabriel Garcia Marquez. One cannot discount the fact that Rushdie is a British writer and a part of the new wave in British fiction, a significant new direction, though not a movement, in a country where tradition dies hard. There is no doubt that with the publication of *Midnight's Children* in 1981 and the subsequent Booker prize he became an important player on the literary scene, if not altogether as an influence, as a source of encouragement. His British contemporaries have not acquired great international fame (who can match Rushdie after the furor of *The Satanic Verses*) but they do represent a new era.

While in his earlier novels such as *A Good Man in Africa* and *An Ice Cream War*, William Boyd did not stray too far from the established tracks of British fiction, in 1988 he published a remarkable novel, *The New Confessions,* which shows the influence of Sterne and Dickens, and perhaps even Rabelais. It is an autobiography of a John James Todd born in 1899, a life and adventures spanning the twentieth century. Todd is working towards his masterpiece, a film of the life of Rousseau, and therefore Rousseau figures almost as a character in the novel. The book has a strong sense of place, describing his life as a boy in Scotland, World War I and the trenches, his role as a director of films in the Berlin of the twenties during the Weimar republic, his subsequent exile to Mexico, Tijuana and Rinion, then on to Los

Angeles and finally in old age, the Mediterranean. The interweaving of personal and international events is fascinating. The writing is of a very high order: the élan of the style makes it almost a romp but it is a tragic one.

Julian Barnes, born in 1946, is another distinguished writer of three fine novels, after his early comedy, *Metroland,* to his credit: *Staring at the Sun, Flaubert's Parrot,* and *A History of the World in 10 1/2 Chapters.* To take *Flaubert's Parrot,* for example: one theme is Life versus Art, as it is appropriate in any consideration of Gustave Flaubert but the novel uses a mind-boggling array of technical devices hardly ever heard of in a novel. These include the straightforward story line, the criss-crossing of flashbacks, chronological tables, the use of a dictionary, literary criticism, a college examination paper, a detective story where the sleuthing is about the whereabouts of the original parrot which Flaubert kept on his desk when he was writing *A Simple Heart.* The life of Geoffrey Braithwaite, a Flaubert scholar, is interwoven with that of Flaubert himself. Other themes are Love, Infidelity instanced in the case of Braithwaite's wife Ellen and the problem of human identity, the difficulty of truly knowing another person, even one's wife:

> We were happy, we were unhappy; we were happy enough to despair wrongs – Isn't it the natural condition of life after a certain age? ... after a number of events what is there left but repetition and diminishment? Who wants to go on living? The eccentric, the religious, the artistic (sometimes); those with a false sense of their own worth. Soft cheeses collapse; firm cheeses indurate. Both go mouldy.

The energy of creation keeps the book at once realistic and bewitching, humorous and sad.

Another interesting young writer, Jeanette Winterson has written excellent, almost idiosyncratic novels: the success of Rushdie's *Midnight Children* must have been a source of inspiration to her: so deft is her mixture of fairy story and myth, which only helps, as in *Sexing the Cherry,* where the contemporary relevance is underscored by the association of the plague in seventeenth-century Europe with the threatening environmental catastrophes of our own time. Other novels are her equally impressive *The Passion,* a story of a bisexual woman, Vilanelle, of intense feelings and of a compelling imagination and a soldier, Henri, a cook for Napoleon, whose doomed relationship is played out against the surreal backdrop of Venice. *Oranges are not the only fruit* was her successful autobiographical first novel. Raised in a charismatic household where the theme song was "What a friend we have in Jesus", the main character realizes she has a lesbian preference and decides to face her state with a rare courage in the face of society's disgust and persecution. The mingling of fantasy with realistic narrative give the book mythic aura: it treats of art and verifiable history, the need to refashion history as a sandwich laced with mustard of one's own.

> Very often history is a means of denying the past ... To fit it, force it, function it, to suck out the spirit until it looks the way you think it should. We are all historians in our own small way. And in some ghastly way Pol Pot was more honest than the rest of us have been. Pol Pot decided to dispense with history altogether. To dispense with the sham of treating the past with objective respect. In Cambodia the cities were to be wiped out, maps thrown away, everything gone. No documents. Nothing. A brave new world. The old world was horrified. We pointed the finger, but big fleas have little fleas on their backs to bite them.

Another interesting novel which must be mentioned is Peter Ackroyd's *Chatterton*, a book purchased by small college libraries in America because it is considered an academic treatise in literary criticism! This novel is a little too contrived for my taste; it is about the plagiarist poet Thomas Chatterton and a portrait of him lying dead in his attic room with another poet, George Meredith, as the model. The story flits ingeniously between the worlds of present-day reality and past history.

And one must not forget to mention Martin Amis, an accomplished writer-son of an established novelist, Kingsley Amis. Martin's first novel about an adolescent's growing up does not really prepare one for the amazing technical novelty of two later books, *Money* and *London Fields*. I cannot help concluding that Rushdie's successes in the immediately preceeding years emboldened Martin Amis' creative energies. The protagonist in the former is mad about money like a Ben Jonson character but the setting is cross-cultural, meaning Britain and the United States and is a savage indictment of twentieth-century culture. The most recent novel, *London Fields,* where a murderee looks for her murderer in a futuristic world, teetering on the verge of disaster, is again an excoriation of modern civilization. The only disquieting note is the apocalyptic tone which is not always expertly managed, but the novel with its manifold technical devices, its inebriated vocabulary and its black humor remains a tour-de-force in English literature. We must not forget that the older masters continued to produce invigorating work; three of them, the late William Golding, whose *Lord of the Flies* I read as an undergraduate, John Fowles and the late Anthony Burgess, who has moved forwards and sideways since he wrote *The Malayan Trilogy,* to which I have devoted a chapter, are the great anticipators of post-modernism. Even those who continue to use traditional forms haven't lost their touch: the late Kingsley Amis has produced in *The Old Devils* work comparable to *Lucky Jim,* the late Iris Murdoch and Muriel Spark seem as feisty as ever, Margaret Drabble in *The Radiant Way* is doing for Thatcherite England, as one blurb writer puts it, what George Eliot did for the Victorian, Anita Brookner writes her crisp and incisive novels about contemporary mores and social habits, Fay Weldon is very current and up-to-date, Ian McEwan, a formidable literary talent, continues to excel and of course there was the inimitable quintessentially British V.S. Pritchett. In the face of such triumph and vitality, it would be foolhardy to offer a recipe for fiction. But the new writers I have commented on represent an original and new development, and it is to this company that my man Salman Rushdie belongs.

I do not want to spend much time trying to see Rushdie in a context of Indians now writing in English as I think, in view of what I have already said, that it would be otiose and limiting. However, it is true that Salman Rushdie's work has been a source of inspiration to Indian writers in English, as one of them, Shashi Tharoor, readily acknowledges. In his own novel, called *The Great Indian Novel,* Tharoor sees the history of twentieth-century India in terms of the ancient epic, *The Mahabharata,* one of the foundations of Indian civilization. Tharoor is very talented and though his satire is close to the bone, he is never mean-spirited. He is still young and one can forgive him when he is not writing at his best: there are parts, especially in the underbelly of the novel, where the writing appears to be journalistic or resembles the prose of official reports. But altogether it is a delightful read and even the satire of Gandhi is done with humor and even with doggerel:

> Groupies with rupees and large solar topis,
> Bakers and fakers and enema takers
> Journalists who promoted his cause with their pen

These were among his favourite men.

Contrasting modern India with its past, Ved Vyas the narrator says

> It was not a land where dharma and duty have come to mean
> nothing, where religion is an excuse for conflict rather than a code of
> conduct; where piety, instead of marking wisdom, masks a crippling
> lack of imagination. It was not a land where brides are burned in
> kerosene-soaked kitchens because they have not brought enough dowry
> with them; where integrity and self-respect are for sale to the highest
> bidder; where men are pulled off buses and butchered because of the
> length of a forelock or the absence of a foreskin.

Kushwant Singh, a doyen of Indian writing in English, is optimistic about the future for literature in English: writers like Alan Sealy, Amitav Ghosh, Rohinton Mistry, Upamanyu Chatterjee are bolder in their interpretation of the Indian scene and their literary strategies while O.V. Vijayan, who writes in Malayalam but translates his work into English, has shown considerable merit.

It is difficult to speak of Rushdie as a direct influence though Bharati Mukherjee's interest in the immigrant communities may well have been fanned by a reading of Rushdie. Amitav Ghosh's *The Circle of Reason*, which has a character Alu who looks like a potato and exhibits an unusual cranium, does recall the narrator of *Midnight's Children* though the physiology and physiognomy are different in each case. This is in no way to diminish Ghosh's talent but to draw attention to the very real, if indirect impact on Rushdie's achievement on contemporary Indian writers.

I don't believe I have yet fully explained why Rushdie is so controversial a writer or why he became such a notorious socio-political and cultural phenomenon. I shall, in conclusion, add some remarks in the hope they will be of some use.

Beginning innocently enough with a work of meta-fiction titled *Grimus*, he saw it fail in popular estimation: I think undeservedly so. I see it classified as Science Fiction in popular libraries: it is clearly more than that, based as it is on a Sufi poem, *Shahnameh*. It shows Rushdie's interest in Sufism which is Islamic Protestantism, believing as it does in inner, mystical knowledge, the dictates of the conscience as against the codes of an organized religion which must always compromise, and adapt itself to the social polity. Sufism speaks the language of Rumi, and also the poetry of the late Faiz Ahmed Faiz whom Rushdie admires enormously and whom I have the pride to have known as a friend. *Grimus* also shows Rushdie's interest in exiledom: it is certainly dystopian but already reveals the strengths of Rushdie's lavish vocabulary and the deployment of multi-form languages: his concern with rootedness is suggested by this sentence: "It is the natural condition of the exile, putting down roots in memory."

One of the main reasons for Rushdie's evocation of strong likes and hates is the close correlation of personal and public histories in his fiction. He had to apologize to Mrs. Indira Gandhi, then Prime Minister of India. This is not surprising when one considers passages such as this in *Midnight's Children:*

> .... the country's corrupt, black economy had grown as large as the official, 'white' variety, which he did by showing me a newspaper photograph of Mrs. Gandhi. Her hair, parted in the centre, was snow-white on one side and black as night on the other; so that, depending on what profile she presented, she resembled either a stoat or an ermine.

Such fiction is perilously close to fact, and soon Rushdie will pay the price. Both his success and impact is due to such closeness. There is sometimes no artistic distance or disguise. *Shame* is about the ruling and influential families of Pakistan, the personal histories are microcosms of public events. Another reason why Rushdie evokes hostility is his irrepressible irreverence, an irreverence which extends not only to Mohammed or the Buddha but to St. Francis's toe.

Midnight's Children is sometimes unimaginable, bizarre, tragic and hilarious at the same time. Conceding that you can suspend your disbelief about 1001 children born on or near the stroke of midnight of the date when India obtained independence, how can you deal with the supernatural powers of these children; nothing like this has appeared in English fiction, before or since.

Indian readers may also have dislike for the book because for them it is an India seen under Western eyes -- irony, parody, absurdism, ghosts of Borges, Marquez, Pynchon float in and out -- and even though the eerie plot is anchored in social reality, the dizzying talent can leave the reader unhinged. The first five hundred pages are brilliant with their descriptions of Grandfather's courtship of his future wife through a perforated bedsheet whereby he acquired microscopic knowledge of unrelated parts of her anatomy, vignettes such as Mary Peresa's guilt ground into green chutney: Rushdie's creativity does not seem to flag even when writing at such length, the pyrotechnical brilliance does not dim. But the novel which best illustrates the case of Salman Rushdie is *The Satanic Verses*. It shows all the strengths of *Midnight's Children* and *Shame*: from the moment when Saladin Chamcha masters the art of eating a kipper and considers it a first step in the conquest of England to the racist incident at the cafe, "'Enjoying your food?' he screamed at Chamcha and Gibreel. 'It's fucking shit. Is that what you eat at home, is it? Cunts.'" The novel moves as though it is powered by a dynamo. It also contains a premonition that readers and viewers could mistake fiction for fact, an eventuality only too real in Rushhdie's own case. *The Satanic Verses* also ends with a reconciliation between Saladin and his dying father, one of the most moving descriptions in modern literature, showing great potential for Rushdie's future growth as a writer: "a serene, and beautiful feeling, a renewing, life-giving thing". Rushdie feels that "we are still capable of exaltation", we can still transcend. The book ends on a note of hope: the magic lamp is returned.

Rushdie's novels are works by an expatriate, a British citizen of foreign origin, though perhaps more acclimatized than an American greencard holder, a class from which a future wave of fiction may crest. This situation is another reason for resistance to Rushdie. His work exemplifies the cross-cultural encounter in one of its extremest forms: as he himself says, "you are not here when you are here, you have not left here when you have left."

Edward Said rightly said that orientalism was a creation of Europeans but it is important to note that Indian writers promulgate similar distortions except when they are exceptionally sensitive. Rushdie is one of the unusually sensitive, and because of this he offends the conventional and commonplace people who make up a large portion of his readership. As elsewhere in this book, I have looked at my chosen texts not only as specimens of cross-cultural literature but as works of art in their own right: in fact my book may be read by a student of the modern novel in English, regardless of any cross-cultural focus of attention. But in the case of Rushdie, I have had to consider the extreme forms this bi-culturality or multi-culturality has taken before assessing the novels as literature.

Of course, exiledom is distinct from emigration but in the area of sentience, they often merge. Displacement is always harrowing, sometimes traumatic, in life as well as in art. Ulysses wandered, Dante was exiled, though to a different part of Italy. Though the known world was small, transportation and communications were poor. But in modern times both exile and emigration are more complex. There are those who are banished, there are others who voluntarily choose to leave due to dissatisfaction with their homeland. Between these are those who want to find a new Utopia or at least a more congenial or delectable setting. Henry James abandoned what he thought was a crude environment for an ampler society which would nourish his creativity. Any important source of creative endeavor, any prod to seeing things anew, is worthy of consideration in a book of aesthetics: all I want to establish is that the modern context is unique. Rushdie is not an exile but has always been acutely conscious of his situation as an immigrant: he is now under sentence of death, and is a prisoner.

The problem with *The Satanic Verses* is not the debasement of the Islamic faith; Rushdie's deep involvement in Sufism, especially the kind emigrants from India carry with them, would seem to discredit such an approach. There are also distinguished forebears in the Islamic tradition itself; Iqbal, for example. The difficulty is simply that most people cannot distinguish fact from fiction (in both senses of the word); they have not read the book, let alone pondered its implications. The first requisite for a critic is to know what fiction is!

The problem also is not blasphemy, as Rushdie himself said, *"The Satanic Verses* is, in part, a secular man's reckoning with the religious spirit"*, and as one of his characters puts it, "Where there is no belief there is no blasphemy." Christians have perhaps had a longer exposure to blasphemy and tend to view it with more composure. Ernest Renan in his *Vie de Jesus* denied Christ's divinity but was able to portray a personality as close to perfection as possible for a human being. There have been more savage blasphemies before and since and they have been received with relative equanimity. But there is a problem in the case of Rushdie: when the work draws its power from the importance and pull of what is blasphemed, it must give the blasphemed object a fair shake, so to speak. This is where Rushdie is most remiss. *The Satanic Verses* is aesthetically maladroit because it does not give Islam a fair trial. It satirizes a considerably smaller thing, and provides a denatured caricature.

But this fault does not warrant a sentence of death: this is one of the barbaric and feral distortions of contemporary politics, totally unworthy both of the Muslim religion and its heritage. Of Rushdie's recently announced conversion to Islam I do not wish to comment. It is a

humiliating commentary on how the human spirit can be broken by
presecution to the extent that he can disavow his life work.

I want Rushdie to thrive as a writer: he still has major
shortcomings. For all his wordy éclat, he moves art too far away from
ordinary human nature and common human concerns: his sympathies
are rarely engaged profoundly, and one is often left with the colorful
display one gets from looking at an aquarium or through a
kaleidoscope. His latest fairy tale is I trust a new beginning.

Since the above chapter was completed, Rushdie has written a long
novel, *The Moor's Last Sigh*, which is fully worthy of comparison with
his earlier masterpiece, *Midnight's Children:* another bold attestation of
his astonishing linguistic imagination. The adoption of Indian English
coinages, whether in actual currency or only in the author's mind, his
novelties, adaptations, inventive borrowings and mélanges from a
variety of languages and traditions is unsurpassed in English literature:
he belongs with James Joyce but the comparison is often to Rushdie's
advantage because his experimental voyages are more intelligible,
accessible and reader-friendly.

But his main character and other characters are often grotesque.
They are in a sense monstrosities. Though there is moral and satiric
passion and abundant, vigorous human interest, the human importance
is curtailed and the reader's sympathy crucially diminished. Which
brings us to the larger doubts and questions about Rushdie's art: no
doubt he celebrates the mongrel joy of multiculturalism but is this an
intrinsic value?

The literary value of *Middlemarch* and *Anna Karennina* are
intimately related to the moral urgencies that went into their making. In
fifty years' time how will Rushdie's work measure up against them? I
have to conclude on this questioning note.

Hard on the heels of my second attempt to conclude this chapter
comes Rushdie with his calling card of a new novel, *The Ground
Beneath Her Feet*, hot off the press. I do not have the space or the time
given by my publisher's deadline to consider this book in any detail but
a few comments and questions must be aired. They relate to issues that
have not been raised in the reviews that have so far appeared.

The pluses of Rushdie's art are abundantly there: the imaginative
blending of the real and the mythic, the linguistic ebullience, the
imagistic bravura, the penchant for the memorable phrase—"we live on
a broken mirror, and fresh cracks appear in its surface every day, "
Vincent Price is a "smooth nocturnal prince of the fanged classes,"

disorientation is a loss of the Orient, Vina finds "a direct line to the world's ashamed unconfident heart".

However, a blurb such as this by Toni Morrison, "This is Rushdie at his absolute, almost insolently global best," must be deconstructed to be nearly meaningless, though I do not normally favor this procedure.

It is not a recreation of the myth of Orpheus and Eurydice; it is a superb take-off on it, but often strikes the reader as an adventure of a creative magpie.

It is offered as a love story, but the love delineated has equal parts of affection and self-will; surely Vina's love is compromised by adultery, though it is committed with the good man in the eternal triangle, Rai the photographer; surely it is besmirched by a ravenous promiscuity. As for Ormus, surely his love is disfigured by a mulish vow of abstinence which is the antithesis of commitment, the negation of spontaneity. It balloons into a monstrous *hubris*.

Rai is the most rounded character in the novel, agnostic, sceptical, the most lovable.

Rushdie's disappointingly inadequate hope for his future novel is that it will move away from India and deal mainly with the West. There has been enough of the West in his work to-date. As a man senior to him and an admirer of his great impact in literature of multi-cultural modes of being, what I want from him is work that would engage more intrinsic moral concerns of human significance, books that would interest my grandchildren in the ways of Shakespeare, Sophocles, Tolstoy and George Eliot. I have no doubt that he has the capacity to write them.

CHAPTER XIX

NO MAN IS AN ISLAND: ROMESH GUNESEKERA'S *REEF*

One of the impressive adventures of the twentieth century is the rapidly burgeoning interpenetration of cultures. A rich fruit of this is a type of moderm literature in which the central experience is cross-cultural and the characters' destinies are shaped in some fashion by the cross-cultural encounter.

Romesh Gunesekera's debut novel, *Reef,* which was short-listed for Britain's prestigious Booker Prize, is a successful example of cross-cultural convergence. Sri Lanka, the book's setting and the land of Gunesekera's birth, has its own ethnic mix. The island nation, which is insulated from the rest of the world by the reef that girds its southern shore, has, however, undergone considerable change because of external influences during some centuries of colonization and foreign rule. Now, even its coral reef is in danger as it is being dug for use in building projects and the sea is fast eroding the frail land mass; the sea, "which would be the end of us all," is only waiting for the motion of its final wave. The sea and the reef have a symbolic weight in the novel, but the fortunes of the central characters are at the center of the stage.

There have been other novels written by Sri Lankans with the island as their setting, but this is the first to win international acclaim. Leonard Woolf's neglected masterpiece, *The Village in the Jungle,* is located in Sri Lanka, but Woolf was an Englishman. Michael

Ondaatje's *Running in the Family,* though it uses the techniques of fiction, is a family history peopled by some exotic, larger-than-life characters. Besides, Ondaatje, though born in Sri Lanka, has long been a Canadian.

But it is important to see Gunesekera also as a Britisher, one of the expatriates who have written novels of diaspora and who are now at the forefront of London literary life. He bids fair to join the likes of V. S. Naipaul, Salman Rushdie, Timothy Mo and Kazuo Ishiguro.

Reef is a *Bildungsroman,* the story of a boy's maturation into an expert cook, an autodidact and even a philosopher. The boy is the narrator, named Triton after the son of the mythological god of the sea, Poseidon. He goes into service as a houseboy in the employ of Salgado, an affluent marine biologist dedicated to the mission of saving the protective reef from its human predators, an able and well-meaning scientist but with little sense of what is going on in the country around him. Salgado's hypothesis is that the delicate polyp is affected even by a minor change in the immediate environment. "Then the whole thing will go. And if the structure is destroyed, the sea will rush in. The sand will go. The beach will disappear."

It is nature, red in tooth and claw: the human cruelty only mirrors nature and what goes on in the jungle on land and under the sea. In Triton's words:

> "The one time I did swim out to Mister Salgado's real reef, back home, I was frightened by its exuberance. The shallow water seethed with creatures. Flickering eyes, whirling tails, fish of a hundred colours darting and digging, sea snakes, sea-slugs, tentacles sprouting and grasping everywhere. Suspended in the most primal of sensations, I slowly began to see that everything was perpetually devouring its surroundings."

This predaciousness in nature has its human parallel in the rumblings of national discontent that soon erupt into a suppurating class and ethnic war in the 1960s. Neither Triton--who plies the culinary arts, learns to make excellent love cakes and other pastries, and knows how to marinate tiger prawns and steam parrot fish--nor his master Salgado, who is a dedicated scientist but also a naif, realizes what is going on until it is too late.

The novel is further complicated by the entry into the bachelor household of Salgado's mistress, Nili, who lifts the monkishness from their house but does little to open their eyes to the real conditions in the country, preferring to bask in Salgado's love and to savor Triton's culinary delicacies.

Gunesekera's style is sensuous and impassioned, almost incandescent. Nature also has its benign and blessed aspect:

> "The sand garden, the clumps of crotons, the vines around the trellises by the kitchen, all seemed to breathe life. Even the furniture seemed stained by the shade, but when I looked up again I would glimpse the sea between the trees bathed in a mulled gold light. The color of it, the roar of it, was overwhelming. It was like living inside a conch: the endless pounding. Numinous."

But whatever is idyllic has to disappear. Nili proves unfaithful; the insurgency and the racial war make it necessary for Salgado to emigrate. Triton is led to reflect: "But are we not all refugees from something? Whether we stay or go or return, we all need refuge from the world beyond our fingertips at some time."

When Salgado hears in England that his former love Nili is homeless after her house was gutted by a mob incensed because she had given refuge to Tamil families, he decides to return to find her. Triton remains in London, "without a past, without a name," hoping to become a restaurateur. But he cannot forget the sights and sounds of his home country: "Most of all I missed the closeness of ... the reservoir. The lapping of the dark water, flapping lotus leaves, the warm air rippling over it and the cormorants rising, the silent glide of the hornbill ... An elephant swaying to a music of its own."

CHAPTER XX

WHERE MULTICULTURALISM RUNS INTO A DEAD END: KERON BHATTACHARYA'S *THE PEARLS OF COROMANDEL*

There has been such a surfeit of novels set in British India--during its prime, apogee, twilight and aftermath--that one would have thought this type of fiction was an endangered species. But the vein is not altogether spent, for here comes a debut novel set in the Empire's declining years.

It may be unfair to compare *The Pearls of Coromandel* with such titans of the novel as Paul Scott's *Raj Quartet* or Kipling's *Kim* or Forster's *Passage to India*, but even when judged on its own merits it is a disappointment. Bhattacharya does make a bold attempt to capture the spirit of segments of society in colonial India, and signs of promise emerge, notably in the depiction of the growing love between an Englishman and an Indian. But these signs fall short of fulfillment because of the author's inadequate literary equipment.

The story concerns a young Britisher, John Sugden, who joins the Indian Civil Service, a prestigious appointment, and embarks with enthusiasm on his career in the service of Empire. He is a believer in the imperialist cause, endowed with a strong sense of duty and of fairness towards the local people over whom he exercises dominion.

Initially he distrusts Gandhi as a troublemaker and a demagogue, but later he changes his opinion and comes to believe that Gandhi's leadership and Home Rule are the only viable options for India.

This change of heart stems from his association with his chief assistant, Ratan Bannerji, and his family. John is invited to attend the wedding of Ratan's daughter Kamala, who is modest and beautiful but with strength of character which surfaces as the story develops.

What triggers the action is the brutal rape of Kamala by eight men, and here Bhattacharya follows in the wake of other novelists of the Raj by making rape into a symbol of the imperialist violation of an entire country. Kamala's father and husband both reject her although she was by no means to blame; they refuse to have her live in their house because she is now considered unclean. Sugden is the only person who can prevent her from having to earn her living as a prostitute: She is taken to the sahib's home and inducted into his domestic staff. The two fall deeply in love. This not only riles the servants but also causes mounting ill will among both Hindus and Moslems. Sugden's superiors compel him to resign; whereupon, with the help of a Belgian missionary, Father Fallon, one of the more empathetic characters in the book, the couple is forced to flee to Pondicherry. Since Kamala is with child, they are married by the priest. Wedding a foreigner is unforgivable, and having a child by a *firinghee* is anathema.

Even with its twists and turns, the plot of *The Pearls of Coromandel is* predictable. But what is more discomfiting is the prose style. The novel is littered with pedestrian expressions and clichés: "exuded magnetic charisma," "electric atmosphere," "an intense glow of unbelievable fervor," "iron-fisted control," "covered him with kisses as love flowed in abundance," "tossing and turning with anxiety".

The characters also leave much to be desired. Apart from Sugden and Kamala, possibly Father Fallon and Bannerji, all the others are stereotypes. But what is most disconcerting about the novel's drift is that it has no positive vision to offer, except that of Sugden's soon-to-be-born child: "Another Sugden coming on to this earth ... Not a Eurasian--but a man who could represent everyone--East and West--because he would understand them, identify himself with them--not as an outside observer, but as part of the global civilization."

This vision of the future belongs more to the realm of pious hopes than to the world of *The Pearls of Coromandel.*

CHAPTER XXI

BOUND FEET & WESTERN DRESS BY PANG-MEI NATASHA CHANG

Although an advocate of "multiculturalism" has become both hero and bogeyman in contemporary polemics, the reality the word denotes is very much alive, and kicking so vigorously that its relevance is likely to grow rather than wane in future years. The trends of easier communications, increasing travel and global modernization in general are irreversible. Consequently, creative literature has to be affected significantly by these trends: *Bound Feet & Western Dress* is but a new instance, albeit a welcome one.

It is a memoir, another example of a genre increasing in provenance as a medium of creative art. Of course, some memoirs tend to trespass into the realm of fiction but this one remains pretty close to the truth, with a detailed chronology of events and a sheaf of photographs. However, it does not lack the gifts of story-telling as the writer, a great-niece, relates the history of her great-aunt largely as disclosed by her, a story replete with familial and historical meaning.

It is only in the first few pages that the reader may wince or even groan at the prospect of yet another tale of an "identity crisis" and a narrative dealing with persons torn "between two cultures." But as soon as the memoirist introduces her great-aunt one's fears are stilled. The writing shows artistic finesse, a flair for reminiscence, a delicacy of response, a touching, even poignant sensibility and an unobtrusive, modest style which draws attention not to itself but to its subject matter.

Functioning almost like a frame for this memoir is a carved mahogany trunk transplanted from China to the writer's home in Connecticut, gripping the ancient Chinese traditions as tenaciously as its tiger-claw feet grip the ground: but what is more important are its contents, the aprons of her amah, her grandmother's robe, her grandfather's tuxedo and dinner jackets, and especially the black cheongsan from her great-aunt Chang Yu-i's shop which binds her to the older woman across the years, till at the memoir's end Pang-Mei places it alongside her own special clothes and then closes her family's chest of remembrances.

Chang Yu-i, the protagonist, was born into changing times. Hailing from an eminent, well-to-do, avant-garde family, rebelling early on against her upbringing by refusing to allow her feet to be bound, she "had two faces, one that heard talk of the old and the other that listened for talk of the new, the part that stayed East and the other that looked West, the spirit in me that was woman and the other that was man." She grew up in the years between the overthrow of the Manchu dynasty (1644-1911) and the Communist Revolution, a time of epochal transition. Pang-Mei Chang, the narrator, also grows up in a world of change, but the changes are more muted, less cataclysmic as they take place in the United States. Chang's main preoccupation was to avoid the "crevice between the cultures," to prevent herself from falling into the crack, to reconcile herself to the clashes between inherited customs and modern, Western influences and to accept the fact that Americans knew she was different and generally spurned her for it.

"Bound feet" becomes a complex symbol in the book. Though a rebel Yu-i married in the conventional way Hsu Chih-mo, a famous poet from an equally distinguished family, a man even more progressive in his views than she was. But her unbound feet proved insufficient for Hsu. When he brought a visitor home and Yu-i remarked that her "bound feet and Western dress did not go together," Hsu blurted out that he wanted a divorce, the first recorded divorce in Chinese history, where such incompatibilities as even the lack of a male heir were overcome by the husband finding a concubine. Her real inadequacy was that her mind was not truly liberated. Even the villagers would snicker "Big feet, big temper;" Lao Ye, Hsu's father, spent evenings in teahouses ogling lily-footed ladies who danced on tables where erotic passion clung to bound feet:

The mincing gait of these maidens, who could not stray beyond the limits of their rooms, bewitched men, young and old alike. He who beat out all others in a drinking game downed his last from one tiny embroidered slipper whose owner lay waiting for him on the top floor of the teahouse. In the intimacy of her chambers she would unravel the bindings of her feet and reveal them to him. That evening, in a final moment of passion, he would lift her tiny unwrapped feet to his shoulders and thrust them into his mouth to suck.

Unbound feet were apparently not enough for freedom and Yu-i was trapped between Hsu's westernized dreams, which she desperately wanted to emulate, and the bound feet of her mother-in-law Lao Taitai, betokening the graces of tradition.

But it is Yu-i who is the more heroic and the even more successful person. Poetic gifts aside, Hsu tends to be more abstract, unfeeling and rather effete. Yu-i joins her husband when he goes to Cambridge University in England to study literature, but soon he tires of her. Yu-i, however, pregnant, abandoned, alone, decides to stay on in Europe for many years with little money and less knowledge of the local languages till she returns to China to direct the Shanghai Women's Savings Bank. The Communist Revolution leads to her emigration to the U.S. where she is the grand old lady of her clan and heroine to her grand-niece Pang-Mei Chang, who herself seems to have eased her cross-cultural woes by going to Harvard, becoming a lawyer and marrying an outsider of her choice.

The most moving part of the memoir, however, is the relationship between Yu-i and Hsu as it is climaxed in the beautifully understated but touching confession Yu-i makes to her great-niece:

> You always ask me if I loved Hsu Chih-mo, and you know, I cannot answer this. It confuses me, this question, because everyone always tells me that I did so much for Hsu Chih-mo, I must have loved him. But that I cannot say, what is love. In my entire life, I have never said to anyone, "I love you." If caring for Hsu Chih-mo and his family was love, then maybe I loved him. Out of all the women in his life, I loved him the most.

CHAPTER XXII

MIRRORWORK: 50 YEARS OF INDIAN WRITING 1947-1997 EDITED BY SALMAN RUSHDIE AND ELIZABETH WEST

When anthologists put together a varied, vibrant, richly composite but in a deeper sense unified collection of a hitherto under-appreciated literature spanning a period of half a century and meant to coincide with India's fifty years of independence, it is a matter for unqualified gratitude. Especially is it so, when one of the editors, Salman Rushdie, is the writer who both by his own work and his championship of Indian writing in English has, more than anybody else, done the most to put this literature on the map of international letters. But let me crave the reader's indulgence for commenting on the shortcomings of this excellent collection before proceeding to considering its strengths.

When Rushdie avers that "'Indo-Anglian literature' represents perhaps the most valuable contribution that India has yet made to the world of books," this remark must surely be an oversight, for he cannot mean that what he is promoting is superior to the *Mahabharata,* the versions of the *Ramayana,* the plays of Kalidasa, the Tamil classics, *et al.!* And how can he so gratuitously put down the sixteen "official languages" of India when he admits he cannot read any of these languages: how can he judge O.V. Vijayan (Malayalam) or V.R.

Ananthamurthy (Kannada) or Nirmal Verma (Hindi) or Amrita Pritam (Punjabi)? When he makes a cursory reference to these writers he is surely guilty of transmitting received opinion or indulging in special pleading.

The next major inadequacy is that a book which purports to cover Indian writing has no selections from Indian poetry written in English. This cannot be due to lack of space: some of the excerpts from prose writers who have not yet proved their mettle could have been left out to accommodate some highly accomplished poets. India has a capacious nest of singing birds, the more interesting of them distinguished by a fistful of poems each, and exhibiting no fruitful threads of development which can be traced by a critic in the way he can chart the variety and plot the growth of poets like Yeats, Eliot or Wallace Stevens. But since it is in poetry that the nuances of human intercourse are most sensitively recorded, it cannot be ignored in a representative anthology of writing. Room, therefore, has to be found for the likes of Nissim Ezekiel, A.K. Ramanujan, Jayanta Mahapatra, Arvind Merhotra, Arun Kolatkar, R. Parthasarathy.

Another disquieting feature is that a high percentage of the writers represented are expatriates from the Indian sub-continent. Rushdie in his introduction celebrates them for holding a "conversation with the world" but the phenomenon should have been addressed more fully and reasons sought for such an exodus.

It is easy to fault anthologies, especially because the process of selection is so much influenced by the vagaries of personal taste and individual judgement, and I will not succumb to this temptation. Given the range of their search among material from India and overseas, given that the English "knowing" public of India could exceed in numbers, if it has not already, the entire population of Great Britain, Rushdie and West have done an extremely fine piece of work.

Their sense of literary sapor is impeccable, and when one is a trifle disappointed with a particular selection, it is because the excerpt cannot give you an adequate sense of why the longer work is so important; this is true even of the much hailed Arundathi Roy, whose novel *The God of Small Things* is now so famous: one cannot determine from the extract whether it is deserved fame, or trendy notoriety. Of course, the great achievers of Indian writing in English are suitably recognized. There is Nirad Chauduri, a maverick autodidact who forged an original Victorian prose-style out of reading books in English, deprived as he was of any English-speaking community of educated peers: but no extract can convey his irreverent, even iconoclastic attitude towards the much vaunted heritage of India. If there is a need for anti-chauvinistic common sense, India needs it more than most: Chauduri was the answer and the antidote. Another mischievous rebel was G. V. Desani whose singleton tour-de-force *All About H. Hatterr* is, as Anthony Burgess called it, a coterie classic; Mulk Raj Anand, a pioneer and a humanitarian, deserves his space though he is not to be compared to R.K. Narayan, who could fill with distinction all the space one could spare. You can also find in these pages Ruth Prawer Jhabvala, a fine writer for the most part but controversial, and Anita Desai, one of the best and most prolific of Indian writers in English. Salman Rushdie, who enriched the English language with Indianizing accretions to the extent that he created not only a new idiom but a new style, is here with his justly celebrated excerpt "The Perforated Sheet" from *Midnight's Children*. There is Rohinton Mistry who may in the end surpass all others. There is Vikram Seth who was a fine poet but became a mediocre and long-winded novelist, though this extract itself is hilariously funny. There is an excerpt from his novella, *A Strange and Sublime Address,* which shows great sensitivity to a sense of place, and therefore to cultural displacement, one of the major themes of modern multi-cultural literature.

I don't share Rushdie's admiration for Allen Sealy though I will withhold my judgement till I have read more than the included extract. Shashi Tharoor could well become an important writer if he would forgo his political, bureaucratic and administrative interests: he straddles the border between creative art and well-written reportage.

But I am personally most grateful to these editors for introducing me to Padma Perera, Bapsi Sidhwa, Sara Suleri, who in *Meatless Days* writes a brilliant prose (and I hope that in the future she writes less about food and more about meatful days and nights), Firdaus Kanga, Amitav Gosh and Kiran Desai, who has a stronger claim to be noticed than that she is Anita Desai's daughter. I will follow their literary futures with interest.

So, while congratulating Salman Rushdie and Elizabeth West on this collection, let me tell them not to dream of literary dynasties, just because Kiran Desai is Anita Desai's daughter. It is to end all dynasties that Jawarharlal Nehru spoke on the attainment of Indian Independence: that was his tryst with Destiny. Let us also not exaggerate the achievement: we must compare 50 years of American or British literary history or the Caribbean Renaissance, from a group of

tiny islands (Derek Walcott, V.S. Naipaul, Caryll Phillips, Roy Heath
et al.) and remember that within fifty years in Russia, we had Tolstoy,
Dostoevsky and Turgenev: let us celebrate but with a sense of
perspective.

CHAPTER XXIII

BITTEN BY DESTINY: SANJAY NIGAM'S *THE SNAKE CHARMER*

Of the new stars which have been spotted in the literary firmament of Indian writers in English, the two most visible are Arundathi Roy, whose first novel *The God of Small Things* has already won the Booker Prize and Vikram Chandra, whose debut novel, *Red Earth and Pouring Rain* won distinguished awards and has now been succeeded by his second, *Love and Longing in Bombay,* which will no doubt receive critical accolades and hosannas in days to come.

Sanjay Nigam's *The Snake Charmer* bids fair to join this select and elect company. Of course, there are differences between individual kinds of creative talent, as for that matter, there are differences between human beings (*Quot homines...*). Nigam does not have Arundathi Roy's linguistic fecundity, comparable only to G. V. Desani's or Salman Rushdie's to limit oneself to Indian writing in English. However, her style is not so overpowering as to intimidate her readers. Nor does Nigam have the skills of Chandra who is almost a conjuror in manipulating situation and plot while capturing in incandescent prose the ongoing life of a vibrant but ugly modern megalopolis.

Nigam's style is sparer but not for that reason less intense, or less effective. The story partly is an allegory, but it is not fantastic. Like Hawthorne's *The Scarlett Letter* it is firmly anchored in reality: in that sense Nigam's novel, to adapt to modern jargon , is "reader friendly."

Since he is not given to verbal pyrotechnics or to adventitious tricks of style, he does not build barriers between himself and his reading public.

Surely, one of the reasons why Indian writers in English are so much admired is that they can lend variety to the somewhat uniform, and even animate the sometimes comatose corpus of the Anglo-American novel. They can introduce new places, situations, attitudes, and visions. They can even inject new venom into an already well immunized body. Nigam does this almost literally, and with considerable brio.

His novel is about Sonalal, a successful snake charmer who wants to be the best in the world. It is about the relationship between him and his snake, Raju, whom he loves more than a father loves his son. But he is martinet enough to drive the snake to the extremes of exhaustion. He wants the Gods to appreciate Raju's dance and to enjoy the music he plays on his *been*, a musical instrument made of a dried disembowelled pumpkin.

One of the themes of the book is the quest for perfection: the protagonist so faceless that even his wife had difficulty identifying him in a crowd—"which now and then proved quite convenient—" has a special need and therefore an impetus for eclat, for exceptional excellence in his vocation. The man-snake relationship is firmly set in a background of family and friends, some genuine, some charlatan: his wife Sarita caring but vengeful in her own way, his children to whom he wants to teach his snake charmer's skills but who are more influenced by their mother and spurn his pedagogical endeavors.

The novelty does not stop with the man-snake relationship: one of the more moving sub-themes is Sonalal's love for his prostitute, also his devoted mistress, Reena, who tries hard to cure him from impotence, a common malady of ageing men but rarely treated in fiction. She succeeds, she is his life-line: humane, devoted and patient she gives him back his manhood.

The main preoccupation and what gives the story its momentum, is the protagonist's sense of guilt. Exasperated by Raju's refusal to cooperate and provoked because he bit his left calf, Sonalal does the unthinkable: he bites his beloved snake in half. From then on, his forehead bore the mark of Cain. Though the novel has few surprises, except that it is itself one big surprise, Sonalal's life is now a stony pathway toward the expiration of his guilt. The term "guilt" is part of the quackery of psychiatric modernism and Dr. Basu, one of his doctors, tells him that the matter with him is called guilt. Another doctor, who is probably a homosexual, dubs him a homosexual. But whatever his disease, Sonalal has to live with it. Apart from Reena, he has a good friend in an older charmer, Jagat, who stresses the centrality of everyday life to creative achievement, and the importance of what we see as mere distractions:

> "and of the distractions you speak of," continued Jagat, "are life itself. The reason you are the best charmer I've ever heard because your music makes me feel that living and everything that goes with it, the things you call distractions—wives and children, coughs and colds, liquor and beedies, lotteries, hot boring days, charming itself—are important in some way. Sona you need those distractions. You must put every one into your music."

Sonalal and his wife often glare at each other with two decades of anger. It is not surprising that some venom seems to have entered his jaws. When Raju's substitute snake also through exhaustion bites his calf, the incensed man nearly bites the snake in return, the way he dismembered Raju, thereby threatening to negate all suffering and penance he has experienced. He pulls back in the nick of time.

He wanted his own sons to follow their ancestors in the long lineage of snake charming "Sonalal, son of Chandilal, grandson of Pannalal, great-grandson of Motilal, great-great-grandson of Heeralal" and he was bitterly disappointed by their lack of enthusiasm.

Midway through the novel, Sonalal consults a blind magician, Ratan the Great, reputed to have performed the Indian rope trick. It is Ratan who tells him of the most potent symbols in the story—the cosmic ether which must be sniffed and the overripe mango which must be eaten in order to know perfection. The ether's wonderful smell could be likened to the mango, rainbow-colored, smooth, curvaceous, capturing within it in its nectar "some essential property of the universe." Though Sonalal claws into the mango and feels a pressure within his dhoti, the sensation is short lived.

Nigam has been able to create a convincing character, who though lowly and of low caste, is able to aspire towards perfection and at least once in his life has sensed it. It is this achievement which makes *The Snake Charmer* an exceptional novel. I cannot do better than quote the book's concluding paragraph.

Sonalal turned his gaze to the sky for he had a vague impulse to plead for divine mercy. Then it occurred to him that he was really after something else – a sign it wasn't only his life that had been so fated. But the sky was so blue and unblemished, so immense and unreal, there seemed no way to communicate with it. The sky seemed part of a perfection that could never be known by a man. And yet, he, Sonalal, had once known it. On a day that suddenly felt like yesterday he had caught a faint whiff of the ether that flows through the universe. Still staring at the sky, he thought the ether must be blue, and way high up there, it smelled like a freshly cut mango.

CHAPTER XXIV

PLACE AS ANIMA

In this brief coda, I would like to illustrate and reinforce one of the concerns of this book, viz, the role of place or setting or landscape in cross-cultural literature. This has been dealt with at some length in preceding essays as well as in the first part of this book but some of the sharper polarities become more overt if we compare extreme examples. Different novels exhibit differing degrees of the function of landscape as soul or character or destiny.

If, for example, we examine J.G. Farrell's *The Siege of Krishnapur*, a remarkable though little known novel, we will find India and the events surrounding the Sepoy uprising of 1857 as strong presences in the fiction. But far more important than the setting of plain and cantonment, the climate of hot sun and monsoonal rain, the atmosphere of disease, the dust and dirt, the proliferation of flies and insects, is the reaction of the besieged British community, the changes of individual characters and even of their ideas, thoughts and ideals in response to the conditions of emergency and crisis.

The "extreme" examples I have chosen are Joseph Conrad's *Heart of Darkness* and the novel *The Quiet American* by a widely read, even popular novelist, Graham Greene. Though no judgements of value are predicated, it would be obvious that Conrad has a more profound, poetic, more tragic sense of place as *anima*, both here and in such novels as *Nostromo*, than Greene though the Greene novel is highly readable and enjoyable. In fact, a class to which I recently taught both

books vastly preferred *The Quiet American*. I am a great admirer of
Greene and do not share the snobbish depreciation of him in some
academic circles merely because he is a popular success and a brilliant
entertainer; he has serious purposes. Even Somerset Maugham, equally
slighted by academics, is, whatever his limits, a master of his craft and
a provider of superb entertainment, like Guy de Maupassant before
him. We must not belittle the value and charm of art as play.

But Vietnam, which is the locale of Greene's novel, with its internal
and internecine struggles and squabbles among and between the South
Vietnamese, the Vietminh, the Communists and the "Third Forces",
governed by the French colonialists in a state of retreat and futility, is
no more than a backdrop, however vividly evoked in isolated scenes.
The story could have been set in Africa, the Caribbean or even the
South Pacific.

Greene is concerned primarily with the growth of a character named
Fowler, an ageing British newspaper correspondent with a history of a
failed marriage and unfulfilled love affairs, who sedulously avoids
taking sides in the conflicts and refuses to commit himself to any
definite moral or intellectual stance. He falls in love with a native
woman, Phuong, not with the buoyancy of desire but rather out of quiet
desperation. With oriental subservience and gentleness she prepares his
opium pipe and lets him feel her thigh beside him in his bed. This
placid state of affairs is interrupted by the intrusion of an innocent
American do-gooder, Pyle, who works in the American Aid Mission.
Pyle not only falls in love with Phuong, he also wants to marry her and
give her love, security and permanence. He is also involved in a highly
dangerous game of supplying plastic dust, via an American exporter,
which could just as easily be used for making toys as plastic bombs for
a Third Force, cynically led by a General Thé.

Landscape is not character, in the Jamesian phrase, in this novel.
Even the differences in the way Fowler and Pyle treat Phuong can be
attributed more to the kindness of an inexperienced American than to
cross-cultural differences arising out of the ingrained superiority
towards the locals acquired by the British as the fruit of longer colonial
experience. It is not a matter of the sophisticated knowledge the
Englishman has of the "locals" and his different expectations from love
in such contexts: what slight cross-cultural difference there may be
between the Englishman and the American is not stressed; rather it is
the difference between two different men of different ages and
dispositions.

Pyle does steal Phuong away from Fowler for a while. But this has nothing to do with Fowler's decision to act when he realizes what Pyle is up to. Fowler decides to take a stand, make a commitment and forestall more deaths and killings. He connives at Pyle's elimination. It is a moral development for Fowler though he becomes an accessory to murder.

Coincident with this decision to take a moral stand in the name of humanity is his recognition of a deeper commitment to Phuong than he had thought possible. It is no longer an old man's convenience on his part, but love. Fowler asks his wife for divorce so as to have Phuong for good to prepare his opium tray, warm his bed and above all to give him a sense of purpose in life through an enduring relationship.

However, for our purposes, we must observe that it is really amazing in a fast-paced book, packed with incident, how thin the setting is: we do not meet the Vietnamese, except for Phuong, and the etiolated French colonialists are represented by a marginal character, a French policeman with the name of Vigot. However, it is important to state that in his major works, *The Power and the Glory* and *The Heart of the Matter*, landscape does become character.

The function of locale in Conrad's *Heart of Darkness* is at the opposite extreme: the setting of the Congo, of river and dense forest, is a palpable and ominous presence, a significant persona in the human drama. The novel is what it is because of the physical ambience, however much of it is treated as a symbol of evil and the search for it, of the need to confront it, and emerge from it safe or inexorably overcome and trapped.

The river represents a search for the deepest layers in human nature, for the heart of evil identified as darkness, a journey into this darkness in order to attain real self-knowledge and understand the human condition which alone can lead to true maturity; one has to weather and overcome evil in order to attain full manhood. The river to darkness flows along with the river of Kurtz's life and the initiation for Marlowe into true adulthood. The forest is a colossal jungle "so dark green as to be almost black." But it is not just the river in the Congo: it is also the more civilized Thames, transposed to an earlier time: it is still a waterway leading to the uttermost ends of the earth.

Man's inhumanity to man is at the heart of the colonial encounter, both in its cruelty and futility; it is paralleled by man's spoliation of Nature. The incredibly pointless sniping at an entire continent is seen against the hostility of Nature itself which will wait patiently for its revenges till it can oust the intruder and revert to its pristine power.

> Once, I remember, we came upon a man-of-war anchored upon the coast. There wasn't even a shed there, and she was shelling the bush. It appears the French had one of their wars going on thereabouts. Her ensign dropped limp like a rag; the muzzles of the long six inch guns stuck out all over the low hull; the greasy, shiny swell swung her up lazily and let her down, swaying her thin masts. In the empty immensity of earth, sky and water, there she was, incomprehensible, firing into a continent. Pop, would go one of the six-inch guns; a small flame would dart and vanish, a tiny projectile would give a feeble screech -- and nothing happened. Nothing would happen. There was a touch of insanity in the proceeding, a sense of drollery in the sight; and it was not dissipated by somebody on board assuring me earnestly there was a camp of natives -- he called them enemies! -- hidden out of sight somewhere.
>
> We gave her her letters (I heard the men in that lovely ship were dying of fever at the rate of three a day) and went on. We called at some more places with farcical names, where the merry dance of death and trade goes on in a still and earthy atmosphere as of an overheated catacomb: all along the formless coast bordered by dangerous surf, as if Nature herself had tried to ward off intruders; in and out of rivers, streams of death in life, whose banks were rotting into mud, whose waters, thickened into slime, invaded the contorted mangroves, that seemed to writhe at us in the extremity of an impotent despair.

The primeval setting highlights and reinforces the themes -- the ambivalence of religious proselytization, the craving for power and how its unbridled use can distort and deform the noblest human motives, the idealism that leads to loathing ("Exterminate the brutes") and to the final agonized cry "The horror, the horror". It is also the locale for the ambiguous moral triumph of Kurtz as he stepped into the abyss, was sucked in before he had his vision of the horror of reality, unlike the majority of mankind who live with the complacent compromises of quotidian experience born of a lack of moral daring. Most people don't even peep over the abyss as Marlowe does though he has the prudence to withdraw in time. Marlowe can even accommodate into his ethics the "white lie" he tells Kurtz's fiancée, the Intended, because human beings cannot bear very much reality. Colonialism is seen as evil both at its outpost in the Congo and its source in the whited sepulchre of Brussels. Kurtz at least had wanted justice: Marlowe finds him but lives with the recognition and the memory. We return to the Thames which also seems to lead into the heart of an immense darkness.

Heart of Darkness is a flawed work: the iteration of words like "brooding," "unspeakable," "inscrutable" "inconceivable" cloaks a failure of imaginative realization. Even in the magnificent evocation of the forest and the river,

> Going up that river was like travelling back to the earliest beginnings of the world, when vegetation rioted on the earth and the big trees were kings. An empty stream, a great silence, an impenetrable forest. The air was warm, thick, heavy, sluggish. There was no joy in the brilliance of sunshine. The long stretches of the waterway ran on, deserted, into the gloom of overshadowed distances. On silvery sandbanks hippos and alligators sunned themselves side by side. The broadening waters flowed through a mob of wooded islands; you lost your way on that river as you would in a desert, and butted all day long against shoals, trying to find the channel till you thought yourself bewitched and cut off for ever from everything you had known once -- somewhere -- far away -- in another existence perhaps. There were moments when one's past came to one, as it will sometimes when you have not a moment to spare to yourself; but it came, in the shape of an unrestful and noisy dream, remembered with wonder amongst the overwhelming realities of this strange world of plants, and water, and silence. And this stillness of life did not in the least resemble a peace. It was the stillness of an implacable force brooding over an inscrutable intention.

The last sentence is a major and embarrassing blemish. Yet the book remains significant, alike in ambition and execution. Despite the charge of racism, which Chinua Achebe, a leading Nigerian writer, levels against the book, a criticism with which I agree to a fair degree, I think that Achebe's remarks are more political and sociological and do not belong altogether to the sphere of literary judgement. It is like belittling Milton for his empathetic and inward portrait of Lucifer. In my opinion Conrad's *Heart of Darkness* raises cross-cultural literature to the status of a masterly form of poetic achievement.

APPENDIX

LITERATURE AND CULTURAL KNOWLEDGE

There are many ways of knowing a culture different from one's own. Perhaps the best, most complete and comprehensive is to take the step, sometimes irretraceable, of living in another culture and learning in a direct way the language or languages of the people – becoming familiar consciously and subconsciously with the customs, social habits, mores, thoughts, religions, literature and art, the "popular" culture and other aspects of the culture's way of life. But for most – indeed all – of us, this way of learning cultures is not practicable. To begin with, it is not at all clear that one has learned another culture merely because one has lived several years in it. Apart from degrees of percipience and discernment, which vary among individuals, too close an identification with the culture one studies leads to a loss of the objectivity which is essential for any kind of balanced study. Again, there is such an overwhelming number and variety of cultures in the world that one has to consider economies not only of time, money and place, but also of spirit. The student of culture has therefore to limit his area, choose his focus, and achieve what is possible given the inevitable brevity of the time he has at his disposal. He has to know the separate ways -- not really separable except as mental conveniences -- of the anthropologist, the sociologist, the philosopher, the historian, the creative writer, the *littérateur*, and the intelligent or merely curious traveller.

However, the study of its literature is a unique, and perhaps the best, way of apprehending a culture in its complex particularities, its nuances and its own characteristic tone.   Literature is an invaluable cultural expression because it springs from its cultural nexus, if it may be so called, with an immediacy, a freshness, a concreteness, an authenticity and a power of meaning which are not easily found in other emanations or through other channels.   When, for example, one reads of the tea ceremony in Japan, as presented by Kawabata, one proceeds from the intricacies of the ceremony to the complexities of Japanese social life; in R. K. Narayan's *The Financial Expert* one is plunged into the actualities of a small town in southern India, and immersed in the vivid realities of a small town's business life.

Obviously, if the writer is great, the importance of his work is not contained by a regional, national or even time-bound frame; but the vividness of the cultural nexus, however mixed the brew may be, is often a necessary condition of his art.   One may illustrate this further by citing some established American examples, such as Mark Twain's *The Adventures of Huckleberry Finn*, Henry James' *The American* or *Portrait of a Lady*, and F. Scott Fitzgerald's *The Great Gatsby*.

Huckleberry Finn is a novel set in the specific context of pre-Civil War America.   It opposes nature and the machine, the pre-industrial and the industrial ways of life.   The novel's morality, however, does not depend on a simple repetition of ethical principles found in currently-accepted codes of conduct, not is it merely illustrative; a kind of gloss on prevalent ethical attitudes.   On the contrary, the novel shows a complex, evolving moral imagination and sensibility, far removed from the conventional Christian ethics of Twain's day.   The current worship of the machine, of money, of what Ruskin called "the Goddess of getting on" is what Mark Twain inveighs against. Elsewhere he describes the offensive credo as follows: "Get money, Get it quickly.   Get it in abundance.   Get it in prodigious abundance. Get it dishonestly if you can, honestly if you must."   Against this he places his sense of the old America, simpler, with its own mix of good and evil, but somehow to be preferred.   The novel has a moral aura, and is symbolic of moral realities.   The concrete setting of the story in a particular time and place is the source of its value as cultural knowledge, and also one of the sources of its artistic excellence.

Henry James' *The American* also belongs to a specific time and place, even though it is engaged with the international theme: with America's relationship to its past, and to the old Europe, the land of ancestral memory. The protagonist, Christopher Newman, embodies a particular aspect of the American dream of that time. As he tells his expatriate friend Tristram:

> I want the biggest kind of entertainment a man can get. People, places, art, nature, everything! I want to see the tallest mountains, and the bluest lakes, and the finest pictures, and the handsomest churches, and the most celebrated men, and the most beautiful women.

He uses a metaphor from his business past when he says that he wants a woman who would be the "best article in the market". Even his business mentality is idealized as having "undefined and mysterious boundaries, which invite the imagination to bestir itself on his behalf".

Even though he is 'crude' compared to the Europeans – he has often admired the "copy" more than the "original" – he has a strong streak of decency; he refuses to exploit his knowledge of the skeleton in their cupboard in order to get even with his European associates. The novel however is too simplified, as it opposes not just American innocence to European sophistication, but American nobility of mind to European villainy. But it does look forward to the later novels, where James was to treat the "international" theme with greater psychological depth and maturity, where the American-European exchange was more subtle and more a two-way business, where James' main preoccupations were the theme of freedom and the circumstances in which freedom had to operate, where he was able to project his opposition between American and European cultures in terms of an ideal civilization which, though nowhere to be found, could nevertheless be posited as a humanly-satisfying scale of reference. It looks forward to *The Portrait of a Lady*, which examines more seriously the possibilities of freedom in the real world of circumstance, and uncovers a tragic reality which endures.

F. Scott Fitzgerald's *The Great Gatsby*, though admittedly a slighter novel, has a complex cultural meaning: it is a later variant of the American dream, and reflects a changed society. I wish to draw attention only to the quality of Gatsby's corrupt greatness, which can still cling to an incorruptible hope. The earlier widespread respect for "getting-rich-quickism" has already turned somewhat sour in American culture, though Gatsby's love for Daisy redeems to some extent his unscrupulously acquired wealth and other major faults of character. The description of Gatsby at the graveside as the "poor son of a bitch" is derogatory as well as pathetic. Gatsby differs from the typical American self-made man by his greater imaginative style for self-renewal, for wanting to be reborn, to spring from his own platonic conception of himself. This feeling, though somewhat individualized in Gatsby, has its links with the original American desire to begin all over again in a new country, with frontiers that had an apparent capacity for expansion without end. One could chart the further disintegration of the American dream in later times, as for example in Arthur Miller's *Death of a Salesman*, where the pressures exercised by the still sufficiently pervasive belief that only "making it" matters, can only lead to disintegration and disaster.

The use of literature for learning about cultures is one of the important new directions taken by literary studies in recent times. Though it has been known for a long time that one of the ways in which culture reveals itself most fully is in the thinking which guides it, shapes its values, and gives rise to its various creative expressions, and that the literary or artistic achievements of a culture are among its deepest and most authentic manifestations, there have been in the past relatively few systematic or sustained attempts to study cultures in this way; to "possess" them intellectually as it were, and to relate the humanistic achievements to the "totality" or "wholeness" of cultures. Traditionally, the teaching of literature has been concerned with the literary text as being worthy of study because of its artistic merit or moral value. The most common way in which the literary text has been extended has been in the direction of relating it to, and seeing it as a part of, the history of literary tradition in a particular language. While the major literary works of past historical periods have been regularly used as source material for the study of the social life of the period in question, little contemporary work has been examined in this way. In recent years, though, there has been growing momentum and development in the belief that the social context of literature is essential to its understanding.

Though the literary critic in particular has resisted any attempt to "sociologize" the work of art, he now seems more willing to approach it through concepts of medium, channel, genre or ambience. The conviction has gained ground that the study of society is a necessary dimension of the study of literature itself; that the sensitive literary critic or the sensitive social scientist will not do any disservice either to literary or to social studies. In fact without sensitiveness, moral sensitivity and imagination, neither the literary critic not the social scientist is likely to be a good practitioner of his own chosen specialty.

Characteristically modern phenomena, such as the lost of a sense of personal identity in a mass society, the concern with aberration, the ecological dangers posed by twentieth-century growth, the intensive bureaucratization of modern life, and the threat to the very survival of the human species in the nuclear age, are reflected in fiction, poetry and drama, and the sociological studies of these matters provide useful background for literary study. On the other hand, the literature is itself important documentation for social studies, and the social scientist cannot ignore it. Particularly since the 1950s there has been a renaissance in the study of the relations of literature and society, the position of the writer in society, and in social problems as material for the creative artist. Anthropologists have been especially imaginative and adventurous in the uses of literary materials to support their research and enforce, if not actually discover, their findings.

However, it must be emphasized that even though literature introduces the reader to the culture with an immediacy and a concreteness which cannot otherwise be duplicated, there are several pitfalls which have to be borne in mind. Most critics and lovers of literature claim that literature is its own end and justification, that one must first learn to read and appreciate literature before moving from it to cultural studies of any kind. In fact they would reverse the process, and say that one must study the culture in order to appreciate the literature – and not vice versa – because literature represents the greater value, and should therefore be the prime concern. More people are interested in Homer than in the specifics of Homeric times.

The work of literature is surrounded by concentric circles. There is the author's character, his life story, his health or illness, his place within his family and immediate social circumstances, his receptivity to the ideas and ideologies current in his time, and remembering T. S. Eliot's remark that a major Western poet should write with a sense of the tradition from Homer onwards in his bones – his place in the literary tradition, which may extend backward for thousands of years. There is also, and importantly, the writer's relation to his own times. In addition to all these there is the quirk of his own creativity, that special gift which is unique to him and which interacts with all the other factors, somewhat in the nature of a catalytic agent, to produce the special and irreplaceable work of art. To be able to read literature well one must be perceptive and sensitive to all these factors: to read it perfectly would therefore be nearly impossible.

It may be that a culture is more accurately studied in some respects by reading its newspapers that its works of serious art. It may also be true that best-sellers are more representative of some aspects of the time that its works of major literature. It is undeniable that popular books such as *Uncle Tom's Cabin* or even *Gone With the Wind*, which have defensible claims to authenticity, are better source-material for the study of the age than the more recondite masterpieces. In our own time, soap operas on television may tell us more about what that indefinable character known as the common man really feels and thinks. The point, however, is that literature is the fruit of the most creative, and often the most interesting, minds in a society. And therefore what is found in them is significant in a different way, and at a different level. Great literature may capture what is happening in the depths of the individual and social mind; it may engage the deeper preoccupations, which in future times may surface and become prominent, so that students of later periods are ready to identify these interests as the most important realities of the times in question. But one has to have the required critical sense to recognize that some works may be merely idealistically nostalgic, or even utopian or future-oriented. The novel may deal with the emergent aspects of the future as, for example, George Orwell's *1984*. The "feel" or reality may be deceptive: if you read Tolstoy's short story *Master and Man*, you cannot conclude that the aristocrat who gave his life to prevent his servant from dying of cold is in any way typical of relations between master and man in nineteenth-century Russia. Tolstoy is more concerned with communicating a human sympathy which transcends time and place. It is in this sense that one has to reckon with literature's engagement in the universal arena of experience. The writer's enduring value may subsist in what he gives to his time, and not so much in what he derives from it. One has therefore to take into account in an interrelated way all these possible facets of a work of art before determining their relevance for cultural knowledge.

Great literature is concerned with truth, while soap operas may merely reflect the fantasies, dreams and pathologies of the producer and the audience. In so far as man is a social animal, even the most private experiences treated in literature have a social context, and therefore they help to determine and complete our knowledge of the human and cultural condition. The Chinese poet's attitude to nature and the passage of time, and Wordsworth's sense of the non-human in nature, tell us not only of the individual sensibilities of the poets concerned, but also of their respective societies and the different periods in which they wrote. As even the most intimate experiences of, say, love, nature or death have a social context, their recreation by artists has profound social meanings.   There is therefore no substitute for the cognitive value of great literature: it is an invaluable source of the on-going movements of communion between individuals and cultures.

There are other tendencies, not yet dominant, but becoming more and more vocal in our culture, which have given the study of literature additional new dimensions. Literature has acquired a special value in the so-called age of science, to the extent to which purely scientific education has been seen to be incomplete. Natural science is not expected to yield values or guide conduct, but the "scientific" approach seen as a total attitude is now largely discredited, if not finally laid to rest. Every partial approach, such as the scientific, however ethically or morally neutral it may appear, creates its own mythologies; and the grey mythologies of science have proved themselves life-defeating.

The social sciences enjoyed until recently a period of fitful bloom, but they too seem to have lost their confidence. More and more people are turning to literature to seek the values whose life-support was once provided by religion and philosophy. Critics and scholars nowadays increasingly tend to busy themselves with the cultural situation in which literature finds itself, and with the insistent demands being made upon literature to provide an education in moral sensibility and critical intelligence. They tend to approach literature with the expectation that the principle which should direct and inform educational effort is to be found primarily in literary study. Since literature expresses the lived actualities of the time, it is seen as an authentic source not only of the realities of society as experienced by its most intelligent and sensitive members, but of life-giving values and value-judgements. Literary study is seen to lead not only to enlargement or refinement of sensibility, but to training in discrimination, aesthetic and moral; the moral judgement is not separate from the aesthetic in the sense that it is subsequently superimposed on it; they are composite, and form a unity.

Unlike in the past, when the experience of literature was sought to clarify or extend moral insights, as for example, one's reading of Blake would modify one's traditional interpretations of Christian world-views, today one goes to literature for the very creation of values. Literature no longer offers the mere alteration of, or escape from, traditional belief systems; it is called upon to provide substitutes for what is no longer believed in.

It is in this context that extreme, and exaggerated, demands are made upon poetry, and nearly impossible claims made on its behalf. For a poet like Wallace Stevens, poetry belongs to the highest rung in the caste-system of human knowledge. He says in one of his essays, "After one has abandoned the belied in God, poetry is that essence which takes its place as life's redemption." This is indeed the supreme claim; it goes far beyond even the Shelleyan position of the poet as the unacknowledged legislator. Stevens may not be representative. There are other views, notably that of T. S. Eliot, a poet equally dedicated to his calling, but for whom the poetic discipline was not self-sufficient, and needed completion by a moral or even theological discipline. But Eliot's view is even less accepted today. For Stevens poetry makes life "complete in itself"; that his assertion is not as fantastic as it appears is seen in his long poem "Notes Toward a Supreme Fiction". The subject is the relation between Imagination and Reality; the imagination which is the golden solvent brings the vivid transparence which in turn renovates experience. Reality is not realism, which is a corruption; it is the "ultimate value", the spirit's 'true centre'. Imagination, "man's power over nature", confronts reality in all its fullness: what ensues is a fruitful interchange, a supreme fiction, a poetry which is life's sustaining ailment:

> Is it he is or is it I that experience this?
> Is it I then that keep saying there is an hour
> Filled with inexpressible bliss, in which I have
>
> No need, am happy, forget need's golden hand
> Am satisfied without solacing majesty,
> And if there is an hour there is a day,
>
> There is a month, a year, there is a time
> In which majesty is a mirror of the self:
> I have not but I am and as I am, I am.

That in a secular age a poet should fabricate an experience which may be described as a "pagan" equivalent of the beatific vision, is in itself an achievement: that he should make it appear so nearly credible is a poetic triumph. In another poem, "The World as Meditation", Stevens expressed the sense in which, even though there is no longer any fury in transcendent forms, his actual candle blazes with artifice. Though God is dead, the imagination takes his place as the mirror and the lamp, the source and giver of life:

> We say God and the imagination are one
> How high that highest candle lights the dark
>
> Out of this same light, out of the central mind
> We make a dwelling in the evening air
> In which being there together is enough.

Despite the fact that high claims are made for literature, and that it has been pressed into service for a variety of scholastic purposes, the most notably recent of which is its use for cultural studies, I would like to conclude by stressing that there is no substitute for the close, unremitting, disinterested reading of the literary text with a view to extracting the total meaning. There is no surrogate for literary analysis and comparison. All cultural study of literature must begin from there, before proceeding to aesthetic, moral or cultural extensions and judgements.   This is not to minimize the information and the knowledge that is afforded by the study of history, sociology and other relevant disciplines, but merely to stress that the realities or portions of reality discovered by the creative personality belong organically to the history and the mythology of the human imagination.

Since the medium is words, with all the weight of denotation, connotation, rhythm and the accumulated inheritances of historical usage, modified by the specificity of the immediate situation, cultural knowledge is most accessible, complete and distinctive in literature. It is not incidental that Aristotle gave poetry a higher place than history. To understand the individual creative personality, one must read the text as carefully as possible, and grow into the reality it embodies, just as the artist grows into his experience in the process of creation. It is only then that the reader can encompass the total experience, and demonstrate how complete or partial, how effective or ineffective, the particular work is.   Only after fully saturating oneself in the work, penetrating and evaluating its significance, can one move into cultural studies. The "movement" into cultural studies must also be informed by an equally intense and sophisticated concern for the dynamics of civilization, which in itself has close relationships to the original creative pressure.